Java for
Students

Pearson Education

We work with leading authors to develop the
strongest educational materials in computing,
bringing cutting-edge thinking and
best learning practice to a global market.

Under a range of well-known imprints, including
Prentice Hall, we craft high-quality print and
electronic publications which help readers to
understand and apply their content, whether
studying or at work.

To find out about the complete range of our
publishing please visit us on the World Wide Web at:
www.pearsoneduc.com

DOUGLAS BELL
MIKE PARR

JAVA
FOR
Students

Prentice
Hall

An imprint of **Pearson Education**

Harlow, England · London · New York · Reading, Massachusetts · San Francisco
Toronto · Don Mills, Ontario · Sydney · Tokyo · Singapore · Hong Kong · Seoul
Taipei · Cape Town · Madrid · Mexico City · Amsterdam · Munich · Paris · Milan

Pearson Education Limited
Edinburgh Gate
Harlow
Essex CM20 2JE

and Associated Companies throughout the world

Visit us on the World Wide Web at:
www.pearsoneduc.com

First published 1998
Second edition published 1999 by Prentice Hall Europe
Third edition published 2002

© Prentice Hall Europe 1999
© Pearson Education Limited 2002

ISBN 0130 32377 2

British Library Cataloguing-in-Publication Data
A catalogue record for this book is available from the British Library

Library of Congress Cataloging-in-Publication Data
Bell, Doug, 1944–
    Java for students / Douglas Bell and Mike Parr.—3rd ed.
      p. cm.
    ISBN 0–13–032377–2 (pbk.)
    1. Java (Computer program language)   I. Parr, Mike, 1949– .   II. Title.

    QA76.73.J38   B45   2001
    005.2'762—dc21   2001021474

10 9 8 7 6 5 4 3 2 1
06 05 04 03 02

Typeset in Galliard 9.75/12pt by 35
Printed in Great Britain by Henry Ling Ltd, at the Dorset Press, Dorchester, Dorset

Contents

Trademark notice

The following designations are trademarks or registered trademarks of the organizations whose names follow in brackets:

Active X, IIS, Internet Explorer, MS-DOS, Visual Basic, Visual Studio.Net, Windows, Word (Microsoft Corporation); Apache (licensed through Apache Software Foundation); Ada (US Department of Defense – Ada Joint Program Office); C+++ (CNS incorporated); Eiffel (Nonprofit International Consortium for Eiffel); Intel, Pentium (Intel Corporation); Java, JavaScript, Sun workstation (Sun Microsystems Inc); Linux (Linus Torvalds); Mac, Macintosh, Apple II (Apple Computers Inc); Netscape Navigator (Netscape Communications); PC (IBM Corporation); Smalltalk (Xerox Corporation); UNIX (licensed through X/Open Company Ltd).

Detailed contents

Appendices

Introduction

What this book will tell you

This book explains:

- how to write Java programs;
- how to run Java programs as free-standing programs;
- how to invoke a Java program from a World-Wide Web browser.

This book is for novices

If you have never done any programming before – if you are a complete novice – this book is for you. This book assumes no prior knowledge of programming. It starts from scratch. It is written in a simple, direct style for maximum clarity. It is aimed primarily at first year undergraduates at universities and colleges, but it is also suitable for novices studying alone.

Why Java?

Java is probably one of the best programming languages to learn and use at the start of the 21st century, because of the following features.

Java is small and beautiful

The designers of Java have deliberately left out all the superfluous features of programming languages; they have cut the design to the bone. The result is a language that has all the necessary features, combined in an elegant and logical way. The design is lean and mean. It is easy to learn, but powerful.

Java is object-oriented

Object-oriented languages are the latest and most successful approach to programming. Object-oriented programming has been the most popular approach to programming in the late 1990s and now into the new millennium. Java is completely object-oriented from the ground up. It is not a language that has had object-orientedness grafted onto it as an afterthought.

Java supports the Internet

The main motivation for Java was to enable people to develop programs that use the Internet and the World-Wide Web. Java programs can easily be invoked from Web browsers like Netscape Navigator and Internet Explorer to provide valuable and spectacular facilities. Also Java programs can be easily transmitted around the Internet and run on any computer.

Java is general-purpose

Although designed for writing World-Wide Web applications, Java is a truly general-purpose language. Anything that C++, Ada etc. can do, so can Java.

Java is platform-independent

Java programs will run on almost all computers – unchanged! Try that with any other programming language. (You almost certainly can't!) This is summed up in the slogan 'write once – run anywhere'.

Java is robust

If a Java program goes wrong (and programs do have that tendency), it won't create mayhem, damage and uncertainty. Because Java programs run inside a protective 'cage', the effects of any errors are confined and controlled. Java programs are even protected against infiltration by viruses.

Java has libraries

Because Java is a small language, most of its functionality is provided by pieces of program held in libraries. A whole host of library software is available to do graphics, Internet access and support graphical user interfaces (GUIs) – as well as the things ordinary programming languages do.

You will need . . .

To learn to program you need a computer and some software. There are several such systems around. A typical system is a PC (personal computer) with a Java Development Environment. This is software that allows you to prepare and run Java programs in a convenient way.

A little history

Java was originally called Oak, after the tree that grows outside the office of its principal designer, James Gosling. He found out, however, that there is already a programming language called Oak. So the team had to think again. They bought their coffee at a local shop and one of the types of coffee was Java. So that was the name they chose.

Java was designed by a team at Sun Microsystems, California. It arose from the need to construct software for consumer electronics – VCRs, TVs, telephones, pagers and perhaps (one day) toasters. The obvious-choice languages of the time, C and C++, had drawbacks – it was not easy to transport software onto a new processor chip. Thus Java was born with the objectives of creating very small, fast, reliable and transportable programs.

● Exercises are good for you

If you were to read this book time and again until you could recite it backwards, you still wouldn't be able to write programs. The practical work of writing programs and program fragments is vital to becoming fluent and confident at programming.

There are exercises for the reader at the end of each chapter. Please do some of them to enhance your ability to program.

There are also short self-test questions with answers throughout the text, so that you can check you have understood things properly.

● What's included?

This book explains the fundamentals of programming:

- variables;
- assignment;
- input and output;
- calculation;
- graphics and windows programming;
- repetition using `while`;
- choice using `if`.

It also covers integer numbers, floating-point numbers and character strings. Arrays are also described. All these are all topics that are fundamental, whatever kind of programming you go on to do.

This book also thoroughly addresses the object-oriented aspects of programming:

- classes;
- objects;
- methods;
- using library classes.

We also look at some of the more sophisticated aspects of object-oriented programming, like:

- inheritance;
- polymorphism.

Last, but not least, this book explains how to write Java applets for World-Wide Web documents.

● What's not included

This book describes the essentials of Java. It does not explain the bits and pieces, the bells and whistles. Thus the reader is freed from unnecessary detail and can concentrate on mastering Java and programming in general.

● Applications or applets?

Because we see the Internet as being tremendously important, we focus on applets here. In addition, applets are simple to construct for the beginner. However, we also explain how Java can create free-standing applications.

● Graphics or text?

Throughout the text we have emphasized programs that use graphical images rather than text input and output. We think they are more fun, more interesting and clearly demonstrate all the important principles of programming. We haven't ignored programs that input and output text – they are included, but they come second best.

● Graphical user interfaces (GUIs)

The programs we present use many of the features of a graphical user interface (GUI), such as windows, buttons, scrollbars and using the mouse in lots of different ways.

● The sequence of material

Programming involves a lot of sophisticated ideas, and one of the problems of writing a book about programming is deciding how and when to introduce new ideas. We introduce simple ideas early and more sophisticated ideas later on. So, for example, ideas on objects appear about one third of the way into the book. Our approach is to start with ideas like variables and assignment, then introduce if statements and looping, and then go on to objects and classes (the object-oriented features). We also wanted to make sure that the fun element of programming was paramount, so we use graphics right from the start.

● Bit by bit

In this book we introduce new ideas carefully one-at-a-time, rather than all at once. So there is a single chapter on writing methods, for example.

● Applications

Computers are used in many different applications and this book uses examples from all these areas:

● information processing;
● games;
● scientific calculations.

We have also included a few exercises which look at the new and exciting idea of artificial life.

The reader can choose to concentrate on those application areas of interest and ignore any of the other areas.

● Different kinds of programming

There are many different kinds of programming – examples are procedural, logic, functional, spreadsheet, visual and object-oriented programming. This book is about one type of programming – object-oriented programming – as practised in languages like Ada, C++, Eiffel and Smalltalk.

● Standard Java

Java is a standardized language with no variations and no dialects. This book sticks to the standard language. This book is about Java in general – not any specific product that supports or complements Java. All the programs in the book work under any manufacturer's implementation of Java.

● Which version of Java?

Java is evolving, but fairly slowly. The current mainstream version of Java is called Java 2 and this is the version that is covered in this book.

● AWT or Swing?

There are two ways of creating a GUI (graphical user interface) in Java. The original way is to use the AWT (Abstract Window Toolkit) and this is the approach used in most of this book. The newer way of creating a GUI is to use Swing; this is becoming popular and we have included a chapter on how to use it.

● Have fun

Programming is creative and interesting, particularly in Java. Please have fun!

● Visit our Web Site

All the programs presented in this book are available on our Web Site accessible via www.booksites.net.

● Any comments on this book?

If you want to email the authors, we are at D.H.Bell@shu.ac.uk and M.Parr@shu.ac.uk. We look forward to hearing from you.

● Authors' acknowledgements

We would like to thank the following for their advice during the revision and development process of *Java for Students, 3rd Edition*:

Michael Casperson (University of Aarhus, Denmark); Robin Clark (University of Stirling, UK); John Crowe (University of Nottingham, UK); Kevin Curran (University of Ulster, UK); Bertil Danielsson (Midsweden University, Sundsvall, Sweden); Rod Farkas (Community College, Allegheny County, Pennsylvania, US); Chris Fenwick (Brunel University, UK); Erik Frendsen (University of Stockholm, Sweden); Jeroen Fokker (University of Utrecht, Netherlands); Ulf Korneliussen (Alesund Hogskolen, Norway); Laszlo Bela Kovacs (University of Copenhagen, Denmark); Ville Leppanen (University of Turku, Finland); Ron Poet (University of Glasgow, UK); Alun Preece (University of Aberdeen, UK).

Many thanks also to all involved at Pearson Education and to all those readers who submitted comments and suggestions on earlier editions.

● Companion Web Site

A Companion Web Site accompanies *Java for Students*, 3e, by Douglas Bell and Mike Parr

Visit the *Java for Students* Companion Web Site at www.booksites.net/bell to find valuable teaching and learning material including:

For Students and Lecturers:

- downloadable code of all the programs in the book
- runnable versions of the programs
- discussion forum
- a bonus chapter on socket programming
- links to many useful Java resources

For Lecturers:

- planning a course – suggestions on how to use the book and what topics to include
- answers to selected exercises
- links to conferences on teaching with Java
- links to useful Java web sites

Also: This regularly maintained site also has search functions.

The scope of Java

In this chapter we set the scene. We see how and why Java came into being and what is new and novel about it.

● The Internet and the Web

The *Internet* is the world-wide collection of computers connected together by a network of communications channels. The communications technology consists of a variety of technologies – satellite, microwave, optical fibre and copper wire. Some networks are private and some are public. Millions of computers are connected together and can exchange information. One form of communication is electronic mail (email), which an individual can use to send mail to another person or to a complete list of addresses. You don't need to know anything about the technology of the communication links in order to use the Internet. All you do is use a software package running on your computer. This software, together with the programs running on the other computers on the Internet, handles all the detail of message passing and routing of messages.

An important form of communication is where someone creates a file of information on a disk (or one that the person rents space on) and then permits access to the information by anyone else in the world. Such a file of information is called a *site*. The information in the file can consist of text, graphics or a combination of the two. Accessing the information at a site is known as *visiting* the site.

The collection of sites across the world that offer information in this way is called the *World-Wide Web*, WWW or (usually) just the Web.

To visit a site, you need to know its address. An address on the Internet is unique, just as an international telephone number is unique. A typical address looks like this:

```
http://www.microsoft.com/
```

which is the address of Microsoft Corporation. Other addresses that might be of interest to you are:

`http://www.LATimes.com/`	is the *Los Angeles Times*, a daily newspaper
`http://www.kpix.com/live/`	is a view across San Francisco Bay, updated every five minutes
`http://www.sun.com/`	is Sun Microsystems, home of extensive information on Java

An address like those above is known as a URL. This is one of those terms that everyone uses but forgets what it stands for. It is short for *uniform resource locator*. A URL is an address that is unique in the whole world.

To get the information from a site (to visit a site) you need a computer and a program called a Web *browser*. A Web browser allows you to type in a site address: a URL. The browser then sends messages soliciting the information from the site. Provided the site is willing, it will send the information, which the browser displays on your screen. Anyone can write browser software, but it turns out that the short history of the Web has led to just two companies dominating the scene, each with their own Web browser. Netscape produces Navigator and Microsoft provides Internet Explorer. (These two firms are in strong competition with each other.)

Many sites have a lot of information to offer, so when you first access the site, what you will get is the *home page*. This is a screenful (or more) of information that is both a welcome mat and a directory of what information there is on offer at the site. If you access a site, you will normally get a choice of information to browse.

The Web is a wonderful international encyclopaedia providing information for free to anyone with a computer connected to the Internet.

● Hypertext

Most pages on the Web have pointers to other pages. When you click the mouse button on a line of text that is highlighted in some way (often by underlining) or click on a graphical image, you get transported to a different page. This new page could be on the same site as the one you just left or it could be anywhere else on the Web. This is called a *hypertext* link. It is common to follow these links, searching for the particular information you need, or simply browsing. This process is commonly called *surfing* the Net, presumably because of its associations with speed and adventure.

Sometimes a hypertext link is simply a pointer to another place within the same Web page. This illustrates that hypertext links are a break with the normal sequential structure of a document; normally we read information starting at the beginning and reading it line by line until we get to the end. Well – sometimes we do! Perhaps with a novel we read it in this way, but with some things we skip fragments and jump around all over the place. In a document with hypertext links the jumps are made explicit; we can read the page sequentially or we can follow any of the links.

You can create a document with hypertext links yourself using an editor with the appropriate facility. The parts of the text that allow people to click on links are written in a language called hypertext markup language (HTML). You can view such a file with a Web browser. If you have permission or money you can offer your information to the world as a page on the Web. There is no magic to hypertext links – they are simply pieces of text that are present in the file but not displayed by the browser. It is like having green ink in a book that is mostly black type and not being able to view the green bits. Appendix C describes the structure of hypertext files. For the purpose of Java programming you need to know a little about the format of hypertext files, but only a little. We will look at this in Chapter 2.

You can also place links to documents at other Web sites by placing the URL of the desired document in your hypertext file.

● Executable documents

The Internet and the Web are wonderful things. You can search for and find interesting information on anything under the sun. You can view beautiful and imaginative graphics. You can follow hypertext links from one site to another. There is one drawback – the information is static. It is static in the sense that it stays the same (although some sites update their pages regularly). It is static in the sense that you cannot interact with the information, except to click on links. Also, there is no animation (movement) of graphical images. So, wonderful as it is, surfing is simply fetching information from files on remote computers.

This is, of course, a slight exaggeration – it is possible to interact with Web pages to a limited degree. For example, you can often fill in fields of information to send back to the remote site – the search engines work in this way. You can also order products using the Web by selecting from menus and supplying your credit card number. But interaction is limited to filling in a field within a box. There is also some limited animation on some Web pages – logos that rotate of their own accord. But, by itself, the Web provides nothing like interaction on the scale of a computer game.

This is where Java comes in. To make the Web more exciting what we need to do is retrieve programs from other Web sites. Programs are essentially dynamic things – they do things. A computer program is virtually unlimited in what it can do. It can:

- animate some graphics;
- play a game with you;
- provide a word-processing facility;
- let you order goods from a catalogue;
- let you see a graph of stocks and shares as the data is actually changing.

What we want to do is fetch a program from a Web site and execute it on our own machine. However, before Java there were several obstacles to doing this. First, there is the danger of catching a computer virus by allowing a rogue program loose on your own machine. Secondly, there is the problem that there are a number of different types of computer in the world (Sun, PC, Macintosh etc.) that work differently and will not normally run the same program.

Java solves these problems by facilitating the construction of both secure programs (programs that will not do damage) and programs that are portable (programs that run on any computer). So now someone can create a Web page with a Java program embedded in it (along with the normal text and graphics), someone else can fetch the page using a Web browser and then execute (run) the Java program. (To do this, the browser does have to be *Java-enabled*.) These Java programs are called *applets*.

Java was designed as a language to allow programs to be securely transmitted across the Internet and securely executed. But Java is more than that: it is a truly general-purpose language that supports the construction of a wide variety of programs.

● What is a program?

In this section we try to give the reader some impression of what a program is. One way to understand is by using analogies with recipes, musical scores and knitting patterns. Even the instructions on a bottle of hair shampoo are a simple program:

```
wet hair
apply shampoo
rub hair
rinse
```

This program is a list of instructions for a human being, but it does demonstrate one important aspect of a computer program – a program is a *sequence* of instructions that is obeyed, starting at the first instruction and going on from one to the next until the sequence is complete.

A musical score and a knitting pattern are similar – they constitute a list of instructions that are obeyed in sequence. In the case of a knitting pattern, there are knitting machines which are fed with the program of instructions and then automatically obey the instructions. This is what a computer is – it is a machine that automatically obeys a sequence of instructions, a program. The set of instructions that are available for a computer to obey typically include:

● input a number;
● input some characters (letters and digits);
● output some characters;
● do a calculation;
● output a number;
● output some graphical image to the screen;
● respond to a button on the screen being clicked by the mouse.

The job of programming is one of selecting from this list those instructions that will carry out the required task. These instructions are written in a specialized language called a programming language. Java is one of many such languages. Learning to program means learning about the facilities of the programming language and how to combine them so as to do something you want.

The example of musical scores illustrates another aspect of programs. It is common in music to repeat sections, for example a chorus line. Musical notation saves the composer duplicating those parts of the score that are repeated and, instead, provides a notation specifying that a section of music is repeated. The same is true in a program; it is often the case that some action has to be repeated: for example, in a word-processing program, searching through a passage of text for the occurrence of a word. *Repetition* (or iteration) is common in programs. It is described in Java using **while**, **for** or **do** statements.

Recipes sometimes say something like: 'if you haven't got shallots use onions'. This illustrates another aspect of programs – they often carry out a test and then do one of two things depending on the result of the test. This is called *selection*, and it is described in Java programs using **if** and **switch** statements.

If you have ever used a recipe to prepare a meal, you may well have got to a particular step in the recipe only to find that you have to refer to another recipe for something that you need for the meal. The other recipe might be on another page in the recipe book. This way of writing instructions has an important analogue in programming, called *methods* in Java and other object-oriented languages. Methods are used in all programming languages, but go under other names, such as functions, procedures, subroutines or subprograms. If a recipe gets very long or very complicated, it is a good idea to split it into a main recipe plus the recipes for each of the components. In programming these are all called methods – because they are a method for doing something. These methods refer to each other, just as recipes refer to each other. Using methods promotes simplicity where there might otherwise be complexity. For example, if you say as part of one recipe: 'prepare a Hollandaise sauce', you are hiding a large amount of detail, which is described somewhere else in another method. Methods have another virtue: once written, a method can be used as part not only of one bigger recipe but of a number of recipes. So we have designed reusable recipes (methods).

To sum up, a program is a list of instructions that can be obeyed automatically by a computer. A program consists of combinations of:

● sequences;
● repetitions;
● selections;
● methods.

These features are shared by all kinds of programming and programming languages. We will now look at what is special about OO programming.

● Object-oriented programming – OOP

The programs that appear in this book and that hopefully you will write are fairly small. But some programs are huge. For example, Microsoft's word-processing program, Word, contains about 400 000 lines of program. At 40 lines per page, this is 10 000 pages, or about 40 paperback books. It is not so much the length of a program like this, it is the complexity. A program is not like a novel that you can understand by reading it sequentially from start to end; it is more like millions of pages on the Web, closely connected by hypertext links.

In order to cope with complexity, programmers have devised ways of splitting programs into smaller, more manageable pieces. Such pieces are sometimes called modules. Splitting 10 000 pages into 40 books would be creating modules. Within each book we could create, say, 14 chapters, which would make the material even more digestible. Within each chapter we could create sections. Of course, we would not choose to split up some text arbitrarily – we would create divisions that are natural and appropriate to the material.

In object-oriented programs (OOPs) the programs are constructed from modules called *objects*. These are the building blocks that allow complex programs to be created. Even small programs benefit from having been built from objects, as we shall see. Java is called an object-oriented language because it provides the facility to construct programs using objects.

One of the key aspects of OOP is *objects*. An object is a grouping of some data together with the instructions that act on the data. Such a combination constitutes a neat self-contained bundle. The selection of data and actions is not arbitrary – the data and the actions must be strongly related so that the object is a meaningful thing. We have already met the idea of having a small self-contained set of instructions; it is named a method. So objects are made up of data and their associated methods.

OOP is also about simulating or modelling real-world problems. A model is built from objects that interact with each other. The programmer attempts to write the program in such a way as to model the problem that he or she wants to solve. In the OOP view, the closer the model is to reality, the better the program will do what is desired. Examples are:

- a word processor – model as objects words, pages, lines, headings;
- airline seat reservation system – model flights, seats, times, destinations;
- a chess game – model the board, pieces etc.

In a word processor, the object named `line` will consist of the line itself (the data), together with methods named create, delete, insert word, display.

In the airline seat reservation system, object `flight` will have as data the time, destination and number of seats. The methods will be book a seat, cancel a seat and calculate the number of free seats.

In the chess game, an object `piece` will have the data that describes the piece (its name, position and colour), together with methods named move, display and remove.

In an OO program the objects interact by using each other's methods. For example, in a word processor, an object `line` provides a method delete. In order to carry out its task, this method uses a method named erase, which is provided by the object `word`. This is like a `washing machine` object which provides as a service to its users the method named wash. This method consists of many instructions, one of which is a request to the object `motor` to rotate the drum.

Objects are tools that provide the programmer with two things:

● modularity – a program consists of separate self-contained objects;
● simulation – a powerful idea for modelling real-world problems.

Classes

In the example of the word processor, we identified an object named `line` as being a likely candidate for modelling the information. But there will, of course, be not just one but a whole collection of lines in a document being handled by a word processor. So there will be a number of line objects. In OOP, rather than describe each and every object, the programmer describes the general type of an object and then creates as many of the objects as are needed. This general type is called a *class*. So in the word processor we would need a class `line`, from which we would create a number of objects of this same type.

This idea of creating a class that describes the properties of a whole number of objects is one we see in many forms of engineering and manufacture. If you are making garden gnomes, there is one mould from which you cast all the copies. If you are manufacturing mass-produced cars, there are blueprints that specify the parts of all of the cars. It's the same with washing machines, computers, TVs – even houses. In the jargon of OOP, a particular washing machine is said to be an *instance* of the class of washing machines of that type. In general, an object is an instance of some class.

In OOP, the programmer describes the nature of the various classes that the program will use. Each class has a name, some data and a number of methods. Then the programmer writes instructions to create particular instances of the classes for use in the program. Each object created in this way has its own unique name plus the data and the methods derived from the class. The particular instruction that creates an object is named **new**.

Classes provide the programmer with generality, the facility to define something once and then make lots of copies of it.

Inheritance

The last of the OO concepts that we are going to explain is called inheritance. When people start thinking about classes they think about classification schemes. The common example is living beings. One classification system looks like the one shown in Figure 1.1. What this diagram means is that any class shares some characteristic with the class immediately above it, the *superclass*. For example, all birds have skeletons. We say that

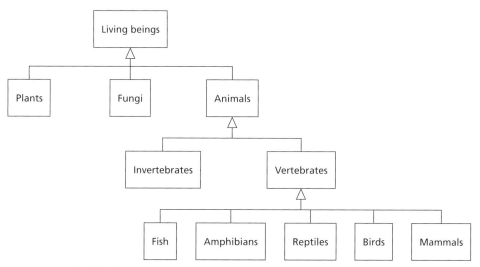

Figure 1.1 A classification scheme to illustrate inheritance.

the class *inherits* the characteristics of the class above it. In fact a class inherits all the characteristics of all the classes above it in the tree. For example, all birds are living things.

The same is true of human-made objects. For example, all washing machines share common characteristics, such as a drum or a soap dispenser. In OOP we often create classes that are related to other classes in a similar way. They inherit certain character-istics (data and/or methods) from their superclass, but they have their additional special characteristics. If we were writing a program that uses windows on the screen, we might make use of a class `window` that provides the border, the title bar and resizing buttons. But we would enhance it to provide the buttons for our special application. We shall see this happen in many examples later in this book.

What inheritance provides for the programmer is reuse; the programmer can create new classes that make use of the facilities of existing classes, extending the facilities as necessary.

We have reviewed some of the main ideas of object-oriented programming (objects, classes, inheritance) in an abstract way. We shall see throughout this book how object-oriented ideas are put into practice using Java.

Summary

● The Internet is the enormous number of computers connected together world-wide by networks.

● The World-Wide Web (Web) is the vast collection of documents resident on the Internet that can be viewed using a browser.

- Java allows Web pages to come alive.

- A program is a list of instructions that are obeyed automatically by a computer.

- Object-oriented programming (OOP) extends the power of lesser languages by providing objects, classes and inheritance.

EXERCISES

1.1 If you have Internet access, use your browser to surf the Net.

1.2 Some browsers have an option that allows you to view the raw hypertext markup language, HTML. Have a quick look at it, just for interest.

ANSWER TO SELF-TEST QUESTION

1.1 *Data:* speed, direction, position of steering wheel, position of accelerator, amount of petrol.

Methods: start engine, stop engine, press gas, release gas, press brake, release brake, turn wheel left, turn wheel right, change gear.

A first Java program

Introduction

To learn how to program in Java you will need access to a computer with software that allows you to prepare Java programs. To prepare and run Java programs you need to make use of a variety of programs that are supplied with your computer. Some of these software tools differ from one computer to another.

This chapter explains:

- how to prepare a Java program;
- how to use the various software tools that are necessary – the operating system, the filing system, the editor, the compiler, the linker, the applet viewer and the browser;
- the structure of a very simple Java program.

Applets and applications

A program is a collection of instructions to a computer. Computer programs are collectively known as software and there are many different types of software. Java is one of many languages for instructing a computer. Java programs are of two distinct types – applications and applets. Both types are programs. The difference is that an application is a completely free-standing program – it is not part of any other program and it doesn't need any other program to launch it. In contrast, an applet is invoked as part of a Web page and therefore needs either a Web browser or an applet viewer to invoke it. There are important differences between the way in which an applet and an application are written in Java. In this book we very largely concentrate on how to write applets, because we believe that this is the main way in which Java will be used in practice.

To summarize:

- An applet is invoked as part of a Web page.
- An application is free-standing.

● Integrated development environments

It may be that you can use an *integrated development environment* (IDE). This is a software package designed to help with the complete process of preparing and running a Java program. Such development environments are available from a number of major software houses. They combine the functions of editor, compiler, linker and applet viewer, which are described below as separate programs. They also provide a debugger, which we shall meet in Chapter 24 on debugging. An integrated development environment provides menus and buttons to make the process of developing a program as easy as possible.

If you use one of these software packages, it is still a good idea to understand the ideas of files, editing, compilation, linking and execution, as described below.

● The operating system

The programs that are automatically loaded and run when the computer is switched on are collectively called the *operating system*. The operating system is usually supplied by the computer manufacturer along with the hardware, or is bought separately from a software company like Microsoft.

The operating system provides you with useful facilities to:

- enter commands from keyboard or mouse. The operating system provides the user interface to the computer;
- run programs that someone else has already written (stored on the disk).

Your operating system may also provide a wealth of other facilities, including the ability to:

- display on the screen the contents of files held on disk;
- send and receive electronic mail, and browse the Web.

● Files

Your computer either has its own disk or is connected to a disk via a network. Information stored on a computer disk is stored in files, just as information stored in filing cabinets in an office is stored in files. A part of the operating system called the filing system allows you to do this.

Normally you set up a file to contain a collection of related information, for example:

● a letter to your mother;
● a list of students on a particular course;
● a list of friends, with names, addresses and telephone numbers.

Each file has its own name, chosen by the person who created it. It is usual, as you might expect, to choose a name that clearly describes what is in the file. A filename has a *suffix* – a bit on the end – that describes the type of information that is held in the file. For example, a file called `letter1` that holds a letter and is normally updated with a word processor might have the suffix `.doc` (short for document) so that its full name is `letter1.doc`. A file that holds a Java program has the suffix `.java`, so that a typical filename might be `game.java`. File suffixes are sometimes called file *extensions*.

On most computers, a group of related files is collected together into a *directory* (sometimes called a *folder*). So, in a particular directory you might hold all letters sent to the bank. In another directory you might store all the sales figures for one year, and in another directory you might hold all your games programs. Certainly you will keep all the files that are used in a single Java program in the same directory. You give each directory a name – usually a meaningful name that helps you to find it. If you have a directory called `myprogs` and a file within it called `game.java`, then the full name of the file is `myprogs\game.java`.

The character '\' (backslash or reverse solidus) separates the directory name from the filename within it. But beware: by a strange quirk of history, the two major camps in the world of operating systems use two confusingly similar symbols for this purpose:

● Microsoft operating systems use \
● The UNIX operating system uses /

You will probably also be using Web addresses, and these feature the / character.

Normally directories are themselves grouped together in a directory. So you might have a directory called `Toms` within which are the directories `myprogs`, `letters`, `games`. So now an even more complete name for the file `game.java` is the name `Toms\myprogs\game.java`. You might think that this will go on forever, and indeed you can set up directories of directories *ad infinitum*. Your computer system will typically have tens of directories and hundreds of files. Some of these will be yours (you can set them up and alter them) and some of them will belong to the operating system (leave them alone!).

So, a file is a collection of information (like a single Java program) with a name. Related files are collected together into a directory, which also has a name.

You need to know how to use the filing system on your particular computer so that you can:

● create a file with a Java applet in it;
● display the applet on the screen;
● run the applet;
● find a file;
● group files together in a directory.

Unfortunately, this book doesn't explain how to use your operating system – because there are a number of them. You will have to do one or more of the following:

- ask someone to show you;
- read a manual or a book;
- follow a tutorial package on your computer (if available);
- experiment.

SELF-TEST QUESTION
....

2.1 What does a filing system do? What is a file? What is a directory (or folder)?

● The editor

The editor is another important part of the operating system. You might think of an editor as a dominating man with a permanent cigarette in a newspaper office, but an editor in computing is a program that helps you to create and change files.

An editor provides facilities to:

- create a new file;
- retrieve an existing file;
- delete text in a file;
- insert text in a file;
- change text in a file;
- move text around in a file;
- search for some text in a file.

Different editors provide these facilities in different ways. Your editor may be built into the software package that assists you in developing Java programs. Again, this book doesn't explain how to use the editor – because there are so many of them. You will need to become fairly fluent at using your editor, because it is common to have to correct programs frequently.

SELF-TEST QUESTION
....

2.2 Find out how to start and use your editor.

● Preparing a Java program

By now you probably know how to run a program that someone else has already written – a game perhaps. Now it's time to write your own program in Java. No computer can directly understand Java. So you have to make use of several programs that help. The programs are, in order:

1. editor;
2. compiler;
3. linker;
4. applet viewer or browser.

We will now look at each of these to see what they do.

● Editing

We have already met the editor. It provides facilities to alter the contents of a file. You will have to familiarize yourself with the editor on your computer.

Using the editor, key in your first small Java program. Do not worry about what it means, at this stage. You will see that the program contains certain unusual characters and two different kinds of bracket. You might have to search for them on your keyboard.

```
import java.awt.*;
import java.applet.Applet;

public class Greeting extends Applet {
    public void paint (Graphics g) {
        g.drawString ("Hello", 50, 50);
    }
}
```

Undoubtedly you will make mistakes when you key in this program. You can use the editor to correct the program. When it looks correct, save the program in a file on the disk. Give the file a suitable name:

```
Greeting.java
```

A file that holds a Java program must have the suffix .java. The first part of the name can be whatever the programmer chooses, but it is compulsory to use the name of the program. This is the name that follows the words `public class` in the Java code.

The first step is now complete.

● Compiling

A *compiler* is a program that converts a program written in a language like Java into the language that the computer understands. So a compiler is like an automatic translator, able to translate one (computer) language into another. Java programs are converted into *byte-code*. Byte-code is not exactly the same as the language that a computer understands (machine code). Instead, it is an idealized machine language that means that your Java program will run on any of a large number of computers. When your program is run, the byte-code is interpreted by a program called the Java Virtual Machine.

Find out how to run your Java compiler and use it to convert your program to byte-code. In the jargon, you wish to *compile* your program. If your operating system uses a command line, the command to invoke the compiler will look like this:

```
javac Greeting.java
```

The name of the compiler is `javac` and it is followed by the name of the file that contains the code of your program.

If you have a Java development system with a graphical user interface (GUI), then you click on a button or menu option to invoke the compilation process.

As it compiles your program, the compiler checks that the program obeys the rules of programming in Java and, if something is wrong, displays appropriate error messages. It also checks that the programs in any libraries that you are using are being employed correctly. It is rare (even for experienced programmers) to have a program compile correctly first time, so don't be disappointed if you get some error messages.

One of the standing jokes of programming is that error messages from compilers are often cryptic and unhelpful. The compiler will indicate (note: not pinpoint) the position of the errors. Study what you have keyed in and try to see what is wrong. Common errors are:

● semicolons missing or in the wrong place;
● brackets missing;
● single quotes (') rather than double quotes (").

Identify your error, edit the program and re-compile. This is when your patience is on test! Repeat until you have eradicated the errors.

● Creating a Web page

To run our Java program, we need to create a Web page with the applet embedded in it. We use the editor to create a file containing hypertext markup language (HTML). (Some integrated development systems create this file automatically.) An appropriate name for the file is:

```
Greeting.html
```

in which the suffix has the obvious meaning. The HTML file contents look like this:

```
<title> Web page with Applet </title>
<applet code="Greeting.class"
     width=300 height=200> </applet>
```

The text sandwiched between `<title>` and `</title>` is the text that appears in the heading of the Web page as displayed by the browser. It can be any text that you choose.

The word `<applet` tells the browser that a Java applet is on its way (and the description of the applet terminates with the `</applet>`). The word `code` introduces the name of the file containing the Java applet – in our case this is `Greeting.class`. The words `width` and `height` specify the size of the area of the screen available for the applet, measured in pixels.

● The libraries

The output from the compiler in the `.class` file is not yet quite ready to run because it is incomplete. Every Java program needs some help from one or more pieces of program that are held in libraries. In computer terms, a *library* is a collection of already-written useful pieces of program, kept in files. Your small sample program needs to make use of such a piece of program to display information on the screen. In order to accomplish this, the requisite piece of program has to be *linked* to your program when it is run.

The libraries are collections of useful parts. Suppose you were going to design a new motor car. You would probably want to design the body shape and the interior layout. But you would probably want to make use of an engine that someone else had designed and built. Similarly, you might well use the wheels that some other manufacturer had produced. So, some elements of the car would be new, and some would be off-the-shelf. The off-the-shelf components are like the pieces of program in the Java library.

Things can go wrong when the compiler checks the links to library software – and you may get a cryptic error message. Common errors are:

● the library is missing or not where you expect it to be;
● you have misspelled the name of something in the library.

● Running the Java program – the applet viewer and the browser

The compiler creates a file on the disk with the suffix `.class`. It contains the byte-code equivalent of your Java program. The first part of the name is the name of the Java program – so in this example the filename is:

```
Greeting.class
```

The next step is to run the program using the *applet viewer* or a *Web browser*. A browser is a program that allows the user to fetch Web pages from a site on the Internet and display them. The most common Web browsers are Netscape Navigator and Microsoft Internet Explorer. An applet viewer is a program that runs a Java applet – without the need for a Web browser. It provides a useful tool for testing Java applets.

If we now point the browser at this page – by entering the filename `greeting.html` in the appropriate box, we will see the output created by the Java program. Alternatively

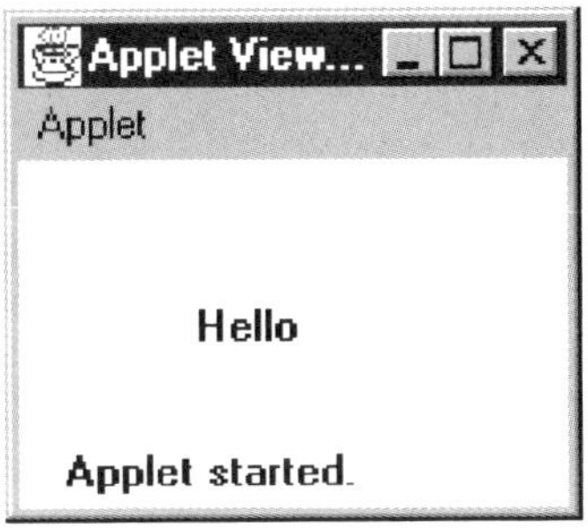

Figure 2.1 Output from the greeting program.

you can run the applet viewer. If your operating system uses a command line, the command to invoke the applet viewer probably looks like this:

```
appletviewer Greeting.html
```

The name of the viewer program is `appletviewer` and it is followed by the name of the file that contains the HTML of your applet.

If you have a GUI-based Java development system, then you click on a button to invoke the applet viewer.

The applet viewer or browser will examine your HTML file, fetch your program, link it and run it.

If all goes well, the applet viewer or Web browser can at last run the Java program and the effect of running this particular program is shown in Figure 2.1. Library software is linked as and when needed as the program is running.

● Demystifying the program

We will now explain the Java program. Even though it is as small as it can be, you can see that the program has quite a lot to it. This is because Java is a real industry-strength language, and even the smallest program needs some heavyweight ingredients.

We give the code of the program here again. This time it has line numbers to help with the explanation. (Line numbers should not and must not be part of a real program.)

```
1. import java.awt.*;
2. import java.applet.Applet;
3. public class Greeting extends Applet {
4.     public void paint(Graphics g) {
5.         g.drawString("Hello", 50, 50);
6.     }
7. }
```

The important piece of this program – and the only piece you need to understand for some time to come – is line 5. This instructs the computer to display some text on the screen. The text is the word 'Hello', which must be enclosed in double quotes. Text in quotes like this is called a string. The two numbers specify the position on the screen at which the string is to be displayed. The position is 50 pixels from the left of the screen and 50 pixels from the top. (As we shall see later, a pixel is the unit of measurement for items displayed on the computer screen.) When this program is run, as shown in Figure 2.1, you can see the brief message displayed on the screen.

Lines 1 and 2 specify information about the library programs that the program uses. The word `import` is followed by the name of a library that is to be used by the program. This program uses the AWT (Abstract Window Toolkit) and the applet library in order to carry out output to the screen.

Line 3 is a heading which announces that this code is an applet and gives its name, `Greeting`. The applet itself is enclosed within the curly brackets on lines 3 and 7.

Line 4 is a heading specifying that the statements that follow are the statements that paint (output images to) the window. The statements that paint the image are grouped inside curly brackets on lines 4 and 6. As we have seen, there is only one such statement in this program, line 5, which outputs the desired message. You will see that it ends with a semicolon, which is the norm for statements in Java.

Programming pitfalls

When you are editing a program, save it every ten minutes or so to guard against losing your work should the computer fail.

Make sure that when you key in a program, you copy the characters exactly as shown.

Make sure that the name of the file matches the name of the class in the file. If your class is called `Elephant`, your file must be called `Elephant.java`, not `elephant.java`.

You will almost certainly make a mistake when you key in a program. The compiler will tell you what the errors are. Try not to get too frustrated by the errors.

Summary

● The operating system is a program that obeys commands entered by the user.

● Information held on a disk is held in files. The filing system is a part of the operating system that organizes files.

● The editor is the program that allows you to make changes to files.

● Compiling a Java program converts it to byte-code and checks it for grammatical errors.

● Linking a program combines a program with the necessary parts from libraries.

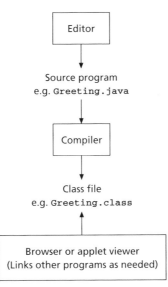

Figure 2.2 The stages of program preparation.

● The applet viewer or a browser launches a Java applet.

● An application is a Java program that runs directly, without the need for an applet viewer or a browser.

The steps involved in preparing a Java program (Figure 2.2) are:

1. Edit (create) the program in a file with suffix .java.
2. Compile.
3. Create a file with HTML commands in it.
4. Run the program using an applet viewer or browser. The library software is linked when it is needed by the program.

Things can go wrong at any stage, and part of the programmer's job is identifying and correcting the errors. Don't forget: it is rare for everything to work smoothly first time. Be careful, be relaxed.

The editor, compiler and applet viewer differ from one computer to another, so we have only described them in outline. Alternatively, you may be using an integrated development environment. Thankfully, the language itself, Java, is standardized and the same on different computers.

SELF-TEST QUESTION

2.3 List and explain the steps involved in preparing a program to run on a computer.

EXERCISES

2.1 Learn about the facilities available on your computer to:

- run programs;
- store information in files;
- edit files.

2.2 Run a program that has already been written – a game perhaps.

2.3 Using the editor, key in the following Java program:

```java
import java.awt.*;
import java.applet.Applet;

public class Love extends Applet {
    public void paint(Graphics g) {
        g.drawString("Hello", 50, 50);
        g.drawString("I love Java", 50, 100);
    }
}
```

Be careful, because it contains lots of unusual characters. When you have keyed it in, check that it is correct, and, if necessary, correct it using the editor.

Again using the editor, create a file with the following HTML in it:

```html
<title> Web page with Applet </title>
<applet code="Love.class"
    width=300 height=200> </applet>
```

Then compile and run the program. You will probably encounter errors that require you to go back and amend the program. Be patient; everyone makes mistakes at programming.

2.4 Alter the program so that it displays your name after the word 'Hello'.

ANSWERS TO SELF-TEST QUESTIONS

2.1 A file is a collection of information, stored on a disk. It has a name. A directory is a collection of files. It also has a name. A filing system organizes the files and directories. It keeps track of file and directory names. It provides the facility to create, load and save files.

2.2 1. Key in the program using an editor program, storing the program text in a file.
2. Compile the program using the compiler.
3. Run the program. The library programs are linked when needed.

Introductory graphics

● Setting the scene

The term 'computer graphics' conjures up a variety of possibilities. We could be discussing a computer-generated Hollywood movie, a sophisticated video game, a virtual reality environment, a static photographic-style image on a VDU, or a rather more simple image built out of lines. The experienced Java programmer can display animated images, but here we will restrict ourselves to the display of still images built from simple shapes.

● A first picture

Here we will look at the graphical equivalent of the greeting program in Chapter 2. It displays a diagonal line on the screen. The program listing is:

```
import java.awt.*;
import java.applet.Applet;
public class FirstLine extends Applet {
    public void paint(Graphics g) {
        g.drawLine(0,0,100,100);
    }
}
```

Figure 3.1 shows what the program produces when it runs via the applet viewer.

Recall that when we run an applet we must provide an HTML file. On some Java programming environments, the HTML file will be automatically created, but if your system doesn't do this, the easiest way to set one up is to copy the HTML file used in Chapter 2, renaming it to `FirstLine.html`, and altering it to use `FirstLine.class`.

Figure 3.1 The output of the `FirstLine` applet.

Here is the altered file, named `FirstLine.html`:

```
<title> Web page with Applet </title>
<applet code="FirstLine.class"
    width=300 height=200> </applet>
```

Again, most Java programming environments will generate this file for you.

To run the above program, create a new file called `FirstLine.java`, and attempt to compile it. When it compiles correctly, use the applet viewer on the `FirstLine.html file`.

● The graphics screen

Java graphics are based on *pixels*. A pixel is a small dot on the screen which can be set to a particular colour. Unfortunately for programmers, different screens have different numbers of pixels, so at this introductory stage we will set up a graphics area that is small enough for any computer: 300 pixels wide and 200 pixels high. We specify this in the HTML code, as shown by the command:

```
width=300 height=200
```

Each pixel is identified by a pair of numbers (its coordinates), starting from zero:

● the horizontal position, often referred to as *x* in mathematics (and in the Java documentation) – this value increases from left to right;
● the vertical position, often referred to as *y* – this value increases downwards.

We use this system when we request Java to draw simple shapes. Figure 3.2 shows the approach.

● Explanation of the program

The only section we will explain (and later alter) is the following. The rest of the program should be taken on trust for now. It merely says that we are writing an applet.

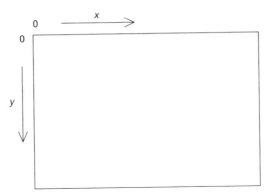

Figure 3.2 The pixel coordinate system in Java.

Remember that we said that Java is an industrial-strength language, and 10-line programs are not its forte!

```
1. public void paint(Graphics g) {
2.    g.drawLine(0,0,100,100);
3. }
```

Line 1 introduces the section of your program which is concerned with displaying shapes on the screen. The { } in lines 1 and 3 show the extent of the display instructions. A section of program such as the above is known as a *method* in Java.

The main feature of our program is the line:

```
g.drawLine(0,0,100,100);
```

You might guess that it is concerned with drawing a line, but what about that 'g.'? It specifies the area where drawing is to take place. In short programs there might be no choice – all we have is the applet window – but later we will see that the screen could be split into separate drawing areas.

The drawLine method is one of the many methods provided by the Java system in a library. The statement shown is an invocation (also known as a call) of the method, asking it to carry out the task of displaying a line. A method is so called because it is a method (or way) of doing something.

When we make use of the drawLine method, we need to supply it with some values for the start and finish points of the line, and we need to get these in the correct order, which is:

1. the horizontal value (*x*) of the start of the line;
2. the vertical value (*y*) of the start of the line;
3. the horizontal value of the end of the line;
4. the vertical value of the end of the line.

The items are known as *parameters* in Java – they are inputs to the drawLine method. Parameters must be enclosed in round brackets and separated by commas. (You may encounter the term 'argument', which is an alternative name for a parameter.) This particular method requires four parameters, and they must be integers (whole numbers). If we attempt to use the wrong number of parameters, or the wrong type, we get an error message from the compiler. We need to ensure that:

● we supply the correct number of parameters;
● we supply the correct type of parameters;
● we arrange them in the right order.

Some methods do not require any parameters. In this case, we must *still* use the brackets, as in:

```
doSomething();
```

A final point – note the semicolon ';' at the end of the drawLine parameters. In Java, a semicolon must appear at the end of every 'statement'. But what is a statement? The answer is not trivial! As you can see from the above program, a semicolon does not occur at the end of *every* line. Rather than provide intricate formal rules here, the advice is to base your initial programs on our examples. However, the use of a method followed by its parameters is in fact a statement, so a semicolon is required.

● The paint method

There are two kinds of method at work in our example:

● those that the programmer writes, which are part of the applet program;
● those that are pre-written in the libraries.

All methods have a name, and most have parameters. The paint method is one which the programmer must write. It is invoked by the browser or applet viewer whenever the screen needs to be drawn. Thus, the programmer must include within paint all the instructions to display the required text and graphics. To observe paint being invoked, resize the applet window with the mouse, and note that the image is re-drawn.

● Methods for drawing

As well as lines, Java provides us with facilities for drawing:

● rectangles;
● ovals (hence circles);
● arcs.

The following shapes can also be drawn, but require additional Java knowledge. We shall omit their parameter details, and won't use them in our programs.

● raised (three-dimensional) rectangles;
● rectangles with rounded corners;
● polygons.

Additionally, the shapes can be filled with a specified colour.

Here we list the parameters for each method, and provide an example program which uses them.

`drawLine`
- the horizontal value of the start of the line;
- the vertical value of the start of the line;
- the horizontal value of the end of the line;
- the vertical value of the end of the line.

`drawRect`
- the horizontal value of the top left corner;
- the vertical value of the top left corner;
- the width of the rectangle;
- the height of the rectangle.

`drawOval`

Imagine the oval squeezed inside a rectangle. We provide:

- the horizontal value of the top left corner of the rectangle;
- the vertical value of the top left corner of the rectangle;
- the width of the rectangle;
- the height of the rectangle.

`drawArc`

An arc is a curve, part of a circle. This method involves specifying angles in a similar style as in mathematics: angles increase in an anticlockwise direction and are measured in degrees, zero degrees being in an easterly direction. We specify the starting angle and the number of degrees in the arc. As usual we specify an enclosing rectangle, which you can imagine as containing the complete 360-degree circle, if we chose to draw it. Figure 3.3 shows the geometry.

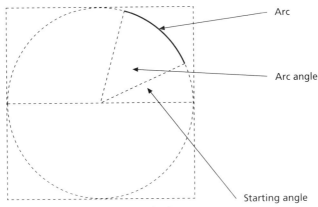

Figure 3.3 The geometry of the `drawArc` method.

The order of parameters is:

- the horizontal value of the top left corner of the rectangle;
- the vertical value of the top left corner of the rectangle;
- the width of the rectangle;
- the height of the rectangle;
- the starting angle;
- the total angle of the arc.

● Filling shapes with colours

It is possible to set the colour to be used for drawing, and the background colour. There are 13 standard colours:

black	blue	cyan	darkGray
gray	green	lightGray	magenta
orange	pink	red	white
yellow			

(cyan is a deep green/blue).

Take care with the spellings – note the use of capitals in the middle of the names. Here is how you might use the colours:

```
setBackground(Color.lightGray);
g.setColor(Color.red);
```

If you don't set a colour, Java chooses a default one.

Additionally, we have a set of methods for filling the shapes:

```
fillRect
fillArc
fillOval
```

Their parameters are identical to those of the `draw` equivalents, their only difference being that `fillArc` produces a pie shape.

● The sequence concept

When we have a number of statements in a program, they are performed top-to-bottom, in sequence (unless we specify otherwise using the later concepts of selection and repetition). Here is a program which draws a variety of shapes. Figure 3.4 shows the resulting output.

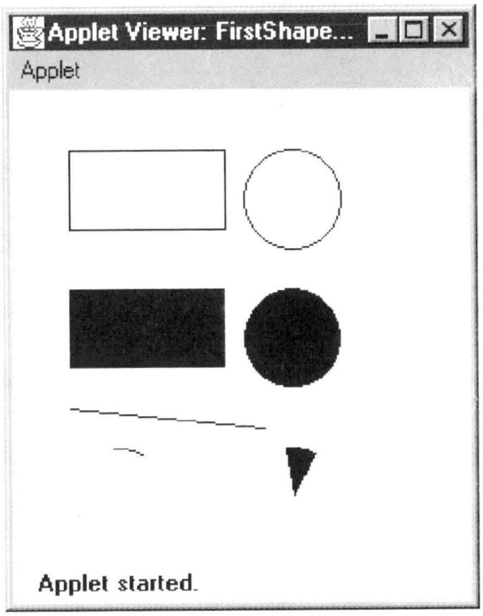

Figure 3.4 The output of the FirstShapes applet.

```java
import java.awt.*;
import java.applet.Applet;

public class FirstShapes extends Applet {
    public void paint(Graphics g) {
        g.drawRect(30,30,80,40);
        g.drawOval(120,30,50,50);
        g.setColor(Color.black);
        g.fillRect(30,100,80,40);
        g.fillOval(120,100,50,50);
        g.drawLine(30,160,130,170);
        g.drawArc(30,180,50,50,60,40);
        g.fillArc(120,180,50,50,60,40);
    }
}
```

The statements are obeyed (executed, performed . . .) from top to bottom, down the page (even though this may be hard to observe on a fast computer).

SELF-TEST QUESTION

3.1 Write and run an applet which draws a large 'T' shape on the screen.

● Displaying characters

In our early programs, we will make extensive use of Java's facilities for displaying messages alongside graphics. We use the `drawString` method, as in:

```
g.drawString("Hello World",30,40);
```

The parameters of `drawString` are:

- a string. The simplest form of string is a sequence of characters enclosed within double-quote characters;
- the horizontal position of the start of the string;
- the vertical position of an imaginary line that the characters rest on. In many fonts, characters like 'g' have a descender that hangs down below this line.

One drawback with mixing text and graphics on the same screen area is that the size of the characters (and their font, i.e. 'style') depends on your computer. The assumption that we will make here is that the default font and size will be satisfactory on all computers for our introductory purposes. However, the experienced Java programmer would produce programs that select a suitable font and size.

● Joining strings with +

We have seen the use of strings, as in:

```
g.drawString("Hello World", 40, 40);
```

In Java, we can join (concatenate) several strings together to build up a single string, by using the + symbol. In Java jargon, + is known as an *operator*.
Here is an example:

```
g.drawString("Hi "+"there "+"Mike" , 100, 100);
```

The use of + results in `"Hi there Mike"` being used by `drawString`.
String concatenation is useful with methods that will only accept a single string as a parameter (like `drawString`). Chapter 4 makes frequent use of this technique.

● Adding meaning with comments

What does the following do?

```
g.drawLine(20,80,70,10);
g.drawLine(70,10,120,80);
g.drawLine(20,80,120,80);
```

The meaning is not instantly obvious, and you probably tried to figure it out with pencil and paper. The answer is that it draws a triangle with a horizontal base, but this is not apparent from the three statements. In Java, we can add *comments* (a kind of annotation) to the instructions, by preceding them by '//'. For example, we might put:

```
// draw a triangle
g.drawLine(20,80,70,10);
g.drawLine(70,10,120,80);
g.drawLine(20,80,120,80);
```

A comment can contain anything – there are no rules. It is up to you to use them to convey meaning.

Comments can also be placed at the end of a line, as in:

```
// draw a triangle
g.drawLine(20,80,70,10);
g.drawLine(70,10,120,80);
g.drawLine(20,80,120,80); //draw base
```

Do not over-use comments. It is not normal to comment every line, as this often involves duplicating information. The following is a poor comment:

```
g.drawString("Hello",100,100); // display Hello
```

Here, the statement says clearly what it does, without the need for a comment. Use comments to state the overall theme of a section of program, rather than restating the detail of each statement. In Chapter 22 you will learn about additional commenting styles which assist in program documentation.

Programming pitfalls

Take care with the punctuation. Commas, semicolons, and round and curly brackets must be exactly as in the examples.

Grammar spot

The order and type of parameters must be correct for each method.

New language elements

- "..." to indicate a string of characters
- +   for string concatenation
- ( )   to enclose parameters
- //   to indicate comments

Summary

- Statements are obeyed in sequence, top to bottom (unless we request otherwise).
- Java has a set of 'draw' methods which you can call up to display graphics. These methods can be placed inside the `paint` method.

● Graphics positioning is based on pixel coordinates.

● Parameter values can be passed into methods.

EXERCISES

In the following, we recommend that you do rough sketches and calculations prior to writing the program. You can use the same HTML and program for each question. Merely add your new statements to the `paint` method.

3.1 Draw a triangle, with one vertical side.

3.2 Draw an empty tic-tac-toe (noughts and crosses) board.

3.3 Design a simple house, and draw it.

3.4 Here are rainfall figures for the country of Xanadu.

1994   150 cm
1995   175 cm
1996   120 cm

(a) Represent the data by a series of horizontal lines.
(b) Use `drawString` to add the numbers alongside the lines.
(c) Instead of lines, use filled rectangles with different colours.

3.5 Design an archery-style target with concentric circles. Then add different colours and use `drawString` to show the score for each ring. The purchase of a rubber sucker gun to fire at the screen is optional.

ANSWER TO SELF-TEST QUESTION

3.1
```
import java.awt.*;
import java.applet.Applet;
public class FirstLine extends Applet {
    public void paint(Graphics g) {
        g.drawLine(20,20,120,20);
        g.drawLine(80,20,80,120);


    }


}
```

Variables and calculations

● Introduction – numeric variables

Numbers of one form or another occur in most programs, for example drawing pictures using screen coordinates, controlling spaceflight trajectories, calculating salaries and tax deductions.

Here we will introduce the two basic types of number:

- whole numbers, known as integers in maths and as the `int` type in Java;
- 'decimal point' numbers, known as 'real' in maths, and as `float` (from the term 'floating point') in Java.

Previously we used whole numbers to produce screen graphics, but for more sophisticated programs we need to introduce the concept of a *variable* – a kind of storage box used to remember values, so that these values can be used or altered later in the program.

Before we get to actual code, it is worth while to spend time exploring a problem faced by new programmers – they know that they need a numeric variable, but can't choose between `int` or `float`.

There are undeniably some `int` situations:

- the number of students in a class;
- the number of pixels on a screen;
- the number of copies of this book sold so far.

And there are some undeniable `float` situations:

- my height in metres;
- the mass of an atom in grams;
- the average of the integers 3 and 4.

However, sometimes the type is not obvious; consider a variable for holding an exam mark – `float` or `int`? The answer is that you don't know yet – you must seek further clarification, e.g. by asking the marker if they mark to the nearest whole number, or if they ever use decimal places. Thus, the choice of `int` or `float` is determined by the problem.

● The nature of `int`

When we use an integer in Java, it can be a whole number in the range –2 147 483 648 to +2 147 483 647 or, approximately –2 000 000 000 to +2 000 000 000.

All integer calculations are accurate, in the sense that information at the least significant (right-hand) end of the number will be preserved correctly.

● The nature of `float`

When we use a `float` number in Java, its value can be between -3.4×10^{38} and $+3.4 \times 10^{38}$. In non-mathematical terms, 3.4×10^{38} means 34 followed by 37 zeros – very large indeed! Numbers are held to an approximate accuracy of seven digits.

The main point about `float` quantities is that they are stored *approximately* in many cases. Try this on a calculator:

$$7 \div 3$$

Using seven digits, the answer is 2.333333, whereas we know that a closer answer is:

2.33333333333333333

Even this is not the exact answer!

In short, because `float` quantities are stored in a limited number of digits, errors can build up at the least-significant end. For many calculations (e.g. exam marks) this is not important, but for calculations involving, say, the design of a space shuttle, it might be. In Java the solution is not to use the `int` type (even though it is precise) but to use the `double` type, which allows us to use decimal-point numbers with around 15 digits of precision. In this book, we will use `float` in examples because it is sufficiently accurate for our purposes.

There are a variety of ways in which we can express float numbers, but for now we will show the simplest form – we write the number followed by the letter `f` (for `float`) as in:

```
12.34f            -32.0f
```

If we omit the `f`, the number is assumed to be `double`.

● Declaring variables

Once the type of our variables has been chosen, we need to *name* them. We can imagine them as storage boxes with a name on the outside and a number (value) inside. The value may change as the program works through its sequence of operations, but the name is fixed. The programmer is free to choose the names, but (as in most programming languages) there are certain rules that must be followed. In Java, names:

● must start with a letter (A to Z, a to z);
● can contain any number of letters or digits (a digit is 0 to 9);
● can contain the underscore '_' or '$';
● can be any length.

Note that Java is 'case-sensitive'. This means that 'A' is different from 'a'. Thus, the following three names are different:

```
length
LENGTH
Length
```

Here are some allowable names:

```
Amount
x
pay2001
```

and here are some unallowable (illegal) names:

```
2001pay
_area
my age
```

Those are the Java rules – and we have to obey the rules. But there is also a Java style – a way of using the rules which is followed when a variable consists of several words. The rules do not allow spaces in names. Rather than use short names or the underscore, the accepted style for variables is to start the first word with a lower-case letter, and to capitalize each following word. Thus, rather than:

```
heightofbox
h
hob
height_of_box
```

we put:

```
heightOfBox
```

The style is similar for class names (covered later), except that a capital letter is used to start the name, as in:

```
Applet
HelloWorld
Calculation1
```

Note that there are also some 'reserved' names that Java uses and which can't be reused by the programmer. You have seen some of them, e.g.:

```
void
extends
int
```

A full list is provided in Appendix F.

SELF-TEST QUESTION

4.1 Which of the following variable names are allowed in Java, and which have the correct style?

```
volume
AREA
Length
3sides
side1
getFirst
lenth
mysalary
your salary
screenSize.
```

Here is an actual program which we will study in detail. It calculates the area of a rectangle. We have assumed that its sides are integer quantities.

```
//calculate area of rectangle -version 1
import java.awt.*;
import java.applet.Applet;

public class Calculation extends Applet {
    public void paint(Graphics g) {
        int length;                            //declarations
        int breadth;
        int area;

        length = 20;                           //assignments
        breadth = 10;
        area = length * breadth;               //* means multiply
        g.drawString("Area is " + area, 100, 100); // display answer
    }
}
```

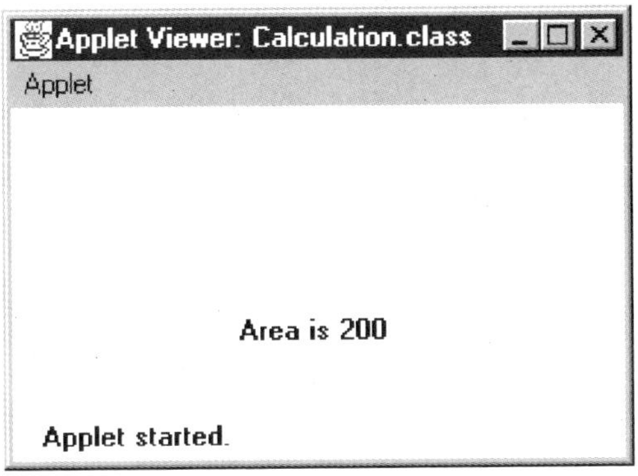

Figure 4.1 The output of the `Calculation` applet.

Before you run this program (we recommend that you do!) you need to create (or rename) your minimum HTML file to 'Calculation.html'. Figure 4.1 shows what you will see on the screen.

In the program we have used three integer variables, which eventually will hold our rectangle data. Recall that we can choose whatever names we like, but have opted for clear names rather that single-letter or funny names. (Funny names are only funny the first time you see them!)

Now that names are chosen, we must *declare* them to the Java compiler. Though this seems like tedious red tape at first, the point of introducing them is to enable the compiler to spot misspellings lower down the program. Here are the declarations:

```
int length;
int breadth;
int area;
```

Note the use of `int` to show that each will hold a whole number, and the semicolon at the end of each statement. Alternatively, we could have put:

```
int length, breadth, area;
```

using commas to separate each name. The style is up to you, but we have a preference for the first style, which enables you to comment each name if you need to. If you use the second form, use it to group related names. For example, put:

```
int pictureHeight, pictureWidth;
int myAge;
```

rather than:

```
int pictureHeight, pictureWidth, myAge;
```

In the majority of programs we will use several types, and in Java we are free to intermingle the declarations, as in:

```
float personHeight;
int examMark;
float salary;
```

Additionally, we can choose to initialize the value of the variable as we declare it, as in:

```
float personHeight = 1.53f;
int examMark = 63;
```

This is good style, but only use it when you really *know* the initial value – don't use arbitrary misleading values (such as zero).

● The assignment statement

Once we have declared our variables, we can place new values in them by means of the 'assignment statement', as in:

```
length = 20;
```

Pictorially, we can imagine the process as in Figure 4.2. We say: 'the value 20 has been assigned to the variable `length`' or '`length` becomes 20'.
    Note:

● The movement of data is from the right of the = to the left.
● Whatever value was in `length` before is now 'overwritten' by 20. Variables have only one value – the current one. And just to give you a flavour of the speed: an assignment takes less than one-millionth of a second.
● For very large (or very small) `float` values, you can express 'scientific' or 'exponent' notation, with e or E, as in:

```
float someFloat = 12.3e+23;
```

which means 12.3 multiplied by 10^{23}.
● We have chosen to put spaces around the =. They are not essential, but we think they make the program easier to read.

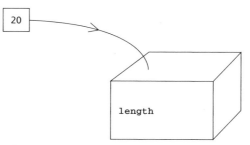

Figure 4.2 Assigning a value to a variable.

● Calculations and operators

Recall our rectangle program, which included the statement:

```
area = length * breadth;
```

This is your gentle introduction to calculations. The general form of the assignment statement is:

variable = expression

An expression can take several forms: for example, a single number or a calculation. In our specific example, the sequence of events is:

1. '*' causes multiplication of the values stored in `length` and `breadth`, resulting in the value 200.
2. The equals symbol '=' causes the 200 to be assigned to (stored in) `area`.

The '*' is one of several 'operators' (so called because they operate on values) and, just as in maths, there are rules for their use.

An understanding of the movement of data is important, and enables us to understand the meaning of code such as:

```
int n = 10;
n = n + 1;
```

What happens is that the right-hand side of the = is calculated using the current value of n, resulting in 11. This value is then stored in n, replacing the old value of 10. In fact, years ago a large number of programs were studied, and statements of the form:

```
something = something + 1;
```

were found to be the most common instructions! Java has a shorthand version of this so-called *increment* instruction, which is written as:

```
something++;
```

The conclusion you can draw from the above is that = does *not* mean 'is equal to' in the algebra sense. You should imagine it as meaning 'becomes' or 'gets'.

● The arithmetic operators

Here we present an introductory set of operators – the arithmetic ones, akin to the buttons on your calculator. By the way, in this context, we pronounce the adjective 'arithmetic' as 'arithMETic'.

Operator	Meaning
*	multiply
/	divide
%	remainder
+	add
-	subtract

Note that we have split the operators into two groups, to indicate their 'precedence' – the order in which they are obeyed. Thus, *, / and % are carried out before + and -. We can also use parentheses (round brackets) to group calculations and force them to be calculated first. If a calculation involves operators of the *same* precedence, the calculation is performed from left to right.

Here are some examples:

```
int result:
result = 3+3;        //result set to 6
result = 3 * 4;      //result set to 12
result = 3+2*4;      //result set to 11
result = (3+2)*4;    //result set to 20
```

SELF-TEST QUESTION

4.2 In the following, what are the values of the variables after each statement?

```
int a, b, c;
a = 2*3 + 1;
b = 1 + 2*3;
c = (1+2)*3;
```

Now we know the rules. But there are still pitfalls for the beginner. Let us look at some maths formulae, and their conversion into Java:

	Mathematics version	Java version
1	$y = mx + c$	```y = m*x + c;```
2	$x = (a - b)(a + b)$	```x = (a - b)*(a + b);```
3	$y = 3[(a - b)(a + b)] - x$	```y = 3*((a - b)*(a + b)) - x;```
4	$y = 1 - \dfrac{2a}{3b}$	```y = 1 - (2*a) / (3*b);```
5	$a = -b$	```a = -b;```

In example 1, we insert the multiply symbol. In Java, `mx` would be treated as one variable name.

In example 2, we need an explicit multiply between the brackets.

In example 3, we replace the mathematics square brackets by parentheses – square brackets have another meaning in Java.

In example 4, we might have gone for this incorrect version:

```
y = 1 - 2*a / 3*b;
```

Recall the left-to-right rule for equal precedence operators. The problem is to do with `*` and `/`. The order of evaluation is as if we had put:

```
y = 1 - (2*a/3)* b;
```

i.e. the `b` is now multiplying instead of dividing. The simplest way to handle potentially confusing calculations is to use extra brackets – there is no penalty in terms of program size or speed.

The use of `+`, `*` and `-` is reasonably intuitive, but division is slightly trickier, as it involves a knowledge of `int` and `float` types. The essential point is that `/`, when operating on integers, will produce an integer answer. Consider:

```
int a , b;
a = 10/5;       // a becomes 2
b = 7/4;        // b becomes 1
```

The first case is as expected, but in the case where the integers don't divide exactly, Java will do the division and truncate (chop off) any decimal places, forcing the answer to be an integer. Incidentally, you might have thought that a better answer would have been 2, but Java (in common with many languages) does not round to the nearest integer. When dividing `float` quantities, Java produces a `float` answer, as you might expect, though with potential inaccuracies in the least-significant decimal places:

```
float x;
x = 6.5f / 2.0f;      // x becomes 3.25
```

SELF-TEST QUESTION

4.3 My salary is $20 000, and I agree to give you half using the following calculation:

```
int half = 20000*(1/2);
```

How much do you get?

Our final operator is %, which operates slightly differently on integers and floats. It produces the remainder, as in:

```
int a;
a = 12 % 4;          //a becomes 0    (divides exactly)
a = 13 % 4;          //a becomes 1    (remainder 1)
a = 15 % 4;          //a becomes 3


float x;
x = 7.0f % 2.0f;     // x becomes 1.0
x = 8.6f % 2.0f;/    // x becomes 0.6
```

This might seem obscure (you don't have it on your calculator) but consider this problem:

Given a whole number of cents, convert it into two quantities – the number of dollars and the number of cents remaining.
    The solution is:

```
int cents = 234;
int dollars, centsRemaining;
dollars = cents / 100;          // 2
centsRemaining = cents % 100;   // 34
```

SELF-TEST QUESTION

4.4 Complete the following, adding assignment statements to split totalSeconds into two variables, hours and seconds:

```
int totalSeconds = 307;
```

● Displaying variables

Our example program needed to display the value of a variable on the screen. Previously we saw that drawString can output strings, as in:

```
g.drawString("Hello", 100, 100);
```

and we also saw that + could be used to join strings, as in:

```
g.drawString("hello" + " there", 100, 100);
```

Recall our example, which contains the statement:

```
g.drawString("Area is " + area, 100, 100);   // display answer
```

In Java, when + operates on a string and a number, the number is converted to a sequence of characters, and is then joined onto the string. The complete string is then displayed. Be careful when displaying calculations – you need to add brackets around numeric calculations, so that they are evaluated as a single number before the string-joining takes place. So, in the following:

```
g.drawString("answer is " +1+2, 100, 100);
```

will display:

```
answer is 12
```

whereas

```
g.drawString("answer is " +(1+2) , 100, 100);
```

displays:

```
answer is 3
```

● Type conversion

Sometimes, we need to convert values from one type to another. The most common cases are converting an int to a float, and a float to an int. Here is how to do it:

```
int ivalue = 33;
float fvalue = 3.9f;
int i;
float x;
x = ivalue;                // x becomes 33.0
i = (int) fvalue;          // i becomes 3
x = (float) (10+11) / 2;   // x becomes 10.5
```

The main points are:

- int can be converted to float in an assignment, without any additional programming. This is safe, as no information can be lost.
- float can be converted to int by using a *cast*, i.e. (int). We have to acknowledge that we require a conversion, because information can be lost or, in the above example, decimal places are truncated.
- We can use casts within expressions. In the last line, we find the average of two integers by adding them, then converting the result (21) to a float (21.0). The divide operation now takes place on a float and int, producing a float answer. This is so because the Java rule is that when an operator manipulates a mixture of int and float values, any integers are temporarily converted to float for the purposes of the calculation. Chapter 12 provides a more in-depth look at this topic.

● The role of expressions

Though we have emphasized that expressions (calculations) can form the right-hand side of assignment statements, they can occur in other places. In fact, we can place an integer expression anywhere we can place a single integer. Recall our use of the `drawString` method, which has two integers specifying the screen position:

```
g.drawString("Hello" , 50, 60);
```

We could (if it was useful) replace the numbers with variables, or with expressions:

```
int x = 100;
int y = 200;

g.drawString("Hello" , 50, 60);
g.drawString("Hello" , x, y);
g.drawString("Hello" , 3*x/2, 4*y);
```

The expressions are calculated, and the resulting values are passed into `drawString` for it to make use of.

Grammar spot

- Note the semicolon after every assignment statement.
- In maths, 'multiply' is expressed by writing two items side-by-side. In Java, the '*' must be used, as in:

```
int a,b,c;
c = a b;      // wrong
c = a*b;      // right
```

Programming pitfalls

- Take care with the spelling of variable names. For example, in:

```
int circle;
circle = 20;
```

there is a misspelling of a variable, using a '1' (one) instead of an 'l'. The Java compiler will complain about the second spelling being undeclared. Another favourite error is using a zero instead of a capital 'O'.
- Compilation errors are tricky to spot at the beginning. Though the Java compiler gives an indication of where it thinks the error is, the actual error could be on the previous line, or even in a declaration at the top of the file.
- Remember to put the letter `f` after `float` numbers.
- Brackets must balance – there must be the same number of '(' as ')', and the same number of '{' as '}'.

New language elements

● `float int`
● `+ - * / %`
● `=` assignment
● casts: `(int) (float)`

Summary

- Variables are used to hold (store) values. They keep their value until explicitly changed (e.g. by another assignment statement).

- Operators operate on values.

- An expression is a calculation which produces a value. It can be used in a variety of situations.

EXERCISES

4.1 Extend the rectangle program provided in this chapter to compute the volume of a box, given its three dimensions.

4.2 Using the following value:

```
float radius = 7.5f;
```

use assignment statements to calculate the circumference of a circle, the area of a circle, and the volume of a sphere, based on the same radius. Display the radius value and the results in a clear format. Here are the formulae:

circumference = $2\pi r$

area = πr^2

volume = $4\pi r^3/3$

You may use your own value for π, but we strongly recommend using the value set up in a Java class, which can be used as in:

```
float circumference;
circumference = 2.0f*(float)Math.PI*radius;
```

4.3 Assume that two students take a Java exam, and the results are assigned to two variables:

```
int mark1 = 44;
int mark2 = 51;
```

Write a program which calculates and displays the average mark as a float value. Check your answer with a calculator.

4.4 Assume that two students take a Java exam, and the results – as produced by a very discriminating examiner – are assigned to two variables:

```
float mark1 = 50.7f;
float mark2 = 55.9f;
```

Write a program which calculates and displays the average mark as a float value. Check your answer with a calculator.

4.5 Assume that individuals are taxed at 20% of their income. Set up an initial value of income using an assignment statement, then calculate and display the initial amount, the amount after deductions, and the deducted amount. Display messages so that the results are understandable.

4.6 Using `float` types, set up a variable containing a Fahrenheit temperature, then display the Celsius (centigrade) equivalent. The formula is:

```
c = (f - 32.0f) * 5.0f / 9.0f
```

4.7 Assign an initial value to a variable:

```
int totalSeconds = 2549;
```

and convert this to hours, minutes and seconds. Do an example with pen and paper before you write the program.

4.8 This problem is to do with electrical resistors, which 'resist' the flow of electrical current through them. An analogy is a hosepipe – a thin one has a high resistance, and a thick one has a low resistance to water. We can imagine connecting two hosepipes in series, resulting in a higher resistance, or in parallel, reducing the resistance (effectively, a fatter pipe).
Starting with:

```
float r1 = 4.7f;
float r2 = 6.8f;
```

calculate and display the series resistance, given by:

series = $r1 + r2$

and the parallel resistance, given by:

$$parallel = \frac{r1*r2}{r1 + r2}$$

4.9 We require some software for installation in a UK drink-dispensing machine. Here are the details: all items cost less than £1, and a £1 coin is the highest value that can be inserted. Given the amount inserted and the cost of the item, your program should give change, using the lowest number of coins. For example, if we had:

```
int amountGiven = 100;
int itemCost = 55;
```

the result should be of the form:

```
Number of 20p coins is 2
number of 5p coins is 1
```

Hint: work in pence, and make extensive use of the % operator. The UK coins are:

100p (i.e. £1) 50p 20p 10p 5p 2p 1p

ANSWERS TO SELF-TEST QUESTIONS

4.1

`volume`	allowed, correct style
`AREA`	allowed, but `area` preferred
`Length`	allowed, but lower-case l preferred
`3sides`	not allowed, starts with a digit
`side1`	allowed, correct style
`getFirst`	allowed, correct style
`lenth`	allowed, but strange spelling of `length`
`mysalary`	allowed, but capital s is preferred
`your salary`	not allowed (space)
`screenSize`	allowed, correct style

4.2
```
int a, b, c;
   a = 2*3 + 1;      //a becomes 7
   b = 1 + 2*3;      //b becomes 7
   c = (1+2)*3;      //c becomes 9
```

4.3 Unfortunately you get zero, as (1/2) is calculated first – as an integer – resulting in 0. A better version is:

```
int half = 20000 /2;
```

4.4
```
int totalSeconds = 307;
int hours, seconds;
hours = totalSeconds / 3600;
seconds = totalSeconds % 3600;
```

Methods and parameters

● Introduction

Large programs can be complex, with the result that they can be difficult to understand and debug. The most significant technique for reducing complexity is to split a program into (relatively) isolated sections. This allows us to focus on an isolated section without the distractions of the complete program. Furthermore, if the section has a name, we can invoke it (cause it to be obeyed) merely by using this name. In a way, it enables us to think at a higher level. In Java, such sections are known as methods. We made extensive use of graphics methods to draw shapes on the screen in Chapter 3.

Recall the `drawRect` method, which we invoke with four parameters in this manner:

```
g.drawRect(20,20,80,50);
```

First, the use of parameters allows us to control the size and position of the rectangle. This ensures that `drawRect` is flexible enough for a variety of circumstances. The parameters modify its actions. Incidentally, the correct Java terminology is *arguments*, but we shall use the more meaningful term *parameters*. Secondly, note that we *could* produce a rectangle by using four invocations of `drawLine` (in fact, if you were to look behind the scenes at the source code of `drawRect`, you would see that this is indeed how a rectangle is drawn). However, bundling up the four `drawLine` instructions inside a method known as `drawRect` is a sensible idea – it enables the graphics programmer to think at a higher level.

● Writing your own methods

Here, we will examine the construction of a method which draws an isosceles (two sides equal) triangle on a flat base, in the form of a tent. *We* are designing the method, so *we* can choose the parameters that will be required. For example, we could require three pairs of coordinates, but for our isosceles flat-based triangles, we will choose:

● the coordinates of the bottom left corner;
● the length of the base;
● the vertical height.

Rather than dive straight into writing a method, we will approach it in stages, introducing the basic statements involved in drawing a triangle, then moving towards bundling them up into a method with parameters.

Here are some Java statements which draw a triangle with a bottom corner 80 pixels in and 200 pixels down, with a base of 100 and a height of 110. First, we draw from the left end of the base to the right. Only the horizontal position changes:

```
g.drawLine(80, 200, 80+100, 200);
```

Secondly, we draw from the right of the base to the apex. We divide the base by 2 to find the mid-point.

```
g.drawLine(80+100, 200, 80+100/2, 200-110);
```

Thirdly, we draw from the apex to the bottom left.

```
g.drawLine(80+100/2, 200-110, 80, 200);
```

Rather than calculating each point as a single number, we have left some of them as expressions to show the calculations involved. Later we will simplify these calculations.

Altering the above triangle is difficult – but we could make it more flexible by introducing variables, as shown in this complete program:

```
import java.awt.*;
import java.applet.Applet;

public class TriangleTry extends Applet {
    public void paint(Graphics g) {
        int bottomX=80;
        int bottomY=200;
        int base=100;
        int height=110;

        g.drawLine(bottomX, bottomY, bottomX+base, bottomY);
        g.drawLine(bottomX+base, bottomY,bottomX+base/2, bottomY-
        height);
        g.drawLine(bottomX+base/2, bottomY-height, bottomX, bottomY);

    }
}
```

It is easy to change the triangle – simply alter the initial values of the variables. But what if we wanted to draw two triangles at different positions? We would have to duplicate the code! Instead we will create our own method, which we will call `drawTriangle`. (The choice of name is up to us.)

● A first method

Figure 5.1 shows a program containing a method named drawTriangle, which is invoked (made use of or called) twice. The resulting output is shown in Figure 5.2.

```
import java.awt.*;
import java.applet.Applet;

public class TriangleMethodDemo extends Applet {
    public void paint(Graphics g) {
        drawTriangle(g,80,200,100,110);
        drawTriangle(g,125,220,60,70);
    }

    private void drawTriangle(Graphics g, int bottomX, int bottomY,
                              int base, int height) {
        g.drawLine(bottomX, bottomY, bottomX+base, bottomY);
        g.drawLine(bottomX+base, bottomY, bottomX+base/2, bottomY-height);
        g.drawLine(bottomX+base/2, bottomY-height, bottomX, bottomY);
    }
}
```

Figure 5.1

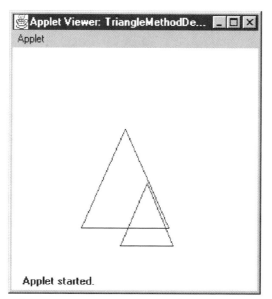

Figure 5.2 The output of the TriangleMethodDemo applet.

Yes, the program is short. However, the concept of methods and parameters is a major skill that all programmers need to master. We will now discuss the program in detail.

● Private and public

Look at the extract:

```
private void drawTriangle(Graphics g, int bottomX, int bottomY,
                          int base, int height)
```

This declares (introduces) the method, and is known as the *method header*. It states the name of the method (which we had the freedom to choose), and the parameters that it will accept. We shall examine parameters below. The rest of the method, enclosed in { }, is known as the *body*. Often the header consists of a long line, and we may choose to split it up at suitable points (though not in the middle of a word).

A vital decision that the programmer must make is: where can the method be invoked from? There are two main choices:

● The method can only be invoked from within the current applet or program. In this case, use the keyword `private`.
● The method can be invoked by another program. In this case, we would use the keyword `public`. (Methods like `drawLine` are examples of methods which have been declared as `public` – they are intended for general use.) Creating public methods involves a deeper knowledge of OO concepts, which we will leave till Chapter 9.

The private and public keywords are known as *access control modifiers*.

Moving on, we have the `void` keyword. This involves further choices:

● Will the method calculate a result and return it to the section of code which invoked it?
● Will the method perform a task without the need to supply an 'answer'?

In the triangle method, no result is produced. (A picture on the screen does not count as a result – if we extended the method to calculate the area of the triangle as well, then *that* would be a result.) This possibility is covered later in the chapter.

● Invoking a method

In Java, you invoke a private method by stating its name, together with a list of para-meters. In our program, the first invocation is:

```
drawTriangle(g, 80, 200, 100, 110);
```

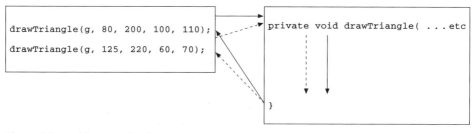

Figure 5.3 Invoking a method.

This statement has two effects:

● The parameter values are automatically transferred into the method. This transferring is a duplication process, in that the original values remain intact.
● The program skips to the body of the method – the part enclosed in { }, and executes the statements. When it runs out of statements and reaches the closing }, it continues its execution at the point where it was invoked from. Figure 5.1 shows `paint` invoking the same method twice.

The second invocation then takes place:

```
drawTriangle(g,125,220,60,70);
```

Figure 5.3 illustrates this. There are two invocations, producing two triangles.

● Passing parameters

It is essential to have an understanding of how parameters are transferred (passed) into methods. In our example, the concept is shown in the following lines:

```
drawTriangle(g,80,200,100,110);
void drawTriangle(Graphics g,int bottomX,int bottomY,int base,int height)
```

Recall our likening of a variable to a box. Inside the method, a set of empty boxes awaits the transfer of parameters. After the transfer, we have the situation shown in Figure 5.4. The transfer takes place in a left-to-right order. The invocation must provide the correct number and type of parameters. If the invoker (the user) accidentally gets parameters in the wrong order, the transfer process won't re-order them! When the `drawTriangle` method executes, the above values control the drawing process. Though we have invoked the method with numbers, we can use expressions (i.e. involving variables and calculations), as in:

```
drawTriangle(g,100,100,50+4,30);
drawTriangle(g,100,startY,60,tall);
```

In the above, the parameters are evaluated (reduced to a single value), then copied into the method. The technical term for this approach to passing parameters is *passing by*

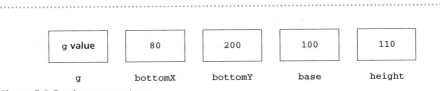

Figure 5.4 Passing parameters.

value, and this is how Java passes the built-in primitive types (`int`, `float`, `boolean` etc.). However, in Chapters 9 and 13 we will encounter a different approach known as *passing by reference*, which Java uses when objects (including arrays) are passed.

There is an additional parameter that we need to perform drawing. As we saw in Chapter 3, the applet viewer supplies us with a drawing area, which we named `g`. To enable other methods to use the same area, we need to pass it to them as a parameter.

● Formal and actual parameters

There are two lists of parameters that we are discussing, and it is important to be clear about the difference:

- The list of parameters that the invocation must supply is termed the *actual* parameters. Imagine this as meaning 'the current parameters at this moment'.
- The list of names and types that the writer of the method decides on is termed the *formal* parameters. Though their values will change, the names stay the same. The writer of the method is free to choose formal parameter names. If similar names are used in other methods, no problem arises – each method has its own copy of its parameters.
- The type of each formal parameter must be chosen – this depends on the particular method. The type name must be placed before each parameter name, and a comma is used to separate the type/name pairs. Look at the `drawTriangle` header to see the arrangement.

SELF-TEST QUESTION

5.1 Explain what is wrong with these invocations:

```
drawTriangle(g,100,100, 50,"10");
drawTriangle(100,g,100,50,10);
drawTriangle(g,100,100,30);
```

● Local variables

Just as we declared variables in `paint`, so we might want to declare them within *any* method. The following program shows the use of variables to simplify the calculations in `drawTriangle`.

```java
import java.awt.*;
import java.applet.Applet;
public class TriangleMethodDemo extends Applet {
    public void paint(Graphics g) {
        drawTriangle(g,80,200,100,110);
        drawTriangle(g,125,220,60,70);
    }
    private void drawTriangle(Graphics g, int bottomX, int bottomY,
                                int base, int height) {
        int rightX = bottomX+base;
        int topX = bottomX+base/2;
        int topY = bottomY-height;

        g.drawLine(bottomX,bottomY,rightX,bottomY);
        g.drawLine(rightX,bottomY,topX,topY);
        g.drawLine(topX,topY,bottomX,bottomY);
    }
}
```

The variables `rightX`, `topX` and `topY` which we have introduced exist only within `drawTriangle`. If variables of the same name exist within other methods, then there is no conflict, in that each method uses its own copy. Another way to look at this is that when *other* programmers are creating methods they can invent local variables without cross-checking with everyone.

The role of local variables is to assist in the work of the method, whatever it is doing. The variables have a limited scope, restricted to their own method. Their existence is temporary – they are created when a method is invoked, and destroyed when it exits.

● Name clashes

In Java, the creator of a method is free to choose appropriate names for local variables and formal parameters – but what happens if names are chosen which clash with other variables? We could have:

```java
private void methodOne(int x, int y) {
    int z = 0;
    // code...
}


private void methodTwo(int z, int x) {
    int w = 1;
    // code...
}
```

Let us assume that the methods have been written by two people. MethodOne has x and y as parameters, and declares an integer z. These three items are all local to methodOne. In methodTwo, the programmer exercises the right of freedom to name local items, and opts for z, x, and w. The name clash of x (and of z) does not give a problem, as Java treats the x of methodOne as different from the x of methodTwo.

Let us summarize the method facilities we have discussed so far. Later we will include the return statement.

● The general form is:

```
private void someName(parameter list) {
body
}
```

The programmer chooses the method name.
● The parameter list is a list of types and names, separated by commas. If a method doesn't need parameters, we use empty brackets for the actual and formal parameters, as in:

```
private void myMethod() {
    body
}
```

and the method invocation is:

```
myMethod();
```

● An applet can contain any number of methods, in any order. The layout is:

```
public class Any extends Applet {
    public void paint(Graphics g) {
        body
    }

    private void someName() {
        body
    }

    private void anotherName() {
        body
    }
}
```

● public **and** paint

There seems to be something different about paint. All our private methods are declared *and* invoked, but paint is only declared! There *is* something different. The applet viewer (or browser) initiates your applet, and expects you to provide a declaration of a method called `paint`. The applet viewer then invokes `paint` as required. This also explains why `paint` cannot be private – it has to be available externally. When we look at event-driven programs in Chapter 6, we will see other similar public methods.

● `return` and results

When discussing parameters, we stressed that their values were copied into the formal parameters – this is a one-way process. If we need to get results *out* of a method, we must use a different mechanism – the `return` statement. Let us look at a simple method which calculates the area of a rectangle, given its two sides as parameters. We put:

```
import java.awt.*;
import java.applet.Applet;
public class ReturnDemo extends Applet {
    public void paint(Graphics g) {
        int answer = areaRectangle(30, 40);
        g.drawString("area of rectangle is "+answer, 100, 100);
    }

    private int areaRectangle(int side1,int side2) {
        int area = (side1 * side2)/2;
        return area;
    }
}
```
(handwritten: `float` next to `int answer`; `/2;` annotation on the area line)

There are a number of new features in this example, which go hand in hand.

Instead of `void`, we have used a type – in this case `int`. This specifies that the method will use a `return` statement to pass back a value of that type. The choice of the type depends on the problem, but it can be `int`, `float`, a string or even a class type which you will encounter later: `Button`, `TextArea`, `Scrollbar` etc.

To return a value, we put:

```
return expression;
```

The expression (as usual) could be a number, a variable or a calculation (or even a method invocation), but it must be of the correct type, as specified in the declaration of the method – i.e. its header. Additionally, the `return` statement causes the current method to stop executing, and returns immediately to where it left off in the invoking method.

A method which returns a value cannot be used as a complete statement, as in:

```
areaRectangle(10,20);    //    wrong
```

Instead, the invoker must arrange to 'consume' the returned value.

Here is an approach to understanding the returning of values: imagine that the method invocation (the name and parameter list) is erased, and is replaced by the returned result. If the resulting code makes sense, then Java will allow you to make such an invocation. Look at this example:

```
answer =    areaRectangle(30,40)   ;
```

The result is 1200, which we imagine as replacing the invocation, effectively giving:

```
answer = 1200;
```

This is valid Java. But if we put:

```
areaRectangle(30,40);
```

the substitution would produce:

```
1200;
```

which is meaningless. Here are some more ways that we might consume the result:

```
int n;
n = areaRectangle(10, 20);
g.drawString("area is " + areaRectangle(10,20), 100, 100);
n = areaRectangle(10, 20) + areaRectangle( 22, 33);
```

SELF-TEST QUESTION
....

5.2 Work through the above statements with pencil and paper, substituting results for invocations.

To complete the discussion of return, note that it can be used with void methods. In this case, we must use return without specifying a result, as in:

```
private void demo() {
    //do something
    return;
    //do something else
}
```

This can be used when we want the method to terminate at a statement other than the last one.

● The flexibility of methods

Let us re-code our example:

```
import java.awt.*;
import java.applet.Applet;
public class ReturnDemo extends Applet {
    public void paint(Graphics g) {
        g.drawString(
            "area of rectangle is"+areaRectangle(30,40), 100, 100);
    }
    private int areaRectangle(int side1, int side2) {
        return side1*side2;
    }
}
```

Because we can use `return` with expressions, we have omitted the variable `area` in `areaRectangle`. Also, because expressions can be used as actual parameters, we have omitted the variable `answer` in `paint`; instead, we have invoked `areaRectangle` from a parameter of `drawString`. However, if we needed to use the same result lower down in `paint`, the use of a variable to memorize the number is more efficient than invoking `areaRectangle` twice.

Such reductions in program size are not always beneficial, because the reduction in meaningful names can reduce clarity, hence leading to more debugging and testing time.

● Building on methods

As an example of methods using other methods, let us create a method which draws a simple house cross-section of the form shown in Figure 5.5. We will choose the parameters to be:

● the bottom left coordinates;
● the width;
● the height of the walls.

All our houses will have similar proportions – the roof height will be half the wall height.

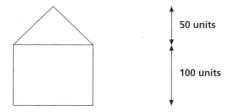

50 units

100 units

Figure 5.5 A simple house cross-section.

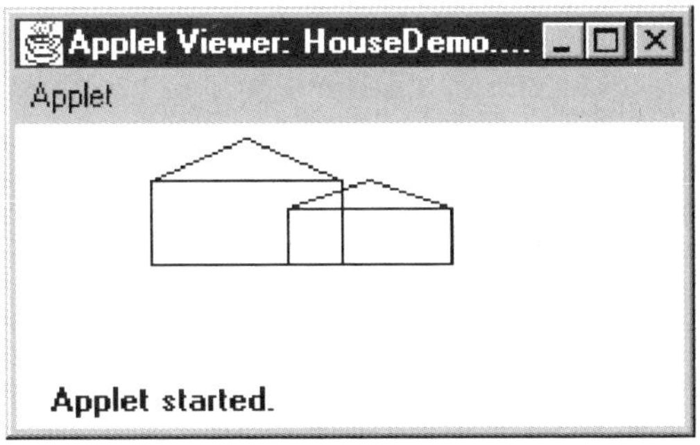

Figure 5.6 The output of the `HouseDemo` applet.

We will use `drawRect` from the Java library, and use our own `drawTriangle`.

This example illustrates the need for the `import` statement: the `drawRect` method is in fact contained in a prewritten library supplied with every Java system. If we omitted the statement:

```
import java.awt.*;
```

then `drawRect` would not be linked to our program. On the other hand, we don't need an include for `drawTriangle`, because it exists within our program.

Here is the program, with the resulting images shown in Figure 5.6.

```
import java.awt.*;
import java.applet.Applet;
public class HouseDemo extends Applet {
    public void paint(Graphics g) {
        drawHouse(g,50,50, 70,30);
        drawHouse(g,100,50,60,20);
    }

    private void drawTriangle(Graphics g,int bottomX, int bottomY,
                              int base,int height) {
        g.drawLine(bottomX, bottomY, bottomX+base, bottomY);
        g.drawLine(bottomX+base, bottomY, bottomX+base/2, bottomY-height);
        g.drawLine(bottomX+base/2, bottomY-height, bottomX, bottomY);
    }

    private void drawHouse(Graphics g,int bottomX,int bottomY,
                           int width,int height) {
        g.drawRect(bottomX, bottomY-height, width, height);
        drawTriangle(g, bottomX, bottomY-height, width, height/2);
    }

}
```

The program is straightforward if you recall that:

● The details about the drawing area (g above) need to be passed to any method that draws.
● Methods return to where they were invoked from, so:

   – paint invokes drawHouse;
   – drawHouse invokes drawRect;
   – drawHouse invokes drawTriangle;
   – drawTriangle invokes drawLine (three times).

● Actual parameters can be expressions, so height/2 is evaluated, then passed into drawTriangle.
● The bottomX and bottomY of drawHouse and the bottomX and bottomY of drawTriangle are totally separate. Their values are stored in different places.

You will see that what might have been a long and complex program has been written as a short program, split into methods with meaningful names. This illustrates the power of using methods.

Grammar spot

● The general pattern for methods takes two forms. First, when the method does not return a result, we declare the method by:

```
private void methodName(formal parameters) {
    body
}
```

and we invoke the method by a statement, as in:

```
methodName(actual parameters);
```

● When the method returns a result, the form is:

```
private int methodName(parameter list) {
    body
}
```

Any type or class can be specified, not only int.
● We invoke the method as part of an expression, e.g.:

```
int n = methodName(a, b);
```

The body of the method must include a return statement featuring the correct type of value.
● When a method has no parameters, we use empty brackets () in both the declaration and the invocation.

● The formal parameter list is created by the writer of the method. Each parameter consists of a type name (e.g. `int`, `float`), followed by a name. Commas separate the parameters.
● The actual parameter list is written by the invoker of the method. It consists of a series of expressions in the correct (matching) order, and of the correct types. Unlike formal parameters, the type names are not used.
● The appropriate `import` is needed when we use methods from library classes.

Programming pitfalls

● The method header must include type names. The following is wrong:

```
private void methodOne(x, f) // wrong
```

Instead we must put, for example:

```
private void methodOne(int x, float f)
```

● A method invocation must not include type names. For example, rather than:

```
methodOne(int y, float b);
```

we put:

```
methodOne(y, b);
```

● When invoking a method, you must supply the correct number of parameters and the correct types of parameters.
● If a method returns a value, you must arrange to consume its result in some way. The following style of invocation does *not* consume a return value:

```
someMethod(e,f);
```

New language elements

● The declaration of a private method:

```
private void someMethod(parameters) {
    body
}
```

● The use of `void` to indicate that a method does not return a result.
● The use of a type instead of `void` to state the type of a returned result.
● The invocation of a method, consisting of the method name and parameters.
● The use of `return` to simultaneously exit and pass a value back from a non-`void` method.
● The use of `return` to exit from a `void` method.

Summary

- Methods contain subtasks of a program.
- We can pass parameters into methods.
- Methods can return a result.
- A class can contain several methods.

EXERCISES

5.1 Code a method which draws a circle, given the coordinates of the centre and the radius. Its header should be:

```
private void circle(Graphics g,int xCentre, int yCentre,
                    int radius)
```

5.2 Code a method which draws a street of houses, using the provide drawHouse method. For the purposes of this question, a street consists of four houses, and there should be a 10 pixel gap between each house. The header is:

```
private void drawStreet(Graphics g, int wallHeight, int bottomX,
                        int bottomY)
```

where we provide the height of a wall, and the position of the bottom of the leftmost wall. The width of each house should be the same as the height.

5.3 Code a method (to be known as drawStreetInPerspective), which has the same parameters as Exercise 5.2. However, each house is to be 20% smaller than the house to its left.

5.4 Code a method drawPerson which draws a stick figure, formed from a circle for the head and lines for the torso, arms and legs. Base the size of the body parts on the height. The method header should be:

```
private void drawPerson(Graphics g, int height, int baseX,
                        int baseY)
```

where caller provides the height and the coordinates of the point between the feet.

5.5 Create a method drawFamily which draws two adults and two children (assumed to be half as tall as the adults). Make use of your drawPerson, and decide on your own parameters.

5.6 Write a method which returns the inch equivalent of its centimetre parameter. An example invocation is:

```
float inches = inchEquivalent(2.5f);
```

Multiply centimetres by 0.394 to calculate inches.

5.7 Write a method which returns the volume of a cube, given the length of one side. A sample invocation is:

```
float vol = cubeVolume(1.2f);
```

5.8 Write a method which returns the area of a circle, given its radius as a parameter. A sample invocation is:

```
a = area(1.25f);
```

The area of a circle is given by the formula `pi*r*r`. An accurate value of π can be obtained by using `Math.PI`, which is available in a library. See Q 4.2 for details.

5.9 Write a method which returns the doubled value of its integer parameter. A sample invocation is:

```
int d = doubled(n);
```

Explain how the following Java code is executed, and check your answer by running the program:

```
int d = doubled(doubled(doubled(10)));
```

ANSWERS TO SELF-TEST QUESTIONS

5.1   `drawTriangle(g, 100, 100, 50, "10");`
        `"10"` should not be in quotes
    `drawTriangle(100,g,100,50,10);`
        g should be the first parameter
    `drawTriangle(g,100,100,30);`
        the number of parameters is incorrect

5.2   `int n;`
    `n = areaRectangle(10,20);`
        n becomes 200
    `g.drawString("area is "+areaRectangle(10,20),100,100);`
        The display is: `area is 200`
    `n = areaRectangle(10,20) + areaRectangle(22,33);`
    n becomes 200 + 726, i.e. 926

Events

Introduction

Imagine that you are about to set off on a car journey – but your car is rather unusual. Before setting off, you have to decide if you want the radio on, which cassette is in the player, whether headlights will be required etc. In short, everything must be predetermined!

Obviously, the design of such a car is absurd. We want cars with the ability to respond to changing situations and options. We are using the car analogy to contrast old-style programs with modern interactive programs.

In a car, we have:

- 'input' controls, e.g. accelerator, brake, radio volume control;
- 'output' displays, e.g. speedometer, current radio settings;
- warning devices, e.g. petrol-low signal.

The driver can manipulate the controls at any time, depending on the current situation.

At the moment, I'm 'driving' a modern word processor. It has around 60 buttons on the screen, and nine pull-down menus, with around 10 options on each one. The creator of this software has designed it to allow a range of options at any instant – the software can respond to 'events'. The set of gadgets on a modern computer screen is called a 'user interface', or a 'graphical user interface', GUI – pronounced 'gooey'.

What is an event?

The term is rather misleading – most people would regard the football World Cup or the death of President Kennedy as an event, but in programming circles, an event is (in most cases) an action taken by the user. In fact, we can list most events:

Figure 6.1 A program viewed as a sequence of instructions.

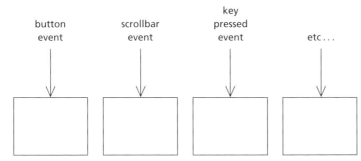

Figure 6.2 An event-driven program.

- The user presses a key or clicks the mouse.
- The user clicks on a button, a scrollbar, a menu option, etc.

So, rather than imagining a program as a long sequence of instructions, as in Figure 6.1, we imagine sections of program which can be activated by an event, as in Figure 6.2.

Before we look at the detail in Java, we must learn one more jargon phrase: *event handling*. When the user produces an event (e.g. clicks on the 'save' button) then obviously we must arrange for the appropriate task to be carried out – i.e. the click must be routed to a section of program which actually carries out the 'save' operation. Detecting the event and carrying out the required task is called 'handling' the event, and programs which rely on this style of user interface are termed 'event-driven'.

● The event loop

As you know, computer users spend a lot of time gazing at the screen, often in puzzlement. What happens inside the computer when this occurs? The answer is that the software cycles round in a loop, waiting for an event. The pattern is shown in Figure 6.3. The event loop structure seems simple. But exactly how do we detect mouse clicks, and how do we distinguish a click from a drag?

Fortunately, Java does part of the work for us. We don't have to code an event loop, and we don't have to do the low-level recognition of events. In Java, we create sections of program – methods – which the Java system will automatically invoke when an event happens, additionally supplying us with details of the event. We then use these details (e.g. the name of the button that was clicked) to ensure that the required processing takes place.

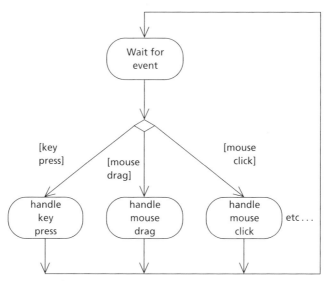

Figure 6.3 The structure of an event loop.

In Java, events are classified. For example, scrollbars are typically used to modify or adjust a value or screen area, whereas buttons are clicked to initiate or terminate a task – a definite action, rather than an adjustment. In Java, these classes are named `ActionListener` and `AdjustmentListener`. Our program must *register as a listener* for particular classes of event. Here is an analogy – assume you are interested in music CDs from a particular company, who produce rock, Latin and jazz recordings. You might register with them by saying 'please send me details when you release a batch of new Latin CDs'. When the event of the CD release happens, the company will send you a mailshot.

In Java, we have to code a method for every class of event in which we are interested (e.g. a method for scrollbar events, a method for button-click events, etc.). Additionally, we have to register as a listener with the component (e.g. scrollbar) which produces the event, so that our method can be invoked automatically when the event happens.

● A first event-driven program

Eventually we will get to the technical detail, together with a framework for you to use in most of your programs. But first we will look at a very simple example – a program to read a number from a scrollbar and display its value as digits on the screen. We recommend that you run the program, which can be done by typing in the Java code and storing it in a file called `FirstEvent.java`. Then (if your programming environment doesn't generate HTML) copy the minimum `.html` file to a new file, renaming it to `FirstEvent.html`. When you compile and run the program, the applet viewer will produce a screen as shown in Figure 6.4.

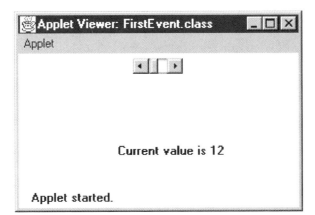

Figure 6.4 The output of the `FirstEvent` applet.

```java
import java.awt.*;
import java.applet.Applet;
import java.awt.event.*;

public class FirstEvent extends Applet
    implements AdjustmentListener {
    private Scrollbar slider;
    private int sliderValue = 0;

    public void init() {
        slider = new Scrollbar(Scrollbar.HORIZONTAL, 0, 1, 0, 100);
        add(slider);
        slider.addAdjustmentListener(this);
    }

    public void paint(Graphics g) {
        g.drawString("Current value is " + sliderValue, 100, 100);
    }

    public void adjustmentValueChanged(AdjustmentEvent e) {
        sliderValue = slider.getValue();
        repaint();
    }
}
```

Let us consider the task of the program in terms of events. (Later in this chapter, we will introduce more detail.) The user will manipulate a scrollbar and the number it is set to will be displayed on the screen as digits. Here is a horizontal scrollbar:

It acts like a slider volume control on a hi-fi, and in its simplest use, the user can drag the slider left or right to decrease or increase the value. You have probably used a vertical one in your editor or word processor to scroll through a long document.

Rather than producing a program which examines the scrollbar very frequently (say every tenth of a second), we use the event-driven approach. We state that we are going to implement a listener for scrollbar events, which are classified in `AdjustmentListener`. Note the capital 'A' – this is a class, not a method. We then register our program as a listener by using the `addAdjustmentListener` method, which in effect causes our `adjustmentValueChanged` method to be invoked when the scrollbar is used. In this simple program, our `adjustmentValueChanged` method simply fetches the new value from the scrollbar, and arranges for it to be painted on the screen.

Here is the essence of the program, expressed in informal English. Trust us that the Java detail will follow!

```
declare a variable sliderValue initially 0

init:
    set up the scrollbar so that it supplies us with integers from 0
    to 100

    register as a listener to the scrollbar

paint:
    display the current value of sliderValue as a number

adjustmentValueChanged:
    get the current value of the scrollbar
    and place it in sliderValue
    invoke the paint method, by using repaint()
```

There is only one thing you can do with this program (apart from stopping it). You can manipulate the scrollbar. Every time you do this, `adjustmentValueChanged` gets the new value, and deposits it in a variable (`sliderValue`) for `paint` to display. It is important to realize that you can manipulate the scrollbar as often as you like.

There are some arbitrary things we chose in the program, for example:

● the name of the scrollbar – we chose `slider`;
● the name of a variable to hold the value of the scrollbar – we chose `sliderValue`;
● the range of numbers we wanted the scrollbar to produce – we opted for 0 to 100.

There are some essential unchangeable parts of the program:

● the import `java.awt.event`;
● the `implements adjustmentListener`;
● an `init` method;
● the use of `addAdjustmentListener` to register as a scrollbar listener;

● an `adjustmentValueChanged` method;
● a `paint` for any screen drawing;
● the use of `repaint` (to invoke `paint`).

When we say unchangeable, we *mean* it. Don't invent your own names, such as `initialize`.

● The event framework

Let us now generalize from the previous example; here is a framework of methods which will serve you for all the examples in this chapter:

The `init` method will be invoked by the system when the applet is run. Use it for creating an initial screen.	`public void init ( ) {`
	
	`}`

Used to display graphic items	`public void paint (Graphics g) {`
	
	`}`

The event-handling method for scrollbars. When such an event occurs, this method will be invoked automatically. Your event-handling code will be inserted here.	`public void adjustmentValueChanged`
	`            (AdjustmentEvent e) {`
	`}`

Note that when we reach the stage of producing more sophisticated programs, we will introduce additional event-handling methods, such as `actionPerformed` to respond to buttons and text fields, and `itemStateChanged` to respond to check boxes.

● Scopes – an introduction

Recall from Chapter 5 that the scope of an item (e.g. a variable) is the region of program in which it can be used. In all our examples so far, we have used variables which are *local* to a single method, and we have used parameters to convey values from one method to another. However, in event-driven programs (and object-oriented programming in general), it is common to use variables that can be accessed by *any* method of a class. So, rather than use purely local scope, we can declare variables outside of (above or below) the methods of a class. They can now be used by any method of a class, and they are known as *instance* variables; we specify them as `private`, to prevent their use by methods of *other* classes. Chapter 9 explains the concept in more detail. Here is the pattern:

```
class Demo extends Applet {
    private int x;
    private void methodOne() {
        int a;          // a is local in methodOne
        x = 42;
        // etc
    }
    private void methodTwo() {
        int b; // b is local in methodTwo
        b = x;
    }
}
```

Here, `x` is declared outside the methods, yet can be used by them. `methodOne` assigns a value to `x`, and `methodTwo` copies its value into `b`.

● The Abstract Window Toolkit

In Chapter 3, we made use of the shape-drawing facilities in the AWT, but its more significant use is in the creation of event-driven programs with 'components' (e.g. buttons, scrollbars) for user interaction. Because Java is intended to be portable, the range of components has been chosen to work with most operating systems: Windows, Macintosh and UNIX. The downside is that the full range of (say) Windows components are not available – we have to make do with a subset.

Though the components are all different, there are similarities in how they are manipulated by a program. Each component is a class and, just as we declare numeric variables, so we must declare our components. Let us look at an imaginary 'gunsight' component, which consists of a circle with cross-hairs. The program will set its initial position, and then the user moves it across the screen to select a target. First, we invent a name for our particular gunsight, and declare it:

```
GunSight laserGun;
```

Note that this is identical to the way in which we declared integers, with a type name followed by our choice of name:

```
int n;
```

In fact, `laserGun` is a `GunSight` object – or, more precisely, is an instance of the class `GunSight`. Now we can create an actual instance of the component with appropriate values. Typically this takes the form of, for example:

```
laserGun = new GunSight(50, 100); // initial position
add(laserGun);
```

Often, we need to detect events from a component, and we will register by invoking the appropriate addListener method.

For many components we need to provide parameters in brackets, which control the initial setup. The details of these depend on the actual component. The next stage is to add it to the currently displayed components.

Once the component has been created, we may want to change the settings, often done by a statement of the form:

```
laserGun.setValue(100, 100);
```

and we will want to access the current value – in our gunsight component, the settings will change as the user moves it around the screen. The typical approach is:

```
int x, y;
x = laserGun.getXValue();
y = laserGun.getYValue();
```

where x and y become the current coordinates of the gunsight.

This style of method invocation, where we use an object name, followed by a point, followed by a method name, is one which you will become very familiar with.

The general point is that values are usually sent to a component by using some form of set method, and that current values can be brought out by some form of get method. Enough of gunsights – let's look at a real component.

The scrollbar component

So far, we have written programs (classes) which performed simple calculations, based on the initial values of variables, as in:

```
length = 20;
```

but in reality it is very rare for the programmer to know the input data in advance. Instead, we will use a scrollbar to input values. As you saw above, the user can drag the slider left or right to decrease or increase the value. Additionally, the end arrow can be clicked to increase the value by a fixed amount (often 1, though this can be altered).

When we create a scrollbar, we can set the integer values that are represented by the extreme left and right.

How do we know when the user changes the value? The answer is that clicking on the scrollbar constitutes an event which our program can be set up to detect. The new current value of the scrollbar can then be accessed by a getValue() method.

An event-driven example

The following program simulates an electronic window blind – when we drag the vertical scrollbar downwards, the window blind lowers. To represent this setup, we draw a

Applet Vie...

Applet

Scrollbar value is 41

Figure 6.5 The output of the `WindowBlind` applet.

rectangle to represent the window frame, and a filled rectangle to represent the blind. To run the program, store it in a file called `WindowBlind.java`, and amend your HTML file if your system does not do it for you.

The example pulls together all we have done on scopes, components and events. The example is short, and we will explain it in detail. When you come to write your own event-driven programs you will find that the structure is familiar. Figure 6.5 shows the output from the program.

```
// Scrollbar example - window blind simulator
import java.awt.*;
import java.applet.Applet;
import java.awt.event.*;

public class WindowBlind extends Applet
    implements AdjustmentListener {
    private Scrollbar slider;
    private int sliderValue;

    public void init () {
        slider = new Scrollbar(Scrollbar.VERTICAL, 0, 1, 0, 100);
        add(slider);
        slider.addAdjustmentListener(this);
    }
```

```
    public void paint (Graphics g) {
        showStatus("Scrollbar value is " + sliderValue);
        g.drawRect(40, 80, 60, 100);
        g.fillRect(40, 80, 60, sliderValue);
    }


    public void adjustmentValueChanged(AdjustmentEvent e) {
        sliderValue = slider.getValue();
        repaint();
    }

}
```

The overall structure consists of three methods, required in most applets. There is an `init` method, a `paint` method, and an `adjustmentValueChanged` method. The unusual thing about them is that we provide them but don't explicitly make use of them – in fact, `paint` and `init` are invoked by the applet viewer or browser, and `adjustmentValueChanged` is invoked by the Java event-handling system.

Let us walk through the applet. We import the event-handling classes, and state that our applet will provide a method for dealing with adjustment events such as those produced from scrollbars:

```
import java.awt.event.*;
public class WindowBlind extends Applet
    implements AdjustmentListener {
```

Then we declare a scrollbar called `slider` as a private instance variable, so that any method of the `WindowBlind` class can access it. We are free to choose its name, and could have opted for `bar`, `scroller` or `blind` for example. We follow the pattern of declaring it, creating the instance, adding it to the screen, and registering with it:

```
private Scrollbar slider;
    //etc.
slider = new Scrollbar(Scrollbar.VERTICAL, 0, 1, 0, 100);
add(slider);
slider.addAdjustmentListener(this);
```

Registration should be regarded as a formality that we must do, but the behind-the-scenes process (which you don't need to understand at this stage) is rather intricate. When we put:

```
slider.addAdjustmentListener(this);
```

we are stating that our current program (in fact the current object, referred to in Java by `this`) requires that its `adjustmentValueChanged` method is to be invoked when `slider` is manipulated.

When we initialize our new slider object, we supply five parameters in brackets. These are:

● Orientation – horizontal or vertical. The use of capitals is mandatory.
● The initial value. This depends on the range of values to be used. Our range will be 0 to 100, so 0 is reasonable.
● Large change. As well as clicking on the end arrows or dragging the slider, we can click in the areas between the arrows and the slider to produce another change. This parameter controls the amount of change, and you might tailor this for particular examples. We will use 1 in every case.
● The minimum and maximum values for the end positions. We opt for 0 to 100, because the window frame was set to 100 – this is a suitable size (in terms of pixels) for most applet viewers.

Now let's look at the overall structure of the class. Every applet needs to provide an init method, which the browser/applet viewer expects, and will invoke when the applet is run. Here we put 'one-off' statements, such as creating an initial screen.

The familiar paint method is then called up by the browser. It makes use of the value placed in the instance variable sliderValue (initially 0, denoting an open window). We could have opted for accessing the scrollbar value in paint, rather than in adjustmentValueChanged, but as a general principle we shall try to restrict paint to deal with graphics output rather than user input.

In paint, we draw the fixed-size window frame followed by a filled rectangle, whose depth depends on the scrollbar. As this is your first event-driven program, we will also display the value of the slider as a number. We could have used drawString, but will use an additional facility, showStatus, which displays text on the status line at the very bottom of the window. It is used in a similar manner to drawString, but doesn't need the pair of screen coordinates.

We prepare the program for events, in the sense of setting up methods that it will invoke. In this case we must provide an adjustmentValueChanged method. We have:

```
public void adjustmentValueChanged(AdjustmentEvent e) {
    sliderValue = slider.getValue();
    repaint();
}
```

What happens is that the above method is invoked, and details about the event are available in the variable e, of class AdjustmentEvent. In our primitive program there is only one event (the scrollbar is changed), so all we do is make use of getValue to fetch the changed position and store this in sliderValue. Then – in recognition that the screen display needs changing – we invoke repaint which, in its basic form, merely calls paint. This causes the drawing of a new window frame and blind.

This concludes the explanation of the class. We have used instance variables, components and event handling.

● Adding labels

In this chapter we are focusing on the concept of events, explored in a practical way with the scrollbar. However, when we have *several* scrollbars on the screen, it is helpful to the user if we display a message near each one to clarify what each one is for.

We have been using add to place a new component on the display, and have (behind the scenes) been using the default layout approach of the AWT for applets, in which components are placed in centred rows from left to right, and overflow to the next row if more space is needed. This is known in the AWT as *flow layout*. The point is that we don't know their location in pixels, and hence we can't use drawString to place text near them. (We could guess the coordinates, but this is not good enough!)

Instead, we can use a *label* component which contains text, and which is added to the layout in the same way as scrollbars. We simply declare the component and initialize it with some text.

Here is an example, which produces the output of Figure 6.6.

```
import java.awt.*;
import java.applet.Applet;
import java.awt.event.*;

public class LabelDemo extends Applet
    implements AdjustmentListener {
    private Scrollbar bar1, bar2;
    private int bar1Value = 0;
    private int bar2Value = 0;
```

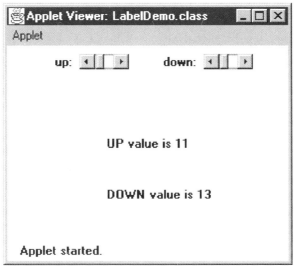

Figure 6.6 The output of the LabelDemo applet.

```
public void init() {
    Label title1, title2; // local scope is sufficient
    title1 = new Label("up:");
    add(title1);
    bar1 = new Scrollbar(Scrollbar.HORIZONTAL, 0, 1, 0, 100);
    add(bar1);
    bar1.addAdjustmentListener(this);
    title2 = new Label(" down:");
    add(title2);
    bar2 = new Scrollbar(Scrollbar.HORIZONTAL, 0, 1, 0, 100);
    add(bar2);
    bar2.addAdjustmentListener(this);
}

public void paint(Graphics g) {
    g.drawString("UP value is " + bar1Value, 100, 100);
    g.drawString("DOWN value is " + bar2Value, 100, 150);
}

public void adjustmentValueChanged(AdjustmentEvent e) {
    bar1Value = bar1.getValue();
    bar2Value = bar2.getValue();
    repaint();
}
}
```

Note:

● A label is not active – clicking on it does not produce an event, and we will not need to refer to a label later on. Thus, the scope can be local to init.
● Though a label is simple, it takes several lines of code to display. In many of our tutorial examples we are attempting to illustrate particular Java facilities, without additionally creating beautiful screens for the user – hence we will often omit labels.

● Scaling the scrollbar

Because we will make extensive use of the scrollbar in our early programs, let us look at an example in which its integer values are not what we require. Consider the problem of converting a number of inches (in the range 0 to 10) to centimetres, where 1 inch equals 2.54 cm. Yes, we could set the scrollbar with a range of 0 to 10, but this would give us low precision. Instead, we will create a '0 to 100' scrollbar and then scale these integers to floats, resulting in steps of 0.1 inches. Here is the program, which produces the output of Figure 6.7. Note its similar structure to the window blind example.

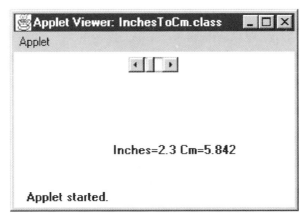

Figure 6.7 The output of the InchesToCm applet.

```
// scrollbar example - inches to cm
import java.awt.*;
import java.applet.Applet;
import java.awt.event.*;

public class InchesToCm extends Applet
    implements AdjustmentListener {
    private Scrollbar slider;
    private float sliderValue;
    public void init() {
        slider = new Scrollbar(Scrollbar.HORIZONTAL, 0, 1, 0, 100);
        add(slider);
        slider.addAdjustmentListener(this);
    }

    public void paint(Graphics g) {
        float cmEquivalent;
        cmEquivalent = sliderValue*2.54f;
        g.drawString("Inches="+sliderValue+
            " Cm="+cmEquivalent, 100, 100);
    }

    public void adjustmentValueChanged(AdjustmentEvent e) {
        sliderValue = (float) slider.getValue()/10;
        repaint();
    }
}
```

Here is where we scale the value:

```
sliderValue = (float) slider.getValue()/10;
```

The reason for using (float) to cast the '0 to 100' value into a '0.0 to 100.0' value is to avoid integer division being used, which always produces an int result. Recall that, when one of the quantities is float, a float result is produced. The final step is to do the conversion and display the result:

```
cmEquivalent = sliderValue*2.54f;
drawString("Inches="+sliderValue+
                    " Cm ="+cmEquivalent, 50, 50);
```

It would have been possible to do the whole thing in drawString, but the following is less clear, in our view:

```
drawString("Inches="+(float)sliderValue/10
    +" Cm="+(float) slidervalue/10*2.54, 50, 50);
```

● Building up graphical output

Sometimes, you may want your program to draw part of a picture, then wait for an event (e.g. a scrollbar movement, or button click) before drawing another part. In such a case, the use of paint and repaint is rather difficult, because paint erases all of the picture before drawing the new part. What we would prefer in some cases is to keep the existing picture, and add a new part when required. This can be done by the use of the getGraphics method, which obtains details of the drawing area. In most of our programs, we obtained this information by making use of the graphics parameter (often named as g) passed to paint. However, in the following program, we do our drawing in the event-handling method. Each time the scrollbar is accessed, the applet displays a new horizontal line representing the current value. Any previous lines are retained on the screen.

```
import java.awt.*;
import java.applet.Applet;
import java.awt.event.*;

public class ScrollbarValues extends Applet
    implements AdjustmentListener {
    private Scrollbar slider;
    private int currentX = 1;
    private int currentY = 5;

    public void init() {
        slider = new Scrollbar(Scrollbar.HORIZONTAL , 0, 1, 0, 100);
        add(slider);
        slider.addAdjustmentListener(this);
    }
```

```
    public void adjustmentValueChanged(AdjustmentEvent e) {
        Graphics g = getGraphics();
        currentX = slider.getValue();
        g.drawLine(0, currentY, currentX, currentY);
        currentY = currentY+5;
    }
}
```

Grammar spot

● Prefix all instance variables with `private`. (When you learn more about the construction of classes, you may choose other options.)
● Ensure that your scrollbar applets have:

```
import java.awt.event.*;
```

and:

```
implements AdjustmentListener;
```

● Register as a listener for each scrollbar by:

```
scrollbarName.addAdjustmentListener(this);
```

● Create an `adjustmentValueChanged` method for reacting to scrollbar manipulation.
● Stick to the provided event framework.

Programming pitfalls

● Attempting to refer to a method's local variables from within another method. This will be detected at compilation time.
● Forgetting to call `repaint` when the display needs updating. You will see an unchanging picture.
● Misspelling and wrong capitalization of the names:

```
AdjustmentListener
addAdjustmentListener
adjustmentValueChanged
```

In particular, if you misspell the method name `adjustmentValueChanged`, the compiler will misleadingly suggest that your class should be 'abstract'.

New language elements

● Local and `private` variables
● AWT components: `Scrollbar`, `label` and `showStatus`
● The use of `init`, `paint`, `repaint`, `addAdjustmentListener`, `adjustmentValueChanged`

Summary

● Events are user actions.

● Scrollbar events cause the method `adjustmentValueChanged` to be invoked.

EXERCISES

6.1 Produce an event-driven applet which converts degrees Celsius (centigrade) entered with a scrollbar to Fahrenheit. Allow for 0 to 100 degrees. The formula is:

$f = (c*9/5) + 32$

Test this with 0°C, which should be 32°F.

6.2 All Java programmers have (or deserve!) swimming pools, and we will create software for calculating the volume of a pool, given its dimensions. The width of the pool is fixed at 5.0 metres and the length is fixed at 20.0 metres. The depths can be different at each end, with the restrictions that the maximum depth of the shallow end is 1.0 metres, and the maximum depth of the deep end is 3.0 metres.

Your applet should contain two scrollbars to adjust the depths, and should draw out the current shape on the screen, for example:

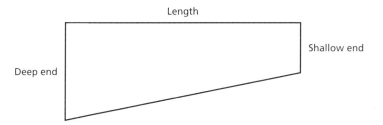

It should also display the volume, which may be calculated by:

```
v = average depth * width * length
```

Hint: don't bother figuring out which scrollbar has been changed. Simply 'get' the current values of each one.

6.3 Create an applet which displays a message of the form:

```
Now I'm at 50, 100
```

and allows the user to control the horizontal and vertical positioning of the message.

6.4 Produce an applet that allows the user to manipulate a filled oval on the screen via two scrollbars – one for the width, and one for the height. Add labels close to the scrollbars to indicate horizontal or vertical change.

6.5 Produce an applet which draws a right-angled triangle on the screen, and which allows the horizontal and vertical sides to be changed. Also display the gradient of the slope as a tangent. The tangent is calculated by:

```
tangent = vertical / horizontal
```

The display should be of the form:

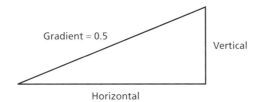

6.6 Superwoman has some steel hoops with which to encircle planets, and she is interested in what size of planet can be encircled by a hoop when the hoop is increased in size by breaking into it and inserting an extra piece. Assist Superwoman by producing an applet in which the circumference of a circle can be set via a scrollbar, and which then draws a circle of the appropriate size, and displays the diameter and circumference as a number.

Hints: use a slider of 1 to 100, where each unit represents 100 miles. Calculate the diameter by using this assignment:

```
diameter = circumference / (float)Math.PI;
```

where `Math.PI` is π, 3.14. . . .

The results may be unexpected – try extending a 1-unit circumference by 1 to 2, and then a 99-unit circle to 100. Note the change in the diameter.

ANSWER TO SELF-TEST QUESTION

6.1 We can amend the value that is used by `drawString`:

```
public void paint(Graphics g) {
    g.drawString("Current value is " + 2*sliderValue, 100,100);
}
```

Decisions – `if` and `switch`

● Introduction

We all make decisions in daily life. We wear a coat if it is raining. We buy a CD if we have enough money. Decisions are also central to computer programs. The computer tests a value and according to the result, takes one course of action or another. Decisions are used a lot in programs. Whenever the program has a choice of actions and decides to take one action or the other, an `if` statement is used to describe the situation.

We have seen that a computer program is a series of instructions to a computer. The computer obeys the instructions one after another in sequence. Often we want the computer to carry out a test on some data and then take one of a choice of actions depending on the result of the test. For example, we might want the computer to test someone's age and then tell them either that they may vote or that they are too young. This is sometimes called selection. It uses a statement (or instruction) called the `if` statement, the central subject of this chapter.

`if` statements are so important that they are used in every programming language that has ever been invented.

This chapter explains:

- how to use `if` statements to carry out tests;
- boolean data.

Along the way, this chapter also explains:

- how to use buttons;
- how to use text fields;
- how to use random numbers.

• The if statement

The voting checker

Our first example is a voting checker program. Users enter their ages using the scrollbar and the program decides whether they can vote or not. The screen is shown in Figure 7.1. We want the program to take different actions depending on whether the value is less than or greater than 18. As in the last chapter, we write the program as a collection of methods – init, paint and adjustmentValueChanged. Method init creates the scrollbar. Method adjustmentValueChanged is invoked whenever the scrollbar value is changed (by the mouse). Method paint displays the decision about voting rights.

```java
import java.applet.Applet;
import java.awt.*;
import java.awt.event.*;

public class Voting extends Applet implements AdjustmentListener {

    private Scrollbar bar;
    private int age = 0;

    public void init() {
        bar = new Scrollbar(Scrollbar.HORIZONTAL, 0, 1, 0, 100);
        add(bar);
        bar.addAdjustmentListener(this);
    }

    public void paint(Graphics g) {
        if (age >17)
            g.drawString ("You may vote", 50, 50);
        g.drawString("Age is " + age, 50, 70);
    }
```

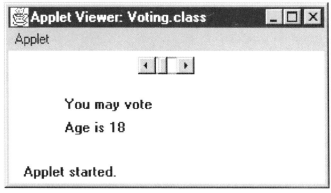

Figure 7.1 Screen for the voting checker program.

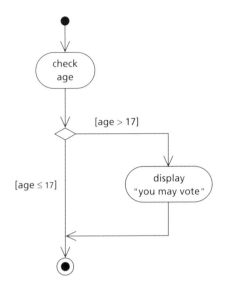

Figure 7.2 Activity diagram for an `if` statement.

```
public void adjustmentValueChanged(AdjustmentEvent event) {
    age = bar.getValue();
    repaint();
  }
}
```

The `if` statement tests the value of the variable age. If the value is greater than 17, the statement immediately below the `if` is carried out. Then the next statement is executed. On the other hand, if the age is not greater than 17, the associated statement is ignored and the next statement is executed.

One way of visualizing an `if` statement is as an activity diagram (Figure 7.2). This shows the above `if` statement in graphical form.

There are two parts to the `if` statement:

● the condition being tested;
● the statement(s) to be executed if the condition is true.

All programs have a sequence of actions. A sequence is still evident here:

1. An age is input from the scrollbar.
2. Then a test is done.
3. If appropriate, a message is output to say that the person can vote.
4. Finally, the statement to output the person's age is (always) executed.

Very often we want not just one, but a complete sequence of actions carried out if the result of the test is true:

```
if (age > 17) {
    g.drawString("congratulations! ", 50, 50);
    g.drawString("you may vote", 50, 70);
}
g.drawString ("Age is "+age, 50, 90);
```

The sequence of statements to be carried out if the test is true is enclosed in curly brackets. Each statement is followed by a semicolon.

The rule is: when just one statement is to be done as part of the `if`, it need not be enclosed in curly brackets (but it can be if you like.)

Indentation

Notice that the lines have been indented to reflect the structure of this piece of program. (Indentation means using spaces to push the text over to the right.) Although indentation is not essential (it is not a mandatory part of the Java language), it is highly desirable so that the (human) reader of a program can understand it easily. All good programs (whatever the language) have indentation and all good programmers use it.

You can create indentation using the space bar on your keyboard or with the aid of the tab key. An indentation of four spaces is generally considered to give good readability and this is used throughout this book.

SELF-TEST QUESTION

7.1 Do these two pieces of Java achieve the same end or not?

```
if (age > 18)
    g.drawString ("you may vote ", 50, 50);


if (age < 18)
    g.drawString ("you may not vote", 50, 50);
```

Very often in a program we want to specify *two* sequences of actions – those that are carried out if the condition is true and those that are carried out if the condition is false:

```
if (age > 17) {
    g.drawString("congratulations! ", 50, 50);
    g.drawString("you may vote", 50, 70);
} else {
    g.drawString("sorry ", 50, 50);
    g.drawString("you may not vote", 50, 70);
}
g.drawString("Age is "+age, 50, 90);
```

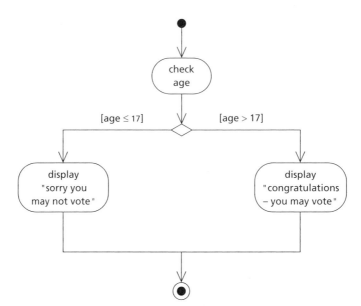

Figure 7.3 Activity diagram for an `if...else` statement.

There are three parts to this `if` statement:

● the condition being tested;
● the statement(s) to be executed if the condition is true;
● the statement(s) to be executed if the condition is false.

The new element here is the word `else`, which introduces the second part of the `if` statement. Notice how the indentation helps considerably in emphasizing the intention of the program. Also, each statement is followed by a semicolon.

Again we can visualize an `if...else` statement as an activity diagram, as shown in Figure 7.3.

● Comparison operators

The program fragments above (excluding the self-test question) used only greater than (>), which is one of several comparison operators. Here is a complete list:

>	means greater than
<	means less than
==	means equals
!=	means not equal to
<=	means less than or equal to
>=	means greater than or equal to

The odd one out in this list is the test for equality, which is two equals signs, rather than one. It is a common mistake to use just one equals sign in a test. So remember that:

```
x = y;
```

means that x becomes equal to y. But the expression:

```
x == y
```

means a test to see whether x is equal to y.

Choosing the appropriate operator often has to be done with great care. In the program to test whether someone can vote, the appropriate test should probably be:

```
if (age >= 18)
    g.drawString("you can vote", 50, 50);
```

Note that it is usually possible to write conditions in either of two ways. The following two program fragments achieve exactly the same result, but use different conditions:

```
if (age >= 18)
    g.drawString("you may vote", 50, 50);
else
    g.drawString("sorry", 50, 50);
g.drawString("good-bye", 50, 70);
```

achieves the same end as:

```
if (age < 18)
    g.drawString("sorry", 50, 50);
else
    g.drawString("you may vote ", 50, 50);
g.drawString("good-bye", 50, 70);
```

Although these two fragments achieve the same end result, the first is probably better than the second, because it spells out clearly the condition for eligibility to vote.

● And, or, not

Often in programming we need to test two things at once. Suppose, for example, we want to test whether someone should pay a junior rate for a ticket:

```
if (age > 6 && age < 16)
    g.drawString("junior rate", 50, 50);
```

The double ampersand (&&) is one of the 'logical operators' and means 'and'.

Brackets can be used to improve the readability of these more complex conditions:

```
if ((age > 6) && (age < 16))
    g.drawString("junior rate", 50, 50);
```

It might be very tempting to write:

```
if (age > 6 && < 18)        // error!
```

but this is incorrect because the conditions have to be spelled out in full:

```
if (age > 6 && age < 18)        // OK
```

The complete list of these logical operators is:

&& means and
| | means or
! means not

The | | operator is actually two | characters, which are there on the keyboard but not used very much other than for this purpose.

Throw of the dice

This example illustrates how to carry out a more complex series of tests. Two dice are thrown in a betting game and the program has to decide what the result is. We will create two scrollbars with a range of 1 to 6 to input the values of each of the two dice (Figure 7.4). To start with, let us make the rule that only a total score of six wins anything.

We saw how to use a scrollbar in Chapter 6. For this program, the two horizontal bars are set up so that:

1. The initial value of the scroll bar is 1.
2. The amount the value is changed if the area between the slider and the end of the range is clicked is 1.
3. The minimum value is 1.
4. The maximum value is 6.

The program is:

```
import java.awt.*;
import java.applet.Applet;
import java.awt.event.*;
```

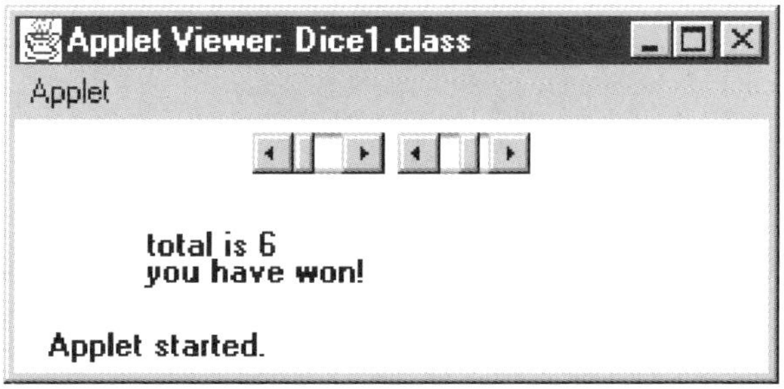

Figure 7.4 The dice program, version 1.

```
public class Dice1 extends Applet implements AdjustmentListener {

    private Scrollbar die1, die2;
    private int value1 = 1, value2 = 1;

    public void init() {
        die1 = new Scrollbar(Scrollbar.HORIZONTAL, 1, 1, 1, 6);
        add(die1);
        die1.addAdjustmentListener(this);
        die2 = new Scrollbar(Scrollbar.HORIZONTAL, 1, 1, 1, 6);
        add(die2);
        die2.addAdjustmentListener(this);
    }

    public void paint(Graphics g) {
        int total;
        total = value1 + value2;
        g.drawString("total is "+total, 50, 50);
        if (total==6)
                g.drawString("you have won!", 50, 60);
    }

    public void adjustmentValueChanged(AdjustmentEvent event) {
        value1 = die1.getValue();
        value2 = die2.getValue();
        repaint();
    }

}
```

To illustrate how to use the `else` option, we could write:

```
if (total == 6)
    g.drawString("you have won!", 50, 50);
else
    g.drawString("you have lost!", 50, 50);
```

Now we will alter the rules and see how to rewrite the program. Suppose that any pair of values wins, i.e. two ones, two twos etc. Then the `if` statement is:

```
if (value1 == value2)
    g.drawString("you have won", 50, 50);
```

Now let's suppose that you win if you get 2 or 7:

```
if ( (total == 2) || (total == 7) )
    g.drawString("you have won", 50, 50);
```

The pair of symbols | | – which you will find on your keyboard – means or. Notice that we have enclosed each of the conditions with brackets. These brackets aren't strictly necessary in Java, but they help a lot to clarify the meaning of the condition to be tested.

SELF-TEST QUESTIONS

7.2 Alter the program so that a win is a total value of 2, 5 or 7.

7.3 Write `if` statements to test whether someone is eligible for full-time employment. The rule is that you must be 16 or above and younger than 65.

The ! operator, meaning **not**, gets a lot of use in programming, even though in English the use of a negative can suffer from lack of clarity. Here is an example of the use of not:

```
if (! (age > 18))
    g.drawString("too young", 100, 100);
```

This means: test to see if the age is greater than 18. If the result is true, make it false. If it is false, make it true. Then, if the outcome is true, display the message. This can, of course, be written more simply without the not (!) operator.

SELF-TEST QUESTION

7.4 Rewrite the above `if` statement without using the not operator.

● Nested `ifs`

Look at the following program fragment:

```
if (age > 6)
    if (age < 16)
        g.drawString("junior rate", 50, 50);
    else
        g.drawString("adult rate ", 50, 50);
```

You will see that the second `if` statement is completely contained within the first. (The indentation helps to make this clear.) This is called *nesting*. Nesting is not the same as indentation – it is just that the indentation makes the nesting very apparent. The meaning of this nested code is as follows:

- If the age is greater than 6, then the second if is carried out.
- If the age is not greater than 6, then nothing is done (and the statements that follow this fragment are executed).

The overall effect of this piece of program is:

- If the age is greater than 6 and less than 16, the rate is the junior rate.
- If the age is greater than 6 but not less than 16, the rate is the adult rate.
- If the age is not greater than 6, nothing happens.

It is common to see nesting in programs, but a program like this has a complexity which makes it slightly difficult to understand. Often it is possible to write a program more simply using the logical operators. Here, for example, the same result as above is achieved without nesting:

```
if ((age > 6) && (age<16))
    g.drawString("junior rate", 50, 50);
if (age >= 16)
    g.drawString("adult rate", 50, 50);
```

We now have two pieces of program that achieve the same end result, one with nesting and one without. Some people argue that it is hard to understand nesting, hence such a program is prone to errors and therefore nesting should be avoided.

Other people counter by saying that the second piece of program will always have to perform two tests, whatever the data, and that this is wasteful of computer time.

This is a matter of program style. The best advice is probably to try to write programs that are as simple as possible for the majority of readers.

SELF-TEST QUESTION
....

7.5 Write a program to input a salary from a scrollbar and determine how much tax someone should pay according to the following rules:

People pay no tax if they earn up to $10,000. They pay tax at the rate of 20% on the amount they earn over $10,000 but up to $50,000. They pay tax at 90% on any money they earn over $50,000.

Tom and Jerry

In this program we create two scrollbars, one called Tom, the other called Jerry. The program compares the values and reports on which one is set to the larger value. The screen is shown in Figure 7.5. The library method fillRect is used to draw a solid rectangle whose width across the screen is equal to the value obtained from the corresponding scrollbar.

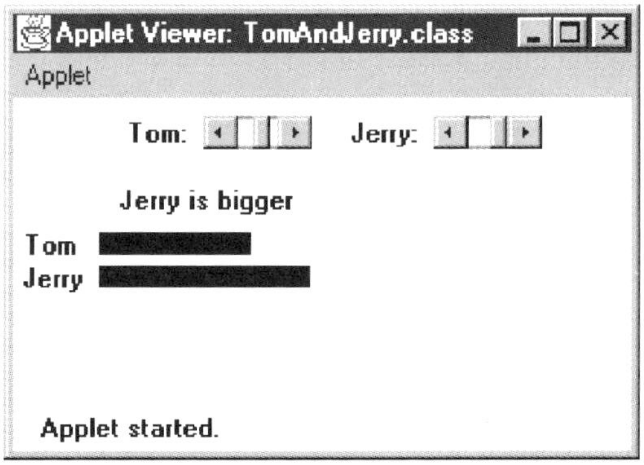

Figure 7.5 Screen for the Tom and Jerry program.

```java
import java.awt.*;
import java.applet.Applet;
import java.awt.event.*;


public class TomAndJerry extends Applet implements AdjustmentListener {

    private Scrollbar tom, jerry;
    private int tomValue = 0, jerryValue = 0;

    public void init() {
        Label toms = new Label("Tom:");
        add(toms);
        tom = new Scrollbar(Scrollbar.HORIZONTAL, 0, 1, 0, 100);
        add(tom);
        tom.addAdjustmentListener(this);

        Label jerrys = new Label("Jerry:");
        add(jerrys);
        jerry = new Scrollbar(Scrollbar.HORIZONTAL, 0, 1, 0, 100);
        add(jerry);
        jerry.addAdjustmentListener(this);
    }

    public void paint(Graphics g) {
        g.drawString("Tom", 5, 70);
        g.fillRect(40, 60, tomValue, 10);
        g.drawString("Jerry", 5, 85);
        g.fillRect(40, 75, jerryValue, 10);
```

```
        if (tomValue > jerryValue)
            g.drawString("Tom is bigger ", 50, 50);
        else
            g.drawString("Jerry is bigger", 50, 50);
    }

    public void adjustmentValueChanged(AdjustmentEvent event) {
        tomValue = tom.getValue();
        jerryValue = jerry.getValue();
        repaint();
    }
}
```

This is fine, but again illustrates the importance of care when using if statements. In this program, what happens when the two values are equal? The answer is that the program declares Jerry to be bigger – which is clearly not the case. We really need to enhance the program to spell things out more clearly:

```
if (tomValue == jerryValue)
    g.drawString("They are equal ", 50, 50);
else
    if (tomValue > jerryValue)
        g.drawString("Tom is bigger ", 50, 50);
    else
        g.drawString("Jerry is bigger", 50, 50);
```

This is another illustration of nested if statements. There are two if statements. The second if is written within the else part of the first if statement. The indentation, while not required, is enormously helpful in visualizing how the ifs are meant to work.

SELF-TEST QUESTION
....

7.6 Write a program that creates three scrollbars and displays the largest of the three values.

● Case studies using if

The amplifier display

Some stereo amplifiers have a display that shows the volume being created. The display waxes and wanes according to the volume at any point in time. Sometimes the display has an indicator that shows the maximum value that is currently being output. This program displays the numerical value of the maximum value that the scrollbar is set to (see Figure 7.6).

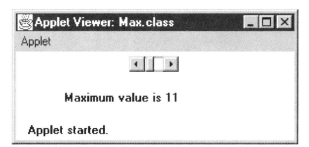

Figure 7.6 Screen for the amplifier display.

```java
import java.awt.*;
import java.applet.Applet;
import java.awt.event.*;

public class Max extends Applet implements AdjustmentListener {

    private Scrollbar volumeControl;
    private int max = 0;
    private int volume = 0;

    public void init() {
        volumeControl = new Scrollbar(Scrollbar.HORIZONTAL,
                                      0, 1, 0, 100);
        add(volumeControl);
        volumeControl.addAdjustmentListener(this);
    }

    public void paint(Graphics g) {
        if (volume > max)
            max = volume;
        g.drawString("Maximum value is " + max, 50, 50);
    }

    public void adjustmentValueChanged(AdjustmentEvent event) {
        volume = volumeControl.getValue();
        repaint();
    }
}
```

SELF-TEST QUESTIONS
....

7.7 Write a program that displays the numerical value of the minimum value that the scrollbar is set to.

7.8 The Young and Beautiful holiday company restricts its clients to ages between 18 and 30. (Below 18 you have no money; after 30 you have too many wrinkles.) Write a program to test whether you are eligible to go on holiday with this company.

● Using buttons

We saw in an earlier chapter how to create and use scrollbars within a program. Now we look at how to use buttons. Figure 7.7 shows a window with a button in it. A button has a label on it – the label is 'Press here' in Figure 7.7. The user can position the mouse over a button and click on it, just like pressing a real button on a stereo or a lift. Buttons are used a lot in graphical user interface (GUI) programs. If you use a word processor, it undoubtedly uses buttons to select options and functions (like cut, paste, select bold), as well as to change the size of the window. So buttons are an important aspect of programming.

As with scrollbars, use of buttons is accomplished using methods in one of the Java libraries, the AWT (Abstract Window Toolkit) library.

Button count

We will start out using only a single button, with a label on it called 'Press here'. When we press the button, by clicking on it with the mouse button, we will get the program to display the number of times the button has been pressed. This will test that the button and our Java code is working properly. When the program is running, the window is shown in Figure 7.7.

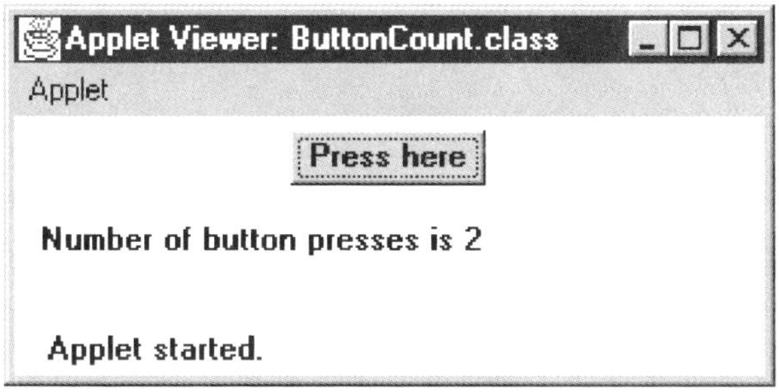

Figure 7.7 Screen for the button counter.

To create a button on the screen, we must first specify that the class implements `ActionListener`.

Then we declare a button among the variables at the start of the program:

```
private Button tester;
```

This declares a variable of type `Button`, which we have chosen to call `tester`. The method `init` is invoked when the program starts, and within `init` we must write the statement to create the button with the required label on it:

```
tester = new Button("Press here");
```

Next, we add the button to the window:

```
add(tester);
```

Finally we register as a listener to button events:

```
tester.addActionListener(this);
```

In total, there are six steps to setting up a button:

1. State that the class implements `ActionListener`.
2. Declare a button variable, giving it a name.
3. Create a new button, giving it a label.
4. Add the button to the window.
5. Inform the button that this object will respond to button events, using `addActionListener`.
6. Provide a method called `actionPerformed` to be invoked when a button click event occurs.

When we use scrollbars, we need to provide a method called `adjustmentValueChanged` to handle the event, but with buttons we have to provide a different method, called `actionPerformed`. The program code is:

```
import java.applet.*;
import java.awt.*;
import java.awt.event.*;

public class ButtonCount extends Applet implements ActionListener {

    private Button tester;
    private int count = 0;

    public void init(){
        tester = new Button("Press here");
        add(tester);
        tester.addActionListener(this);
    }
```

```
public void actionPerformed(ActionEvent event) {
    count++;
    repaint();
}

public void paint(Graphics g) {
    g.drawString("Number of button presses is " + count, 10, 50);
}

}
```

When the event happens the browser (or applet viewer) invokes `actionPerformed`, providing a set of information in the parameter `event`. The most useful item is the method `getSource()`, which enables us to detect which component caused the event.

In this particular program, only one kind of event can occur – someone clicking the mouse on the button. So in the method `actionPerformed` we can safely assume that any event is the button and therefore increment the count.

The count, initially zero, is displayed by the method `paint`.

Suppose we had a program that uses two buttons. For example, sometimes you see people at the roadside carrying out a census of road usage. Let us suppose that they are using a computer to record how many cars and how many trucks are passing. The program will display two buttons – one marked truck and the other marked car. It also displays the total number of cars and trucks. When an event occurs, it could be either the truck button or the car button that has been pressed. So we need to use `if` statements in conjunction with the method `getSource` to distinguish between them:

```
public void actionPerformed(ActionEvent event) {
    if (event.getSource() == truckButton)
        truckCount++;
    if (event.getSource() == carButton)
        carCount++;
    repaint();
}
```

So, in general, when there are two or more buttons, we need to use `if` statements to identify the source of an event. What about a program that uses both buttons and scrollbars? There is no extra problem here – we can use `actionPerformed` and `adjustmentValueChanged` in the same program. The class header becomes:

```
public class ButtonAndBar extends Applet implements ActionListener,
                                                  AdjustmentListener
```

● Boolean variables

All of the types of variable that we have met so far are designed to hold numbers. Now we meet a new kind of variable. It is a special type of variable, called a `boolean`, that can only hold either the value `true` or the value `false`. The words `boolean`, `true` and `false` are reserved in Java and cannot be used for any other purpose. This type of variable is named after the 19th century British mathematician George Boole who made a large contribution towards the development of mathematical logic, in which the ideas of true and false play a central role.

We can declare a variable of type `boolean` like this:

```
boolean finished;
```

and we can assign either of the values `true` and `false`:

```
finished = true;
```

Equally importantly, we can test the value of a `boolean` in an `if` statement:

```
if (finished)
    g.drawString("Good bye", 10, 10);
```

The value of `finished` is tested, and if it is `true` the accompanying statement is executed. An alternative, but slightly more cumbersome, way of writing the same test is:

```
if (finished == true)
    g.drawString("Good bye", 10, 10);
```

Boolean variables are used in programming to keep a record of the state of some action. Suppose we want to display the message 'OUCH' the first time that a button is pressed (see Figure 7.8). We will use a boolean variable to say whether or not the button had been pressed. The variable, named `clickedYet`, has the value `false` if the button has not yet been clicked and `true` if it has been clicked. Initially, the value must be `false`. When the button is clicked, it must be made `true`. When the method `paint` sees that `clickedYet` is true, it displays the required message:

```
import java.applet.*;
import java.awt.*;
import java.awt.event.*;
```

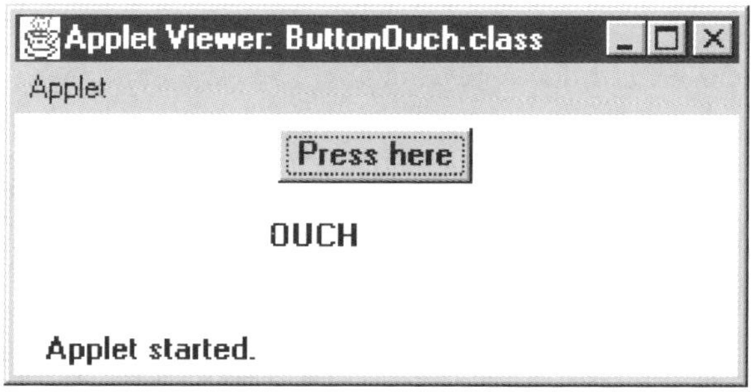

Figure 7.8 The output of the ButtonOuch applet.

```
public class ButtonOuch extends Applet implements ActionListener {

    private Button tester;
    private boolean clickedYet = false;

    public void init() {
        tester = new Button("Press here");
        add(tester);
        tester.addActionListener(this);
    }

    public void paint(Graphics g) {
        if (clickedYet)
            g.drawString("OUCH", 100, 50);
    }

    public void actionPerformed(ActionEvent event) {
        clickedYet = true;
        repaint();
    }
}
```

A method can return a boolean value. For example, suppose we need a method to check whether three numbers are in numerical order:

```
public boolean inOrder(int a, int b, int c) {
    if ((a <= b) && (b <= c))
        return true;
    else
        return false;
}
```

SELF-TEST QUESTION
....

7.9 Write a method that tests whether its three float parameters are valid lengths for the sides of a triangle. (In a triangle, the sum of the lengths of any two of the sides must be greater than the length of the third side.)

● Random numbers

We will return to the dice-throwing program discussed earlier. Instead of inputting the dice values via the scrollbars, we will change the program so that the computer decides

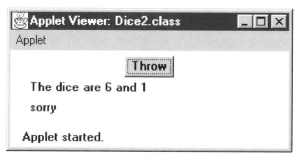

Figure 7.9 The dice program, version 2.

the die values randomly. We will create a button, labelled 'Throw'. When it is clicked, the program will get two random numbers and use them as the die values (Figure 7.9).

Creating random numbers is a very common thing to want to do in game programs of all kinds. If the game behaved the same way every time you played it, it would be very boring. Randomness creates variety, whether it is the arrival of aliens, the bounce of a ball or the layout of a maze.

To get a random number in Java, we invoke a library method. There are a number of methods, including one named `random`, which is in the maths library. The method `random` returns a random number, a `double` in the range 0.0 up to but not including 1.0. What we need for our purpose is an integer in the range 1 to 6. So we need to convert the numbers that `random` produces into the ones that we want:

1. `random` creates numbers evenly distributed in the range 0.0 to 0.999999. . . . If we multiply by 6, we will get random numbers evenly distributed in the range 0.0 to 5.999. . . .
2. If we now convert the floating point number to an integer using the cast operator (`int`), we will get the integers 0 to 5. Remember that (`int`) truncates the floating point number, so that for example 5.7 becomes 5.
3. Finally we add 1 to get random integers in the range 1 to 6.

The complete formula is thus:

```
die = (int)(Math.random() * 6) + 1;
```

Transforming the size of random numbers in a manner similar to this is often necessary. The program to throw two dice looks like this:

```
import java.awt.*;
import java.applet.Applet;
import java.awt.event.*;

public class Dice2 extends Applet implements ActionListener {

    private Button throwDice;
    private boolean thrown = false;
```

```
public void init() {
    throwDice = new Button("Throw");
    add(throwDice);
    throwDice.addActionListener(this);
}

public void actionPerformed(ActionEvent event) {
    thrown = true;
    repaint();
}

public void paint(Graphics g) {
    int die1, die2;
    if (thrown) {
        die1 = (int)(Math.random() * 6) + 1;
        die2 = (int)(Math.random() * 6) + 1;
        g.drawString("The dice are " + die1 + " and " + die2, 20, 40);
        if (die1 == die2)
            g.drawString("a win", 20, 60);
        else
            g.drawString("sorry" , 20, 60);
    }
}
}
```

The random numbers that are obtained using the library method random are not truly random. Because a computer is a machine that can only carry out a well-defined series of actions, a computer cannot create random numbers. What it does instead is to create what look like random numbers – numbers that are indistinguishable from random numbers. These are called pseudo-random numbers. These are created as a series. The next number is created from the last, and so on. A formula is used to derive one value from the next in such a way that the next number seems to be random.

There are some other random number methods, one of which is called nextInt. When invoked it produces an integer random number in the complete range of the type int. This method is in a package called jav.util (util is short for utilities), and to use it another import statement must appear at the head of the program, along with the others:

```
import java.util.*;
```

● Case studies using buttons

Little and Large

In this program we create two buttons. The program draws a circle. Clicking on one button makes the circle bigger; the other makes it smaller (Figure 7.10).

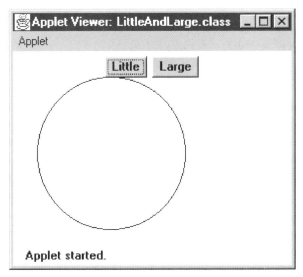

Figure 7.10 Little and Large.

When the user clicks the mouse, the browser (or applet viewer) detects the event. It then invokes the method called `actionPerformed` that we have written to handle the event. We must provide this method (if we want to respond to events) as part of the program we write. The method carries out tests to identify which particular event happened – which button was pressed.

```
import java.applet.Applet;
import java.awt.*;
import java.awt.event.*;

public class LittleAndLarge extends Applet implements ActionListener {

    private int diameter = 20;
    private Button little, large;

    public void init() {
        little = new Button("Little");
        add(little);
        little.addActionListener(this);
        large = new Button("Large");
        add(large);
        large.addActionListener(this);
    }

    public void paint(Graphics g) {
        g.drawOval(25, 25, diameter, diameter);
    }
```

```
    public void actionPerformed(ActionEvent event) {
        if (event.getSource() == little)
            diameter = diameter - 10;
        if (event.getSource() == large)
            diameter = diameter + 10;
        repaint();
    }
}
```

The library method drawOval needs as its first two parameters the x- and y-coordinates of the top left of a rectangle that just encloses the oval. The third parameter is the width of the oval and the last parameter is the height of the oval. (If the width and height are the same we get a circle.)

The safe

This program represents the combination lock on a safe. The program displays three buttons, one for each of the digits 1, 2 and 3 (Figure 7.11). The user has to press three buttons, in an attempt to guess the combination correctly.

```
import java.applet.*;
import java.awt.*;
import java.awt.event.*;

public class Safe extends Applet implements ActionListener {

    private int guess = 0;
    private int combination = 321;
    private Button one, two, three, again;

    public void init() {
        one = new Button("1");
        add(one);
```

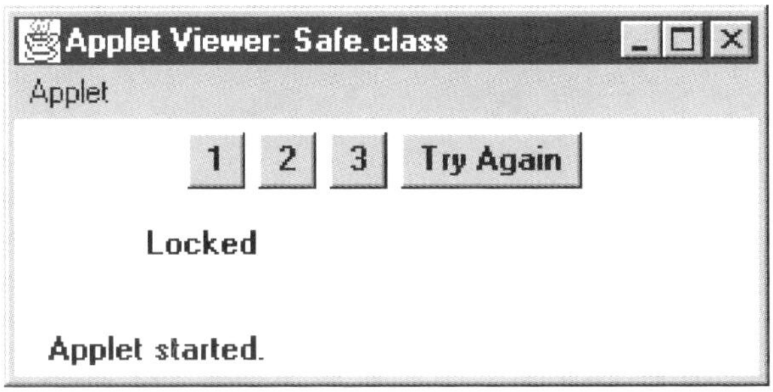

Figure 7.11 The safe.

```
        one.addActionListener(this);
        two = new Button("2");
        add(two);
        two.addActionListener(this);
        three = new Button("3");
        add(three);
        three.addActionListener(this);
        again = new Button("Try Again");
        add(again);
        again.addActionListener(this);
    }

    public void paint(Graphics g) {
        if (guess == combination)
            g.drawString("Unlocked", 50, 50);
        else
            g.drawString("Locked", 50, 50);
    }

    public void actionPerformed(ActionEvent event) {
        if (event.getSource() == one)
            guess = guess*10 + 1;
        if (event.getSource() == two)
            guess = guess*10 + 2;
        if (event.getSource() == three)
            guess = guess*10 + 3;
        if (event.getSource() == again)
            guess = 0;

        repaint();
    }
}
```

It might be frustrating to play with this program because you could try for a very long time before you got the correct combination. A less frustrating game is set as an exercise at the end of the chapter.

● switch

The switch statement is another way of doing a lot of if statements. But it is actually not used very often and, if you wish, you can skip this section. We have included an explanation of the switch statement for completeness, and when you feel confident about programming you may want to come back and read all about it.

If you find that you are writing a lot of if statements together, it may be worth rewriting them as a switch statement. For example, suppose we need a piece of program to display a date. Suppose that the day of the week is represented by an integer called day, which has one of the values 1 to 7, representing the days Monday to Sunday. We could write:

```
if (day == 1)
    g.drawString("Monday", 50, 50);
else
    if (day == 2)
        g.drawString("Tuesday", 50, 50);
else
    if (day == 3)
        g.drawString("Wednesday", 50, 50);
else
    if (day == 4)
        g.drawString("Thursday", 50, 50);
else
    if (day == 5)
        g.drawString("Friday", 50, 50);
else
    if (day == 6)
        g.drawString("Saturday", 50, 50);
else
    if (day == 7)
        g.drawString("Sunday", 50, 50);
```

Notice that we have chosen to write the elses underneath each other. An alternative style would be to indent them, one from the other, so that successive lines would march rightwards across the page. (See Chapter 22 for a further discussion of the style of a series of nested if statements.)

Now although this piece of coding is fairly neat, clear and well-structured, there is an alternative that has the same effect using the switch statement:

```
switch (day) {
    case 1 : g.drawString("Monday", 50, 50); break;
    case 2 : g.drawString("Tuesday", 50, 50); break;
    case 3 : g.drawString("Wednesday", 50, 50); break;
    case 4 : g.drawString("Thursday", 50, 50); break;
    case 5 : g.drawString("Friday", 50, 50); break;
    case 6 : g.drawString("Saturday", 50, 50); break;
    case 7 : g.drawString("Sunday", 50, 50); break;
}
```

This now shows the symmetry of what is to happen more clearly than the equivalent series of if statements.

The word break means go to the end of the switch statement.

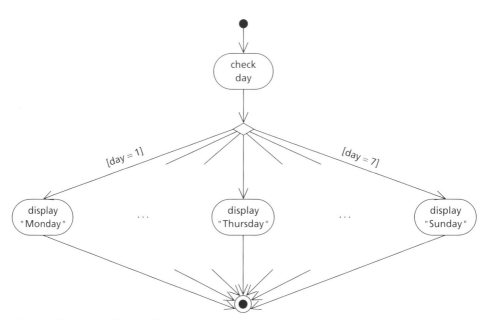

Figure 7.12 Activity diagram for a switch statement.

Notice the brackets around the variable that acts as the control for the switch statement. Notice also the colon following each occurrence of the value of the variable. Curly brackets enclose the complete set of options.

A switch statement like this can be visualized as an activity diagram in Figure 7.12.

SELF-TEST QUESTION
....

7.10 Write a method that converts the integers 1, 2, 3 and 4 into the words diamonds, hearts, clubs and spades respectively.

More than one statement can follow an option. For example, one of the options could be:

```
case 4 : g.setColor(RED);
        g.drawString("Thursday", 50, 50);
        break;
```

Several options can be grouped together, like this:

```
switch (day) {
    case 1 : case 2: case 3: case 4: case 5:
        g.drawString("weekday", 50, 50); break;
    case 6 : case 7: g.drawString("weekend", 50, 50); break;
}
```

Another sometimes useful part of the switch statement is the default option. Suppose in the above example that the value of the integer denoting the day of the week is input from a scrollbar. Then there is the distinct possibility that the number entered will not be in the range 0 to 7. Any decent program needs to take account of this, in order to prevent something odd happening. The switch statement is very good at dealing with this situation, because we can supply a 'catch-all' or default option that will be invoked if none of the others are valid:

```
switch (day) {
    case 1 : g.drawString("Monday", 50, 50); break;
    case 2 : g.drawString("Tuesday", 50, 50); break;
    case 3 : g.drawString("Wednesday", 50, 50); break;
    case 4 : g.drawString("Thursday", 50, 50); break;
    case 5 : g.drawString("Friday", 50, 50); break;
    case 6 : g.drawString("Saturday", 50, 50); break;
    case 7 : g.drawString("Sunday", 50, 50); break;

    default : g.drawString("illegal day", 50, 50); break;
}
```

If a default option is not written as part of a switch statement and if none of the cases corresponds to the actual value of the variable, then all the options are ignored.

SELF-TEST QUESTION
....

7.11 Write a method to convert integers as follows. If the number is in the range 1 to 5, return the string 'weekday'. If it is 6 or 7 return the string 'weekend'. Otherwise return the string 'error'.

The switch statement looks very useful, but unfortunately it is not as flexible as it could be. Suppose, for example, we want to write a piece of program to output two numbers, with the smallest first, followed by the larger. Using if statements, we have:

```
if (a > b)
    g.drawString(b + " is greater than " + , 50, 50);
else
    if (b > a)
        g.drawString(a + " is greater than " + , 50, 50);
    else
        g.drawString("they are equal", 50, 50);
```

We may be tempted to rewrite this using the switch statement as follows:

```
switch (?) { // beware! illegal Java
    case a>b : g.drawString(b + " is greater than " + , 50, 50); break;
    case b>a : g.drawString(a + " is greater than " + , 50, 50); break;
    case a == b : g.drawString("they are equal", 50, 50); break;
}
```

but this is not allowed because, as indicated by the question mark, switch only works with a single integer or character variable as its subject.

● Text fields

Text fields are another graphical user interface component for inputting information from the user of a program. Until now we have used scrollbars for the input of numbers – which is convenient and intuitive. But a text field allows a number to be input more directly than a scrollbar. (A text field can also be used to input textual information, as we shall see later.) For example, Figure 7.13 shows the window for a program that acts as the voting checker, which we presented at the beginning of this chapter. However, in this new version of the program the voter's age is entered into a text field. To enter a number into a text field the cursor is positioned within the field. Then the characters are keyed in. They can be altered as much as you like by using the backspace and delete keys. When the user is satisfied with the number, the enter key is pressed.

Here is the program that displays the text field, gets the number and checks it – the voting checker program:

```
import java.applet.*;
import java.awt.*;
import java.awt.event.*;

public class AgeCheck extends Applet implements ActionListener {

    private TextField ageField;
    private int age;
```

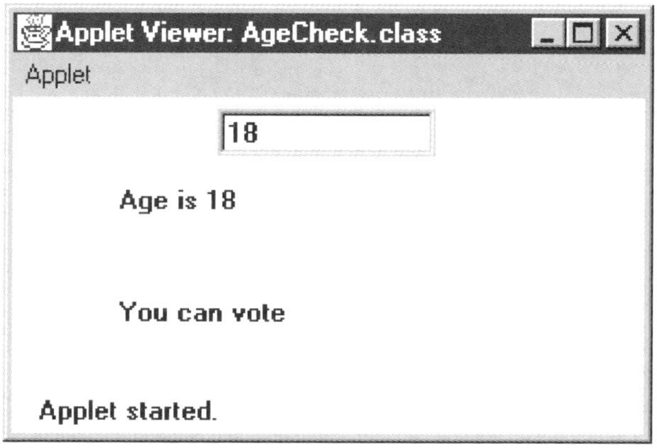

Figure 7.13 Age check program using a text field.

```
public void init() {
    ageField = new TextField(10);
    add(ageField);
    ageField.addActionListener(this);
}

public void actionPerformed(ActionEvent event) {
    age = Integer.parseInt(ageField.getText());
    repaint();
}

public void paint(Graphics g) {
    g.drawString("Age is " + age, 50, 50);
    if (age >= 18)
        g.drawString("You can vote", 50, 100);
    else
        g.drawString("You cannot vote", 50, 100);
}

}
```

Setting up a text field is similar to setting up a button. First we declare a variable of type
`TextField`:

```
private TextField ageField;
```

with a name chosen by the programmer. This is declared with any other variables at the
top of the program. Next we create the text field when `init` is invoked:

```
ageField = new TextField(10);
```

The parameter for the method `TextField` is the width, in characters, of the text field
displayed on the screen.

Next, the text field is added to the window display:

```
add(ageField);
```

Finally, we tell the event-handling mechanism to notify us when an event occurs:

```
ageField.addActionListener(this);
```

When the user of the program presses the enter key, the method `actionPerformed` is
invoked by the applet viewer or the browser. We must provide such a method to handle
the event. In this program there is only one possible event, so we have no need to distinguish it from any others. (Note that the methods associated with handling events
from text fields are the same as those used with buttons.)

We can go on to process the data that was entered. The library method `getText()`
does this, and in our case `ageField.getText()` inputs the characters from the text field.

Finally we need to convert the characters into an integer number using the library method `Integer.parseInt`. A string of characters such as 123 may look like a number, but in fact is simply three characters – the character 1, the character 2 and the character 3. If we want to convert them into a number, we need to do so explicitly. The method `parseInt` is so called because the word parse means to scan or process some text. In summary, inputting an integer from a text field involves:

1. Use `getText` to input the text.
2. Use `Integer.parseInt` to convert the text to an integer.

If the characters entered into a text field are not digits – for example, if they are letters or punctuation characters – then the program will stop with an error message. (There is a way to avoid this, but we will not see how until Chapter 16 on exception handling.)

We will use text fields in later chapters to input floating-point numbers and to input character strings. The process is similar. In the case of floating-point numbers, various library methods are used to convert the characters into a number (see Chapter 12 on calculations). In the case of inputting a string, no conversion is necessary.

If a program uses two or more text fields, or a text field and a button, the method `actionPerformed` that handles the events from these components needs to distinguish between the sources of an event, using `if` statements in the following manner:

```
public void actionPerformed(ActionEvent event) {
        if (event.getSource() == ageField)
            age = Integer.parseInt(ageField.getText());
        if (event.getSource() == yearField)
            year = Integer.parseInt(yearField.getText());
        repaint();
    }
```

A text field can also be used to output (display) text, using the method `setText` as shown in the following code. Note that the text field needs to be sufficiently wide to accommodate the text.

```
TextField message = new TextField(25);
message.setText("Your message here");
```

A text field is used for the input (or output) of just one line of text. If you need to input (or output) several lines of text, a GUI component called a text area is what you need. These are described later in this book.

Grammar spot

● The first kind of `if` statement has the structure:

```
if (condition)
    statement;
```

or

```
if (condition) {
    statement1;
    statement2;
}
```

The second type of `if` statement has the structure:

```
if (condition)
    statementA;
else
    statementB;
```

or

```
if (condition) {
    statement1;
    statement2;
} else {
    statement3;
    statement4;
}
```

● Several aspects of using `if` statements require care:

   – The condition is enclosed in round brackets.
   – Within an `if`, more than one statement must be enclosed in curly brackets.
   – Each and every statement within an `if` must be followed by a semicolon.

● The `switch` statement has slightly complicated grammar and must be used carefully. For example, it uses colons and semicolons. The best approach is simply to copy a `switch` statement from a book or an existing program. Luckily, it is not something that you will use very often.

Programming pitfalls

● Do not forget to enclose the condition being tested in an `if` statement in brackets like this:

```
if (a > b)...
```

● Don't forget that, in a test, the test for equality is not = but ==, so

```
if (a = b)...
```

will not compile correctly, whereas:

```
if (a == b)...
```

is probably what you want to write. This is a very common error.

● You might find that you have written an `if` statement like this:

```
if (a > 18 && < 25) ...
```

which is wrong. Instead, the && (meaning **and**) must link two complete conditions, preferably in brackets for clarity, like this:

```
if ((a > 18) && (a < 25)) ...
```

Programming principles

● The computer normally obeys instructions one-by-one in a sequence. An `if` statement or a `switch` statement causes the computer to test the value of some data and then take a choice of actions depending on the result of the test. This choice is sometimes called *selection*. The test of the data is sometimes called a *condition*.
● The `if` statement comes in two flavours, one with an `else` part and one without. When you use an `if` statement with an `else` part, the two alternative actions are clearly distinguished. When you use an `if` statement without an `else`, the actions are only performed if the condition is true.
● After an `if` statement is completed, the computer continues obeying the instructions in sequence.
● A `boolean` variable can only have one of two values – `true` and `false`.

New language elements

● Control structures for selection:

  – `if`, `else`
  – `switch`, `case`, `break`, `default`

● `Boolean` variables.

Summary

● `if` statements allow the programmer to control the sequence of actions by making the program carry out a test. Following the test, the computer carries out one of a choice of actions.

● There are two varieties of the `if` statement, one with an `else` part and one without.

● A `boolean` variable can take on either the value `true` or the value `false`.

● The `switch` statement carries out a test, but provides for an unlimited set of outcomes. However, the `switch` statement is restricted to tests on integers.

EXERCISES

7.1 **Random number** Write a program to display a single random number each time a button labelled 'next' is pressed. The program should display:

1. the random number obtained by invoking `Math.random`, which is in the range 0.0 to 0.999 . . . ;
2. a random integer in the range 1 to 10;
3. a random integer in the range 0 to 100;
4. a random boolean value (`true` or `false`).

7.2 **Deal a card** Write a program with a single button on it which, when clicked, randomly selects a single playing card. First use the random number generator method in the library to create a number in the range 1 to 4. Then convert the number to a suit (heart, diamond, club, spade). Next use the random number generator to create a random number in the range 1 to 13. Convert the number to an ace, 2, 3 etc. and finally output the value of the chosen card. (Hint: use `switch` as appropriate.)

7.3 **Sorting** Write a program to input numbers from three scrollbars, or text fields, and output them in increasing numerical size.

7.4 **Cinema price** Write a program to work out how much a person pays to go to the cinema. The program should input an age from the scrollbar or a text field and then decide on the following basis:

● under 5, free;
● aged 5 to 12, half price;
● aged 13 to 54, full price;
● aged 55, or over, free.

7.5 **Betting** A group of people are betting on the outcome of three throws of the dice. A person bets $1 on predicting the outcome of the three throws. Write a program that uses the random number method to simulate three throws of a die and displays the winnings according to the following rules:

● all three throws are sixes: win $20;
● all three throws are the same (but not sixes): win $10;
● any two of the three throws are the same: win $5.

7.6 **The digital combination safe** Write a program to act as the digital combination lock for a safe. Create three buttons, representing the numbers 1, 2 and 3. The user clicks on the buttons, attempting to guess the correct numbers (say 331121). The program remains unhelpfully quiet until the correct buttons are pressed. Then it congratulates the user with a suitable message. A button is provided to allow users to give up when they become frustrated.

   Enhance the program so that it has another button which allows the user to change the safe's combination.

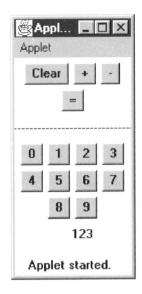

Figure 7.14 The calculator.

7.7 **Rock, scissors, paper game** This is a game for two humans to play. Each player simultaneously chooses one of rock, scissors or paper. Rock beats scissors, paper beats rock and scissors beats paper. If both players choose the same, it is a draw. Write a program to play the game. The player selects one of three buttons, marked rock, scissors or paper. The computer makes its choice randomly using the random number method. The computer also decides and displays who has won.

7.8 **The calculator** Write a program which simulates a simple desk calculator (Figure 7.14) that acts on integer numbers. It has one button for each of the 10 digits, 0 to 9. It has a button to add and a button to subtract. It has a clear button, to clear the display, and an equals (=) button to get the answer.

When the clear button is pressed the display is set to zero and the (hidden) total is set to zero.

When a digit button is pressed, the digit is added to the right of those already in the display (if any).

When the + button is pressed, the number in the display is added to the total (and similarly for the – button). The display is set equal to zero.

When the = button is pressed, the value of the total is displayed.

7.9 **The elevator** Write a program to simulate a very primitive elevator. The elevator is represented as a rectangle and there are two buttons – one to make it move up the screen and one to make it move down.

7.10 **Reaction timer** Write a program that acts as a reaction timer. It uses the library method `currentTimeMillis( )` which returns the current time in milliseconds as a `long`. A millisecond is one thousandth of a second. This method is invoked like this:

```
long timeNow = System.currentTimeMillis( );.
```

When the program starts up the `init` method should create and display a button labelled 'Now!' and record the time. When the user hits (clicks on) the button, the program gets the time and displays how long it took the user to respond. (Times of less than 0.1 of a second are suspect and may have resulted from cheating!)

For interest, the time is measured from 1 January 1970 (the so-called epoch). It is called UTC (Coordinated Universal Time) and is essentially the same as Greenwich Mean Time (GMT).

7.11 Turtle graphics Turtle graphics is a way of making programming easy for young children. Imagine a pen fixed to the belly of a turtle. As the turtle crawls around a floor, the pen draws on the floor. The turtle can be issued with commands as follows:

- pen up
- pen down
- turn left 90°
- turn right 90°
- go forward *n* pixels

Initially the turtle is at coordinates 0, 0 and facing to the right.

So, for example, we can draw a rectangle using the sequence:

```
pen down
go forward 20 pixels
turn right 90°
go forward 20 pixels
turn right 90°
go forward 20 pixels
turn right 90°
go forward 20 pixels
```

Write a program that behaves as the turtle, with one button for each of the commands. The number of pixels, *n*, to be moved is input via a scrollbar.

ANSWERS TO SELF-TEST QUESTIONS

7.1 No, because they treat the age of 18 differently. The two `if` statements also create different messages.

7.2
```
if ((total == 2) || (total == 5) || (total == 7))
    g.drawString("you have won", 50, 50);
```

7.3
```
if (age >= 16)
    if (age < 65)
        g.drawString("Yes", 10, 10);
```

7.4
```
if (age <= 18)
    g.drawString("too young", 100, 100);
```

7.5
```
salary = bar.getvalue();
int tax = 0;
if ((salary > 10000) && (salary <= 50000))
    tax = (salary - 10000)/5;
if (salary > 50000)
    tax = 8000 + ((salary - 50000) * 9 / 10);
```

7.6
```
int a = bar1.getvalue();
int b = bar2.getvalue();
int c = bar3.getvalue();
int t;

if (b > c)
    t = b;
else
    t = c;
if (a > t)
    t = a;

g.drawString("largest value is " + t, 20, 20);
```

7.7 The essential part of this program is:
```
if (volume < min)
    min = volume;
g.drawString("Minimum value is " + min, 50, 50);
```

7.8
```
private boolean isTriangle(float a, float b, float c) {
    if ((a + b) <= c)
        return false;
    if ((b + c) <= a)
        return false;
    if ((c + a) <= b)
        return false;
    return true;
}
```

7.9
```java
private String convert(int s) {
    String suit;

    switch(s) {
        case 1 : suit = "diamonds"; break;
        case 2 : suit = "hearts"; break;
        case 3 : suit = "clubs"; break;
        case 4 : suit = "spades"; break;
    }
    return suit;
}
```

7.10
```java
private String checkDay(int day) {
    String status;
    switch (day) {
        case 1 : case 2 : case 3 : case 4 : case 5 :
            status = "Weekday"; break;
        case 6 : case 7 :
            status = "Weekend"; break;

        default : status = "error"; break;
    }
    return status;
}
```

Repetition – `while`, `for` **and** `do`

Introduction

We humans are used to doing things again and again – eating, sleeping and working. Computers similarly routinely perform repetition. Examples are:

- searching files for some desired information;
- solving a mathematical equation iteratively, by repeatedly obtaining better and better approximations:
- making a graphical figure move on the screen (animation).

Part of the great power of computers arises from their ability to perform repetitions extremely quickly. In the language of programming, a repetition is called a *loop*.

There are three ways in which the Java programmer can instruct the computer to perform repetition:

- `while`
- `for`
- `do`

Any of these can be used to carry out repetition, but there are differences between them, as we shall see.

We have already seen that a computer obeys a *sequence* of instructions. Now we shall see how to repeat a sequence of instructions a number of times.

In this chapter we explain how to write programs that carry out repetition using `while`, `for` or `do` statements.

● while

We are going to illustrate loops by writing some programs to display patterns of asterisks on the screen.

We can output a line of eight asterisks like this:

```
g.drawString("********", 10, 10);
```

but another way is to view this as repeating the output of a single asterisk. In order to do this, we will need a counter. The counter, initially zero, is incremented by one each time a single asterisk is output. We need to repeat the output until the counter reaches the desired total:

```
int counter, x = 10;
counter = 0;
while (counter < 8) {
    g.drawString("*", x, 20);
    x = x + 10;
    counter++;
}
```

The output from this piece of program is shown in Figure 8.1. It uses a `while` loop. The word `while` signifies that a repetition is required. The sequence in the curly brackets is repeated. The expression in brackets following the word `while` is the condition for the loop to continue. It says: 'if the condition is true, the loop is executed'. Another way to interpret a `while` statement is to say that 'such and such is repeated while ever the condition is true'. You might also imagine `while` as meaning 'as long as'.

The sequence of statements to be repeated (the body of the loop) is enclosed in curly brackets and each statement is followed by a semicolon.

Notice that within the loop we have made use of the shortcut way of adding one to the value of a variable:

```
counter++;
```

It is very common to see this shortcut operator used inside a loop. The loop repeats with counter equal to 0,1,2, . . . until it finally has the value 8. The condition is no longer true, so the loop terminates. Eight asterisks have been output.

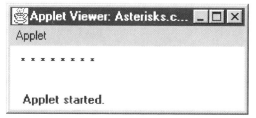

Figure 8.1 Screen showing the display of asterisks using `while`.

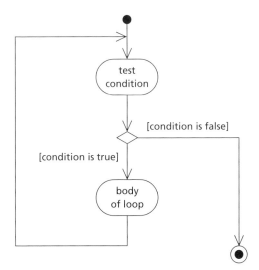

Figure 8.2 Activity diagram for a `while` loop.

Each time the loop is repeated the *x*-coordinate of the asterisk is increased by 10 pixels to provide sufficient space for each asterisk.

One way to visualize a `while` loop is using an activity diagram, as shown in Figure 8.2. The computer normally obeys instructions in sequence from top to bottom as shown by the arrows. A `while` loop means that the condition is tested before the loop is executed and again before any repetition of the loop. When, finally, the condition is false, the body of the loop ceases to be executed and the repetition ends.

The above program fragment used the less than (<) operator. This is one of a number of available comparison operators, which are the same as those used in `if` statements. Here, again, is the complete list of the comparison operators:

>   means greater than
<   means less than
==   means equals
!=   means not equal to
<=   means less than or equal to
>=   means greater than or equal to

The odd one out in this list is the test for equality, which is two equals signs, rather than one. It is a common mistake to use just one equals sign in a test. This will result in a compilation error.

SELF-TEST QUESTION

8.1 What would this program fragment do?

```
int counter, x = 100;
counter = 0;
while (counter <= 8) {
    g.drawString ("*", x, 100);
    x = x + 10;
    counter++;
}
```

Parallel lines

As another illustration of the use of the `while` statement, we will use it to output some horizontal parallel lines, as in Figure 8.3.

We will use the library method `drawLine` to output a single line. We will use a `while` statement to say that we want to draw several lines:

```
import java.awt.*;
import java.applet.Applet;

public class Lines extends Applet {

    public void paint(Graphics g) {
        int n = 0;
        int x = 20;
        int y = 20;
        while (n < 5) {
            g.drawLine(x, y, x + 100, y);
            y = y + 10;
            n++;
        }
    }
}
```

You will see that the structure of the loop is similar to that used above to draw asterisks. A count is initially zero. Each time the loop is repeated, the count is incremented by one. The `while` loop checks the value of the count and allows the loop to repeat while the value is less than 5. This means that when the value becomes equal to 5, the repetition ceases. So the loop is repeated five times – we get five parallel lines.

Figure 8.3 Screen layout for the parallel lines program.

SELF-TEST QUESTIONS

8.2 Write a program to draw five vertical parallel lines.

8.3 Chessboard Write a program to draw a chessboard with 9 vertical lines, 10 pixels apart, and 9 horizontal lines, 10 pixels apart.

8.4 Write a program that uses a scrollbar to input the number of horizontal lines that are required to be drawn and then draws them.

8.5 Pile of sticks Write a program to draw 10 lines with random start coordinates (*x* and *y* between 10 and 100 pixels) and with similar random end coordinates. Chapter 7 describes how to use the library random number method `Math.random`, which produces a random `double` in the range 0.0 to 0.999. . . .

Steps

This program draws a number of steps leading downwards, as shown in Figure 8.4. The number of steps is determined by the setting of a scrollbar.

```java
import java.awt.*;
import java.applet.Applet;
import java.awt.event.*;

public class Steps extends Applet implements AdjustmentListener {

    private Scrollbar steps;
    private int count, numberOfSteps;

    public void init() {
        steps = new Scrollbar(Scrollbar.HORIZONTAL, 0, 1, 0, 100);
        add(steps);
        steps.addAdjustmentListener(this);
    }
```

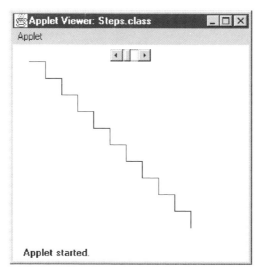

Figure 8.4 Screen layout for the steps program.

```
public void paint(Graphics g) {
    int count = 0;

    int x = 20;
    int y = 20;
    while (count < numberOfSteps) {
        g.drawLine(x, y, x + 20, y);
        g.drawLine(x + 20, y, x + 20, y + 20);

        x = x + 20;
        y = y + 20;
        count++;
    }
}

public void adjustmentValueChanged(AdjustmentEvent e) {
    numberOfSteps = steps.getValue();
    repaint();
}
}
```

Notice that, even if the number of steps is zero, the program works correctly (no steps are drawn). This is an important feature of while loops and ensures that they can be used very generally.

● for

In the for loop, many of the ingredients of the while loop are bundled up together in the statement itself. Here again is the program to display a row of asterisks on the screen. The number of asterisks is input from a scrollbar:

```
import java.awt.*;
import java.applet.Applet;
import java.awt.event.*;


public class Asterisks extends Applet implements AdjustmentListener {

    private Scrollbar bar;
    private int count, numberRequired = 8;

    public void init() {
        bar = new Scrollbar(Scrollbar.HORIZONTAL, 0, 1, 0, 100);
        add(bar);
        bar.addAdjustmentListener(this);
    }

    public void adjustmentValueChanged(AdjustmentEvent event) {
        numberRequired = bar.getValue();
        repaint();
    }

    public void paint(Graphics g) {
        int count;
        int x = 10;
        for (count = 0; count < numberRequired; count++) {
            g.drawString("*", x, 30);
            x = x + 10;
        }
    }
}
```

Within the brackets of the for statement there are three ingredients, separated by semi-colons:

● an initial statement – what is to be done once before the loop is started
  (count = 0);
● a condition – what is tested prior to any execution of the loop
  (count < numberRequired);
● a statement that is carried out just before the end of each repetition (count++).

The condition determines whether the loop is executed or completed:

● If the condition is true, the loop continues.
● If the condition is false, the loop ends.

This rule is the same as in the `while` statement. Similarly, the test is carried out before the loop.

The above loop works like this. Initially the count is equal to zero. This is less than 8, so the loop is carried out and an asterisk is output. Then the count is incremented to 1. This is still less than 8, so the loop is carried out again. This continues until the final asterisk is output, the count becomes 8 (which is not less than 8) and the loop is over.

If two or more statements are to be repeated, then curly brackets are needed around them. If only one statement is to be repeated, the curly brackets are not needed (but you can write them if you like).

Because using a counter in a `for` statement is so common, Java allows us to declare the counter as part of the `for` statement, so that the above loop can be written like this:

```
int x = 100;
for (int count = 0; count < numberRequired; count++) {
    g.drawString("*", x, 30);
    x = x + 10;
}
```

This example of a `for` loop is typical; `for` loops are normally used when the number of repetitions is known in advance. For example, in the above case, we know how many asterisks are to be displayed.

One way to visualize how a `for` statement works is to study an activity diagram, as shown in Figure 8.5. Notice that, as in the `while` statement, the test on the condition is made at the start of the loop.

SELF-TEST QUESTIONS
....

8.6 Write a program that uses a `for` statement to display eight rectangles across the screen. Use the library method `drawRect` to draw an individual rectangle. When invoked like this:

```
g.drawRect (x, y, width, height);
```

all the parameters are integers, representing a pixel number. `x`, `y` are the coordinates of the top left of the rectangle.

8.7 Rewrite the above `for` loop to display five rectangles down the screen.

You always have to exercise great care when you write loops to make sure that the counting is done properly. A common error is to make the loop repeat one too many

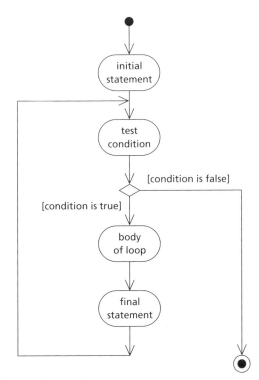

Figure 8.5 Activity diagram for a `for` loop.

times or one too few times. Sometimes a loop is written so as to start with a count of 0 and the test is to see whether it is less than the number required:

```
for (int count = 0; count < numberRequired; count++) {
    // loop
}
```

Alternatively it is written to start with a count of 1 and the test is to see whether it is less than or equal to the number required:

```
for (int count = 1; count <= numberRequired; count++) {
    // loop
}
```

Both of these styles are used in this book.

● `do...while`

If you use `while` or `for`, the test is done at the beginning of the loop. In the `do` loop, the decision is made at the end of the loop. This means that the loop is guaranteed to be done once at least. This is suitable for some programming situations, but not others.

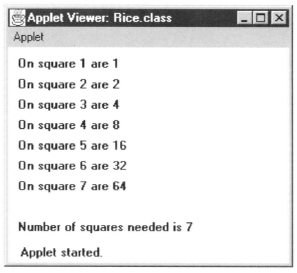

Figure 8.6 Screen layout for the grains of rice program.

Grains of rice

We have seen how to use loops to repeat something a fixed number of times. We knew in advance how many lines were needed. In some situations, we don't know how many repetitions will be needed. Do you remember an old folk tale about someone who is asked what they wanted as a reward for some daring deed? The response was that he would like as many grains of rice as you would get if you put one on the first square of a chess board, two on the second, four on the third, and so on, doubling the amount on the previous square. Let us write a program to find out how many squares would be needed to get 100 grains of rice. The screen looks like Figure 8.6.

We need a loop, and we don't know in advance how many repetitions will be needed – this is what we want to find out. But we do know that we will need at least one loop. Therefore the program uses a do statement, with the test at the end of the loop. Initially the number of grains is 1 and the number of squares is 1. Each time we move to a new square, we add one to the number of squares and double the number of grains on the new square. The Java code is:

```
import java.awt.*;
import java.applet.Applet;

public class Rice extends Applet {

    public void paint(Graphics g) {
        int countOfSquares = 0;
        int riceOnThisSquare = 1;
```

```
int totalRice = 0;
int y = 20;
do {
    countOfSquares++;
    g.drawString("On square "+countOfSquares +
        " are " + riceOnThisSquare, 10, y);
    totalRice = totalRice + riceOnThisSquare;
    riceOnThisSquare = riceOnThisSquare * 2;
    y = y +20;
} while (totalRice < 100);

g.drawString("Number of squares needed is " +
            countOfSquares, 10, y + 20);
    }

}
```

SELF-TEST QUESTION

8.8 Alter this program so that the rule for the number of grains of rice on any square is that it is the number of the square times itself, so that, for example, the number of grains on square 5 is $5 \times 5 = 25$. Make the program display the number on each square and the running total.

As with `while` and `for` loops, the condition at the end of the `do` loop determines whether or not the loop is repeated. So the sequence is:

1. The loop is done once.
2. If the condition is true, the loop is repeated.
3. If the condition is false, the loop is not repeated.

Because the test is at the end of the loop, the repetition is always performed once, at least. In contrast, loops constructed using `while` or `for` may not be executed at all, depending on circumstances. Put another way, a `while` or a `for` loop may repeat zero times, but a `do` loop is always carried out at least once. Thus the `while` and `for` loops are actually more powerful and general-purpose than a `do` loop. `while` and `for` are interchangeable. Anything you can accomplish with a `do`, you can accomplish with a `for` or a `while`, but not vice versa. `do` loops tend to be used only occasionally in programming, when the occasion is suitable.

We can visualize a `do...while` statement using an activity diagram, as in Figure 8.7. You will notice that the test on the condition is carried out after the loop is executed. This is the opposite of what happens with `while` and `for` loops.

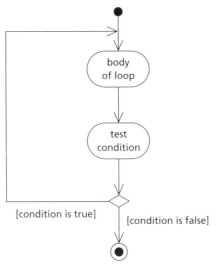

Figure 8.7 Activity diagram for a `do...while` loop.

● And, or, not

On occasions, the condition that controls a loop is more complex and we need the **and**, **or** and **not** operators. You'd use these in everyday life if you wanted to say 'I'm going for a walk until it starts raining or it is 5 o'clock.' The list of these logical operators is:

`&&`	means and
`||`	means or
`!`	means not

(We've already met these in Chapter 7 on decisions using the `if` statement.)

If we wanted to describe how long we are going walking for using a `while` statement, we would say 'While it is not raining and it is not 5 o'clock, I am going walking.' Notice that each of the two conditions (raining, 5 o'clock) is preceded by a 'not' and that the two conditions are linked by an 'and'. This is what tends to happen when you write a loop with a `while` statement – and you have to be very careful to write the condition very clearly.

We will revisit the grains of rice program. Suppose we want to tot up the number of grains as before. But this time we want to stop either when we have got to 64 squares (the number on a chessboard) or when the total is 10 000 grains. So we want the loop to continue while the total is less than 10 000 and the number of squares is less than or equal to 64. The program is:

```
import java.awt.*;
import java.applet.Applet;


public class Rice extends Applet {

    public void paint(Graphics g) {
        int countOfSquares = 1;
        int riceOnThisSquare = 1;
        int totalRice = 1;
        while (totalRice < 10000 && countOfSquares <= 64) {
            countOfSquares++;
            riceOnThisSquare = riceOnThisSquare * 2;
            totalRice = totalRice + riceOnThisSquare;
        }
        g.drawString("the number of squares is "
                            + countOfSquares, 100, 100);
        g.drawString("the number of grains is "
                            + totalRice, 100, 120);
    }
}
```

You will see that, after the repetition, the program displays both the number of repetitions and the total accumulated rice grains. So we can see which happened first – a total of 10 000 or 64 squares.

SELF-TEST QUESTION
....

8.9 Rewrite the loop using `for` instead of `while`.

● Nested loops

A nested loop is a loop within a loop. Suppose, for example, we want to display the output shown in Figure 8.8, which is a crudely drawn block of apartments. There are four floors, with five apartments on each floor. Each line is repeated. But also, within each line, the letter 'A' is repeated. The loop that draws an individual floor is:

```
x = 0;
for (int apartment = 0; apartment < 5; apartment++) {
    g.drawString("A", x, y);
    x = x + 20;
}
```

Figure 8.8 Display of apartment block.

and the loop that draws a number of floors is:

```
y = 0;
for (int floor = 0; floor < 4; floor++) {
    y = y + 20;
}
```

What we need is the combination of these two loops, with a number of apartments for each of the number of floors. So the loops are nested:

```
y = 20;
for (int floor = 0; floor < 4; floor++) {
    x = 0;
    for (int apartment = 0; apartment < 5; apartment++) {
        g.drawString("A", x, y);
        x = x + 20;
    }
    y = y + 20;
}
```

and you will see that both the indentation and the brackets help considerably in understanding the program.

SELF-TEST QUESTION

8.10 Write a program that displays an apartment block as a collection of rectangles, three floors high, with five apartments on each floor.

● Combining control structures

In the last chapter we looked at selection using the `if` statement and in this chapter we have looked at repetition using `while`, `for` and `do`. Most programs consist of combinations of these control structures. In fact most programs consist of:

- sequences;
- loops;
- selections;
- invocations of library methods;
- invocations of methods that we, the programmer, write.

We will now look at an example where both repetition and selection are used.

The bouncing ball

In this program a ball bounces around the screen, as shown in Figure 8.9. This is called animation. Its position at any time is specified by its *x*- and *y*-coordinates. Initially it starts at the top left-hand corner of the window. It moves in increments of 7 pixels in the *x* direction, and 2 in the *y* direction, and leaves a series of images as it moves. The library method `fillOval` is used to draw the ball, with diameter 10 pixels. When the ball hits any of the four walls, its direction is reversed. The ball appears to bounce randomly round the rectangle, because of the values chosen for the increments, but eventually the ball retraces the same path.

First a rectangle is drawn using the library method `drawRect`. A `for` loop causes the ball to move through 1000 repetitions. `if` statements check whether the boundary has been encountered. Movement is achieved by first deleting the ball and then immediately drawing it again a short distance from where it was. Provided the computer is fast

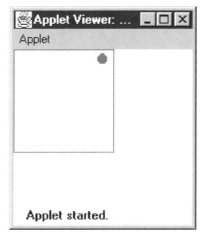

Figure 8.9 The bouncing ball.

enough, the human eye will see a continuous movement. To delete the ball, a small trick is used. The same ball is drawn, but in the colour of the background. Whatever this colour is, it can be obtained by invoking the library method getBackground.

```
import java.awt.*;
import java.applet.Applet;

public class Ball extends Applet {

    private int x = 7, xChange = 7;
    private int y = 2, yChange = 2;
    private int diameter = 10;

    private int rectLeftX = 0, rectRightX = 100;
    private int rectTopY = 0, rectBottomY = 100;

    public void paint(Graphics g) {
        g.drawRect(rectLeftX, rectTopY,
                      rectRightX - rectLeftX, rectBottomY - rectTopY);

        for (int n = 1; n < 1000; n++) {
            Color backgroundColour = getBackground();
            g.setColor(backgroundColour);
            g.fillOval(x, y, diameter, diameter);

            if (x <= rectLeftX)
                xChange = -xChange;
            if (x >= rectRightX)
                xChange = -xChange;

            if (y <= rectTopY)
                yChange = -yChange;
            if (y >= rectBottomY)
                yChange = -yChange;

            x = x + xChange;
            y = y + yChange;

            g.setColor(Color.red);
            g.fillOval(x, y, diameter, diameter);
        }
    }
}
```

This is a typical example of a program in which loops and selection are used together.

Programming pitfalls

● Be very careful with the conditions in looping statements. It is a very common error to make a loop finish early or else to repeat too many times.

Grammar spot

● There are three varieties of looping statement – `while`, `for` and `do`.
● The `while` loop has the structure:

```
while (condition) {
    statement1;
    statement2;
}
```

where:

– the test is carried out before any repetition of the loop. If it is true the loop continues. If it is false, the loop ends.

● The `while` loop is generally used when the number of repetitions is not known in advance.
● The `for` loop has this structure:

```
for (initial statement; condition; repeated statement) {
    statement1;
    statement2;
}
```

where:

– `initial statement` is done once, before the loop is executed.
– The test is carried out before any repetition of the loop. If it is true the loop continues. If it is false, the loop ends.
– `repeated statement` is carried out each time the loop is repeated – as the last statement in the loop.

● The `for` loop is generally used when the number of repetitions is known in advance.
● The `do` loop has the structure:

```
do {
    statement1;
    statement2;
} while (condition);
```

where:

– The test is carried out *after* a repetition of the loop. If it is true the loop continues. If it is false, the loop ends.

- The do loop is used when at least one repetition of the loop is needed.
- In while, for and do loops:
  - If only one statement is to be repeated, it does not need to be enclosed in curly brackets. When two or more statements are to be repeated, they must be enclosed in curly brackets. Each statement is followed by a semicolon.
  - The condition is always enclosed in round brackets.

New language elements

- Control structures for repetition:

  ```
  while
  for
  do
  ```

Summary

- A repetition in programming is called a loop.

- There are three ways of instructing the computer to loop – while, for and do.

- Use while when you do not know in advance how many repetitions will have to be performed.

- Use for when you do know in advance how many repetitions will have to be performed.

- do is used occasionally, when a loop is to be performed at least once.

EXERCISES

8.1 **Display integers** Write a program to display the numbers 1 to 10 using a loop.

8.2 **Random numbers** Write a program to display 10 random numbers using a loop. Use the library method Math.random to obtain random numbers in the range 0.0 to 0.999. . . .

8.3 **The milky way** Write a program that draws 100 circles at random positions in the window and with random diameters up to 100 pixels. Use the library method drawOval to draw an individual circle. It is invoked like this:

```
g.drawOval(x, y, width, height);
```

All the parameters are integers, representing a pixel number. x, y are the coordinates of the top left of an imaginary rectangle that would just enclose the oval.

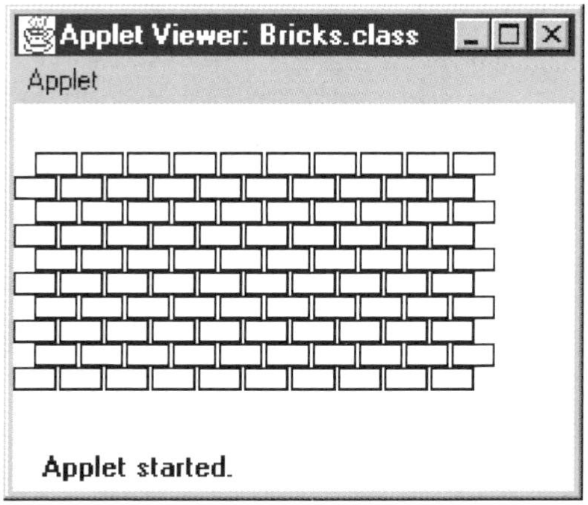

Figure 8.10 The wall.

8.4 **Wall** Write a program to draw a wall of bricks, as shown in Figure 8.10. Use the library method `drawRect` to draw each brick. This is invoked like this:

```
g.drawRect(x, y, width, height);
```

All the parameters are integers, representing a pixel number. `x`, `y` are the coordinates of the top left of the rectangle. Hint: use nested loops.

8.5 **Digital clock** Write a program to display a digital clock continuously on the screen as the time changes. It uses the library method `currentTimeMillis()`, which returns the current time in milliseconds as a `long`. A millisecond is one thousandth of a second. Set up a loop that repeats until 20 seconds have gone by. (You will probably be bored with it by then.)

8.6 **Sum of the integers** Write a program that adds up the numbers 0 to 39 using a loop. Check that it has obtained the right answer by using the formula for the sum of the numbers 0 to n:

$$sum = n \times (n + 1)/2$$

8.7 **Saw-tooth pattern** Write a program to display the following (saw-tooth) pattern on the screen:

```
s
ss
sss
ssss
sssss
s
ss
sss
ssss
sssss
```

8.8 **Multiplication table** Write a program to display a multiplication table, such as young children use. For example, the table for numbers up to 6 is:

```
   1  2   3    4    5    6

1  1  2   3    4    5    6
2  2  4   6    8   10   12
3  3  6   9   12   15   18
4  4  8  12   16   20   24
5  5 10  15   20   25   30
6  6 12  18   24   30   36
```

The program should be capable of displaying a table of any size, specified by an integer like this:

```
private int size=6;
```

8.9 **Fibonacci** The Fibonacci series is the series of numbers:

```
1  1  2  3  5  8  13...
```

Each number (except for the first two), is the sum of the previous two numbers. The first two numbers are 1 and 1. The series is supposed to govern growth in plants. Write a program to display the first 20 Fibonacci numbers.

8.10 **Sum of series** Write a program to calculate and display the sum of the series:

$$1 - 1/2 + 1/3 - 1/4 + \ldots$$

until a term is reached that is less than 0.0001.

8.11 **Nim** is a game played with matchsticks (unused or used, it does not matter). It doesn't matter how many matches there are. The matches are put into three piles. Again, it doesn't matter how many matches there are in each pile. Each player goes in turn. A player can remove any number of matches from any one pile, but only one pile. A player must remove at least one match. The winner is the person who causes the other player to take the last match.

   Write a program to play the game. Initially the computer deals three piles, with a random number (in the range 1 to 200) of matches in each pile. One player is the computer, which chooses a pile and an amount randomly. The other player is the human user, who specifies the pile number and quantity using scrollbars, before clicking on a 'go' button.

8.12 **Bouncing ball** Enhance the bouncing ball program so that it has a button that you click on to start the ball bouncing. Make the ball bounce slightly randomly when it hits a wall as follows. Instead of simply reversing the change in *x* or *y*, reverse it by a random factor in the range 0.5 to 1.0.

ANSWERS TO SELF-TEST QUESTIONS

8.1 Draws nine asterisks across the screen.

8.2
```
import java.awt.*;
import java.applet.Applet;

public class VerticalLines extends Applet {

    public void paint(Graphics g) {
        int n = 0;
        int x = 20;
        int y = 20;
        while (n < 5) {
            g.drawLine(x, y, x, y + 100);
            x = x + 10;
            n++;
        }
    }
}
```

8.3
```
import java.awt.*;
import java.applet.Applet;

public class ChessBoard extends Applet {
    public void paint(Graphics g) {
        int x = 20;
        int y = 20;
        int horiz = 1;
        while (horiz <= 9) {
            g.drawLine(x, y, x + 80, y);
            y = y + 10;
            horiz++;
        }

        int x = 20;
        int y = 20;
        int vert = 1;
        while (vert <= 9) {
            g.drawLine (x, y, x, y + 80);
            x = x + 10;
            vert++;
        }
    }
}
```

8.4
```
import java.awt.*;
import java.applet.Applet;
import java.awt.event.*;

public class VariableLines extends Applet implements
                                AdjustmentListener {

    private Scrollbar lines;
    private int numberOfLines;

    public void init() {
        lines = new Scrollbar(Scrollbar.HORIZONTAL, 0, 1, 0,
                            100);
        add(lines);
        lines.addAdjustmentListener(this);
    }

    public void adjustmentValueChanged(AdjustmentEvent event) {
        numberOfLines = lines.getValue();
        repaint();
    }

        public void paint(Graphics g) {
            int count = 1;
            int x = 20;
            int y = 20;
            while (count < numberOfLines) {
                g.drawLine(x, y, x + 100, y);
                y = y + 10;
                count++;
            }
        }
    }
```

8.5
```
import java.awt.*;
import java.applet.Applet;

public class RandomLines extends Applet {

    public void paint(Graphics g) {
        int n = 1;
        int x, xEnd;
        int y, yEnd;
        while (n <= 10) {
```

```
                    x = (int)(Math.random() * 100) + 10;
                    y = (int)(Math.random() * 100) + 10;
                    xEnd = (int)(Math.random() * 100) + 10;
                    yEnd = (int)(Math.random() * 100) + 10;

                    g.drawLine (x, y, xEnd, yEnd);
                    n++;
                }
            }
        }
```

8.6
```
    import java.awt.*;
    import java.applet.Applet;

    public class Boxes extends Applet {

        public void paint(Graphics g) {
            int x = 20;
            int y = 20;
            int width = 10;
            int height = 10;
            for (int count = 1; count <= 8; count++) {
                g.drawRect(x, y, width, height);
                x = x + 15;
            }
        }
    }
```

8.7
```
    import java.awt.*;
    import java.applet.Applet;

    public class Boxes extends Applet {

        public void paint(Graphics g) {
            int x = 20;
            int y = 20;
            int width = 10;
            int height = 10;
            for (int count = 1; count <= 5; count++) {
                g.drawRect(x, y, width, height);
                y = y + 15;
            }
        }
    }
```

8.8 The following line in the program:

```
riceOnThisSquare = riceOnThisSquare * 2;
```

becomes:

```
riceOnThisSquare = countOfSquares * countOfSquares ;
```

8.9
```
for (int countOfSquares = 1;
     totalRice < 10000 && countOfSquares <= 64;
     countOfSquares++) etc
```

8.10
```
import java.awt.*;
import java.applet.Applet;


public class Apartments extends Applet {

    public void paint(Graphics g) {
        int flats = 5;
        int floors = 3;
        int yCoord = 10;
        for (int floor = 0; floor < floors; floor++) {
            xCoord = 10;
            for (int flat = 0; flat < flats; flat++) {
                g.drawRect(xCoord, yCoord, 20, 20);
                Coord = xCoord + 20;
            }
            yCoord = yCoord + 20;
        }
    }
}
```

Objects and classes

Introduction

So far we have looked at the basics of programming. We have also looked at a number of small programs that work very well. It is now time to look at some of the essential features of object-oriented programming (OOP) – objects and classes. In later chapters we will look at other aspects of OOP.

Objects

Object-oriented programming is about constructing programs from objects. An *object* is a combination of some data (variables) and some actions (methods). Ideally an object is designed so that the data and the actions are closely related, rather than being randomly collected together.

As our first illustration we will use as an example a program to display and manipulate a balloon. This uses the ideas of the Little and Large program used in Chapter 6. We are going to use the Java instructions from that chapter and repackage them in a different way. The program simply displays a balloon as a circle on the screen, as shown in Figure 9.1. Buttons are provided to change its size. A balloon has data associated with it – for example, its size (diameter) and its position. We can represent these in Java like this:

```
int diameter;
int xCoord, yCoord;
```

The *x*- and *y*-coordinates are the coordinates of the top left of a box that perfectly encloses the balloon.

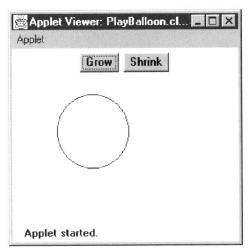

Figure 9.1 Screen layout for the Balloon program.

A balloon also has actions associated with it – e.g. to change its size. We can write these actions as Java methods. Changing the size is accomplished by:

```
public void changeSize(int change) {
    diameter = diameter + change;
}
```

This combination of data and actions (methods) can be packaged up into a unified bundle called an *object*. The object contains everything that is known about an object – all the data and all the actions. In a short time we will explain why the word `public` is used in the heading of this method, rather than our familiar `private` of Chapter 5.

SELF-TEST QUESTIONS

9.1 Write a method that moves a balloon upwards only. Name the method `moveUp`.

9.2 Extend the balloon object so that it has a variable that describes the colour of the balloon. Write a method to change the colour.

9.3 It is planned to write a program that manipulates a building brick. It is in reality just a rectangle. Devise some data and actions that represent a brick and its behaviour.

● Classes

In Java, as in all OOP languages, it is not possible to directly write instructions that define a balloon as a single object. Instead the language makes the programmer define what all balloon objects look like. This is so that if we later find we need a number of balloons, we have already got the template or the master plan to make any number of them. The declaration of the structure of all balloons is called a *class*. A class is a generalization of an object.

The idea of classes is a common idea in most design activity. It is usual before actually constructing anything to create a design for the object. This is true in automobile design, architecture, construction – even in fine art. Some kind of a plan is drafted, often on paper, sometimes on a computer. Sometimes it is called a blueprint. Such a design specifies the desired object completely, so that if the designer gets run over by a bus, someone else can carry out the construction of the object. Once designed, any number of identical objects can be constructed – think of cars, books or computers. So the design specifies the composition of one or any number of objects. The same is true in OOP – a class is the plan for any number of identical objects. Once we have specified a class, we can construct any number of objects with the same behaviour.

Looking at the balloon again, what we need to do is to write down the declaration of what each and every balloon object will look like.

So in OOP, a class is the specification for any number of objects that are the same. Once a class has been described, a particular object is constructed by creating an *instance* of the class. It's a bit like saying we have had an instance of influenza in the house. Or, this Model T Ford is an instance of the Model T Ford design. Your own bank account is an instance of the bank account class.

We will now start to describe a balloon in Java. Remember that we must first describe the general class of balloons before we create a particular instance. The first part of a class description is a header in which the programmer gives the class a name:

```
class Balloon {
    // the variables and methods appear here
}
```

The class heading is followed by declarations of the variables and methods, all enclosed in curly brackets. We will now look at each of the ingredients of a class, one by one.

● Initialization and constructors

When a balloon is first created, the position and size of the balloon need to be given some values. This is called initializing the variables. One good way to do this is to initialize the variables in their declaration, as usual, like this:

```
private int diameter = 10;
private int xCoord = 20;
private int yCoord = 20;
```

This ensures that every new object of this class will have the variables initialized to these values.

An alternative way to initialize an object is to write a special method to do the initialization. This method is named a *constructor* method or simply a constructor (because it is involved in the construction of the object). Such a method has the same name as the class itself. (We will see the very good reason for this later.) It has no return value, but it can have parameters. Also, it does not need to be declared as `public`, even though it is used from outside the class. Here is such a method for the `Balloon` class:

```
public Balloon(int initialDiameter, int initialX, int initialY) {
    diameter = initialDiameter;
    xCoord = initialX;
    yCoord = initialY;
}
```

This method places the values of the parameters (the size and position) in the appropriate variables within the object. We will shortly see this method in use when an object is created. If a variable is not explicitly initialized by the programmer, the Java system gives every variable a default value. This is zero for any numbers, `false` for a boolean, `\u0000` for `char` (see Chapter 15 on strings) and the value `null` (see below) for any object. It is regarded as very bad practice to rely on this method of initialization of variables. Instead, it is better to do it explicitly.

Note that local variables (those declared within a method) are not given an initial default value and so there is even more reason to initialize them explicitly.

SELF-TEST QUESTION
....

9.4 Write a constructor method to initialize a brick object.

● Public or private?

Let us now collect together all the parts of the class. As we do so, we will give attention to the privacy of the items in the class. Some things we want to make publicly available to other pieces of program. This includes the methods, which, after all, we have designed to be provided for the use of others. This includes any constructor methods. To signify that they are publicly available, we must precede their header with the Java word `public`. By contrast, we do not want anybody to be able to access the variables in the class, so we precede their declarations with the word `private`. We can now write the complete description of the class:

```
class Balloon {
    private int diameter;
    private int xCoord, yCoord;
```

```
    public Balloon(int initialDiameter, int initialX, int initialY) {
        diameter = initialDiameter;
        xCoord = initialX;
        yCoord = initialY;
    }

    public void changeSize(int change) {
        diameter = diameter + change;
    }

}
```

Note the curly brackets. One pair encloses the entire class. But pairs of curly brackets also enclose the body of each method, as usual. The variables xCoord, yCoord and diameter are declared outside of the methods and therefore can be accessed by any of the methods in the class. They are called instance variables. These variables are usually written at the start of the class, as shown – though they can be written anywhere outside a method. Note also that the layout of the class is enhanced using blank lines.

Later we will provide an additional method for balloons to display themselves when requested to do so.

We have now distinguished clearly between those items that we are making publicly available and those that are private. This is very much part of the philosophy of OOP. Data (variables) and actions (methods) are bundled up together, but in such a way as to hide some of the information from the outside world. This is termed *encapsulation* or *information hiding.*

SELF-TEST QUESTIONS
....

9.5 Look at the methods and variables that you have designed to add colour to the class Balloon and decide whether they should be public or private. Enhance their declarations appropriately.

9.6 Write a class to describe a building brick.

A class or object has the general structure shown in Figure 9.2. This is the view as seen by the programmer who writes it; it consists of variables and methods.

The view of an object as seen by its users is shown in Figure 9.3. The view to its users, to whom it is providing a service, is very different. Only the public items (usually methods) are visible – all the others are hidden within an impenetrable box. We are used to this idea in everyday life. Examples are a vending machine, a TV, an ATM.

Local variables, those declared within a method, are implicitly private to the method and therefore do not need to be labelled as such.

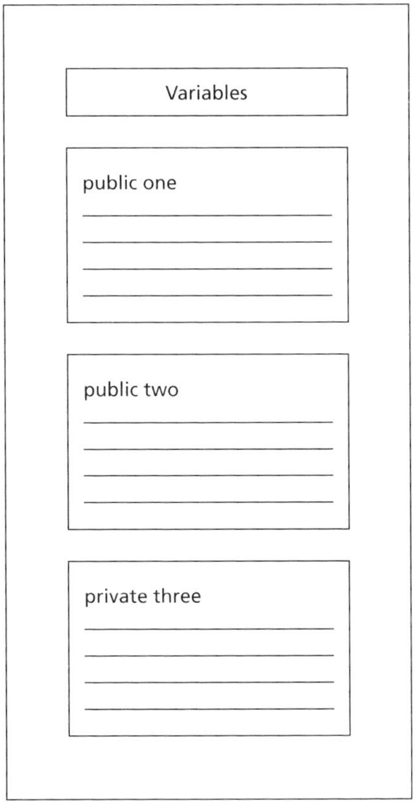

Figure 9.2 Structure of an object or class as seen by the programmer who writes it.

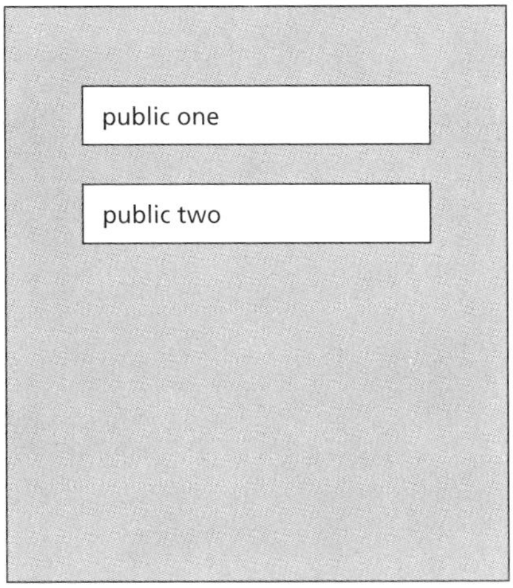

Figure 9.3 Structure of an object or class as seen by its users.

● **Creating an object using** new

It is time now to create some objects, because so far we have only described a class. Declaring a new class is very much like defining a new type to add to those that are already built in to Java (int, float, char, etc.). So the declaration of an object looks like any other variable declaration. Thus:

```
Balloon myBalloon;
```

declares an object of type Balloon with the name myBalloon. But we have not finished yet. Unlike integers and other built-in variable types, we have to explicitly create a new object. To create an object we use the small but powerful Java word new:

```
myBalloon = new Balloon(20, 50, 50);
```

This brief statement creates an object called myBalloon that consists of all the variables and all the methods described in the class Balloon. It also places the values of the size and position in the relevant places within the newly created object – it initializes the object using the constructor method Balloon. You can see that all the work of devising and creating an object is spent in describing the class. Once the class has been written, creating an object is easy. You can see that new is very powerful. It creates a whole new object from the class, with all of the variables and methods of the class.

We can now see why the class name is the same as the name of the method that is used to initialize it – creation and initialization are carried out at the same time. When you ask new to create a new object, it both creates the object and invokes its initialization method.

An object is sometimes referred to as an *instance* of a class and creating an object as instantiating a class. An instance is an occurrence or an example of something. It is like saying that my car is an instance of a Ford Mustang or that there has been an instance of influenza at the university.

Because we have a class that describes balloons in general, we can easily declare a second object of type Balloon like this:

```
Balloon anotherBalloon;
```

and create an object at a different place, with different coordinates:

```
anotherBalloon = new Balloon(20, 100, 100);
```

We now have a second object – again with all the variables and all the methods that were declared in the class description.

SELF-TEST QUESTIONS
....

9.7 Remind yourself of the difference between a class and an object.

9.8 Write a statement to create a balloon called happyBirthday, with parameters of your choice.

9.9 Write instructions to create a brick object.

We have seen how to declare and then separately to create an object of the class `Balloon`. It is often appropriate to do things in this way. Sometimes, however, we can conveniently do both things at once:

```
Balloon myBalloon = new Balloon(20, 50, 50);
```

It is very common to see a statement like this in Java programs. At first sight it may look a little strange to see the word `Balloon` (in this example) twice within the same statement. Java programmers quickly get used to it. Remember that `Balloon` on the left means that we want to declare our intention to use an object of the type `Balloon`. On the right-hand side we use `new` to create an instance (an object) of the class `Balloon`.

Now we look at an example of how to use one of the classes in the library. The example we choose is a text field, as used in several programs earlier in this book. A text field is a GUI component that appears as a box on the screen. It enables a line of text to be entered and processed by a program. To create an object from the library class `TextField`, we use `new` as usual:

```
TextField data = new TextField();
```

which creates a new object called `data` as an instance of the class `TextField`.

● Displaying an object

So far we have declared a class for `Balloon` objects that represents the data and actions associated with it. But there is as yet no way for a balloon to be displayed on the screen. (This was one of the requirements for the program.) We need a method that displays a balloon. The universal guideline in OOP is that an object is responsible for displaying itself. The rightful place, therefore, for the method that is to display a balloon is within the `Balloon` class. Here is the code:

```
public void display(Graphics g) {
    g.drawOval(xCoord, yCoord, diameter, diameter);
}
```

This simply makes use of the library method `drawOval` that we used earlier in the book. This method needs to go in along with all the other constituent methods for the class `Balloon`.

Remember that this method will be invoked from some piece of program that we have still to write. As usual, the method `display` needs to know the graphics context, which is passed to it as the parameter called `g`.

● Using objects

We will now use the balloon object we have created. We need a piece of program to invoke the methods that we have written. Before we do that, let us look again at a very simple program, the Hello program:

```
import java.awt.*;
import java.applet.Applet;

public class Greeting extends Applet {
    public void paint(Graphics g) {
        g.drawString("Hello", 35, 10);
    }
}
```

As you can see this is a class called Greeting. When the browser or applet viewer runs this program it implicitly carries out a

```
new Greeting();
```

statement to create an object from this class. You will not see this instruction in any program. But the browser (or applet viewer) is a program itself and acts as if it executes this instruction. Thus the browser or applet viewer acts as a god, creating the first object in the world. This object can then go on to create other objects. (This particular object is so small that it doesn't create any other objects, but we will soon see others that do.)

The object created by the browser (or the applet viewer) provides the user interface to the other objects in the program. It provides the method paint, which the browser invokes as necessary to redraw the graphics and text in the window. It also provides the method init, which sets up the buttons we need for the program. init is invoked by the browser (or applet viewer) as its first act after creating the object. Finally, the user interface object handles the events that arise when the buttons are pressed. In our new program, init must also create the myBalloon object using new:

```
private Button grow, shrink;
private Balloon myBalloon;

public void init() {
    grow = new Button("Grow");
    add(grow);
    grow.addActionListener(this):

    shrink = new Button("Shrink");
    add(shrink);
    shrink.addActionListener(this);

    myBalloon = new Balloon(20, 50, 50);
}
```

The method actionPerformed handles the events that happen when either of the two buttons are pressed (clicked on by the mouse). It is invoked by the browser or applet viewer, which is continually watching for events like this.

```
public void actionPerformed(ActionEvent event) {
    if (event.getSource() == grow)
        myBalloon.changeSize(10);
    if (event.getSource() == shrink)
        myBalloon.changeSize(-10);
    repaint();
}
```

Finally, we need to ensure that the balloon will be displayed on the screen. To do this we need to make paint invoke the display method:

```
public void paint(Graphics g) {
    myBalloon.display(g);
}
```

This now completes all the coding that is needed. Our final act is to incorporate all these declarations and methods within the class that defines the user interface object. We choose to name this class PlayBalloon.

The complete balloon program consists of two main objects:

1. The user interface object created from the class PlayBalloon. This is created by the browser or applet viewer.
2. The balloon object, myBalloon, created from the class Balloon. This is created by the user interface object.

Note that the import statements appear only once, at the very beginning of the program.

```
import java.applet.Applet;
import java.awt.*;
import java.awt.event.*;


public class PlayBalloon extends Applet implements ActionListener {

    private Button grow, shrink;
    private Balloon myBalloon;

    public void init() {
        grow = new Button("Grow");
        add(grow);
        grow.addActionListener(this);

        shrink = new Button("Shrink");
        add(shrink);
        shrink.addActionListener(this);

        myBalloon = new Balloon(20, 50, 50);
    }
```

```
        public void actionPerformed(ActionEvent event) {
            if (event.getSource() == grow)
                myBalloon.changeSize(10);
            if (event.getSource() == shrink)
                myBalloon.changeSize(-10);
            repaint();
        }

        public void paint (Graphics g) {
            myBalloon.display(g);
        }
    }


class Balloon {

    private int diameter;
    private int xCoord, yCoord;

    public Balloon(int initialDiameter, int initialX, int initialY) {
        diameter = initialDiameter;
        xCoord = initialX;
        yCoord = initialY;
    }

    public void changeSize(int change) {
        diameter = diameter + change;
    }

    public void display(Graphics g) {
        g.drawOval(xCoord, yCoord, diameter, diameter);
    }
}
```

The structure of this program can be shown graphically in a UML collaboration diagram, Figure 9.4. Each object is shown as a rectangular box. Figure 9.4 shows the four objects:

- the unnamed object of the class PlayBalloon
- object myBalloon of the class Balloon
- object grow of the library class Button
- object shrink of the library class Button

As you can see, the name of an object is followed by a colon and then the name of its class. The complete name is underlined. Either the object name or the class name can be omitted. But if the object name is omitted, the colon and class name remain.

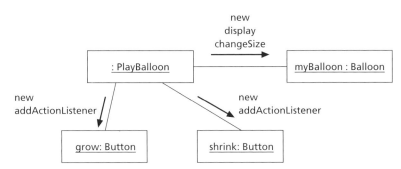

Figure 9.4 Collaboration diagram showing the objects in the balloon program

The relationship between the objects is shown as a line connecting their boxes. Method invocations are shown as small arrows indicating the direction of the invocation, and the method name appears alongside the arrow. A special case is when one object creates another using the Java word `new`. This is shown in the same way as a method invocation. In the illustration (Figure 9.4), the unnamed object of the class `PlayBalloon` invokes methods `new`, `changeSize`, and `display` on the object `myBalloon`.

Diagrams like this can help people understand the structure of a program and how it works.

We shall see this structure repeated many times throughout this book. All the programs use the widgets (buttons, scrollbars, etc.) provided by the Java library software. So all the programs need a user interface object. The other main object in the programs is the object that carries out the functions specific to the particular application. In a more complex program the application will be modelled by two or more objects.

This program makes use of some additional objects, like the `Button` objects `grow` and `shrink`. These are created, using `new`, as instances of the library class `Button`. Another GUI component used widely in this book is text fields. A text field is created using `new` as usual:

```
TextField data = new TextField();
```

Thereafter we can invoke a method of the text field object, for example:

```
String input = data.getText();
```

The output from the program is shown in Figure 9.1.

● Public data

We have seen that the normal practice is to hide the data within an object and therefore to declare such data as `private`. The option exists, but it is rarely used, to make some or any of the data `public`. For example, it might be decided (unusually) to make the *x* and *y* coordinates of a balloon object public. This would mean that they were accessible from outside a balloon object, so that some other object could calculate whether the balloon had hit the floor, for example.

The coordinates would be declared like this:

```
public int xCoord;
public int yCoord;
```

and some other object would refer to one of them like this:

```
if (myBalloon.yCoord >= floorLevel) ...
```

Notice that the reference to the data item looks very much like a method being invoked, using the object name followed by a period. However, the vital brackets that characterize a method invocation are missing.

Finally, be aware that normally it is regarded as very bad practice to do this – the data within an object are usually kept well hidden as part of the policy of information hiding.

● Private methods

The whole purpose of writing a class is to allow the creation of objects which then present useful facilities to other objects. These facilities are the public methods that the object offers. Sometimes a class or object needs to use one or more methods that do not need to be made public. For example, in the `Balloon` class, suppose we wanted to create a method that allowed another object to find out the area of a balloon. Let us name this method `area`. This would be provided as a `public` class. But we might decide that the actual calculation of the area is a little bit complicated and therefore should be packaged up within another `private` method named `calcArea` that `area` invokes when it needs to. We have created a `private` method that acts in support of the public methods in the class:

```
private float calcArea() {
    float radius;
    radius = diameter/2.0f;
    return 3.142f*radius*radius;
}
```

To invoke a private method, you do it like this:

```
float a = calcArea();
```

giving the name of the method and any parameters as usual. If the method was invoked by another object, it would have to be prefixed by the name of an object. But because it is invoked from within a method already within the same object, the object is implicit.

SELF-TEST QUESTION

9.10 Write the `public` method `area` for the class `brick`.

Depending on its size and complexity a class might have a number of private methods. Their purpose is to clarify and simplify the class.

● Names of classes, objects and methods

The programmer chooses the names of classes, objects and methods. Usually you make them as meaningful as possible. The rules for names are:

- They consist of letters (upper-case and lower-case) and digits (0 to 9).
- They must start with a letter.

The Java convention is that names of classes start with a capital letter. Examples are `PlayBalloon`, `Applet` and `Button`. The names of objects and methods start with lower-case letters. Examples are `balloon`, `button` and `paint`. If a name consists of two or more words, the first letters of the new words are capitalized, as in `PlayBalloon` and `myBalloon`.

● this

Imagine that you could follow the computer, pointing with a finger, as it executes a Java program. Your finger follows the sequence of actions, one instruction after another. From time to time a method invocation means that you go from one object to another. At any point in time your finger is within one of the objects that make up the program. This object, the current object, is given the special name `this`.

So, if a method needs to refer to the object that it is currently working on, it can refer to it using `this`. There are a number of occasions in which this can be useful. The first example is one that has been used many times in the programs in this book, in order to accomplish event handling. Suppose a program is using a scrollbar, declaring it as follows:

```
private Scrollbar slider;
```

Then we make sure that the event-handling mechanism knows which object to notify when the value of the scrollbar is altered:

```
slider.addAdjustmentListener(this);
```

This statement states that the method `addAdjustmentListener` of the object `slider` is invoked with parameter `this`. The word *this* says that it is this particular object that should be told when an event happens (and not some other object within the program).

Often a program needs to invoke one of the methods within the current object. If the method is called `calcArea`, for example, this would be normally written:

```
float a = calcArea();
```

But this is completely equivalent to:

```
float a = this.calcArea();
```

This second style serves to spell out which object is involved in the method invocation. Please note that it is not usual to write the second of these two versions; the first is overwhelmingly the normal style.

Another use of `this` is when the programmer might want to emphasize – as a point of style – that the variables of the current object are being used, like this:

```
this.xCoord = this.xCoord + change;
```

which is completely equivalent to:

```
xCoord = xCoord + change;
```

This style is very useful when the names of parameters coincide with those of variables, for example:

```
private int x, y;

public void setCoordinates(int x, int y) {
    this.x = x;
    this.y = y;
}
```

in which `this.x` means the variable and `x` means the parameter.

● Built-in types

Many of the variables that are used in Java programs are true objects (as described above), but some variables are not. Variables which are `boolean`, `char`, `byte`, `short`, `int`, `long`, `float` and `double` are not objects, but are called built-in types. When you declare a built-in variable, it is immediately usable:

```
int i;

i = 10;
i++;
```

This declaration both declares the variable `i` and creates it. In contrast, the declaration of an object such as:

```
Button b;
```

merely declares the variable. It then has to be created, using `new`, before it can be used:

```
b = new Button("Press");
```

Built-in variables come with a whole collection of things you can do with them. For example, with variables of type `int` you can:

- declare variables;
- assign values using =;
- carry out arithmetic;
- compare using >=, <=, != etc.;
- use as parameters;
- return as values from a method.

We shall see in the next section that you cannot necessarily do all these things with objects.

On occasion we need numbers that are actually proper objects. For this purpose the library provides several classes, called *wrapper* classes, to represent the various types of numbers (plus boolean and characters). These classes are Boolean, Character, Integer, Long, Float and Double. These classes are used by classes that need to treat all kinds of data in a uniform way. They also have other occasional uses, and we will see later some examples of their use.

In summary, variables in Java are:

1. Built-in types: boolean, char, byte, short, int, long, float and double. These are not objects.
2. Objects created from classes using new.

Operations on objects

What can you do with an object? The answer is that when you write a class, you define the set of operations that can be performed on objects of that type. With the Balloon class, for example, we have defined the operations changeSize, move and display. Do not readily assume that you can do anything else to a balloon. The only things that you can do with a Balloon object are:

1. changeSize;
2. move;
3. display;
4. create an object of type Balloon (using new);
5. use a Balloon object as a parameter and a return value;
6. assign a Balloon object to Balloon variables.

In Java programs many things that are used are objects. But in addition there are the built-in types – boolean, char, byte, short, int, long, float and double. These are not objects. The language provides ready-made facilities to do operations with these variables – operations such as arithmetic, compare them, use them as parameters, and assign values. And it is tempting to assume that it is possible to use all these operations with any object. This is not so. Take the string type, for example. You cannot compare strings using == in an if statement, like this:

```
String s1 = "abc";
String s2 = "abc";
if (s1 == s2) etc. // do not do this
```

It is very tempting and very intuitively natural to write this, but it is incorrect. This code does actually carry out a test, but not the one you want. The operator == tests to see whether the items being compared are actually the same object. In this case, the strings s1 and s2 are two different objects and so can never be equal. The moral is that you cannot always assume that apparently obvious facilities are available to every type of object. This might become clearer if you think of comparing two balloons. What does it mean to test whether two balloons are equal?

In fact, the library does provide a method for comparing strings. It is invoked like this:

```
if (s1.equals(s2)) etc.
```

This has the following meaning. s1 is a string object. The method equals within the string object s1 is invoked with the parameter s2.

If we wanted a way of comparing two balloons we should provide a method to do it. Suppose that two balloons are considered to be the same if they have equal areas. Suppose there is a method area, discussed above, that returns the area of a balloon. Then we can write the method equals as follows:

```
public boolean equals(Balloon balloon) {
    return(balloon.area() == (this.area());
}
```

and would make use of it by, for example:

```
Balloon b1, b2;
```

```
if (b1.equals(b2)) etc.
```

The moral of this story is that if you are going to use an object, then find out precisely what methods it has available for use. Don't assume that you can do everything that you can do with the built-in variables such as numbers. However, you can assume as a minimum that for every object:

● you can create it;
● you can use it as a parameter and as a return value;
● you can use the methods that are provided as part of its class;
● you can assign it to a variable of the same class.

SELF-TEST QUESTION
....

9.11 Write down a list of operations that are possible with an object of the class Balloon and give examples.

When an object is used as a parameter, there is something to be aware of. The built-in types are different from objects in this respect: when a variable which is a built-in type is passed as a parameter to a method, it is passed by value. This means that a copy of the value is made and passed as the parameter to the method. The consequence is that, whatever the method does to the parameter, it has no effect on the value used in the invoking method. A method passes back a value as the return value of the method. So passing built-in types to methods as parameters is always safe. But objects are different, and when an object is used as a parameter it is passed as a *reference*. A reference is not a copy of the object, but a pointer to the object. So a method can access the methods of an object parameter, and can change the state of the object as held in its private variables. Hence, care is needed if you plan to manipulate objects passed as parameters.

● Object destruction and garbage collection

We have seen how objects are created, using the powerful word new. How do they die? They certainly die when the program ceases to run. They can also die when they cease to be used by the program. For example, if we do:

```
Balloon myBalloon = new Balloon(20, 100, 100);
```

and then:

```
myBalloon = new Balloon(40, 200, 200);
```

what happens is that the first object lived a brief and quiet life. It died when the program no longer had any knowledge of it; its value was usurped by the newer object. The memory that was used to store the values of its variables is reclaimed for other uses. This is termed *garbage collection*. In Java, garbage collection is automatic. (In some other languages it is not and the programmer has to keep track of objects that are no longer needed.)

● Method overloading

A class can have two or more methods with the same name. This may seem initially confusing, and certainly it needs to be done with some care, but there are circumstances in which it is useful. In the case of the class Balloon, for example, suppose we have a method moveRight which moves a balloon towards the right of the screen. Here is one version:

```
public void moveRight(int distance) {
    xCoord = xCoord + distance;
    repaint();
}
```

We might also need another method that also moves a balloon to the right, but moves it a fixed distance. We can write:

```
public void moveRight() {
    xCoord = xCoord + 20;
    repaint();
}
```

We now have two methods with the same name. One method has a single parameter and the other method has no parameters. Java regards them as valid distinct methods. The same name is used for both methods and this is why this technique is known as method overloading. When a method named moveRight is invoked, the Java compiler finds the method which has the matching number of parameters, the matching types of parameters and the matching return type. It then uses that version. Thus there is no ambiguity.

> **SELF-TEST QUESTION**
> ....
>
> **9.12** Write sample invocations on the two methods moveRight.

Method overloading is useful when two or more methods have (nearly) identical purposes.

Method overloading is also sometimes useful with constructor methods. For the Balloon class, we can write two (or more) constructor methods like this:

```
public Balloon(int initialX, int initialY) {
    xCoord = initialX;
    yCoord = initialY;
}

public Balloon(int initialX, int initialY, int initialDiameter) {
    xCoord = initialX;
    yCoord = initialY;
    diameter = initialDiameter;
}
```

As usual with overloaded methods, when a method called Balloon is invoked to create a new Balloon object, the appropriate method is invoked – the one with matching parameters. If Balloon is invoked with no parameters, then the object is simply created without invoking a constructor method. So all classes have an implicit constructor with no parameters.

> **SELF-TEST QUESTIONS**
> ....
>
> **9.13** Write invocations of the above constructor methods for the class Balloon, including the constructor with no parameters.
>
> **9.14** Write two constructor methods for the class brick.

Method overloading is also widely used within the library classes. For example, there are several versions of the constructor method of the class TextField. Here are two examples of creating text fields using two different constructor methods:

```
TextField field1 = new TextField();
TextField field2 = new TextField(10);
```

The first constructor has no parameters, while the second constructor method takes an integer parameter that specifies the width of the text field.

Do not confuse overloading with *overriding*, which we will meet in Chapter 11 on inheritance.

● static

A method or a variable can be described as `static`. This means that it belongs to a class and not to any individual objects that are created as instances of the class. There is only one copy of the item and it is associated with the class.

You will see if you look in Appendix B, which lists selected library methods, that a number of them are labelled as `static`. For example, the method `sqrt` in the class `Math` is static. This is because it does not act on a specific object. It merely accepts a parameter, a number, and calculates the square root. For convenience, `sqrt` is declared within a class, the class `Math`, that groups together a number of useful mathematical operations. But none of the methods is associated with an object, so they are all described as `static`. As in the example above, each of these methods is invoked by preceding the method name with the class name, as follows:

```
y = Math.sqrt(x);
```

The class `Math` also contains several `static` variables, including the mathematical constant π. This variable is referred to as `Math.PI`, again preceding the variable name by the class name. Making data values `public` like this is very unusual in object-oriented programming, because normally variables are labelled `private` in the spirit of information hiding. Access to the mathematical constants is an exception to this general rule.

Another commonly used `static` method is `toString` within the class `Integer`, used like this in order to convert an integer into a string:

```
String string = Integer.toString(number);
```

Here is an example of a class that provides some very simple `static` methods and a public `static` variable:

```
class Calcs {
    public static int magic = 42;

    public static int sum(int x, int y) {
        return x + y;
    }

    public static int diff(int x, int y) {
        return x - y;
    }

}
```

And here is a class that uses the static methods and the variable:

```
public class UseStatics {

    public void useThem() {
        int a = 2, b = Calcs.magic;

        int z = Calcs.sum(2, 3);
        z = Calcs.diff(a,b);
    }
}
```

(If you decided that you did not like object-oriented programming, you could write Java programs that used nothing but static methods in this manner. This would probably not be one of your best decisions.)

A second way of using static variables and methods is illustrated by the following example. Suppose we wanted to know how many balloons had been created by instantiating class Balloon. We use a static variable to record the number:

```
static int count = 0;
```

We write a static method addOne that is invoked by the constructor method whenever a balloon is created:

```
private static void addOne() {
    count++;
}
```

and at any time we can display the value of the count using:

```
public static void displayCount(Graphics g) {
    g.drawString("Number of balloons created is " + count, 10, 10);
}
```

Neither of these methods is any part of an individual object. They belong to the class itself.

The method displayCount of the class Balloon is invoked from outside the class like this:

```
Balloon.displayCount(g);
```

in which the class name Balloon is followed (after a period) by the method name.

SELF-TEST QUESTION
····························

9.15 Write a static method that gives each balloon that is created a unique serial number, starting at 1 for the first balloon.

The description static does not mean that a static variable cannot be changed. It means that, unlike non-static variables, a copy of the variable is not created when an object is created from the class. Similarly, a copy of a static method is not created for each instance of an object.

Note that the constructor method or methods of a class are essentially static methods, though not marked as such.

It is a rule that static methods can only access static variables and other static methods, but no others. This is logical, because any other (non-static) variables and methods are the property of individual objects.

We have seen that there are two uses for static methods and variables:

- methods and variables that are associated with a class as a whole, rather than individual instances of the class;
- methods and variables that are not associated with an individual object.

In summary, there are two ways of using the two types of methods:

- A static method is invoked by preceding the method name by the class name.
- A non-static method is invoked by preceding the method name by the object name.

A similar distinction applies to static and non-static variables.

null

The word null is one of the Java keywords. It means an object that does not exist. If you declare:

```
Ball redBall;
```

and then:

```
redBall.display();
```

your program will abruptly stop with an error message that says there is a null pointer exception. This is because you have declared an object but not created it (with new). The object redBall does not exist. More accurately, it has the value null – which amounts to the same thing. In most elementary programming you do not make use of null – except if you inadvertently forget to use new. But in more advanced programs that use dynamic data structures (beyond the scope of this book), use of null is made explicitly.

If you ever wanted to explicitly destroy an object (and there is no reason why you should because any objects that are not used are automatically destroyed by the garbage collection system, mentioned above) you can assign the value null to the object.

● Classes and files

If a program consists only of a single class, the Java source code is placed in a file which has the same name as the class, but with the suffix `.java`. Thus a class called `Game` goes in a file called `Game.java` and the header for the class is:

```
public class Game extends Applet
```

Any `import` statements must precede this header. The compiler compiles the Java code to byte code, which it places in a file called `Game.class`.

If a program consists of more than one class, there are two alternatives:

1. Place all the classes in one file.
2. Place each class in a file by itself.

Both alternatives are equally satisfactory. With small, novice programs it is usual to place all the classes in the same file. On the other hand, placing classes in their own files provides greater generality. We now look at these two schemes in turn.

If all the classes are placed in a single file, the first class in the file must be declared `public`, but subsequent classes must not be `public`. The filename must correspond to the first class in the file. All the required `import`s must be at the start of the file. For example:

```
import java.awt.*;
import java.applet.Applet;

public class PlayBalloon extends Applet {
    // body of class PlayBalloon
}

class Balloon {
    // body of class Balloon
}
```

If each class is placed in its own file, the filenames must match the class names and all the classes must be declared `public`. If an `import` is needed it must appear at the start of the class. For example, in file `PlayBalloon.java`:

```
import java.awt.*;
import java.applet.Applet;

public class PlayBalloon extends Applet {
    // body of class PlayBalloon
}
```

In file `Balloon.java`:

```
public class Balloon {
    // body of class Balloon
}
```

When classes are placed in different files, all the files associated with a program should be in the same directory or folder.

Whether the Java code for the classes is in one file or in different files, the compiler creates one byte code file for each class, with the suffix `.class`.

● Scope rules (visibility)

In programming, the term *scope rules* or *visibility* means the rules for accessing variables and methods. For humans, scope rules are like the rule that in Australia you must drive on the left, or the rule that you should only enter someone's house via the front door. In a program, rules like these are rigidly enforced by the compiler, to prevent deliberate or erroneous access to protected information. Scope rules constrain the programmer, but help the programmer to organize a program in a clear and logical manner. The scope rules associated with classes and methods allow the programmer to encapsulate variables and methods in a convenient manner.

The programmer can describe each variable and each method as either `public` or `private`. Within a class, any instruction anywhere in the class can invoke any method, `public` or `private`. Also any instruction can refer to any variable, `public` or `private`. The exception is that local variables, those declared within a method, are only accessible by instructions within the method.

When one class refers to another, only those methods and variables labelled as `public` are accessible from outside a class. All others are inaccessible. It is good design practice to minimize the number of methods that are `public`, restricting them so as to offer only the publicly available services offered by the class. It is also good practice never (or very rarely) to make variables `public`. If a variable needs to be inspected or changed, a method should be provided to do the job.

In summary, a variable or a method within a class can be described as either:

1. `public` – accessible from anywhere;
2. `private` – accessible only from within the class.

Programming pitfalls

- Novices often want to code an object straight away. You can't; you have to declare a class and then create an instance of the class.
- Do not forget to initialize instance variables. Explicitly initialize them (either in the variable declaration or by means of a constructor method) and do not rely on Java's default initialization. Local variables (those declared within a method) are *not* initialized automatically by Java. So do not forget to initialize them also.
- Giving a constructor method a return type, say `void`, does not precipitate a compilation error, but instead a `NullPointerException` error when the program runs.

Grammar spot

● A class has this structure:

```
class ClassName {
// declarations of variables

// declarations of methods
}
```

● One or more of the methods in the class may have the same name as the class. One of these constructor methods may be invoked (with appropriate parameters) to initialize the object when it is created.
● Each public method has the structure:

```
public returnType methodName(parameters) {
    // body
}
```

● To declare and create (instantiate) an object:

```
ClassName objectName = new ClassName(parameters);
```

● To invoke a method of an object:

```
objectName.methodName(parameters);
```

● A static method is prefixed by the word static in its header:

```
public static returnType methodName(parameters) {
    // body
}
```

● To invoke a static method of a class:

```
ClassName.methodName(parameters);
```

Programming principles

● Objects and classes are central to OOP. A program is built from a collection of collaborating objects.
● An object is a logical bundling together of variables and methods. It forms a self-contained module which can be easily used and understood. The principle of information hiding or encapsulation means that users of an object have a restricted view of an object. An object provides a set of services as public methods that others can use. The remainder of the object, its variables and the instructions that implement the methods are hidden from view. This enhances abstraction and modularity.

- A class is a generalization of a set of objects. It is not possible to directly declare an object. Instead, the variables and methods of any of a set of objects are declared as a class.
- Creating an object is called instantiating an instance of a class. It is achieved when a program is running by executing the built-in instruction `new`. This creates a new copy of an object with its own name.
- In computer science a class is sometimes called an *abstract data type* (ADT). A data type is a kind of variable, like an `int`, a `float` or a `boolean`. These are types built into the Java language and immediately available for use. Associated with each of these types is a set of operations. For example, with an `int` we can do assignment, addition, subtraction and so on. Classes allow the programmer to construct types additional to the built-in types – hence the name abstract. The `Balloon` class described above is an example of an ADT. It defines some data (variables), together with a set of operations (methods) that can carry out operations on the data.
- The source code of an object-oriented program consists of a number of class descriptions. When the program runs, instances of the classes are created (using `new`). The methods of these objects are invoked in an appropriate order to achieve the desired aim of the program.
- In Chapter 21 we shall see how to design a program as a collection of objects.

New language elements

- `class`   appears in the heading of the description of a class;
- `public` the description of a variable or a method that is accessible from anywhere;
- `private` the description of a variable or a method that is only accessible from within the class;
- `new`   used to create a new instance of a class (a new object);
- `this`   the name of the current object;
- `null`   the name of an object that does not exist;
- `static` the description attached to a variable or method that belongs to a class as a whole, not to any instance created as an object from the class.

Summary

- An object is a collection of data, called variables, and the associated actions, called methods, that can act upon the data. Java programs are constructed as a collection of objects.

- The programmer does not describe an object directly. Instead the programmer describes a class. A class is a generalization of a number of objects. When a Java program executes the word `new`, it causes a new object to be created with all the characteristics of a named class.

● One particular method carries out the initialization of a newly created object. This method, called a constructor, must have the same name as the class.

● Items in a class can be declared to be `private` or `public`. A `private` item can only be referred to from within the class. A public item can be referred to by anything (inside or outside the class). In designing a Java program, `public` items are normally kept to a minimum so as to enhance information hiding. In particular, data items are usually kept private.

● Overloading means providing two or more methods within a class that have the same name. They are unambiguously distinguishable by having different parameters (in number and/or type). The constructor method can be overloaded.

● Most simple programs consist of two objects that are written by the programmer. One is the user interface object, created by the browser or applet viewer. The other object carries out the tasks required by the application. Such a program usually makes use of other objects provided by the library – like strings and buttons.

● The description `static` means that the variable or method belongs to the class and not to particular objects. A `static` method can be invoked directly, without any need for instantiating an instance of the class. A `static` method is useful when a method does not need to be associated with an object, or for carrying out actions for the class as a whole.

EXERCISES

9.1 Balloons Add to the class `Balloon` some additional data, a `String` that holds the name of the balloon and a variable that describes its colour. Add the code to initialize this to the initialization method and add the code to display it.
Enhance the balloon program with buttons that move the balloon.

9.2 Bricks Create a class that represents a brick and various operations that can be performed on it (a brick is simply a rectangle):

● initialize its position and size;
● move it left 20 pixels;
● move it right 20 pixels;
● shrink its size by a set amount (20 pixels);
● make it grow in size by a set amount (20 pixels);
● rotate the brick through 90 degrees.

Write code to create a program with buttons that allow these manipulations to be performed on a brick.

9.3 The amplifier display Some stereo amplifiers have a display that shows the volume being output. The display waxes and wanes according to the volume at any point in time. Sometimes the display has an indicator that shows the maximum value that is currently being output.

This program displays the numerical value of the maximum and minimum values that a scrollbar is set to in a manner similar to the display in Figure 7.6.

Write the user interface as one class and the piece of program that remembers the values, compares them and displays them as a second class.

9.4 Bank account Write a program that simulates a bank account. A text box allows deposits (a positive number) to be made into the account and withdrawals (a negative number) to be made. The state of the account is continually displayed and, if the account goes into the red (negative balance), a suitable message is displayed. Create a class named Account and a user interface class that will use it.

9.5 Scorekeeper Design and write a class that acts as a scorekeeper for a computer game. It maintains a single integer, the score. It provides a method to initialize the score to zero, a method to increase the score, a method to decrease the score, and a method to display the score. Write instructions to create a single object and use it.

9.6 Dice Design and write a class that acts as a die, which may be thrown to give a value 1 to 6. Initially write it so that it always gives the value 6. Write a class that creates a die object and uses it. The screen displays a button, which when pressed causes the die to be thrown and its value displayed.

Then alter the die so that it gives the value one higher than when it was last thrown, for example 4 when it was 3.

Then alter it so that it uses the library random number generator.

Some games like backgammon and Monopoly need two dice. Write Java statements to create two instances of the dice object, throw them and display the outcomes.

9.7 Random number generator Write your own random number generator as a class that uses a formula to obtain the next pseudo-random number from the previous one. A random number program works by starting with some 'seed' value. Thereafter the current random number is used as a basis for the next by performing some calculation on it which makes it into some other (apparently random) number. A good formula to use for integers is:

```
r = ((r * 25173) + 13849) % 65536;
```

which produces numbers in the range 0 to 65535. The particular numbers in this formula have been shown to give good results.

9.8 Complex numbers Write a class called Complex to represent complex numbers (together with their operations). A complex number consists of two parts – a real part (a float) and an imaginary part (a float). The constructor method should create a new complex number, using the floats provided as parameters, like this:

```
Complex c = new Complex(1.0f, 2.0f);
```

Write methods `getReal` and `getImaginary` to get the real part and the imaginary part of a complex number and which is used like this:

```
float f = c.getReal();
```

Write a method to add two complex numbers and return their sum. The real part is the sum of the two real parts. The imaginary part is the sum of the two imaginary parts. An invocation of the method looks like:

```
Complex c = c1.sum(c2);
```

Write a method to calculate the product of two complex numbers. If one number has components x_1 and y_1 and the second number has components x_2 and y_2:

the real part of the product is the product $= x_1 \times x_2 - y_1 \times y_2$
the imaginary part of the product $= x_1 \times y_2 + x_2 \times y_1$

ANSWERS TO SELF-TEST QUESTIONS

9.1
```
public void moveUp(int amount) {
    yCoord = yCoord - amount;
}
```

9.2
```
public Color color;
public void setColor(Color newColor) {
    color = newColor;
}
```

9.3
```
int height, width;
int xCoord, int yCoord;

public void moveUp(int amount) {
    yCoord = yCoord - amount;
}
public void wider(int amount) {
    width = width + amount;
}
```

9.4
```
public Brick(int startWidth, int startHeight, int initialX,
             int initialY) {
    width = startWidth;
    height = startHeight;
    xCoord = initialX;
    yCoord = initialY;
}
```

9.5 The variable `color` should be `private` and the method `setColor` should be public.

9.6
```
public class Brick {

    private int height, width;
    private int xCoord, int yCoord

    public Brick(int startWidth, int startHeight,
                    int initialX, int initialY) {
        width = startWidth;
        height = startHeight;
        xCoord = initialX;
        yCoord = initialY;
    }

    public void moveUp(int amount) {
        yCoord = yCoord - amount;
    }

    public void wider(int amount) {
        width = width + amount;
    }
}
```

9.7 A class is the generalization of any number of objects. It describes what is common to all objects.

9.8
```
Balloon happyBirthday = new Balloon(100, 200, 200);
```

9.9
```
Brick houseBrick = new Brick(20, 10, 20, 20);
```

9.10
```
public int area() {
    return width * height;
}
```

9.11
```
Balloon b = new Balloon();
b.changeSize(20);
b.display(g);
Balloon b2 = b;
```

9.12
```
balloon.moveRight();

balloon.moveRight(20);
```

9.13
```
Balloon b1 = new Balloon(20, 20);
Balloon b2 = new Balloon(20, 20, 100);
```

9.14
```
public Brick(int startWidth, int startHeight) {
    width = startWidth;
    height = startHeight;
}

public Brick(int startWidth, int startHeight, int startX, int
          startY) {
    width = startWidth;
    height = startHeight;
    xCoord = startX;
    yCoord = startY;
}
```

9.15
```
private static int serialNumber = 0;

public static int getSerialNumber() {
    serialNumber++;
    return serialNumber;
}
```

Applet architecture

Introduction

We have seen that an object-oriented program consists of a number of objects. Each object consists of a number of methods providing services to other objects, and some private data. This collection of objects acts as a model or a simulation of something of interest. We will use the balloon program as an example. When the program runs the screen is as shown in Figure 10.1. The purpose of the program is to represent and display a balloon in the window on the screen. Buttons are provided to:

- enlarge the balloon (Grow);
- reduce the size of the balloon (Shrink);

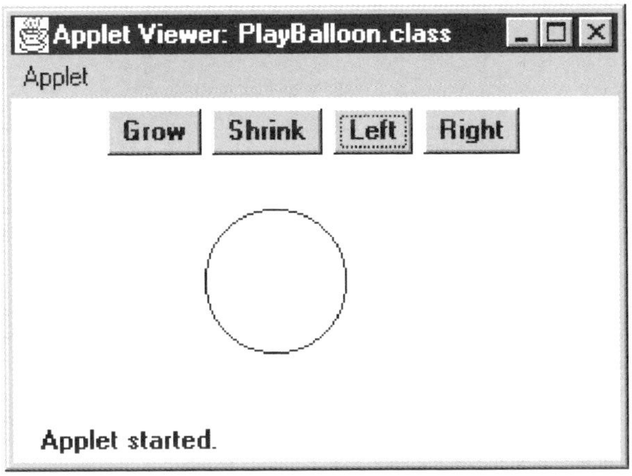

Figure 10.1 Screen display for the balloon program.

- move the balloon to the right (Right);
- move the balloon to the left (Left).

The code for this program is given below. We will spend the whole of this chapter on dissecting this program and identifying the different elements within it – with particular reference to those parts that constitute the user interface to the program. The program consists of two classes – the user interface class and the class Balloon that models the application.

```java
import java.applet.Applet;
import java.awt.*;
import java.awt.event.*;


public class PlayBalloon extends Applet implements ActionListener {

    private Button grow, shrink, left, right;
    private Balloon myBalloon;

    public void init() {
        grow = new Button("Grow");
        add(grow);
        grow.addActionListener(this);
        shrink = new Button("Shrink");
        add(shrink);
        shrink.addActionListener(this);
        left = new Button("Left");
        add(left);
        left.addActionListener(this);
        right = new Button("Right");
        add(right);
        right.addActionListener(this);

        myBalloon = new Balloon();
    }

    public void actionPerformed(ActionEvent event) {
        if (event.getSource() == grow)
            myBalloon.grow();
        if (event.getSource() == shrink)
            myBalloon.shrink();
        if (event.getSource() == left)
            myBalloon.left();
        if (event.getSource() == right)
            myBalloon.right();
        repaint();
    }
```

```
    public void paint(Graphics g) {
        myBalloon.display(g);
    }
}

class Balloon {

    private int diameter = 10;
    private int xCoord = 20, yCoord = 50;

    public void display(Graphics g) {
        g.drawOval(xCoord, yCoord, diameter, diameter);
    }

    public void left() {
        xCoord = xCoord - 10;
    }

    public void right() {
        xCoord = xCoord + 10;
    }

    public void grow() {
        diameter = diameter + 5;
    }

    public void shrink() {
        diameter = diameter - 5;
    }
}
```

The user interface to the balloon consists of two parts:

1. the buttons that allow the balloon to be controlled;
2. the display of the balloon in the window.

The program for the balloon application and indeed any application with any signific-ant graphical user interface (GUI) features consists of three complementary sections of code:

1. the controller;
2. the model;
3. the view.

These three elements collaborate to make the complete program work. Some of these components are written by the programmer and some are borrowed from the library. In simple programs, like the balloon program, there are just two objects:

1. the user interface object that handles the controller;
2. the application object that models the application and displays the view of the application.

In more complex programs, the application is modelled by a number of objects.

● The model, view, controller architecture

The primary task of an object-oriented program is to model the application of interest. A model or simulation of an application is not sufficient – it would be deaf, blind and dumb. Some way of connecting the model to its user is needed. In the balloon object, numbers represent its position and size, but these are merely invisible bit patterns inside the computer's memory. We need a way to control a balloon – alter its position and size (we call this the controller) and a way to display it in the window (we call this the view). If we write software to represent a car, we need a model of the engine and its transmission. This model will be invisible. What will be visible are the instruments which tell us what the car is doing (the view) and the controls that enable the user to alter what is going on (the controller). See Figure 10.2.

Thus every OOP consists of:

● the model (e.g. the car engine, the balloon);
● the view (for the balloon, a display of a circle; for the car, the speedometer or the petrol gauge);
● the controller (for the balloon, buttons to change its position and size; for the car, the brake pedal or the steering wheel).

The model itself is usually invisible (except as Java code). The view is visible on the computer screen as a graphical image, dials, graphs etc. The controls are visible as scrollbars, buttons, text fields etc. The controller is the inputs to the model and the view is the outputs from the model.

Most of the view and the controller are borrowed from class `Applet` in the Abstract Window Toolkit (AWT). But some of the view and controller software is written by the programmer. We use methods like `actionPerformed` as part of the controller and methods like `paint` for the view.

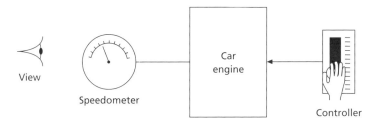

Figure 10.2 Model, view and controller for a car engine.

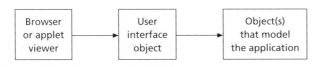

Figure 10.3 Object creation when an applet is initiated.

● In the beginning

When a browser (or an applet viewer) runs a program its first act is to create a user interface object from the user interface class (Figure 10.3). It effectively carries out the statement:

```
PlayBalloon playBalloon = new PlayBalloon();
```

You will not see this written in any program, because it is buried somewhere inside the code of the browser or applet viewer.

Once the user interface object has been created, the browser (or applet viewer) invokes one of its methods – the method `init`. The programmer writes the method `init` whose main tasks are to create the required widgets (buttons etc.) in the window and to create the application object or objects using `new` (Figure 10.3). Creating a button involves invoking the constructor method of the class `Button`. Next the button is added to the current object, the user interface object. Finally, the button object is notified that the current object (`this`) is the object to be notified of any events.

Here is the code for `init` in the balloon program.

```
public void init() {
    grow = new Button("Grow");
    add(grow);
    grow.addActionListener(this);
    shrink = new Button("Shrink");
    add(shrink);
    shrink.addActionListener(this);
    left = new Button("Left");
    add(left);
    left.addActionListener(this);
    right = new Button("Right");
    add(right);
    right.addActionListener(this);

    myBalloon = new Balloon();
}
```

The objects are now ready to carry out the tasks of the program.

The next thing that the browser does is to invoke the method `paint` (which the programmer writes) to draw the required initial graphics in the window. You can see that in this case, `paint` displays the initial view of the balloon. The buttons are also displayed automatically.

The scene is now set for the user to initiate some activity.

● The controller

The controller consists of a number of methods. Their role is to respond to events that the user initiates – events like moving the mouse, clicking on a button or entering a number into a text field. The controller carries out the following series of actions (Figure 10.4):

1. The user causes an event such as clicking the mouse over a button.
2. The browser (or applet viewer) detects the event.
3. The browser (or applet viewer) invokes a method to handle the event.
4. The programmer provides a method that responds to the event from the user – a method such as `actionPerformed`.
5. The event handler method (`actionPerformed`, for example) invokes the appropriate method within the object that models the application.
6. The method within the object changes the data within the model.
7. The event handler invokes the method `repaint` to cause the graphical image of the application to be redrawn.

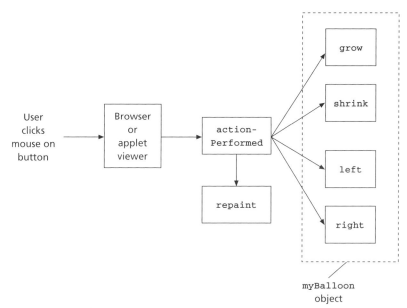

Figure 10.4 Sequence of method invocations when the user clicks on a button.

Here is the relevant piece of the balloon program:

```
public void actionPerformed(ActionEvent event) {
    if (event.getSource() == grow)
        myBalloon.grow();
    if (event.getSource() == shrink)
        myBalloon.shrink();
    if (event.getSource() == left)
        myBalloon.left();
    if (event.getSource() == right)
        myBalloon.right();
    repaint();
}
```

The model

The model is the collection of objects that model the application of interest. In the case of the balloon program, there is only one object. When the controller acts upon the model the view usually changes. Examples are: you move the balloon, you make a change to a document in a word processor or you press the accelerator in a car.

The responsibilities of an object that forms part of an application (model) are:

1. Each object in the model must provide methods that enable it to be controlled.
2. Each object in the model must provide a method or methods to display itself, that is to provide the view or views when requested.

Here is the complete code for the class `Balloon`, illustrating these responsibilities.

```
class Balloon {
    private int diameter=10;
    private int xCoord = 20, yCoord = 20;

    public void display(Graphics g) {
        g.drawOval(xCoord, yCoord, diameter, diameter);
    }

    public void left() {
        xCoord = xCoord - 10;
    }

    public void right() {
        xCoord = xCoord + 10;
    }

    public void grow() {
        diameter = diameter + 5;
    }
```

```
public void shrink() {
    diameter = diameter - 5;
}
}
```

The view

The view is responsible for making sure that an up-to-date picture of the model is displayed in the window on the screen. The actual code to display the picture is contained within the application object. The view is concerned with deciding when a new display is required.

One of the pieces of software that has a responsibility in ensuring that the picture is current is the browser (or applet viewer). The browser (or applet viewer) must invoke the method paint whenever something new needs to be drawn on the screen. When is this? There are a number of circumstances. The first and obvious situation is initially when there is nothing in the window, except the widgets (buttons, scrollbars etc.). It is now that paint is invoked by the browser or applet viewer to display the initial view of the model. In the balloon program, this is the graphic representing the balloon.

Suppose that the user moves the window on the screen, or reduces the size of the window, or increases the size of the window. Then the window needs to be redrawn and method paint invoked (Figure 10.5). Similarly, if some other window is placed on top of the window, either fully or partially obscuring it, then again paint needs to be invoked when the window is back on top again. On all of these occasions nothing has changed in the model; only the user's use of the windowing system has changed.

Most significantly, the view of the model will change when something in the model changes. The only way that the browser or applet viewer knows if the model has changed is if someone tells it. For example, in the balloon program, if the position of the balloon changes because the method move has been invoked, then the view should change. And the only entity that knows something has changed is the actionPerformed method that has been written to handle the pressing of the move button. In order to notify the system that the view has changed, it must invoke the method repaint. Invoking repaint is like

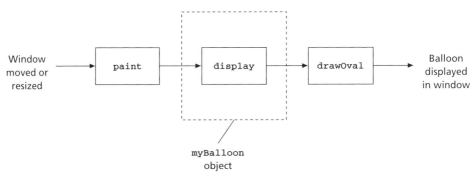

Figure 10.5 Sequence of method invocations when the window is moved or resized.

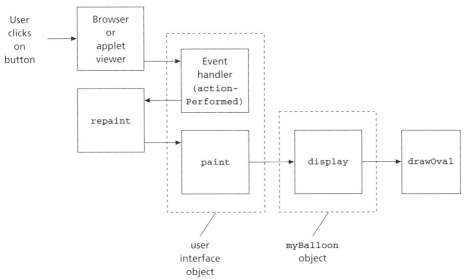

Figure 10.6 Sequence of method invocations when the object changes.

saying 'Something has changed in the model and consequently in the view of the model. Therefore what is displayed in the window needs to change. So please invoke paint.'

The view carries out the following sequence of actions (Figure 10.6):

1. The event handler realizes that something has changed. (This happens in response to a user event like a click on a button.)
2. The event handler invokes the method repaint to signify to the browser (or applet viewer) that something has changed.
3. The browser (or applet viewer) invokes method paint.
4. paint is written by the programmer. It invokes the method within the application object to display the object.
5. The method within the model displays the object appropriately.

Here is the relevant fragment of coding for the balloon program to show what is used when the balloon grows in size:

```
public void actionPerformed(ActionEvent event) {
    if (event.getSource() == grow)
        myBalloon.grow();
    if (event.getSource() == shrink)
        myBalloon.shrink();
    if (event.getSource() == left)
        myBalloon.left();
    if (event.getSource() == right)
        myBalloon.right();
    repaint();
}
```

`repaint` is a method in the library which invokes:

```
public void paint(Graphics g) {
    myBalloon.display(g);
}
```

which in turn invokes:

```
public void display(Graphics g) {
    g.drawOval(xCoord, yCoord, diameter, diameter);
}
```

Summary

Here is a summary of the methods that the programmer writes to provide the input–output interface (view and controller) for a model.

Method	Invoked when	Role
init	Program is started.	**1.** Create the objects for the model. **2.** Create any widgets that are needed.
actionPerformed	A button is pressed by the user.	Handle the event by passing an instruction to the model (invoking a method in the model object).
paint	Something different needs to be displayed – the window needs painting.	Display anything and everything that needs displaying in the window.

Note that there is an important difference between `paint` and `repaint`:

- `paint` is provided by the programmer and invoked by the browser (or applet viewer).
- `repaint` is provided in the library and is invoked by the programmer.

Method	Invoked when	Role
repaint	When the model has changed and therefore the view of the model in the window needs to change.	Notify the browser or applet viewer that something in the window has changed and that it needs to be redrawn.
paint	When the window contents need to be drawn.	Draw the contents of the window.

The model of the application is embedded within the view and the controller, relying on them for instructions and to provide services. Instructions are initiated by the user of the program via the controller. For example, in the balloon program, a user clicks on a button to move the balloon. This is passed on to the balloon object as an invocation of its `move` method. When the balloon object needs to display itself, it invokes the library method `drawOval`. There is thus a symbiotic relationship between the model, the view, the controller and the browser (or applet viewer). If we follow the flow of control, it passes to and fro between all of these.

To use an analogy, suppose your mother asks you to buy a loaf of bread (an instruction). You might respond by saying 'OK, but can I use your car, please?' – a request. So you are making a request of the person who gave you an instruction. Two people are collaborating to achieve some goal by making requests of each other. The same happens with a program – one object makes a request of (invokes) a method within another. The second method then invokes a method within the first.

EXERCISE

10.1 Add further controls to the balloon program, so that you can move a balloon up the screen or down the screen. Add the facility to control the balloon size using a scrollbar. Make the balloon display its x- and y-coordinates as a pair of integers on the screen. If the balloon gets too big, make it display a message in the window. Add the facility to colour the balloon.

Inheritance

Introduction

We have already seen in the last chapter how an object-oriented (OO) program is built from objects. Each object is an instance of a class. A class is the way of describing the general properties of a whole number of objects; it is a template or a generalization. In constructing a program you first describe the classes and then create the objects. For example, we could describe a class Person like this:

```
class Person {
    private String name;

    public void setName(String newName) {
        name = newName;
    }
}
```

Then we can create an instance (a single object) of this class by:

```
Person alice = new Person("Alice");
```

If the class Person doesn't do exactly what you want, you can define a new class that enhances its facilities. For example, you might need a class to handle the person's telephone number and address as well as their name. Such a class uses (inherits) the facilities of the class Person, but adds some more. This mechanism helps the programmer make use of existing pieces of program (classes).

The Java library provides dozens of ready-made classes for the programmer to use. Every program uses at least one class from the library. Most programs consist of descriptions of new classes, which augment the library classes, thus making use of inheritance. This OO approach to programming means that instead of starting programs from scratch, you build on the work of others. In this chapter we will explore inheritance and see how powerful it can be.

● Using inheritance

We start with a class similar to one used already several times in this book. It is a class to represent a sphere. A sphere has a radius and a position in space. When we display a sphere on the screen, it will be shown as a circle. Here is the class description for a sphere:

```
class Sphere {
    protected int x = 100, y = 100;

    public void setX(int newX) {
        x = newX;
    }

    public void setY(int newY) {
        y = newY;
    }

    public void display(Graphics g) {
        g.drawOval(x, y, 20, 20);
    }
}
```

You will notice that when an object of type `Sphere` is instantiated, both of the coordinates of a box just enclosing the sphere are set to 100 pixels. The method to display a sphere simply invokes the library method `drawOval`. The diameter of the sphere is fixed at 20 pixels. We have only modelled the x- and y-coordinates of a sphere (and not the z-coordinate) because we are displaying only a two-dimensional representation on the screen.

Let us suppose that someone has written and tested this class, and made it available for use. But now for a new program let us assume that we need a class very like this, but one that describes bubbles. This new class, called `Bubble`, will allow us to change the size of a bubble and move it vertically – to do new things. The problem with class `Sphere` is that it describes objects that do not move and whose size cannot change. We need a new method that will allow us to set a new value for the radius of the bubble. We can do this without altering the existing class, instead writing a new class that uses the code that is already in `Sphere`. We say that the new class *inherits* variables and methods from the old class. Alternatively we say that the new class *extends* the old class. The new class is a *subclass* of the old. The old class is called the *superclass* of the new class. The use of `protected` is described below. This is how we write the new class:

```
class Bubble extends Sphere {
    private int radius = 10;

    public void setRadius(int newRadius) {
        radius = newRadius;
    }

    public void display(Graphics g) {
        g.drawOval(x, y, 2 * radius, 2 * radius);
    }
}
```

This new class has the name `Bubble`. Within its header it says that it `extends Sphere`. This means that it inherits all the `public` variables and all the `public` methods within class `Sphere`. It is as if the new class `Bubble` has all the public methods of `Sphere`. But you can see that the new class goes on to declare an additional variable and an additional method. The new variable is `radius`, which is additional to the existing variables (`x` and `y`) in `Sphere`. The number of variables is thereby extended.

The new class also has the method `setRadius` in addition to those in `Sphere`. Finally, we have written a new version of the method `display`. This is because the new class has a radius which will change. (In class `Sphere`, the radius was fixed.) This new version of `display` in `Bubble` supersedes the version in the class `Sphere`. We say that the new version *overrides* the old version.

In summary, in the extended class we have:

● added an additional variable;
● added an additional method;
● overridden a method (provided a method which is to be used instead of the method that is already provided).

Do not confuse overriding with overloading, which we met in Chapter 9 on writing classes and objects. Overloading means writing a method in the same class that has the same name, but different parameters. Overriding means writing a method in a subclass that has the same name and parameters.

Let us sum up what we have accomplished. We had an existing class called `Sphere`. We had a requirement for a new class, `Bubble`, that was similar to `Sphere`, but needed additional facilities. So we created the new class by extending the facilities of the old class. In so doing we reused an existing class to create a new one. This is inheritance at work. We have made maximum use of the commonality between the two classes, and we have avoided rewriting pieces of program that already exist.

Making an analogy with human families, inheritance means you can spend your own money and also that of your mother.

Both of the classes we have written, `Sphere` and `Bubble`, are of course still available to use. (In family terms, you can inherit from your mother while she is still alive.) We can create an instance of `Sphere` and an instance of `Bubble`:

```
Sphere sphere = new Sphere();
Bubble bubble = new Bubble();
```

Notice that we are following the usual Java convention of giving classes a name that begins with a capital letter, and giving objects names that begin with a lower-case letter.

We can display the two objects as follows:

```
sphere.display();
bubble.display();
```

In each case the appropriate version of `display` is invoked. There are two methods with the same name (`display`), but they are different. The Java system makes sure that the correct one is selected. The Java system knows which class every object belongs to because the class is specified when an object is created. Java keeps a record of which class every object belongs to and always selects the method associated with the class of the object. So when `display` is invoked for the object `sphere`, it is the method defined within the class `Sphere` that is invoked. When `display` is invoked for the object `bubble`, it is the method defined within the class `Bubble` that is invoked. We shall return to this issue later in this chapter.

As a detail we note that it is easily possible to override variables – to declare variables in a subclass that override variables in the superclass. We will not discuss this further for two reasons: one, there is never any need to do this, and two, it is very bad practice. When you subclass a class (inherit from it) you only ever:

- add additional methods;
- add additional variables;
- override methods.

● Scope rules (visibility)

We have seen how variables and methods are encapsulated within objects and are explicitly labelled `public` or `private`. With inheritance, however, we now have `protected`. The rules are simple:

1. If a variable or method is labelled `public`, it can be referred to by instructions in any subclass (or any class at all). As a rule, all instance variables should be declared as `private`.
2. If a variable or method is labelled `private`, its use is restricted to instructions in the class in which it is declared. As a rule, any methods offering a service to users of a class should be labelled as `public`.
3. Local variables, those declared within a method, are never accessible from outside the particular method.
4. If a variable or method is labelled `protected` it can be used by a subclass of the superclass, but not by a class that merely makes use of the superclass.

● Protected

(Don't read this section unless you are completely happy with the ideas of inheritance.)

In some programs, `private` is just too private and `public` is just too public. If a class needs to give its subclasses access to particular variables or methods, but prevent access from any other classes, it can label them as `protected`. Such an item is accessible to all subclasses. So, in the family analogy, a mother lends out her car keys to her descendants but not to anyone else.

Here is an example to illustrate the use of `protected`. Suppose that a class represents a graphical object such as a circle. The circle is described by three integers:

```
int x, y, radius;
```

where `x` and `y` are the coordinates of the top left of a bounding rectangle. Remembering the principles of information hiding, we would probably decide to label these variables as `private`, so that they can only be accessed from within the class:

```
private int x, y, radius;
```

This is a sound decision, but there may be a better idea. It might be that someone later writes a class that extends this class by providing a method to calculate the area of the circle. This method will need access to the variable `radius` – which is unfortunately inaccessible because it has been labelled `private`. So to anticipate this possible future use, we might instead decide to label this variable as `protected`. Similarly, it might be that some subclass might need access to the *x*- and *y*-coordinates of the circle – perhaps to check whether the circle has collided with some other object. So again, it might be wise to describe these variables as `protected`:

```
protected int x, y, radius;
```

This declaration now protects these variables against possible misuse by any arbitrary classes, but permits access by certain privileged classes – the subclasses.

Suppose we had declared these variables as `private`, as originally planned. The consequence is that it would have been impossible to reuse the class as described. The only option would be to edit the class, replacing the description `private` by `protected` for these particular items. But this violates one of the principles of object-oriented programming, which is never to alter an existing class which is tried and tested. So when we write a class we strive to think ahead about possible future users of the class. The programmer who writes a class always writes it in the hope that someone will reuse the class by extending it. This is another of the principles of object-oriented programming. Careful use of `protected` instead of `public` or `private` can help make a class more attractive for reuse.

In summary, the three levels of accessibility of a variable or a method in a class are:

1. `public` – accessible from anywhere;
2. `protected` – accessible in this class and in any subclass;
3. `private` – accessible only in this class.

(There is an additional level of access which we will meet when we look at packages in Chapter 26.)

So a class can have good, but controlled, access to its immediate superclass and the superclasses above it in the class hierarchy, just as if the classes are part of the class itself. If we make the family analogy, it is like being able to freely spend your mother's money or that of any of her ancestors – provided that they have put their money in an account labelled `public` or `protected`. People outside the family can only access `public` methods.

● The class hierarchy

A good way to visualize inheritance is by using a *class diagram*, as shown in Figure 11.1. Each class is shown as a rectangle. A class joined to another class by an arrowed line is a subclass. A class like `Sphere`, which has no explicit superclass, is a subclass of the class `Object`. This class is at the top of the class tree for all Java classes. Every class (in the library or written by the programmer) fits within a class hierarchy. If you write a class beginning with the heading:

```
class Sphere
```

it implicitly resides immediately beneath class `Object`.

Figure 11.2 shows another class diagram in which another class, called `Orb`, is also a subclass of `Sphere`. The diagram is now a tree structure, with the root of the tree, `Object`, at the top. In computer science, trees grow upside down with a single root at the top and the branches dangling down below. This is like a family tree, except that it only shows one parent.

If you write a new class that begins like this:

```
class MyClass extends ClassX
```

then the new class resides immediately beneath `ClassX` in the tree. As we have seen, `MyClass` is called the *subclass* of `ClassX`. `ClassX` is called the *superclass* of `MyClass`.

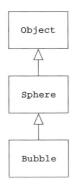

Figure 11.1 Class diagram for classes `Sphere` and `Bubble`.

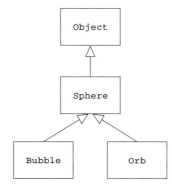

Figure 11.2 Class diagram showing a tree structure.

As the class `Bubble` shows, a class often has a superclass, which in turn has a super-class, and so on up the inheritance tree. It is not only the `public` and `protected` items in the immediate superclass that are inherited, but all the `public` and `protected` variables and methods in all of the superclasses up the inheritance tree. So you inherit from your mother, your grandmother and so on.

The Java language allows a class to inherit from only one immediate superclass. This is called single inheritance. In the family analogy it means that you can inherit from your mother but not from your father.

SELF-TEST QUESTIONS
....

11.1 A balloon is like a bubble, but with some colour. Write a new class named `Balloon` that extends `Bubble` to provide a colour which can be set when the balloon is created. This is accomplished using a constructor method, so that your class should enable the following to be written:

```
Balloon balloon = new Balloon(Color.red);
```

Draw the new class hierarchy diagram showing the relationship between the classes `Sphere`, `Bubble` and `Balloon`.

11.2 Although a balloon can only move up and down, a ball can move horizontally as well. Write a class called `Ball` which extends the class `Balloon` by allowing an object to move in the *y*-direction by providing a method `changeY`.

Suppose we create an object `balloon` from the class `Balloon`:

```
Balloon balloon = new Balloon();
```

What happens if we make this invocation?

```
balloon.setRadius(200);
```

Now `balloon` is an object of the class `Balloon` but the method `setRadius` is a method of a different class `Bubble`. The answer is that all the methods labelled `public` (and `protected`) within the immediate superclass (and all the superclasses in the class hierarchy) are available to a subclass. And since `Balloon` is a subclass of `Bubble`, `setRadius` is available to objects of class `Balloon`.

The rule is that when a method is invoked, the Java system first looks in the class description of the object to find the method. If it cannot find it there, it looks in the class description of the immediate superclass. If it cannot find it there, it looks at the class description for the superclass of the superclass, and so on up the class hierarchy until it finds a method with the required name. In the family analogy, you implicitly inherit from your grandmother, your great grandmother and so on.

● Restricting functionality using inheritance

Extending a class will always mean providing additional variables and/or methods, but these additions may not always extend the functionality – they may restrict it. Take the balloon for example. We will create a class `PoolBall` in which we restrict the movements of a ball to a rectangle on the screen, corresponding to the cushions bordering a pool table. The methods that provide this functionality in the subclass restrict movement that is allowed in the superclass. Here is the code assuming that an object of the class `PoolBall` is restricted to the rectangle 100, 100 (top left *x*- and *y*-coordinates) to 200, 300 (bottom right *x*- and *y*-coordinates):

```
class PoolBall extends Ball {

    public void setX(int newX) {
        if ((newX >= 100) && (newX <= 200))
            x = newX;
    }

    public void setY(int newY) {
        if ((newY >= 100) && (newY <= 300))
            y = newY;
    }
}
```

SELF-TEST QUESTION
....

11.3 Draw the class hierarchy chart showing where `PoolBall` resides in the class hierarchy.

In the human analogy, just because your mother could play the violin does not mean that you can.

● Allowed operations

We have seen how to describe new classes that inherit from, or extend, an existing class. We can then create objects from a new class. But what operations can we carry out on these new objects? We can always assume as a minimum that for every object:

- ● We can create it.
- ● We can use it as a parameter and as a return value.
- ● We can use the methods that are provided as part of its class.
- ● We can use the methods of any of the superclasses above the class in the inheritance tree, provided that they are labelled as public or protected. (This is the whole purpose of inheritance.)
- ● We can assign it to a variable of the same class.

● super

A class will sometimes need to invoke a method in its immediate superclass or one of the classes up the tree. There is no problem with this – the methods in all the classes up the inheritance tree are freely available, provided that they are labelled as public (or protected). The only problem that can arise is when the desired method in the superclass has the same name as a method in the current class. To fix this problem, the subclass prefixes the method name with the word super. For example, Balloon has a variable that represents the colour of a balloon and when a balloon is displayed the colour must be set using setColor. But otherwise the instructions for displaying a balloon are the same as those for displaying a bubble. So the display method in Balloon can use the display method in Bubble as follows:

```
public void display(Grahics g) {
    g.setColor(colour);
    super.display(g);
}
```

Generally this is neater and shorter than duplicating instructions and can help make a program more concise. It can help with making the maximum use of existing methods. (In this particular example, the advantage is marginal.)

You may remember that the Java word this means the current object. Similarly, the word super means the superclass of the current object.

SELF-TEST QUESTION

11.4 There are words for the current object and for the superclass. Why is there no word for the subclass of a class? Hint: how many superclasses does a class have? How many subclasses does a class have?

● Inheriting from library classes

We have already seen in Chapter 9 on objects and classes how most programs make use of the classes that are available in the Java library, like the class `String`. These classes define the data types and all of the operations that can be carried out on them. Frequently programs make explicit use of methods within these classes, such as in:

```
int x;
String s;
s = Integer.toString(x);
```

in which `toString` is a `static` method within the class `Integer`.

We now look at how programs use the library in a different way – by making use of inheritance. Nearly every program in this book uses inheritance. Every program starts with a line like:

```
class MyProg extends Applet
```

This says that the class `MyProg` inherits features from the library class `Applet`. The features in `Applet` include methods for creating graphical user interface (GUI) widgets like buttons and scrollbars. Also provided are the methods to handle the events that arise when these widgets are clicked on with the mouse.

The methods provided by class `Applet` (or one of the classes above it in the inheritance tree) – such as `add`, `repaint` – are simply invoked as and when needed. For example:

```
Button b = new Button("Press Me");
add(b);
```

Methods like `add` are used as if they are methods of the class written by the programmer, but they are in fact `public` methods provided by the superclass `Applet` (or one of the classes above it in the inheritance tree).

Some of the methods provided by `Applet` (or its superclasses) must be overridden by the programmer. These include:

● `init` – the method that is initiated when the program starts to run;
● `paint` – the method invoked to display information on the screen;

Extending the class `Applet` is the main way in which the classes in this book extend the library classes. In a later chapter we shall also see how class `Thread` is extended to carry out multithreading.

● `final`

Inheriting and overriding are all about changing the behaviour of classes and objects. Inheritance is very powerful, but sometimes it is reassuring to have some things fixed and unchanging. For example, it is good to know precisely what `sqrt` does, what `drawString` does and so on. In OO programming there is always a danger that someone will extend the classes that these belong to and thereby change what they do. This could be by error or in a misplaced attempt to be helpful. To prevent this, the programmer can describe a method as `final`. This means that it cannot be overridden. Most of the library methods are described as `final`. This means that whenever you use them you can be completely confident of what they do.

As we have seen from an early stage in this book, variables can also be declared as `final`. This means also that their values cannot be changed. They are constants. For example:

```
final float CmPerInch = 2.54f;
```

declares a variable whose value cannot be altered. Thus the prefix `final` has the same meaning, whether it is attached to a variable or to a method.

A whole class can be described as `final`, which means that it cannot be subclassed. In addition all of its methods are implicitly `final`.

Making a class or a method `final` is a serious decision because it prevents inheritance – one of the power tools of OOP.

● final static

`final` `static` variables are used to declare constants that are used in a number of different classes throughout a program. For example:

```
public class UsefulConstants {
    public final static float C = 3.0E+8f;
    public final static int SCREEN_WIDTH = 640;
}
```

As we saw in Chapter 9, `static` variables are not associated with any specific object. The word `final`, as we have seen, means that the value of the variable cannot be changed – its value is fixed. By convention, variables which are `final` `static` are given names in capitals, with words separated by the underline character. The value of π is available in the library class `Math` as a `final` `static` variable and can be referred to as follows:

```
area = Math.PI * r * r;
```

● Browsing

If you want to use inheritance, you need to know what classes are available in the Java library and what they do. There are two ways to do this. The first way is to look in a book, in a manual or on a Web page to see the specification of available classes. (Appendix B lists some of the most useful library classes.) The other way is to use a program called a browser that helps you see what classes are available and what they do. Very often the code of the classes can be inspected using the browser, so that you can clarify what they do. This makes inheriting easier and more reliable.

● Programming principles

Inheritance is the way in which OO programming provides enormous potential for reusability. Very often programmers reinvent the wheel – they write new software when they could simply make use of existing software. One of the reasons for writing new software is that it is fun. But software is increasingly becoming more complex, so there simply is not enough time to rewrite. Imagine having to write the software to create the GUI components provided by the Java libraries. Imagine having to write a mathematical function like sqrt every time you needed it. It would just take too long. So a good reason for reusing software is to save time. It is not just the time to write the software that you save, it is the time to test it thoroughly – and this can take even longer than actually writing the software.

One reason why programmers sometimes don't reuse software is that the software on offer doesn't do exactly what they need it to do. Maybe it does 90 per cent of what they want, but some crucial bits are missing or some bits do things differently. One approach would be to modify the existing software to match the new needs. This, however, is a dangerous strategy because modifying software is a minefield. Software is not so much soft as brittle – when you try to change it, it breaks. When you change software it is very easy to introduce new and subtle bugs into it, which necessitate extensive debugging and correction. This is a common experience, so much so that programmers are very reluctant to modify software. This is where OO programming comes to the rescue. In an OO program, you can inherit the behaviour of those parts of some software that you need, override those (few) methods that you want to behave differently, and add new methods to do additional things. Often you can inherit most of a class, making only the few changes that are needed using inheritance. You only have to test the new bits, sure in the knowledge that all the rest has been tested before. So the problem of reuse is solved. You can make use of existing software in a safe way. Meanwhile, the original class remains intact, reliable and usable.

This idea of reusing OO software is so powerful that many people think of OO programming entirely in this way. In this view OO programming is the process of extending the library classes so as to meet the requirements of a particular application. OO programming means building on the work of others. The OO programmer proceeds like this:

1. Clarify the requirements of the program.
2. Browse the library for classes that perform the required functions.
3. Extend the library classes as necessary to achieve the desired results.

This is why OO programs are usually much shorter than conventional programs – they consist simply of the extra bits required to extend the library classes. There is a minor downside to this – the programmer needs a very good knowledge of the libraries. However, the learning time is more than compensated by the saving in programming and testing time.

Inheritance provides the facility to design a new class which makes use of an existing class in any of the following ways:

● To add new methods. The subclass defines new methods that are additional to the methods that it inherits. This is the most common way of extending a class.
● To redefine methods. The behaviour of a method (what is does) is changed by overriding it: for example a method to draw a subclass object that looks different from a superclass object.
● To provide different implementations. A method carries out the same function but does it differently: for example using a different lookup algorithm for an object of a particular type.
● To disinherit. The superclass provides some methods that the subclass does not need. (This facility is not provided by Java.)

Programming pitfalls

● Novice programmers use inheritance of the library classes, like `Applet`, from their first program. But learning to use inheritance within your own classes takes time and experience. It usually only becomes worth while in larger programs. Don't worry if you don't use inheritance (except for library classes) for quite some time.
● It is common to confuse overloading and overriding:

  – *Overloading* means writing two or more methods in the same class with the same name (but different parameters).
  – *Overriding* means writing a method in a subclass to be used instead of the method in the superclass (or one of the superclasses above it in the inheritance tree).

New language elements

● `extends` – means that this class extends (inherits from) another named class;
● `super` – the name of the superclass of a class, the class it extends;
● `protected` – the description of a variable or method that is accessible from within the class or any subclass (but not from elsewhere);
● `final` – the description attached to a variable, method or class that cannot be changed in any way (even by overriding).

Summary

● A subclass extends or inherits the facilities of its immediate superclass and all the superclasses above it in the inheritance tree.

● A class has only one immediate superclass. (It can only inherit from one class.) This is called *single inheritance* in the jargon of OOP.

● A class hierarchy diagram is a tree showing the inheritance relationships.

● A class can extend the facilities of an existing class by providing one or more of:

   – additional methods;
   – additional variables;
   – methods that override (act instead of) methods in the superclass.

● Extending (inheriting) the facilities of a class is a good way to make use of existing parts of programs (classes).

● A variable or a method can be described as having one of three types of access:

   – `public` – accessible from any class. Inherited by the subclasses.
   – `private` – accessible only from within this class. Not accessible from subclasses.
   – `protected` – accessible only from within this class and any subclass. Inherited by subclasses. (This is occasionally used by experts for either data or methods.)

● The prefix `final` means that the variable or method cannot be changed (variable) or overridden (method). It is useful for defining constant data items and for ensuring that a method does what it is specified to do. A class can override a method in the superclass (or one of the classes above it in the inheritance tree), but not if the class has labelled the method or variable as `final`. This is to prevent people inadvertently changing the behaviour of vital methods.

● The description `static final` is used to declare constants that are used throughout a program.

● The name of the superclass of a class is referred to by the word `super`.

EXERCISES

11.1 Footballs Write a class `FootBall` that describes an American football. An American football is oval, but otherwise it behaves exactly like a `PoolBall` object. Make maximum use of extending the classes shown in the text.
   Draw a class hierarchy chart to show how the different classes are related.

11.2 Spaceship Write a class `SpaceShip` that describes a spaceship. A spaceship is oval, but otherwise it behaves exactly like a `Ball` object. Make maximum use of extending the classes shown in the text.
   Draw a class hierarchy chart to show how the different classes are related.

11.3 The bank A bank maintains the accounts for a number of customers. The data describing each account consists of the account number, the customer's name and the current balance. Write a class to implement such a bank account. The constructor method should accept as parameters the account number and name. Methods should be provided to deposit an amount of money, to withdraw an amount of money and to get the current balance.

The bank offers its customers two types of account – a checking account and a savings account. A checking account can go overdrawn (the balance can be less than zero) but a savings account cannot. At the end of each month interest is calculated on the amount in a savings account. This interest is added to the balance. Write classes to describe each of these types of account, making maximum use of inheritance. The savings account class should provide a method that is invoked to calculate the interest.

ANSWERS TO SELF-TEST QUESTIONS

11.1
```
public class Balloon extends Bubble {
    private Color color;

    public Balloon(Color newColor) {
        color = newColor;
    }
}
```
Diagram is as follows:

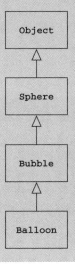

11.2
```
class Ball extends Balloon {

    Ball() {
        super(Color.red);
    }

    public void changeY(int change) {
        y = y + change;
    }
}
```

11.3 Diagram is as follows:

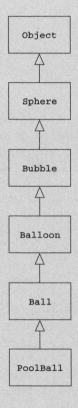

11.4 A class can have many subclasses – one or more classes that inherit from it. So it would be ambiguous to have a Java language word for subclass.

Calculations

Introduction

We have already seen in Chapter 4 how to carry out simple calculations. This chapter is about more serious calculations. It enhances the earlier explanation and brings together all the information you need to write programs that carry out calculations. If you are not interested in programs that do calculations, skip this chapter.

Calculations arise in many programs – not just programs that carry out mathematical, scientific or engineering calculations. In information systems, calculations arise in payrolls, accountancy and forecasting. In graphics, calculations are necessary to scale and move images on the screen.

Integer types

As we saw in Chapter 4, integers are held exactly in a computer; this can be very important. The snag is that the range of numbers that can be held in an integer variable is limited, though as you can see from the table below it is plenty big enough for many things.

The most common use for integers in programs is probably as counters in `for` loops and as the subscripts in arrays (see the later chapters on arrays). But there are, of course, many other uses – for example, the length of a string, a font size, the pixel coordinates on the screen, an annual salary or a product number.

If an integer is the right kind of way to represent some data then the next choice is between the different types of integer. The four different types offer sizes of number as follows:

Type	Size	Minimum value	Maximum value
byte	8 bits	−128	127
short	16 bits	−32768	32767
int	32 bits	−2147483648	2147483647
long	64 bits	−9223372036854775808	9223372036854775807

The range of floating-point numbers that can be held is much greater than for integers. The range of values is huge, as you can see from the table below. The snag with floating-point numbers is that they are only represented to a particular degree of accuracy – a number of digits of precision. The accuracies or precisions are given in the table below.

Type	Size	Largest value	Smallest value	Precision
float	32 bits	±3.4E+38	±1.4E−45	6–7 significant figures
double	64 bits	±1.79E+308	±4.94E−324	14–15 significant figures

For floats, the space available for the value of a number is 24 bits, which equates to space available for a little over six significant figures. For a double, the precision amounts to a little over 14 significant figures. In each case, the exact precision depends on the value of the number being represented.

The only reason for knowing the size of numbers in bits is to get some idea of how much space they take up in computer memory. A double is clearly twice the length of a float, hence the name. Worrying about the space taken up is not usually an issue unless you have lots of variables – for example, if you have a large array of numbers (see Chapter 13).

● Declaration and assignment

Integers and floating-point numbers are declared as shown in the following examples:

```
int salary;
float length;
```

A variable can be given a value in an assignment statement:

```
salary = 100000;
length = 12.34f;
```

As we saw in an earlier chapter, you can also both declare a variable and give it an initial value at the same time:

```
int salary = 100000;
float length = 12.34f;
```

A value like 12.34 is named a *literal* in the jargon of programming languages.

A floating-point literal can either have the decimal point in it, or not. It is usually advisable to follow a floating-point literal with an f or F (for float) or a d or D (for double) to describe how big the number is.

If a value like 12.34 is used in a Java program, it is assumed by the compiler to be a double value. If you leave out the letter F or D, Java assumes that you are defining a double. If, therefore, you want a value to represent a float, it has to be written explicitly as 12.34f or 12.34F. Java is very careful about the different types of data, so that if you write:

```
float x = 10.0; // error
```

the compiler will complain that you are trying to place a double value (10.0) into a float variable. Therefore a good way to remedy this is to write:

```
float x = 10.0f;
```

Extremely big or small floating-point literals can be written using E-notation:

● 0.0001f is the same as .0001f, .0001F, 1.0e-4f, 1.0e-4F, 0.f
● 10000000.d is the same as 1e7d, 1.0e7d, 1.0e7D

So for example E4 means $\times 10^4$.

SELF-TEST QUESTION

12.1 Write these quantities as float literals:

3 000 000

-1.0×10^5

0.635×10^{-4}

Write these quantities as double literals:

5 000 000 000

$-0.000\ 000\ 56$

● Input–output

A convenient way to input integer numbers is from a text field, as introduced in Chapter 7. The input must be converted from the input string to the computer's internal representation using the library methods `Integer.parseInt or Long.parseLong`, as in:

```
int number = Integer.parseInt(inputField.getText());
```

where `inputField` is the name of the text field object.

Inputting a floating-point number from a text field is similar, using the library method `parseFloat` as follows:

```
float value = Float.parseFloat(inputField.getText());
```

where `inputField` is the name of the text field. The user can enter the number in any of several formats, for example:

```
123.45
.006
1.234e2
1.234E3
1901
```

and as the example illustrates, a number can be entered as an integer (which is converted into the internal floating-point representation).

If it is necessary to enter a double-precision floating-point number, then a similar method `parseDouble` is available.

Numbers can be output to the window using the library function `drawString`. If you do this then either you need to use the string concatenation operator `+` like this:

```
g.drawString("Here is the answer" + number, 10, 10);
```

or else explicitly convert the number to a string like this:

```
g.drawString(toString(number), 10, 10);
```

We will see a complete example involving the input and output of numbers later in this chapter.

● Operator precedence

As we saw in Chapter 4, operators follow precedence rules, which say that some operators have higher importance (precedence) than others. Thus:

- ● `*`, `/`, `%` have highest precedence and are done first;
- ● `+`, `-` have lowest precedence and are done last.

Thus `3/4+1` actually means `(3/4)+1`.

If two operators have equal precedence, then the expression is calculated left-to-right. Thus `3/4*2` means `(3/4)*2`.

SELF-TEST QUESTION

12.2 What do these mean? Put brackets in to confirm their meanings:

```
2 + 3 + 4
2 - 3 + 4
2 * 3 / 4
2 / 3 * 4
1 + 2 * 3 + 4 / 5 - 6 * 7 + 8
a * b + c - d / e
```

● Library mathematical functions

It is very common in mathematical, scientific or engineering programs to use certain functions like sine, cosine and log. In Java, these are provided in one of the libraries – the maths library. To use one of the functions, you do not need an `import` statement at the head of the program, but you do have to precede the method name with the word `Math.` like this:

```
x = Math.sqrt(y);
```

which calculates the square root of the parameter `y`.

Some of the more widely used functions in the mathematics in the Java library are given below. The parameters must be floating-point numbers.

`cos(x)`	cosine of the angle `x`, where `x` is expressed in radians
`sin(x)`	sine of the angle `x`, expressed in radians
`tan(x)`	tangent of the angle `x`, expressed in radians
`abs(x)`	the absolute value of `x`, sometimes written $\lvert x \rvert$ in mathematics
`min(x, y)`	the smaller of `x` and `y`
`max(x, y)`	the larger of `x` and `y`
`round(x)`	rounds a float to the nearest integer
`log(x)`	natural logarithm of `x` (to the base e)
`random()`	provides a pseudo-random number in the range 0.0 to 1.0
`sqrt(x)`	the positive square root of `x`
`pow(x, y)`	`x` raised to the power of `y`, or x^y
`exp(x)`	e^x

When you use these methods, you have to be careful (as ever) about the type of the variables or literals used as parameters. For example, the method `abs` can be passed an `int`, `long`, `float` or `double`. But the method `cos` can only be passed a `double`. Appendix B specifies the valid parameters and return values.

In addition to these functions, the mathematical constants π and e are available as constants in the maths library and can be referred to as `Math.PI` and `Math.E` (both in upper-case).

The maths library also provides a method named `Math.random` that provides a pseudo-random number, a double with a random value between 0.0 and 1.0. There is also a separate more comprehensive collection of random number methods in another library named `java.util`.

A selection of mathematical library functions is listed for reference in Appendix B.

● Constants

Constants are values that don't change while the program is running. We have already met two, `E` and `PI`, that are already provided for use in the maths library. But it is often the case that there are other values in a program that will not change. Examples could be the conversion factor for Celsius to Fahrenheit temperature conversion, the velocity of light or the acceleration due to gravity. One approach is to write the values for these quantities directly into the program, like this:

```
energy = mass * height * 9.8f;
```

Another better approach is to declare such numbers as variables that have a constant value and give them a name, for example:

```
final float g = 9.8f;
```

(`g` is the usual symbol for the acceleration due to gravity.) A variable declared like this cannot be changed (by an assignment for example) when the program runs. In fact the compiler will reject any attempt made to give such a variable a new value. The word `final` conveys that the value of the variable is finalized. (The judge's decision is final.) We can then use the name in the calculation:

```
energy = mass * height * g;
```

This is clearer because we are using the programming language to explain what we are doing, rather than using unexplained numbers. If we need to change the program or the value of `g` (if we go to the Moon where its value is smaller), it is easy to see what to change.

● Comparison

`if` statements are commonly used in programs that do calculations. Here we will simply illustrate their use by writing the method `abs`, which gives the absolute value of its parameter. (This method is actually provided in the maths library.)

```
public float abs(int a) {
    if (a > 0)
        return a;
    else
        return -a;
}
```

● Iteration

It is quite common in numerical programming to write iterations – loops that continue searching for a solution to an equation until the solution is found to sufficient accuracy.

As an example of using iteration, there is a formula for the sine of an angle:

$$\sin(x) = x - x^3/3! + x^5/5! - x^7/7! + \ldots$$

(If we need the sine of an angle in a program, we don't need to use this formula, because sine is available as a standard function.)

We can see that each term is derived from the previous term by multiplying by:

$$-x^2/(n+1) \times (n+2)$$

so we can construct a loop that iterates until the new term is less than some acceptable figure, say 0.0001.

```
float sin, x, term;

sin = 0.0f;
term = x;
n = 1;
while (Math.abs(term) >= 0.0001f) {
    sin = sin + term;
    term = -term*x*x/((n+1)*(n+2));
    n = n + 2;
}
```

in which the library method `abs` (mentioned above) calculates the absolute value of its parameter.

● Mixing data types and casting

Java distinguishes carefully between integer and floating-point numbers. It also distinguishes between the various types of integers and floating points. It is common to write expressions that mix the different types of data, for example:

```
float value1, value2, average;

average = (value1+value2)/2;
```

This particular case is perfectly OK and will work as expected, as we shall see below. This is called a mixed-type expression because it contains a mixture of `float` variables and an integer value.

The rule for mixed-type expressions is as follows:

the type of each value is converted to the type of the higher type in the expression

For this purpose, the hierarchy of types is:

```
double   highest type
float
long
int
short
byte     lowest type
```

Thus in the above, `value1 + value2` is carried out as a `float` operation. The subsequent division is also carried out as a `float` operation.

Remember that if you use a floating-point literal like `123.45`, it is regarded by Java as a `double`. If you want it to be a `float`, it has to be written as `123.45f`. Thus in:

```
float f;
f = f * 123.45;
```

the multiplication is carried out as a `double` operation. The compiler will issue an error message because the statement is asking to place a `double` value into a `float` variable.

SELF-TEST QUESTION
••••••••••••••••••••••••••

12.4 Work out the types that all stages of this calculation are carried out in:

```
int i, j;
float f, g;
double d, e;

d = (i + j) * (f + g) * (d + e) * (i + f) * (f + d);
```

What about the assignment of the result of a calculation to a variable? This is fine if the type of the receiver is equal to or bigger than the result. For example:

```
int i;
float f = i;
```

This is valid. It is called *implicit* conversion. It works because a `float` of 32 bits can always represent any 32 bit `int`. Look at the table of ranges of values given above to check that this is so. Notice, though, that this conversion may result in some loss of precision of the number. But if the size of the receiving type is too small for the result, then the compiler will not allow the conversion. For example, in:

```
float x;
int i = x;
```

the assignment will be flagged as an error by the compiler. In a case like this it is necessary to perform *casting* with the use of a cast operator like this:

```
int i = (int) x;
```

Here `int`, in brackets, is the cast operator that converts its parameter (the expression that follows) to an integer. Casting means explicitly converting one data type to another. All of the numeric types (`byte`, `short`, `int`, `long`, `float`, `double`) can be used as cast operators in this way. These operators look a little strange at first because we have grown used to seeing brackets enclosing parameters, rather than an operator.

Java gives us the freedom to convert data types from a lower position in the hierarchy to a higher position. It is always necessary to specify casting of a type that is higher in the hierarchy to a type lower in the hierarchy. (The compiler gives an error if you don't.) This is to force the programmer to be aware that information may be lost in the process.

Casting does the best it can in converting one value into another. In particular, when a floating-point number is converted into an integer the fractional part is lost by truncating it (chopping it off). Thus `(int)3.7` is 3.

The conclusion is that if you want to be completely explicit and deliberate in converting from one type to another, use casting. Where appropriate the compiler will remind you that you must be more explicit.

● Case study – money

We will now trace the development of a program to do calculations with money. In most countries, money comes in two parts – dollars and cents, pounds and pence, francs and centimes. We have a choice – we can represent an amount of money either as a float (like 20.25 dollars) or as an integer (2025 cents). If we use cents, we will have to convert amounts into dollars and cents and vice versa. We will opt to use `float` variables to represent values.

We will construct a program that calculates compound interest. An amount is invested at a particular annual interest rate and accumulates in value. The user enters the initial amount (an integer) and an interest rate (a floating-point number) into text fields. The user then clicks on a button to see the amount accumulate each year, as shown in Figure 12.1. We start by declaring the main quantities:

```
float interestRate;
float oldAmount, newAmount;
```

When the user enters the initial amount (an integer) and the interest rate (a floating-point number) into the text fields, we extract the values in the way that we have seen before.

Figure 12.1 Screen display of interest calculation.

When the button is pressed to move on to the next year, the program must calculate:

```
newAmount = oldAmount + (oldAmount * interestRate / 100.0f);
```

Before displaying the new amount, we need to make sure that the value is a whole number of dollars and cents, so that if the value is 127.2341 dollars for example, we need to convert it to 127 dollars and 23 cents.

First the dollar part. Simple use of the cast operator (int) converts the floating-point number to an integer, truncating the fractional part:

```
dollars = (int)newAmount;
```

Next the cents part. We need to get rid of the dollars part of the number. We can do this by subtracting the whole number of dollars so that a number like 127.2341 will become 0.2341. Now multiply by 100.0 to convert to cents, so that 0.2341 becomes 23.41. Finally use Math.round to convert to the nearest integer (23):

```
cents = Math.round(100.0 * (newAmount - dollars));
```

We can now display the values properly converted. Finally,

```
oldAmount = newAmount;
```

which is what investment is all about.

The complete program follows and the screen is shown in Figure 12.1. You can key in an amount and an interest rate in the text fields, each followed by the enter key. You can click on the button to make a year go by.

The program consists of two classes. First is the user interface class. It creates a button and two text fields. It handles the events when these are used.

```
import java.awt.*;
import java.applet.Applet;
import java.awt.event.*;
```

```
public class Accumulate extends Applet
    implements ActionListener {

    private Button year;
    private TextField interestField, amountField, outcome;
    private Investment myMoney;

    public void init() {
        Label amountLabel = new Label("Enter amount:");
        add(amountLabel);

        amountField = new TextField(8);
        add(amountField);
        amountField.addActionListener(this);

        Label rateLabel = new Label("Enter interest rate");
        add(rateLabel);

        interestField = new TextField(4);
        add(interestField);
        interestField.addActionListener(this);

        year = new Button ("Another Year");
        add(year);
        year.addActionListener(this);

        Label outcomeLabel = new Label
                    ("Your money at the end of the year is");
        add(outcomeLabel);

        outcome = new TextField(20);
        add(outcome);

        myMoney = new Investment();
    }

    public void actionPerformed(ActionEvent event) {
        if (event.getSource() == amountField) {
            float amount = Integer.parseInt(amountField.getText());
            myMoney.setInitialAmount(amount);
        }
        if (event.getSource() == interestField) {
            float rate = Float.parseFloat(interestField.getText());
            myMoney.setRate(rate);
        }
```

```
            if (event.getSource() == year) {
                myMoney.anotherYear();
                float newAmount = myMoney.getNewAmount();
                int dollars = (int) newAmount;
                int cents = Math.round(100.0f * (newAmount - dollars));
                outcome.setText(dollars + " dollars " + cents + " cents");
            }
        }
    }
```

Next is the class that maintains the numbers. When the user enters a new rate and a new
amount into the text fields, it is invoked to alter them. Then, whenever the button is
pressed to make a year go by, it is invoked to calculate the accumulated amount.

```
    class Investment {

        private float interestRate;
        private float oldAmount, newAmount;

        public void setInitialAmount(float amount) {
            oldAmount = amount;
        }

        public void setRate(float rate) {
            interestRate = rate;
        }

        public void anotherYear() {
            newAmount = oldAmount + (oldAmount * interestRate / 100.0f);
            oldAmount = newAmount;
        }

        public float getNewAmount() {
            return newAmount;
        }
    }
```

● Graphs

It is common to present mathematical, engineering and financial information graphically. We will now look at a program to draw mathematical functions. Suppose we want
to draw the function:

$$y = ax^3 + bx^2 + cx + d$$

with values for a, b, c, and d input via scrollbars as in Figure 12.2.

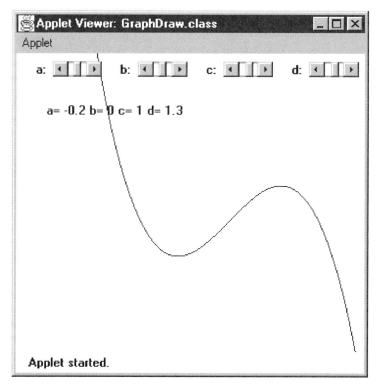

Figure 12.2 Screen of the graph drawer program, with cubic function displayed.

We must resolve several design issues. First we want to see the graph with the *y* coordinate going up the screen, whereas *y* pixel coordinates measure downwards. We will distinguish between *x* and its equivalent pixel coordinate `xPixel`, and between *y* and `yPixel`.

Next we have to ensure that the graph will fit conveniently on the screen, that it is not too small to see or too big to fit. Solving this problem is called scaling. We will assume that the available area on the screen is 400 pixels in the *x* direction and 400 pixels in the *y* direction. We will design the program to display *x* and *y* values in the range −5.0 to +5.0. So 1 unit of *x* (or *y*) is 40 pixels.

Finally, since we will be using `drawLine` to draw the graph, we will have to draw a curved shape as a large number of small lines. We will move along the *x* direction, one pixel at a time, drawing a line from the equivalent *y* coordinate to the next. For each *x* pixel, the program:

1. calculates the *x* value from the *x* pixel value;
2. calculates the *y* value, the value of the function of *x*;
3. calculates the *y* pixel value from the *y* value;

using the following statements:

```
x = scaleX(xPixel);
y = theFunction(x, a, b, c, d);
yPixel = scaleY(y);
```

The program then goes on to the next *x* pixel and again calculates the equivalent *y* pixel:

```
nextXPixel = xPixel + 1;
nextX = scaleX(nextXPixel);
nextY = theFunction(nextX, a, b, c, d);
nextYpixel = scaleY(nextY);
```

Finally the small section of the curve is drawn:

```
g.drawLine(xPixel, yPixel, nextXPixel, nextYPixel);
```

You will see that the program uses several private methods to help simplify the logic.
  Here is the complete code for this graph-drawing program. The screen display is shown in Figure 12.2. Once again the program consists of two classes – one to act as the user interface and one to calculate and display the data.

```
import java.awt.*;
import java.applet.Applet;
import java.awt.event.*;


public class GraphDraw extends Applet implements AdjustmentListener {

    private Graph myGraph;
    private Scrollbar aScrollbar, bScrollbar, cScrollbar, dScrollbar;

    public void init() {
        myGraph = new Graph();

        Label aLabel = new Label("a:");
        add(aLabel);
        aScrollbar = new Scrollbar(Scrollbar.HORIZONTAL,
            50, 10, 0, 100);
        add(aScrollbar);
        aScrollbar.addAdjustmentListener(this);
        Label bLabel = new Label("b:");
        add(bLabel);
        bScrollbar = new Scrollbar(Scrollbar.HORIZONTAL,
            50, 10, 0, 100);
        add(bScrollbar);
        bScrollbar.addAdjustmentListener(this);
        Label cLabel = new Label("c:");
```

```
        add(cLabel);
        cScrollbar = new Scrollbar(Scrollbar.HORIZONTAL,
            50, 10, 0, 100);
        add(cScrollbar);
        cScrollbar.addAdjustmentListener(this);
        Label dLabel = new Label("d:");
        add(dLabel);
        dScrollbar = new Scrollbar(Scrollbar.HORIZONTAL,
            50, 10, 0, 100);
        add(dScrollbar);
        dScrollbar.addAdjustmentListener(this);
    }


    public void adjustmentValueChanged(AdjustmentEvent event) {
            int aValue = aScrollbar.getValue();
            int bValue = bScrollbar.getValue();
            int cValue = cScrollbar.getValue();
            int dValue = dScrollbar.getValue();
            myGraph.setParameters(aValue, bValue, cValue, dValue);
            repaint();
    }


    public void paint(Graphics g) {
        myGraph.draw(g);
    }
}


class Graph {

    private final int xPixelStart = 10, xPixelEnd = 410, xOrigin = 215;
    private final int yPixelStart = 10, yPixelEnd = 410, yOrigin = 215;
    private final float xStart = -5.0f, xEnd = 5.0f;
    private final float yStart = -5.0f, yEnd = 5.0f;
            private final float scale = (xPixelEnd - xPixelStart) /
                                        (xEnd - xStart);

        private float a, b, c, d;

        private float theFunction(float x, float a,
                float b, float c, float d) {
            return a*x*x*x + b*x*x + c*x+d;
        }
```

```
private float scaleX(int xPixel) {
    float value = (xPixel - xOrigin) / scale;
    return value;
}

private int scaleY(float y) {
    int pixelCoord;
    pixelCoord = Math.round(-y * scale) + yOrigin;
    return pixelCoord;
}

public void setParameters(
    int aValue, int bValue, int cValue, int dValue) {
    a = scale(aValue);
    b = scale(bValue);
    c = scale(cValue);
    d = scale(dValue);
}

private float scale(int coefficient) {
    return ((coefficient - 50) / 10.0f);
}

public void draw(Graphics g) {
    float x, y, nextX, nextY;
    int xPixel, yPixel, nextXPixel, nextYPixel;

    g.drawString("a= "+a+" b= "+b+" c= "+c+" d= "+d, 30, 60);

    for(xPixel = xPixelStart; xPixel < xPixelEnd; xPixel++) {
        x = scaleX(xPixel);
        y = theFunction(x, a, b, c, d);
        yPixel = scaleY(y);
    nextXPixel = xPixel + 1;

        nextX = scaleX(nextXPixel);
        nextY = theFunction(nextX, a, b, c, d);
        nextYPixel = scaleY(nextY);

        g.drawLine(xPixel, yPixel, nextXPixel, nextYPixel);
    }
}
}
}
```

If you run this program you can alter the scrollbar values to see the effect of changing the parameters. You can also draw quadratics (by making the coefficient a equal to zero) and straight lines, of course.

Incidentally, there is a small comment to be made about the event handling in this program. The method valueChanged is invoked whenever any of the four scrollbars is changed. But, as written, the method simply looks up the values of all the four scrollbars. It would be easily possible to write a series of nested if statements in order to ascertain which particular scrollbar had changed, but the solution adopted is cleaner and no less efficient.

SELF-TEST QUESTIONS

12.5 Add code to prevent the program drawing the graph outside the designated area.

12.6 Change the function to one of your choosing. (How about the sine function?)

● Exceptions

If you are reading this chapter for the first time, you should probably skip this section, because it deals with things that don't happen very often.

When you write a program that does calculations you have to watch out that you don't exceed the size of numbers that are allowed. It is not like doing a calculation on a piece of paper, where numbers can get as big as you like – it is more like using a calculator, which has a definite upper limit on the size of numbers that it will hold.

So if for example you declare an integer:

```
short number;
```

you must be aware that the biggest number that can be held in a short is 32767. Then if you write this:

```
number = 32767;
number = number + 32767;
```

the variable will not accommodate the result. This is called *overflow*. It can happen much more subtly than this, of course, particularly when data is being entered from the keyboard and its size is less predictable.

You can see that even with a simple calculation that looks quite harmless, vigilance is required.

Another similar thing that can happen is that the program inadvertently divides some number by zero, or tries to. The computer cannot represent numbers above a certain size, let alone infinity. Again, this is likely to arise in the middle of what may be a lengthy calculation and so may not be obvious. As an example it could arise in the calculation of the roots of a quadratic $ax^2 + bx + c = 0$, discussed above, if the value of the first coefficient a happened to be zero:

```
root1 = (- b + Math.sqrt(d)) / (2.0f * a);
```

Integers

With integers, exceptional situations like division by zero cause what is called an *exception* (see below) and the program will terminate abruptly unless something is done about it.

The circumstances and outcomes of these unusual situations are shown in the following table:

Operator	Circumstance	Default action
+ - *	Result too big	Continue, result is reduced to fit space
/ %	Divide by zero	Exception is raised, program stops

With integer arithmetic, there are several ways to deal with this type of situation:

● Ignore it, hope it will not happen, and be prepared for the program to crash and/or give strange results when it does. This is OK for novice programs, but may be less than ideal for real programs designed to be robust.
● Plan so that it will not arise by careful selection of data type (byte, short, int, long), screening any input and scrutinizing the calculations that are to be carried out.
● Allow the exception to arise but change the default action by writing an exception handler as described later in Chapter 16.

Floating point

With floating-point calculations, whatever happens, the program continues relentlessly, no exception arises and the program will not crash. This is called *non-stop arithmetic*. However, these situations do not pass without note. For example, division by zero causes the answer to have a special value, a constant called POSITIVE_INFINITY or NEGATIVE_INFINITY. The program can test a value to see whether this has happened using the library method isInfinite like this:

```
if (root1.isInfinite()) etc.
```

Another status that can arise, for example by dividing zero by zero, is the intriguingly-named Not-a-Number (NaN), which again can be tested for using a library method isNaN.

The table below lists the circumstances and the outcomes of unusual floating-point arithmetic.

x	y	Result of x/y	Result of $x\%y$
finite	±0.0	±infinity	NaN
finite	±infinity	±0.0	x
±0.0	±0.0	NaN	NaN
±infinity	finite	±infinity	NaN
±infinity	±infinity	NaN	NaN

With floating-point arithmetic, there are several ways to deal with this type of situation:

● Ignore it, hope it will not happen, and be prepared for the program to give strange results when it does. This may be less than ideal.
● Plan so that it will not arise by careful selection of variable types (`float` or `double`), screening any input data, and the calculations that are to be carried out.
● Allow it to happen, but then carry out a test on the result to see whether it has become infinite or Not-a-Number, as shown above.
● Avoid it by writing in checks to ensure that such a situation is prevented. For example, in the quadratic, write:

```
if (a == 0)
    g.drawString("No Roots", 10, 10);
```

(But see below.)

This last solution is not really safe enough, because the value of a could be non-zero but still small enough to cause overflow. So a safer preventative measure is to write:

```
if (Math.abs(a) < 0.1E-20f)
    g.drawString("No Roots", 10, 10);
```

The use of `parseInt` and `parseFloat` to convert input strings to numbers can also cause exceptions when the characters that are input are not part of valid numbers. We shall see how to deal with this in Chapter 16 on exceptions.

Programming pitfalls

● Writing:

```
float x = 10.0;
```

will give a compilation error, because the literal 10.0 is assumed by the compiler to be a `double` and an attempt is being made to place a `double` value into a `float` variable. This could instead be written:

```
float x = 10.0f;
```

● Integer division can lead to strange results for the unwary, because it truncates the result. For example, 3/5 is zero.

● Either learn the operator precedence rules or else (probably better) put brackets into expressions to make them clear. For example, `(a+b)*(c+d)` is clear; `a+b*c+d` is less clear (and means something else).
● Mixing different types in an assignment needs care.
● Exceptional situations such as trying to divide by zero can lead to strange results or else the program terminating. Make your programs robust.

Programming principles

● Many programs in science, engineering, mathematics and statistics employ lots of calculations. But even small programs that might not obviously need to do computations often use some arithmetic.
● The first and key step is deciding what types of variable to use to represent the data. The main choice is between integer and floating point.
● It is common to use iteration in numerical computation as the solution converges towards the answer.
● The library of mathematical functions is invaluable in programs of this type.
● Exceptional situations, like overflow, can arise during calculations and should be anticipated if the program is to work robustly in all circumstances.

Summary

● Numbers can be represented as either integers or floating point. These provide different ranges and precision.

● Input, output, calculations, comparisons and loops are all readily possible and widely used.

● Library functions provide the common mathematical functions, e.g. sine.

EXERCISES

12.1 **Calculate area** Write a program to input two numbers using text fields, representing the measurements (length and breadth) of a room, and display the area of the room.

12.2 **Cost of phone call** A phone call costs 10 cents per minute. Write a program that inputs the duration of a phone call, expressed in hours, minutes and seconds, and displays the cost of the phone call in cents.

12.3 **Measurement conversion** Write a program to input a measurement expressed in feet and inches and convert the measurement to centimetres.
There are 12 inches in a foot. One inch is 2.54 centimetres.

12.4 **Cash register** Write a program that represents a cash register. Amounts of money can be entered into a text field and are automatically added to the running total. The running total is displayed. A button allows the sum to be cleared (made zero).

12.5 **Sum of integers** The sum of the integers from 1 to n is given by the formula:

sum = $n(n + 1)/2$

Write a program that inputs a value for n from a text field and calculates the sum two ways – first by using the formula and second by adding up the numbers using a loop.

12.6 **Random numbers** Random numbers are often used in computational and simulation programs, the so-called Monte Carlo methods. The maths library has a method named `random`, which when invoked returns a pseudo-random float number in the range 0.0 to 1.0. For example:

```
float r;
r = Math.random();
```

Write a program to check out the random number generator method, either by writing a loop that repeatedly invokes the method and displays the value or by creating a button that when pressed displays the next random number.

12.7 **Series for e** The value of e^x can be calculated by summing the series:

$e^x = 1 + x + x^2/2! + x^3/3! + \ldots$

Write a program to input a value of x from a text field and calculate e^x to a desired degree of accuracy. Check the value against the value obtained by referring to the constant E in the maths library.

12.8 **Tax calculation** Write a program that carries out a tax calculation. The tax is zero on the first £10 000, but is 33 percent on any amount over that amount. Write the program to input a salary in £s from a text field and calculate the tax payable. Watch out for errors when you perform the calculation – the answer needs to be accurate to the nearest penny!

12.9 **Area of triangle** The area of a triangle with sides of length a, b, c is:

area = $\sqrt{s(s - a)(s - b)(s - c)}$

where

$s = (a + b + c)/2$

Write a program that inputs the three values for the sides of a triangle and uses this formula to calculate the area. Your program should first check that the three lengths specified do indeed form a triangle. So, for example, $a + b$ must be greater than c.

12.10 Square root The square root of a number can be calculated iteratively as shown below. Write a program to do this for a number input using a text field.

● The first approximation to the square root of x is $x/2$.
● Then successive approximations are given by the formula:

nextApproximation = (lastApproximation + (x/lastApproximation))/2

Check the value against that obtained by using the library method sqrt.

12.11 Mathematical calculator Write a program that acts as a mathematical calculator. It provides buttons with which to enter numbers, which are displayed like the display on a desk calculator. Buttons are also provided to carry out standard mathematical calculations like sine, cosine, In (natural log) and square root.

12.12 Interest calculator Rewrite the calculation part of the program in the text so as to use an integer number (instead of a floating-point number) to represent an amount of money (expressed in cents).

Alter the program so that it displays the information as a table, showing the initial investment and then the year-on-year amount, for six years, as shown in Figure 12.3. One way to make this change is to use the object-oriented features of Java so as to make maximum use of the program that is already written. Extend the class Invest to override method display Interest and make use of the other existing methods to display the changing figures over the six-year period.

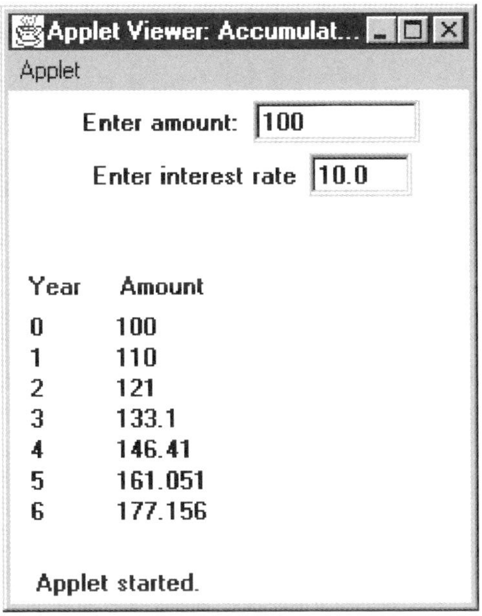

Figure 12.3 Screen display for a revised interest calculation program.

12.13 Graph drawer Enhance the graph-drawing program in the program text so that it:

- draws the x- and y-axes;
- prevents drawing outside the assigned area;
- inputs the coefficients from text boxes instead of scrollbars (to give precision);
- inputs a horizontal and a vertical scaling (zoom) factor from scrollbars;
- draws a second graph of the same function, but with separate coefficients. (Make maximum reuse of the existing program by creating a new instance of class Graph.);
- draws the graphs of some other functions. One way to do this would be to re-write the method theFunction in class Graph. A better, and more object-oriented way, is to write a new class that extends class Graph by overriding method theFunction with a method that calculates the new function.

12.14 Numerical integration Write a program that calculates the integral of a function y using the 'trapezium rule'. The area under the graph of the function is divided into n equal strips of width d. Then the area under the curve (the integral) is approximately the sum of all the (small) trapeziums:

$$\text{area} \cong d(y_0 + 2y_1 + 2y_2 + \ldots + 2y_{n-1} + y_n)/2$$

or:

$$\text{area} = (\text{half the width of the strip}) \times (\text{first} + \text{last} + \text{twice the sum of the others})$$

Use a function for which you know the answer, and experiment by using smaller and smaller values of d.

12.15 Mandelbrot set. The Mandelbrot set is a famous and striking image (Figure 12.4) produced by repeatedly evaluating a formula at each point in a two-dimensional space. Take a point, with coordinates x_{start} and y_{start}. Then repeatedly calculate new values of x and y from the old values using the formulae:

$$x_{new} = x_{old}^2 - y_{old}^2 - x_{start}$$
$$y_{new} = 2x_{old}y_{old} - y_{start}$$

The first values of x_{old} and y_{old} are x_{start} and y_{start}. For each iteration, calculate $r = \sqrt{x_{new}^2 + y_{new}^2}$. Repeat until $r > 10\,000$ or 100 iterations, whichever comes first. If r is greater than 10 000 colour the pixel corresponding to this coordinate white, otherwise black.

Repeat for all points with x between −1.0 and +2.0 and y in the range −2.0 to +2.0.

As the iteration proceeds, starting from particular values of x_{start} and y_{start}, the value of r sometimes remains reasonably small (around 1.0). For other values of x_{start} and y_{start}, the value of r quickly becomes very large and tends to shoot off to infinity.

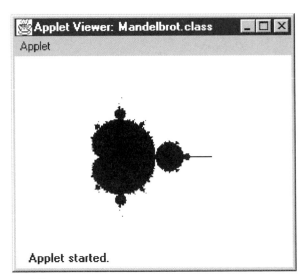

Figure 12.4 The Mandelbrot set.

ANSWERS TO SELF-TEST QUESTIONS

12.1   3e6f

-1.0e5f

0.635e-4f

5e9d

-0.56e-6d

12.2

Without brackets	With brackets
2 + 3 + 4	2 + 3 + 4
2 - 3 + 4	(2 - 3) + 4
2 * 3 / 4	(2 * 3) / 4
2 / 3 * 4	(2 / 3) * 4
1 + 2 * 3 + 4 / 5 - 6 * 7 + 8	(1 + (2 * 3) + (4 / 5) - (6 * 7)) + 8
a * b + c - d / e	(a * b) + c - (d / e)

12.3
```
float max(float x, float y) {
    if (x > y)
        return x;
    else
        return y;
}
```

12.4

Expression	Carried out as
(i + j)	int
(f + g)	float
(d + e)	double
(i + f)	float
(f + d)	double
(i + j) * (f + g)	float
(i + j) * (f + g) * (d + e)	double
(i + j) * (f + g) * (d + e) * (i + f)	double
(i + j) * (f + g) * (d + e) * (i + f) * (f + d)	double

12.5 To prevent the program from drawing outside the appropriate area, check the values of the *y* pixel coordinates in method `draw`:

```
if ((yPixel > yPixelStart) && (yPixel > yPixelEnd)
&&
(nextYPixel > yPixelStart) && (nextYPixel < yPixelEnd))
g.drawLine(xPixel, yPixel, nextXPixel, nextYPixel);
```

12.6 To use a new function, replace the definition of the function in method `theFunction`:

```
return a * Math.sin(b * x);
```

Another approach is to create a new class which inherits from the class `Graph` and overrides the method `theFunction`. In order to do this, the method would need to be described as either `public` or `protected`, rather than `private`, to allow the new class to override the old method as follows:

```
class NewGraph extends Graph {

    protected float theFunction(float x, float a, float b) {
        return a * Math.sin(b * x);
    }

}
```

Arrays and array lists

● Introduction

So far in this book, we have described data items (variables) that are individual and isolated. For example:

```
int count, sum;
String name;
```

These live on their own, performing useful roles in programs as counters, sums or whatever. We can think of these variables as places in memory that have individual names attached to them.

In contrast, we very often in life deal with data that is not isolated, but grouped together into a collection of information. Sometimes the information is in tables. Examples are a train timetable, a telephone directory or a bank statement. In programming, these things are called data structures. The information in a table is related in some way to the other information within the table. One of the simplest types of data structure in programming is an array. An array can be regarded simply as a table, with a single row of information. (Alternatively you can visualize a table as a single column of information.) This could be a table of numbers, a table of strings, or a table of anything.

In this chapter we will look at arrays of numbers, arrays of strings and arrays of other objects, such as playing cards and graphical objects.

Here is an array of numbers:

| 23 | 54 | 96 | 13 | 7 | 32 |

which might represent the ages of a group of people at a party.

And here is a table of words, which holds the names of the members of a famous band:

John	Paul	George	Ringo

In Java, a table like this is called an array. In programming, an item in an array is known as a *component* and we refer to a component by its position in the array, called the *index*. (In the world of programming, the term *element* is sometimes used instead of component, and the term *subscript* instead of index.) To us humans, the name John is in the first position in this table, but in Java the first position in an array is called the zeroth position. Successive positions in an array are the zeroth, first, second, third etc. Thus the string Ringo is in the third position in the above array. The position of a component in an array is called the index. We can therefore picture an array, together with its indices, like this:

array:	John	Paul	George	Ringo
indices:	0	1	2	3

Remember that the indices aren't held in the computer's memory – only the data. The indices are the way that we locate information in an array.

Here is another array, this time containing numbers. The indices for the array are also shown:

array:	34	78	54	12	21	35
indices:	0	1	2	3	4	5

In a program (as in real life) we typically have to carry out the following operations on arrays:

● Create the array – say how long it is and what sort of things it will contain.
● Put some values in the array (for example, enter some numbers into a personal telephone directory).
● Display the contents of the array on the screen (an array is held in the computer memory and it is therefore invisible).
● Search the array to find some value (for example, searching the train timetable to find a train at a convenient time).
● Add up the contents of the array (for example, working out how much a customer spent at the supermarket).

During this chapter we shall see how to carry out these actions one by one and build up to doing all these things in a complete program. We shall start by looking at arrays of numbers. Our plan is to develop a program with the screen layout shown in Figure 13.1. An array holds the data on the rainfall for the seven days in a week (Monday to Sunday). The user of the program can click with the mouse on a component of the array and then enter a value for that component using the text field. A button controls whether the array is displayed on the screen or hidden. Another button causes the sum of the numbers in the array to be displayed (the total rainfall for the week).

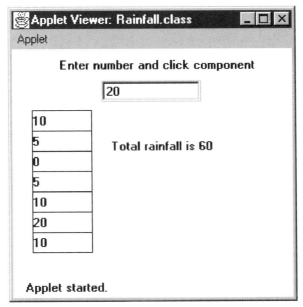

Figure 13.1 Screen layout for the rainfall data program.

● Creating an array

In Java, an array is declared just like any other variable, usually either at the top of a class or at the top of a method. An array is an object and must therefore be created using the operator `new` to create an instance of the class `array`. The programmer gives the array a name, like this:

```
int[] ages;
String[] band;
```

The variable named `ages` is now ready to refer to an array of integers. As with any other variable, it is usual (and a good idea) to choose a name for the array that describes clearly what it is going to be used for. The name is the name for the complete array – the complete collection of data. The rules for choosing the name of an array are the same as for choosing any other variable name in Java.

When you create an array with `new`, you say how long it is (how many items it is going to contain) and what type of objects are going to be contained in the array:

```
ages = new int[6];
band = new String[4];
```

The array called `ages` is big enough to contain six numbers, with indices going from 0 to 5.

The array called `band` is big enough to contain four strings. The indices go from 0 to 3. You can both declare an array variable and create the array all in one statement, like this:

```
int[] ages = new int[6];
String[] band = new String[4];
```

SELF-TEST QUESTION

13.1 Declare an array to hold data for the rainfall for each of the seven days in the week.

● Indices

The way that a program refers to an individual item in an array is to specify an index value (sometimes called an index). Thus `ages[3]` refers to the component in the array with index 3 – the value 12 in this case. Similarly, `band[2]` contains the string George. Remember that indices start at 0, so an array of length 4 has indices that go from 0 to 3. A reference to `ages[5]` is an error. If the program is a free-standing application, it will stop and an error message will be displayed. If the program is an applet, an error message will be displayed and it will continue running, but with an unpredictable outcome. It is usual to use `int` variables as indices, but `short`, `byte` or `char` types can be used.

We can input a value for a component of an array using a text field:

```
ages[2] = Integer.parseInt(inputField.getText());
band[3] = inputField.getText();
```

and similarly output values:

```
g.drawString("the first age is" + ages[0], 10, 10);
g.drawString("the 4th Beatle is" + band[3], 10, 10);
```

This latter example shows how careful you have to be with array indices.

You can change the values of individual components of an array with assignment statements, like this:

```
ages[3] = 99;
band[2] = "Mike";
```

In all these program fragments, we are referring to individual components in an array by specifying the value of an index.

13.2 Given the declaration:

```
int[] table = new int[2];
```

how long is the array and what is the valid range of indices?

Very often we want to refer to the *n*th component in an array, where *n* is a variable. This is how the power of arrays really comes into its own. Suppose, for example, we want to add up all the numbers in an array (of numbers). Let's suppose that we have an array with seven components that hold the number of computers sold in a shop during each day in a week:

```
int[] sale = new int[7];
```

We will insert values into the array with assignment statements. Suppose that on Monday (day 0), 13 computers are sold:

```
sale[0] = 13;
```

and so on for the other days:

```
sale[1] = 8;
sale[2] = 22;
sale[3] = 17;
sale[4] = 24;
sale[5] = 15;
sale[6] = 23;
```

Next we want to find the total sales for the week. The clumsy way to add up the sales would be to write:

```
sum = sale[0]+sale[1]+sale[2]+sale[3]+sale[4]+sale[5]+sale[6];
```

which is quite correct, but does not exploit the regularity of an array. The alternative is to use a `for` loop. A variable called **day** is used to hold the value of the index representing the day of the week. The index is made initially equal to 0 and then incremented each time the loop is repeated:

```
int day, sum;

sum = 0;
for (day = 0; day < 7; day++) {
    sum = sum + sale[day];
}
```

Each time the loop is repeated, the next value in the array is added to the total. This program fragment is actually no shorter than what it replaces. But it would be considerably shorter if the array had 1000 items to add up! The other advantage is that the code explicitly shows that it is performing a systematic operation on an array.

Indices are the one place in programming when it is permissible (sometimes) to use a name that is a little cryptic. In the above program fragment, however, using the name `day` as the index is clear and relates strongly to the problem being solved.

SELF-TEST QUESTION
························

13.3 What would this program fragment do?

```
int[] table = new int[10];

for (int s = 0; s <= 10; s++) {
    table[day] = s;
}
```

● The length of an array

A program can always find out how long an array is. For example, if we have an array declared like this:

```
int[] table = new int [10];
```

you can refer to its length like this:

```
int l;
l = table.length;
```

or:

```
if (table.length < 12) ...
```

We shall see that this facility is very useful. The word `length` is a public variable in the array object, available to reference but not to change.

Once you have created an array, you cannot change its length. Arrays are not made of elastic; they are made of quick-setting concrete. This can sometimes be a problem. When you are developing a new program you must think about how big an array you are going to need. Make it plenty big enough to hold the information. Write statements that check to see that the program is not going beyond the boundaries of the array. If the array you have is inadequate, you can always create another that is big enough.

We have seen that an array, once created, has a definite, fixed size. More advanced data structures in the Java libraries provide greater flexibility – such data structures can expand and contract as needed.

● Passing arrays as parameters

As we have seen in earlier chapters of this book, methods are very important in programming. An important aspect of using methods is passing information to a method
as parameters and returning a value. We now explain how to pass and return arrays.

Suppose we want to write a method whose job it is to calculate the sum of the components in an array of integers. Being perceptive programmers, we want the method to
be general-purpose, so that it will cope with arrays of any length. But that is OK because
the method can simply obtain the length of the array. So the parameter to be passed to
the method is simply the array and the result to be returned to the user of the method
is a number, the sum of the values.

A sample invocation of the method looks like this:

```
int[] table = new int[24];

total = sum(table);
```

The method itself is:

```
int sum(int[] array) {

    int total = 0;
    for (int s = 0; s < array.length; s++)
        total = total + array[s];
    return total;
}
```

Notice that in the header for the method the parameter is declared as an array, with
square brackets. But there is no parameter that spells out how long the array actually is.
Because it will accept an array of any length, this method is general-purpose and potentially very useful. This is highly preferable to a special-purpose method that will only
work when the array is, say, eight components long.

The name used for the index in this method is simply s. This is an example of where
the name that has been chosen is cryptic. Because the method is general-purpose, we
do not know the purpose of the array or the meaning of the index. So a name that simply means any index is OK.

SELF-TEST QUESTION
....

13.4 Write a method that displays an array of strings, one per line, on the screen. The
parameter of the method is the array.

In the above example, the method merely uses the array, without changing its value.
Now we look at an example where the method *does* change the array. Suppose we want

a method to fill an array with zeros; this obviously involves changing the array. An invocation of the method would typically be:

```
int[]table = new int[8];

fillZero(table);
```

and the method itself is:

```
void fillZero(int[] array) {
    for (int s = 0; s < array.length; s++)
        array[s] = 0;
}
```

An array is a fully fledged object in Java, and when an object is used as a parameter it is passed as a reference. So when an array is passed as a parameter to a method, a *reference* to the array is passed. A reference is not a copy of the array, but a pointer to the array. So if and when a method changes an array parameter, it changes the array in the piece of program that invoked the method. This is what happens in the above example.

The normally recommended practice in programming is to pass parameters to a method for it to use. The method does not change the values of the parameters, but simply uses them. Any result produced by the method is passed back to the invoker as the return value of the method. When a parameter that is one of the built-in types is passed as a parameter, it is passed by value. A copy of the variable is passed to the method, which cannot therefore change the value in the invoking method. So passing built-in types to methods as parameters is always safe. However, with objects, the method can change the value of the variable. What we see here is an exception to the usual way that parameters are used.

SELF-TEST QUESTION

13.5 Write a method that puts zeros into the first *n* components of an array of integers. It leaves the remaining components unchanged. The parameters for the method are the array and *n*.

● Typical operations on arrays

In this section we look at a number of useful things that are commonly done with arrays. These are:

1. Input some values for the components of the array.
2. Carry out some action on the array (for illustration, multiply each of the components of the array by itself).
3. Output the values in the array.

We will now look at each of these in turn.

First let us set up an array to hold seven integers – the data for the rainfall on each of the seven days in a week:

```
int[] rain = new int[7];
```

Then we can request that the user of the program enters a value into a text field by displaying a message:

```
private void requestInput() {
    g.drawString("enter rainfall for day " + day + " now", 10, 10);
}
```

When the user presses the enter key after keying in a number into the text field, an event is created as usual which is handled by method `actionPerformed` as follows, putting the number into the array:

```
public void actionPerformed(ActionEvent event) {
    int number = Integer.parseInt(inputField.getText());
    rain[day] = number;
    repaint();
}
```

If we wanted to multiply each of the components of the array by itself:

```
for (int day = 0; day < 7; day++)
    rain[day] = rain[day] * rain[day];
```

Finally, we can output the values of the array like this:

```
for (int day = 0; day < 7; day++)
    g.drawString(Integer.toString(rain[day]), 20, 20*day);
```

so that the numbers are displayed in a column down the screen.

You will see that it is very common to use the `for` statement in conjunction with arrays. They go together like a horse and carriage, in the words of the song. It is, of course, because a `for` loop makes the maximum use of the uniformity of arrays.

Another illustrative action that can be performed on an array is finding the largest value. One approach is to start by assuming that the first item is the largest. Then we look at the remainder of the components in turn, comparing them with this largest value. If we find a value that is larger than the one we have already got, we update our largest value.

```
int[] rain = new int[7];
int largest, day;

largest = rain[0];

for (day = 1; day < 7; day++)
    if (rain[day] > largest)
        largest = rain[day];
```

SELF-TEST QUESTION
....

13.6 Alter the piece of program which finds the largest item in an array so that it also finds the position (index number) of the largest component.

● Using constants

In a program with several arrays, there are the declarations of the arrays and almost certainly lots of `for` loops. The arrays, together with their lengths, will be passed around the program as parameters. There is plenty of scope for confusion, particularly if two different arrays have the same length.

Suppose, for example, we are writing a program to analyse marks that students obtain in assignments. Suppose there are 10 students. We want one array to hold the average mark for each student:

```
int[] studentMark = new int[10];
```

By coincidence, there are also 10 courses. We also want a second array to hold the average mark for each course:

```
int[] courseMark = new int[10];
```

The problem is that, wherever we see the number 10 in the program, we do not know whether it is the number of students or the number of courses. As things stand, of course, it doesn't matter – because they are the same! But suppose we needed to alter the program so that it deals with 20 students. We would very much like to change every occurrence of the number 10 to the number 20 using a handy text editor. But because the arrays are the same length, this would cause great damage to the program.

One way to clarify such a program is to declare the lengths of the arrays as constants, and then to use the constants in `for` loops like this:

```
final int students = 10;
int[] studentMark = new int[students];
final int courses = 10;
int[] courseMark = new int[courses];

for(int s = 0; s < students; s++) ...
```

We can make changes to the program with supreme confidence, simply by changing one number in the constant declaration.

13.7 A program is to store and manipulate rainfall figures for each day of the week. An array is to be used to store the seven values. Write Java statements to declare the array and to fill it with zeros. Make use of constant values as appropriate.

● Initializing an array

Initializing means giving a variable an initial or starting value. If you write this:

```
int[] table = new int[10];
```

then an array is set up in memory and each element is initialized to a value. This value depends on the type of the array. Numeric arrays are initialized to zero and all objects (including strings) are initialized to a null value.

A common way of initializing an array is to do it when the array is declared. The following initialization:

```
int[] ages = {23, 54, 96, 13, 7, 32};
```

is equivalent to:

```
int[] ages = new int[6];
ages[0] = 23;
ages[1] = 54;
ages[2] = 96;
ages[3] = 13;
ages[4] = 7;
ages[5] = 32;
```

Another example, using an array of strings is:

```
String[] band = {"John", "Paul", "George", "Ringo"};
```

Another way to initialize an array is to use a loop as we saw earlier, like this:

```
for (int i = 0; i < 10; i++)
    table[i] = 0;
```

If the program needs periodically to reset the array back to its initial values, then the way to do it is by using the for loop as shown above.

SELF-TEST QUESTION
....

13.8 Declare an array named `numbers` of 10 integers and fill it with the numbers 1
to 10 as part of the declaration.

● A sample program

Now we will combine all the things we have looked at into a program to input some
numbers, put them in an array, display them and add them up. The screen is shown in
Figure 13.1. The data is the rainfall for the seven days in a week (Monday to Sunday).
The user of the program enters a value into the text field and then can click with the
mouse on an component of the array to insert the value into the array. The sum of the
numbers in the array is displayed (the total rainfall for the week).

The array is displayed as a series of seven rectangles using `drawRect`, one below the
other on the screen. The mouse click event is passed to the method `mouseClicked`
which obtains the coordinate. The *y*-coordinate is then converted by the program into
an index value in the range 0 to 6.

```java
import java.awt.*;
import java.applet.*;
import java.awt.event.*;

public class Rainfall extends Applet implements ActionListener,
                                                   MouseListener {

    private Table rainData;
    private TextField value;

    public void init() {
        rainData = new Table();

        Label l = new Label("Enter number and click component");
        add(l);
        value = new TextField(10);
        add(value);
        value.addActionListener(this);
        addMouseListener(this);
    }

    public void paint(Graphics g) {
        rainData.display(g);
    }
```

```
    public void actionPerformed(ActionEvent event) {
        int newValue = Integer.parseInt(value.getText());
        rainData.setValue(newValue);
        repaint();
    }

    public void mouseClicked(MouseEvent event){
        int yCoord = event.getY();
        rainData.selectComponent(yCoord);
        repaint();
    }

    public void mouseReleased(MouseEvent event){
    }

    public void mousePressed(MouseEvent event){
    }

    public void mouseEntered(MouseEvent event){
    }

    public void mouseExited(MouseEvent event){
    }

}

class Table {

    private final int tableSize = 7;
    private int[] rain = new int[tableSize];
    private int index;
    private int newValue;
    private int sum = 0;

    private final int startX = 20;
    private final int startY = 60;
    private final int boxHeight = 20;
    private final int boxWidth = 60;

    public void display(Graphics g) {
        int y = startY;
        for(int s = 0; s < rain.length; s++) {
            g.drawRect(startX, y, boxWidth, boxHeight);
            g.drawString(Integer.toString(rain[s]),
                    startX, y + boxHeight * 3 / 4);
```

```
            y = y + boxHeight;
        }
        addValues();
        g.drawString("Total rainfall is " + sum, 100, 100);
    }
    public void selectComponent(int y) {
        index = (y - startY)/boxHeight;
        rain[index] = newValue;
    }

    public void setValue(int value) {
        newValue = value;
    }

    private void addValues() {
        sum = 0;
        for (int s = 0; s < rain.length; s++)
            sum = sum + rain[s];
    }
}
```

There is some new event handling in this program. The Rainfall class implements the MouseListener interface, so that the program can respond to mouse click events. Such an event causes the mouseClicked method to be invoked. But the declaration to implement MouseListener requires the program to supply several other methods as shown. In this particular program these methods are empty; they do nothing, because this particular program does not need to do anything in response to these events. If in some other program these events were of interest, the methods would need appropriate bodies to handle the events. The five methods are invoked under the following circumstances:

mouseClicked – the mouse button has been clicked and released without moving the mouse.

mouseReleased – the mouse button has been released after the mouse has been dragged.

mousePressed – the mouse button has been pressed.

mouseEntered – the mouse has entered this window.

mouseExited – the mouse has left this window.

● Arrays of objects

Arrays can hold anything – integers, floating-point numbers, strings, buttons, scrollbars, any object in the library, any object that the programmer constructs. The only constraint is that all the objects in an array must be of the same type. We will now illustrate some of these with examples.

We will see in the next section that it is easy to set up an array with each component containing a name and a telephone number. We declare a class to describe each component of the array:

```
public class Entry {
    public String name;
    public String number;
}
```

Then we can go on to create the array:

```
Entry[] directory = new Entry[1000];
```

and put something into it:

```
directory[0].name = "Douglas Bell";
directory[0].number = "01 0114 253 3103";
```

Later we will see how to search such an array.

Next we will set up an array of buttons. This is a good illustration of an array of objects. Each button will be like a digit button on a calculator (Figure 13.2). We will construct 10 of them, bearing the digits 0 to 9:

```
Button[] digit = new Button[10];
```

This statement creates an array that is capable of holding 10 buttons. But the buttons cannot be used until they have been correctly initialized like this:

```
for (int b = 0; b < 10; b++) {
    digit[b] = new Button(Integer.toString(b));
    add(digit[b]);
    digit[b].addActionListener(this);
}
```

When a button is pressed, an event occurs and we provide a method `actionPerformed` to handle it, as usual. The parameter can be used in conjunction with the method `getActionCommand` to obtain the label on the button, a string. This string is then

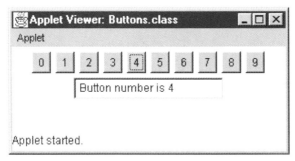

Figure 13.2 An array of buttons displayed in the window.

converted to an integer using `parseInt`. After these conversions, `buttonNumber` holds the digit corresponding to the button that was pressed.

```
public void actionPerformed(ActionEvent event) {
        String buttonCaption = event.getActionCommand();
        buttonNumber = Integer.parseInt(buttonCaption);
        display.setText("Button number is " + buttonNumber);
    }
```

Next we will study a graphical object, described earlier in the book. It is a balloon object (really just a circle) that has a size and a position on the screen. Methods are provided as part of the object to move it, change its size and display it. Here is an illustrative part of the class description:

```
class Balloon {

        private int x; // x pixel co-ordinate of centre
        private int y; // y pixel co-ordinate of centre
        private int radius;
        public Balloon () {
            x = 50;
            y = 50;
            radius = 20;
        }

        public void display(Graphics g) {
            g.drawOval(x-radius, y-radius, radius*2, radius*2);
        }

        public void changeSize(float factor) {
            radius = (int) (radius * factor);
        }
    }
```

We can now create an array of balloons:

```
Balloon[] party = new Balloon[10];
```

But this only creates the array, ready to hold all the balloons. We now need to create the balloons as follows:

```
for (int b = 0; b < 10; b++)
    party[b] = new Balloon();
```

We can now give the balloons different sizes:

```
for (int b = 0; b < 10; b++)
    party[b].changeSize(b/10.0f);
```

and display them:

```
for (int b = 0; b < 100; b++)
    party[b].display(g);
```

The advantage of having them all in an array is that we can do something with them all in a convenient way.

Finally we will look at an example which might be part of a game using playing cards. Each card is described by the class:

```
public class Card {
    public int rank;
    public String suit;
}
```

We will create a class that holds a complete deck of cards. The constructor method Deck initializes the array.

```
public class Deck {

    private Card[] deck = new Card[52];
    final String[] suit = {"hearts", "diamonds", "spades", "clubs"};

    public Deck() {
        int cardNumber = 0;
        for (int suitNo = 0; suitNo < 4; suitNo++)
            for (int rank = 1; rank < 14; rank++) {
                deck[cardNumber] = new Card();
                deck[cardNumber].suit = suit[suitNo];
                deck[cardNumber].rank = rank;
                cardNumber++;
            }
    }
}
```

● Lookup and searching

Part of the power of arrays is that you can look up something very easily and quickly. In the rainfall program, we can extract the value of Tuesday's rainfall simply by referring to rain[1]. The same is true of any information that can be referred to by an integer index. For example, if we have a table showing the average height of people according to age, we can index the table using the age:

```
float[] height = new float[100];

float myHeight = height[25];
```

Similarly, if we have numbered the days of the week as 0 to 6, we can convert the number to a text string like this:

```
int day;
String dayName;
String[] name =
    {"Monday", "Tuesday", Wednesday", Thursday", "Friday"};

dayName = name[day];
```

You could do this in another way, using a switch statement, which would be slightly longer and probably more cumbersome.

Using an array to look up something is extremely useful, simple and exploits the power of arrays.

Another way of accessing information in an array is to search for it. This is what humans do in a telephone directory or a dictionary. Using an array index directly is impossible, because there is no appropriate integer to use. We will consider a telephone directory. Each entry in the directory consists of an object – a name and a number. We will first create a class to represent such an entry:

```
public class Entry {
    public String name;
    public String number;
}
```

We will set up an array, called `directory`, in which each component of the array consists of one of these objects. The declaration of the directory is:

```
Entry[] directory = new Entry[100];
```

This declaration merely creates variables of the required type, each initialized to the value `null`. It is necessary to create each of the components of the array as a separate step. For example, we can create the first component like this:

```
directory[0] = new Entry();
```

If this instruction to create the array component is omitted, then a `NullPointerException` will arise when we try to use it. Now that it is created, we can place some data in it:

```
directory[0].name = "Douglas Bell";
directory[0].number = "01 0114 253 3103";
```

Assume now that the directory contains some entries. A simple and effective way to search the directory is to start at the beginning and go from one entry to the next until we find the name that we are looking for. However, the name we seek might not be in the directory, and we must cater for that situation arising. So the search continues until either we find what we are looking for or we get to the end of the entries. We could check that we have got to the end of the array, but a more convenient approach is to put a special entry into the array to signify the end of the useful data. This end marker will consist of an entry with the name END.

Now we can write the loop to search for a desired telephone number. Notice that all the work is carried out in the condition of the `while` statement, which is very bulky indeed, leaving the body of the loop nearly empty. Notice also that we use the library method `equals` to compare two strings.

```
String wanted = "Albert";
int s = 0;
while (! directory[s].name.equals(wanted)
       &&
       ! directory[s].name.equals("END"))
    s++;

if (directory[s].name.equals("END"))
    display.setText("name not found");
else
    display.setText("the number of " + wanted +
                " is " + directory[s].number);
```

This is called a *serial* search. It starts at the beginning of the array, with the index zero, and continues searching item by item, adding one to the index. The search continues until either the wanted item is found or until the special name END is reached.

This type of search makes no assumptions about the order of the items in the table – they can be in any order. Other search techniques exploit the ordering of items in the table, such as alphabetical ordering. These techniques are beyond the scope of this book.

Information like telephone numbers is normally stored in a file, rather than an array, because data held in a file is more permanent. Usually the file is searched for the required information rather than an array. Alternatively, the file is input into memory, held in an array and searched as shown above.

● Bar charts and pie charts

It is common in any sphere of life to display data in charts of various types – bar charts and pie charts are two popular types. Bar charts are useful for data like rainfall or changes in house prices. Pie charts show the proportions of quantities and are therefore useful for data like personal budgets or company budgets. Before data can be displayed in a chart it needs to be stored in an array. In the case of a pie chart, the data has to be scaled so that each item represents a segment of a circle (a slice of pie). The library method fillRect can be used to draw bars and the method fillArc can be used to draw pie slices.

Let us suppose that we have some integer values in an array named data and we want to display them as a bar chart as in Figure 13.3. We will develop a method called displayBars that does all this work. First we must find the largest data value so that we can set the scale for the height of the bars. Then we scale all the values, placing them in a second array. Finally we display rectangles whose heights represent the data values.

```
public void displayBars(int[] data, Graphics g) {

    int largest;
    int[] scaledData = new int[data.length];

    int yStart = 20;
    int yHeight = 200;
    int xStart = 20;
    int width = 30;
    int gap = 10;

    largest = findLargest(data);
    scaledData = scaleValues(data, largest, yHeight);
```

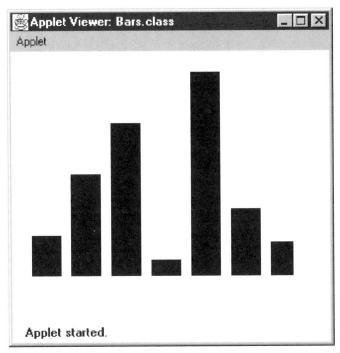

Figure 13.3 Output from a bar chart program.

```
    int x = xStart;
    for (int count = 0; count < scaledData.length; count++) {
        g.fillRect(x, yStart + yHeight - scaledData[count],
                    width, scaledData[count]);
        x = x + width + gap;
    }
}
```

This constitutes the main part of the method, leaving the private methods `scaleValues` and `findLargest` for the reader to complete.

● Array lists

Arrays are excellent structures for modelling many structures. However, sometimes a different structure is more appropriate: for example, arrays have the disadvantage that, once created, they have a fixed size. Thus if you have more information than the array will hold, then your program will not cope. However, the Java library provides a range of more powerful data structures, which are called collections. One of these data structures is called an array list. An array list will expand automatically to cope with additional information. It also allows items to be inserted and deleted from the middle of the structure. Like an array, items in an array list are referred to by an index – an integer value. As with arrays, index values start at zero. But the square bracket notation [] is not used; instead methods are provided to access an array list.

An array list accommodates any type of object, and different types of object can be held within the same array list. This makes array lists very flexible. (But an array list cannot store any primitive type such as `int`.)

Note that earlier versions of the Java library supported a structure called the vector, which had similar functionality to the array list.

To use an array list, the following import declaration is needed at the head of the program:

```
import java.util.*;
```

A program must create an array list object in exactly the same way as any other object is created in the classic Java manner, using `new`:

```
ArrayList arrayList = new ArrayList();
```

A number of methods are provided to place things in an array list:

`add(element)` adds a new element at the end of the list
`add(index, element)` inserts a new element at the specified position
`set(index, element)` replaces an element at the specified position

Note that when a new element is inserted using method `add(index, element)`, the element that was at this position is moved up one position. Also all the elements with a greater index are moved up one position. Thus the original data remains in the list. The size of the array list expands as necessary to accommodate the new information.

Some methods allow items in an array list to be accessed, without removing items:

`get(index)` – gets a copy of the object at the specified position
`size` – returns the size of the array list, that is the number of elements it contains
`isEmpty` – tests whether the array list is empty (returns true or false)

Finally, these methods remove items from an array list:

`clear` – empties the array list
`remove(index)` – removes the element at the specified position. All elements with a greater index are moved down.

You will see that there is never a gap in an array list. If something is removed, elements are moved down to fill the gap.

The methods provided to use an array list are summarized in Appendix B.

Our example program helps maintain a list of the most popular pop stars. (Or it could be used to display a football league table.) A typical view of the applet is shown in Figure 13.4. With the aid of an array list it allows new names to be entered into a list at any position in the list. It also allows entries to be deleted. Note that what is

Figure 13.4 Display from the HitList program using an array list.

displayed is not the array list. The array list itself is held in main memory (RAM) and is therefore invisible. The program extracts and displays the data from the array list in a convenient way.

```java
import java.applet.Applet;
import java.awt.*;
import java.awt.event.*;
import java.util.*;

public class HitList extends Applet implements ActionListener,
                                                  MouseListener {

    private ArrayList artists = new ArrayList();
    private String text;
    private boolean itemSelected = false;
    private int indexSelected = -1;
    private Button add, remove, insert, right;
    private TextField textField;
    private Artist artist;
    private int stepSize = 40;
    private int startY = 60;
```

```java
public void init() {
    add = new Button("add at end");
    add(add);
    add.addActionListener(this);
    remove = new Button("remove");
    add(remove);
    remove.addActionListener(this);
    insert = new Button("insert");
    add(insert);
    insert.addActionListener(this);
    textField = new TextField("", 10);
    add(textField);
    addMouseListener(this);

    artist = new Artist("Elvis");
    boolean result =artists.add(artist);
}

public void actionPerformed(ActionEvent event) {
    text = textField.getText();
    if (event.getSource() == add)
        add();
    if (event.getSource() == remove)
        remove();
    if (event.getSource() == insert)
        insert();
    itemSelected = false;

    repaint();
}

public void mouseClicked(MouseEvent event) {
    int yCoord = event.getY();
    indexSelected = (yCoord - startY) / stepSize;
    itemSelected = true;
    repaint();
}

public void mouseReleased(MouseEvent mouse) {
}

public void mousePressed(MouseEvent mouse) {
}
```

```
    public void mouseEntered(MouseEvent mouse) {
    }

    public void mouseExited(MouseEvent mouse) {
    }

    private void add() {
        artist = new Artist(text);
        artists.add(artist);
    }

    private void remove() {
        if (itemSelected)
            artists.remove(indexSelected);
    }

    private void insert() {
        artist = new Artist(text);
        if (itemSelected)
            artists.add(indexSelected, artist);
    }

    public void paint(Graphics g) {
        for (int i = 0; i < artists.size(); i++) {
            artist = (Artist) artists.get(i);
            int x = 20;
            int y = stepSize * i + startY;
            if (i == indexSelected && itemSelected)
                artist.display(g, x, y, true);
            else
                artist.display(g, x, y, false);
        }
    }
}

class Artist {

    private int height = 25, width = 75;
    private String name;

    public Artist(String name) {
        this.name = name;
    }
```

```
public void display(Graphics g, int x, int y, boolean selected) {
    if (selected) {
        g.setColor(Color.lightGray);
        g.fillRect(x, y, width, height);
        g.setColor(Color.black);
    }
    else
        g.drawRect(x, y, width, height);
    g.drawString(name, x + 5, y + 20);
    }
}
```

There are several noteworthy components in this program. The creation of the GUI is straightforward. Mouse click events are handled in the same way as the array program (Figure 13.1) earlier in this chapter. Similarly the position of a mouse click is translated into the position of an artist in the display. The array list `artists` holds any number of `Artist` objects, declared as a separate class at the end of the program. These objects are rather simple – they only contain a simple string, position information and code to display an object.

When the user clicks on the add button, a new object is created containing the desired text and it is added to the end of the array list using the `add` method. In a similar fashion, the method `remove` is used to delete an entry in the array list. Method `add` is used to insert a new object within the array list. Remember that when an item is removed or inserted, the remainder of the information in the array list moves to accommodate the change. This is reflected in the display of the information.

A `for` loop is used to extract and display the array list contents. Within the loop, the statement:

```
artist = (Artist) artists.get(i);
```

extracts an element from the array list. In an array list, information is held as objects, instances of the ultimate superclass `Object`. But when objects are extracted from an array list for use, they need to be converted back to their original status. So the above statement casts the object to the Artist class. This is needed so that a method such as `display` can be applied to the object `artist`, as in the subsequent statement:

```
artist.display(g, x, y, true);
```

In summary, an array list is the appropriate data structure in circumstances where the number of items is unknown and it is necessary to insert and delete items from the middle of the structure.

Programming pitfalls

A common error in Java is to confuse the length of an array with the range of valid indices. For example, the array:

```
int[] table = new int[10];
```

has 10 components The valid range of indices for this array is 0 to 9. Reference to `table[10]` is a reference to a component of the array that simply does not exist. Luckily the Java system checks for violations like this as the program is running and will issue an error message.

Here is a common example of how to do things wrongly:

```
int[] table = new int[10];

for (int s = 0; s <= 10; s++)
    table[s] = 0;
```

This will place a zero in all of the components of the array `table`, but then go on to try to place a zero in whatever data item happens to be immediately after the array in the computer memory. It is always worthwhile carefully checking the condition for terminating a `for` loop like this.

Programming principles

● An array is a collection of data. The complete structure has a single name. All the items in an array are of the same type. Individual components in an array are identified by means of an index, an integer. So if for example an array of integers is named `table`, an individual component is referred to as `table[2]`, where 2 is the index. You can similarly refer to a component of an array using a variable, an integer, as an index, like `table[s]`. It is this facility that makes arrays powerful.
● Once created, an array has a fixed length, which cannot be changed as the program executes. (The contents of the array can, of course, be changed.) The length of an array can be accessed by referring to `theArrayName.length`.
● Arrays can hold data of any type – for example `int`, `double`, `float`, `Button`, `Textfield`. (But in any one array the data must all be of the same type.) The particular component is still identified using an integer index.
● Like an array, an array list is a collection of data, accessed via an index. But the advantage of an array list is that it can expand as the program is running, to accommodate additional data. Also, items can be removed from the body of an array list. But access to an array list is generally slower than access to an array.

Summary

● An array is a collection of data. It is given a name by the programmer. All the items in an array must be of the same type (e.g. integers).

● An array is declared, along with other variables, like this:

```
int[] harry = new int[24];
```

in which 24 is the length of the array (the number of items it will contain).

● An individual component in an array is referred to by an integer index, for example:

```
harry[12] = 45;
```

● Indices have values that start from zero and go up to one less than the length of the array.

● It is common to use the `for` loop in conjunction with arrays.

● Like an array, an array list holds a collection of data, and each element is referred to by an index. The square bracket notation is not used; instead methods are used to manipulate an array list. An array list can expand to accommodate additional data.

EXERCISES

Extensions to the programs in the text

13.1 **Balloons** Write code to describe a class which is an array of balloons. It has methods to:

1. create an object with *n* balloons;
2. blow up all the balloons by the same factor;
3. move all the balloons by the same amount.

(Don't forget to use what is already written.)

Games

13.2 **Nim** The human plays against the computer. At the start of the game there are three piles of matches. In each pile there is a random number of matches in the range 1 to 20. The three piles are displayed throughout the game. A random choice determines who goes first. Players take it in turns to remove as many matches as they like from any one pile, but only from one pile. A player must remove at least one match. The winner is the player who makes the other player take the last match. Make the computer play randomly, that is it chooses a pile randomly and then a number of matches randomly from those available.

13.3 **Safe combination** Set up an array to contain the six digits that open a safe. Ask the user to input six digits one-by-one from buttons labelled with the digits 0 to 9, and check whether they are correct. (Use an array of buttons as described in the text.) When a digit is entered, tell the user whether it is correct or not and give them three tries before making them start from the beginning again.

13.4   Pontoon (vingt-et-un) Write a program to play this card game. The computer acts as the dealer. The dealer first deals you two playing cards. These are random cards. (In the real game, the dealer has an enormous hand of cards which is several shuffled packs.) Your aim is to get a score higher than the dealer's, without going beyond 21 (vingt-et-un). Ace counts either as 1 or 11. At any time, you can say 'twist', which means that you want another card, or 'stick', which means you are content with what you have. You may also have gone 'bust', which means you have more than 21. When you finally stick or bust, it is the dealer's turn to deal cards for him- or herself. The dealer's aim is to get a bigger score than you, without going bust. But the dealer does not know your score and so gambles on what you might have.

Provide buttons to start a new game, twist and stick. Display both sets of cards that are dealt.

Basic operations on arrays

13.5   Rain data Complete the program to handle rainfall data by including the following operations:

● Improve the program so that it ignores mouse clicks that are outside the area of the displayed data.
● Input values via a text field for all the components of the array.
● Display all the values.
● Hide all the values.
● Add up the values and display the total.
● Find the largest value, the smallest value and display them.

13.6   String array Write a program that uses an array of 10 strings. Write methods that carry out each of the following operations:

● Input from the keyboard via a text field values for all of the components of the array.
● Display the values. (You can now observe that they have been entered correctly into your array.)
● Input a word from the keyboard and search to see whether it is present in the array. Display a message to say whether it is present in the array or not.

13.7   Bar chart Complete the methods that draw a bar chart from an array of integer data.

13.8   Pie chart Write a class that displays a pie chart of the data that is passed to its method as an array.

13.9 **Graph drawer** Write a class that provides a method to draw a graph of a function given as an array of *x*-coordinates and an array of corresponding *y*-coordinates. It has the heading:

```
public void drawGraph(float[] x, float[] y)
```

The method draws straight lines from one point to another. It also draws the axes.

Statistics

13.10 Write a program that inputs a series of integers into an array. The numbers are in the range 0 to 100.
Calculate and display:

- the largest number;
- the smallest number;
- the sum of the numbers;
- the mean of the numbers.

Display a histogram (bar chart) that shows how many numbers are in the ranges 0 to 9, 10 to 19 etc.

Random numbers

13.11 Check to see that the random number generator method is working correctly. Set it up to provide random numbers in the range 1 to 100. Then invoke the method 100 times, placing the frequencies in an array as in the last exercise. Finally display the frequency histogram, again as in the last exercise. Random numbers should be random, so the histogram should have bars of approximately equal height.

Words

13.12 **Word perm** Write a program that inputs four words and then displays all possible permutations of the words. So, for example, if the words 'mad', 'dog', 'bites' and 'man' are entered, then the following are output:

```
man bites mad dog
mad man bites dog
mad bites man dog
etc.
```

(Not all of the sentences will make sense!)

Information processing – searching

13.13 **Dictionary** Set up an array to contain pairs of equivalent English and Spanish words. Then input an English word, look up its Spanish equivalent and display it. Make sure you check to see whether the word is in the dictionary. Then add the facility to translate in the opposite direction, using the same data.

13.14 Library code Each member of a library has a unique user code, an integer. When someone wants to borrow a book, a check is made that the user code is valid.

Write a program that searches a table of user codes to find a particular code. The program should display a message saying that the code is either valid or invalid.

Information processing – sorting

13.15 Sorting Write a program that inputs a series of numbers, sorts them into ascending numerical order and displays them.

This program is not the easiest to write. There are very many approaches to sorting – in fact there are whole books on the subject. One approach is as follows.

Find the smallest number in the array. Swap it with the first item in the array. Now the first item in the array is in the right place. Leave this first item alone and repeat the operation on the remainder of the array (everything except the first item). Repeat, carrying out this operation on a smaller and smaller part of the array until the complete array is in order.

Array lists

13.16 Enhance the HitList program given in the text in the following ways:

- so that all entries can be deleted using an additional button;
- so that a selected name can be replaced by another, using an additional button;
- add error checking so that it checks that the user is not trying to delete an entry with index value –1;
- add a cut-and-paste operation, so that when an entry is deleted, it is displayed in the text field, ready to be inserted into the list at a new position.

13.17 Use the ArrayList class to implement a queue (line in North America) class. A queue provides three operations:

- remove from the front of the queue;
- add to the end of the queue;
- test whether the queue is empty.

13.18 Use the ArrayList class to implement a stack class. (Note that this class already exists in the library.) A stack provides three operations:

- remove from the front of the stack;
- add to the front of the stack;
- test whether the stack is empty.

ANSWERS TO SELF-TEST QUESTIONS

13.1   `int[] rain = new int[7];`

13.2   The length is 2. Valid indices are 0 and 1.

13.3   The array `table` has 10 components, with a maximum index of 9. This program fragment tries to place the numbers 0 to 10 into the components of the array, but attempts to access a non-existent component with index value of 10. So the program will fail.

13.4
```
void display(String[] array, Graphics g) {
        for(int s = 0; s < array.length; s++)
            g.drawString(array[s], 10, s * 20);
    }
```

13.5
```
void fillZero (int[] array, int n) {
        for(s = 0; s < n; s++)
            array[s] = 0;
    }
```

13.6
```
int largest = rain[0];
int position = 0;

for (int day = 0; day < rain.length; day++)
        if (rain[day] > largest) {
            largest = rain[day];
            position = day;
}
```

13.7
```
final int days = 7;
int[] rainfall = new int[days];

for (int s = 0; s < rainfall.length; s++)
    rainfall[s] = 0;
```

13.8   `int[] numbers = {1, 2, 3, 4, 5, 6, 7, 8, 9, 10};`

13.9   We need an additional constructor method that allows the size and position of a balloon object to be specified when a balloon is created:

```
public Balloon(int x, int y, int radius) {
    this.x = x;
    this.y = y;
    this.radius = radius;
}
```

Then we can use this constructor to create a number of balloons with different random characteristics:

```
    Balloon[] party = new Balloon[20];
    for (int b = 0; b < 20; b++) {
        int x = (int)(Math.random() * 100);
        int y = (int)(Math.random() * 100);
        int radius = (int)(Math.random() * 50);
        party[b] = new Balloon(x, y, radius);
    }
```

Blow up all the balloons by a factor of 2.0:

```
    for (int b = 0; b < 20; b++) {
        party[b].changeSize(2.0);
```

Display the balloons:

```
    for (int b = 0; b < 20; b++) {
        party[b].display(g);
```

Move all the balloons down 10 pixels:

```
    for (int b = 0; b < 20; b++) {
        party[b].changeY(10);
```

This needs a new method as part of the class `Balloon`:

```
    public void changeY(int y) {
        this.y = this.y + y;
    }
```

13.10
```
    Deck hand = new Deck();


    public void display(Graphics g, int x, int y) {
        g.drawString("rank is " + rank, x, y);
        g.drawString("suit is " + suit, x + 60, y);
    }


    public void display(Graphics g) {
        int x = 15, y = 15;
        for(int card = 0; card < 52; card++) {
            deck[card].display(g, x, y);
            y = y + 15;
        }
    }
```

13.11
```
    privateString name(int monthNumber) {
        String[] months =
            { "Jan", "Feb", "Mar", "April", "May", "June",
              "July", "Aug", "Sep", "Oct", "Nov", "Dec"};
```

```
        String month = months[monthNumber - 1];
        return month;
    }


    privateString name(int monthNumber) {
        String month;
        switch (monthNumber) {
            case 1 : month = "Jan"; break;
            case 2 : month = "Feb"; break;
            case 3 : month = "Mar"; break;
            case 4 : month = "April"; break;
            case 5 : month = "May"; break;
            case 6 : month = "June"; break;
            case 7 : month = "July"; break;
            case 8 : month = "Aug"; break;
            case 9 : month = "Sep"; break;
            case 10 : month = "Oct"; break;
            case 11 : month = "Nov"; break;
            case 12 : month = "Dec"; break;
        }
        return month;
    }
```

The first solution is smaller and neater.

Arrays – two-dimensional

● Introduction

Two-dimensional arrays, or tables, are very common in everyday life:

- a chessboard;
- a train timetable;
- a spreadsheet.

In the last chapter, we looked at one-dimensional arrays. Java provides a natural extension of one-dimensional arrays to two dimensions. So, for example, the declaration:

```
int[][] sales = new int[4][7];
```

declares a two-dimensional array of integers. It holds figures for the sales of computers at each of four shops on each of the seven days in a week; see Figure 14.1. The array

	0	1	2	3	4	5	6
0	22	49	4	93	0	12	32
1	3	8	67	51	5	3	63
2	14	8	23	14	5	23	16
3	54	0	76	31	4	3	99

Column numbers (days)

Row numbers (shops)

Figure 14.1 An array of sales figures.

257

is called `sales`. We can think of it as having four rows and seven columns. Each row represents a week at a particular shop. Each column represents a single day at each of the four shops. The indices for the rows go from 0 to 3. The indices for the columns go from 0 to 6. Column 0 is Monday, column 1 is Tuesday, etc.

SELF-TEST QUESTION

14.1 Which column number represents Saturday?
How many computers were sold on Thursday at shop 3?
Which row number and column number is this?

● Declaring an array

An array is declared along with other variables, either at the top of the class or at the top of a particular method. The programmer gives the array a name, like this:

```
int[][] sales = new int[4][7];
String chessBoard[][] = new String[8][8];
```

As with any other variable, it is usual (and a good idea) to choose a name for the array that describes clearly what it is going to be used for. The name is the name for the complete array – the complete collection of data. The rules for choosing the name of an array are the same as for choosing any other name (variable, class, object or method) in Java; see Appendix E.

When you declare an array, you say how many columns and how many rows it has.

The array called `sales` has four rows – one for each of four shops. It has seven columns – one for each day in the week. The array contains sales figures for each of four shops for each day of the week.

```
int[][] sales=new int[4][7];
```

We might also set up an array, called `temps`, to hold information about the temperatures in each of 10 ovens, each hour during a 24 hour period:

```
float[][] temps=new float[10][24];
```

SELF-TEST QUESTION

14.2 Declare an array to represent a chessboard. A chessboard is eight squares by eight squares. Each position in the array should hold a single string.

● Indices

With a two-dimensional array, the way that the program refers to an individual item is to specify the values of two integer indices (sometimes called subscripts). Thus `sales [3] [2]` refers to the component in the array with row 3 and column 2, meaning shop number 3 and the day Wednesday. Similarly, `chessBoard[2] [8]` might contain the string `"pawn"`. It is usual to use `int` variables as indices, but `short`, `byte` or `char` types can be used.

We can input a value for a component of an array like this:

```
sales[2][3] = Integer.parseInt(inputField.getText());
```

```
// place a piece on a square
chessBoard[3][4] = inputField.getText();
```

and similarly output values:

```
g.drawString("Salesperson 0 sold" + sales[0][1]
    + "on Tuesday", 20, 20);
g.drawString(chessBoard[3][8], 20, 20);
```

We can change the values with assignment statements, like this:

```
sales[3][2] = 99;
chessBoard[2][7] = "knight"; // place a knight on a square
```

In all these program fragments, we are referring to individual components in an array by specifying the values of the indices that identify the particular component that we are interested in.

Very often, we want to refer to a component in an array by specifying *variables* for each of the two indices. This is the way in which the power of arrays really comes into its own. Suppose, for example, we want to add up all the numbers in an array of numbers. An array holds data on sales of computers in four shops over a period of seven days. The array has four rows, each holding the number of computers sold in one of four shops. The array has seven columns, one for each day in a week. So the array holds the sales figures for each shop, for each day of the week:

```
int[][] sales=new int[4][7];
```

The clumsy way to add up the sales would be to write:

```
sum =
    sale[0][0]+sale[0][1]+sale[0][2]+sale[0][3]
    +sale[0][4]+sale[0][5]+sale[0][6]

    +sale[1][0]+sale[1][1]+sale[1][2]
    +sale[1][3]+sale[1][4]+sale[1][5]+sale[1][6]

    + etc
```

which is longwinded, difficult to understand, prone to error – but quite correct. However, it does not exploit the regularity of an array. The alternative would be to use a `for` loop. Variables are used to hold the values of the indices. Each index is made initially equal to 0 and then incremented each time the loop is repeated:

```
int[][] sales = new int[4][7];
int sum;

sum = 0;
for (int shop = 0; shop < 4; shop++)
    for (int day = 0; day < 7; day++)
        sum = sum + sales[shop][day];
```

which is considerably shorter and much neater than if we had written out all the sums in explicit detail.

SELF-TEST QUESTION
····························

14.3 Write Java statements to place the string "no piece" on every square of an 8 × 8 chessboard that is represented as a two-dimensional array of strings.

● The size of an array

Once created using `new` like this:

```
float[][] info = new float[20][40];
```

an array has a fixed size that cannot expand or contract. If you subsequently need a bigger array, you can always create a new one, assigning it to the same array variable:

```
info = new float[100][200];
```

but the original values are lost.

The size of an array can always be inspected using the word `length`. For the above array:

```
int numberOfRows = info.length;
```

and:

```
int numberOfColumns = info[0].length;
```

The word `length` has the following meaning. Remembering that an array is an object and that objects have methods and variables associated with them, `length` is a public variable – but one that cannot be changed. You will see that the number of columns is expressed as the length of row 0. This is fine because all the rows have the same length. We could have written `info[1].length`, `info[20].length` or whatever.

● Passing arrays as parameters

Methods are a vital ingredient in programming and a major feature is passing information to and from them as parameters. We now look at how to pass two-dimensional
arrays as parameters.

Suppose we want to write a method whose job it is to calculate the sum of the components in an array of integers. Being perceptive programmers, we want the method
to be general-purpose – able to deal with arrays of any size. So we will pass the name
of the array to the method as the parameter, and the result to be returned to the user
of the method is a number – the sum of the values.

An invocation of the method looks like this:

```
int[][] sales = new int[24][12];
total = sum(sales);
```

The method itself is:

```
public int sum(int[][] array) {
    total = 0;
    for (int row = 0; row < array.length; row++)
        for (int col = 0; col < array[0].length; col++)
            total = total + array[row][col];
    return total;
}
```

Suppose we want a method to fill an array with zeros to represent the sales at the
beginning of the week. An invocation of the method would typically be:

```
int[][] sales = new int[4][7];

fillZero(sales);
```

and the method itself is:

```
public void fillZero(int[][] array) {
    int rowLength = array.length;
    int colLength = array[0].length;

    for(int row = 0; row < rowLength; row++)
        for(int col = 0; col < colLength; col++)
            array[row][col] = 0;
}
```

You will see that the method changes the values in the array which was passed to it as
the parameter. Like other objects, arrays are passed as reference parameters. This means
that when the method changes the array parameter, the value is changed back in the
method that invoked the method.

● Typical operations on arrays

In this section we look at a number of useful things that are often done with arrays.
A common sequence is to:

1. Input values for the components of the array.
2. Carry out some action on the array (for illustration, multiply each of the components of the array by a constant).
3. Add up the components of one of the columns of the array.
4. Display the values in the array.

We will now look at each of these in turn.
Given an array:

```
int[][] sales = new int[4][7];
```

we can input a value via a text field from the keyboard and place it in the array like this:

```
sales[row][col] = Integer.parseInt(inputField.getText());
```

Now we multiply each of the components of the array by a constant, say the price of a single computer:

```
for (int row = 0; row < 4; row++)
    for (int col = 0; col < 7; col++)
        sales[row][col] = sales[row][col] * price;
```

Next we might want to add up the numbers in a particular column of an array, say column 3, which is the total sales for Thursday:

```
int sum=0;

for (int row = 0; row < 4; row++)
    sum = sum + sales[row][3];
```

Finally, we display the values of the array on the screen like this, with a layout that reflects the structure of the array:

```
yCoord = 20;
for (int row = 0; row < 4; row++) {
    xCoord = 20;
    for (int col = 0; col < 7; col++) {
        g.drawString(Integer.toString(sales[row][col]), xCoord, yCoord);
        xCoord = xCoord + 20;
    }
    yCoord = yCoord+20;
}
```

You will see again that it is very common to see nested `for` statements used with two-dimensional arrays, because they make the maximum use of the uniformity of arrays.

SELF-TEST QUESTIONS

14.4 Rewrite the above sample operations on arrays (output the values, multiply each component by a constant) as methods that are as general-purpose as possible.

14.5 Write a method that adds up the second row of an array of integers.

● Constants

In a program with several arrays, there are the declarations of the arrays and almost certainly lots of `for` loops. The arrays will be passed around the program as parameters. There is plenty of scope for confusion, particularly if two different arrays have the same length. For example, in the program to analyse the sales figures of computers at a number of shops over a number of days, we used a two-dimensional array to hold the figures. Each column represents a day. The rows are the data for each shop. Now suppose that, by coincidence, there are seven shops. The array is:

```
int[][] sale = new int[7][7];
```

The problem is that, wherever we see the number 7 in the program, we do not know whether it is the number of shops or it is the number of days. As things stand, of course, it doesn't matter – because they are the same! But suppose we needed to alter the program so that it deals with eight shops. We would very much like to change every occurrence of the number 7 to the number 8 using a handy text editor. This is impossibly dangerous because lengths are the same.

An excellent way to clarify such a program is to declare the lengths as constants, like this:

```
final int days = 7;
final int shops = 7;
```

and then the array as:

```
int[][] sales = new int[shops][days];
```

Now if the number of shops changes, we can make the corresponding change to the program with confidence, simply by changing one number in the constant declaration.

● Initializing an array

Initializing means giving a variable an initial or starting value. If you write this:

```
int[][] table = new int[10][10];
```

then an array is set up in memory and each element is initialized to a value. This value depends on the type of the array. Numeric arrays are initialized to zero and all objects (including strings) are initialized to a null value.

One way to initialize an array is to use nested loops, like this:

```
for (int row = 0; row < 10; row++)
    for (int col = 0; col < 10; col++)
        table[row][col] = 0;
```

Another way of initializing an array is to declare it like this:

```
int [][] table = {
    {1, 0, 1},
    {0, 1, 0},
    };
```

Note the use of curly brackets and commas. This both creates an array with two rows and three columns and gives it initial values. The initialization is carried out once, when the array is created. If the program changes the value of a component in the array, the value will not change back to its original value – not until the program is run again.

If the program needs periodically to reset the array back to its initial values, then the way to do it is with the `for` loops as shown above.

SELF-TEST QUESTION
....

14.6 Write the declaration of a 3 × 3 array of strings in such a way that the array is filled with the words one, two, three, ...

● A sample program

In this program we bring together many of the techniques described above. The program maintains a two-dimensional array of integers. These represent the sales of various items in several different shops. The screen is shown in Figure 14.2.

A number is then entered in the text field. The user clicks the mouse on a cell of the array to specify which component of the array they want to change. The program calculates and displays the grand total of all the sales.

The array is displayed as a grid of rectangles using `drawRect`. The position of a mouse click event is obtained by the method `mouseClicked` as x and y pixel coordinates. These are converted by the program into index values for the array. (The mouse handling methods are described in Chapter 13 on one-dimensional arrays.)

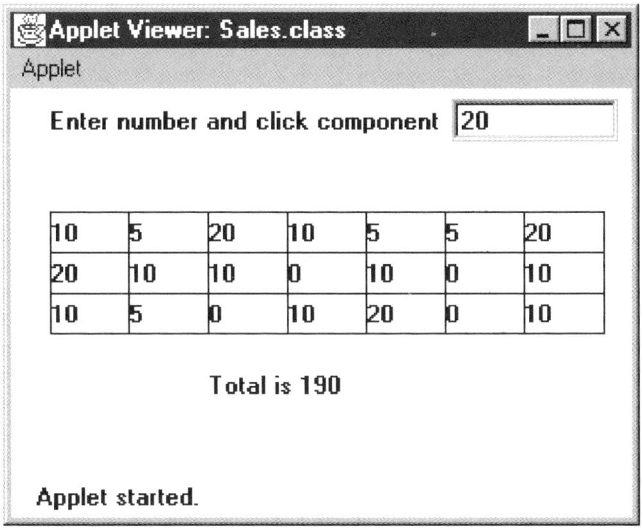

Figure 14.2 Screen for sales figures program.

```java
import java.awt.*;
import java.applet.Applet;
import java.awt.event.*;


public class Sales extends Applet implements ActionListener,
                                                        MouseListener {

    private Table sales;
    private TextField value;

    public void init() {
        sales = new Table(3, 7);
        Label l = new Label("Enter number and click component");
        add(l);
        value = new TextField(8);
        add(value);
        value.addActionListener(this);
        this.addMouseListener(this);
    }


    public void paint(Graphics g) {
        sales.display(g);
    }
```

```
        public void actionPerformed(ActionEvent event) {
            int newValue = Integer.parseInt(value.getText());
            sales.setValue(newValue);
            repaint();
        }

        public void mouseClicked(MouseEvent event){
            int x = event.getX();
            int y = event.getY();
            sales.selectComponent(x, y);
            repaint();
        }

        public void mouseReleased(MouseEvent e){
        }

        public void mousePressed(MouseEvent e){
        }

        public void mouseEntered(MouseEvent e){
        }

        public void mouseExited(MouseEvent e){
        }

    }

    class Table {

        private int[][] data;
        private int rowIndex;
        private int colIndex;
        private int newValue;

        private int sum;

        private final int xStart = 20;
        private final int yStart = 60;
        private final int boxHeight = 20;
        private final int boxWidth = 40;

        public Table(int rows, int columns) {
            data = new int[rows][columns];
```

```
                for(int row = 0; row < rows; row++)
                    for(int col = 0; col < columns; col++)
                        data[row][col] = 0;
        }
        public void display(Graphics g) {
            for(int row = 0; row < data.length; row++) {
                for(int col = 0; col < data[0].length; col++) {
                    int x = xStart + col * boxWidth;
                    int y = yStart + row * boxHeight;
                    g.drawRect(x, y, boxWidth, boxHeight);
                    g.drawString(Integer.toString(data[row][col]),
                            x, y + boxHeight*3/4);
                }
            }
            calculateSum();
            g.drawString("Total is " + sum, 100, 150);
        }

        public void selectComponent(int x, int y) {
            rowIndex = (y - yStart)/boxHeight;
            colIndex = (x - xStart)/boxWidth;
            data[rowIndex][colIndex] = newValue;
        }

        public void setValue(int value) {
            newValue = value;
        }

        private void calculateSum() {
            sum = 0;
            for (int row = 0; row < data.length; row++)
                for (int col = 0; col < data[0].length; col++)
                    sum = sum + data[row][col];
        }
    }
```

Programming principles

● A two-dimensional array is a collection of data, with a single name (for example, rainData). An array can be visualized as a two-dimensional table, with rows and columns. Suppose we want to represent the rainfall data for each of seven days at each of three places. Components in such an array are distinguished by specifying two indices, which are integers, for example rainData[4][2].

You can think of the first index as describing the row number and the second as describing the column number.

● An array is regarded as an object and therefore is created by means of an invocation of new:

```
int[][]  rainData = new int[7][3];
```

● All the components in an array must be of the same type – int in this example. When the array is created the size of the array is specified – seven rows and three columns in this example. The valid indices always start at 0 and go up to (length-1).

In this example the row indices go from 0 to 6 and the column indices from 0 to 2.

● The components of an array can be any type – int, float, String, or any other object.

Programming pitfalls

● A common error in Java is to confuse the length of an array with the range of valid indices. For example, the array:

```
int[][]  table = new int[10][10];
```

has 10 rows and 10 columns. The valid range of indices (for the rows and for the columns) is 0 to 9. Reference to table[10][10] will give rise to the program stopping and an error message being issued.

Summary

● A two-dimensional array is a collection of data in a table, with rows and columns.

● An array is given a name by the programmer.

● An array is declared, along with other variables, like this:

```
int[][]  alice = new int[24][23];
```

in which 24 is the number of rows in the array and 23 is the number of columns.

● An individual component of an array is referred to by an integer index, for example:

```
alice[12][3] = 45;
```

● It is common to use nested for loops in conjunction with two-dimensional arrays.

Basic operations on two-dimensional arrays

14.1 Data handler Write a program that uses a 4 × 7 array of numbers similar to the sales figures program (with output as shown in Figure 14.2). Extend the array processor program to carry out the following functions:

- When a button is pressed marked 'sums', add up the values for each of the seven columns and add up all the values of each of the four rows and display them.
- When a button marked 'largest' is pressed, find the largest value in each row, the largest in each column and the largest value in the complete array.
- When a button marked 'scale' is pressed, multiply every number in the array by a number entered into a text field.

Statistical measures

14.2 Extend the array processor program so that it provides a button to calculate the average sales per day for each shop. So for example the average sales of computers per day in shop 2 might be 23.

Extend it further to provide a button to calculate the mean and standard deviation of the daily sales in any shop. So for illustration, the mean number of computers sold in any shop could be 19, with a standard deviation of 6.4.

Bar charts and pie charts

14.3 Extend the array processor program so that the user can click on a button, then select a row of the table by clicking the mouse on the row. There is also a button to allow the user to similarly select a column. The information is then displayed as a bar chart.

Extend the program to display optionally the information in a single row or a column as a pie chart.

(Displaying information as bar charts and pie charts is explained in Chapter 13 on one-dimensional arrays.)

Mathematical operations

14.4 Transpose The transpose of an array is the technical term used to describe swapping the components in an array across one of the diagonals. The numbers on the diagonal do not change. So if an array is:

1	2	3	4
6	7	8	9
10	11	12	13
14	15	16	17

then its transpose is:

1	6	10	14
2	7	11	15
3	8	12	16
4	9	13	17

Write a program to input the components of an array in the same manner as the data handler program. It transposes the array when a button is pressed and displays it.

Games

14.5 Tic tac toe Tic tac toe (or noughts and crosses) is played on a 3 × 3 grid, which is initially empty. Each of two players goes in turn. One places a cross in a blank square; the other places a nought in a blank square.

The winner is the person who gets a line of three noughts or three crosses. Thus a win for noughts might look like this:

```
o x o
x o
x     o
```

Games can end in a draw, where neither side has obtained a line.

Write a program to play the game. One player is the computer, which plays as noughts and which decides where to play on a random basis.

This is a fun game and it is very interactive. There is just one button – to start a new game. The human player specifies a move by clicking with the mouse on the place where the cross is to be placed.

If you have read Chapter 20 on using graphics, then make the program show graphical noughts and crosses, as shown in Figure 14.3.

14.6 Battleships is a game normally played by two people using paper and pencil. In this version, a person plays the computer. The computer also records and displays the status of the game. When it is the computer's turn to play, it always plays completely randomly. The game is also slightly simplified.

Two 10 × 10 grids are shown on the screen. The home grid represents an ocean showing where your battleships are. The enemy grid shows where you have fired a shot, but you cannot see the enemy. You don't know where the computer has placed its ships, and the computer doesn't know where yours are.

Initially you place 10 battleships somewhere on your grid. You do this by clicking the mouse on the squares that you want. The computer also places its own 10 ships somewhere hidden on the target grid. The computer places its ships randomly, but you can, of course, play with a strategy.

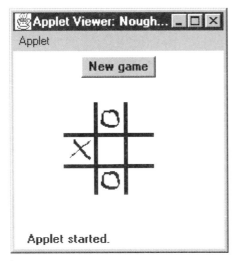

Figure 14.3 Noughts and crosses.

The computer determines randomly who goes first. The computer and you then play in turn.

You 'fire' a shot at the enemy (the computer), by clicking on a square on the target grid. The computer displays the position on the grid, so that you can see where you have fired your shots. The computer displays whether or not one of its ships has been sunk.

Then it is the computer's turn to fire at you. Although it holds the data on where your ships are, it does not use this data in choosing (randomly) where to fire at you. But the computer remembers where it has already fired.

Play continues until one player sinks all the enemy's ships. Mid-way through a game the grids might look like this:

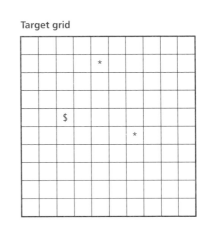

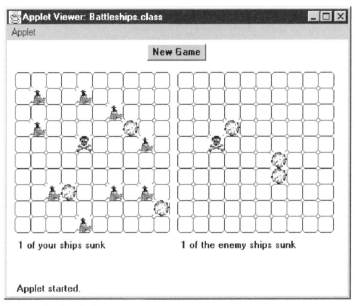

Figure 14.4 Screen for battleships game.

b shows where you have placed your battleships
! shows where the enemy has fired at you
* shows where you have fired at the enemy
$ shows where you have sunk an enemy ship

You can display characters as shown above to describe the status of the fleets. Alternatively you could display coloured circles or rectangles using the `drawRect` or `drawOval` methods. In Chapter 20 we explain how to display graphical images on the screen as shown in Figure 14.4. You can see how to make this game display more exciting images.

Artificial life

14.7 Cellular Life An organism consists of single cells that are on (alive) or off (dead). Each generation of life consists of a single row of cells. Each generation of life (each row) of the organism depends on the previous one (just like real life). Time moves downwards, from top to bottom. Each row represents a generation. The lives look like this:

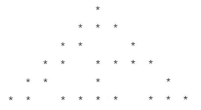

or, without the encompassing array lines:

```
                          *
                      *   *   *
                   *  *           *
                *  *     *  *  *  *
             *  *        *           *
          *  *     *  *  *  *     *  *  *
```

In the beginning, there is just one cell alive. Whether a cell is alive or dead depends on a combination of factors – whether or not it was alive in the last generation and whether or not its immediate neighbours were alive in the last generation. You can see that, even after only five generations, a pattern is emerging. These patterns are very subtle and mimic the patterns found in real living organisms. The rules are as follows.

A cell lives only if:

● it was dead, but only its left neighbour was alive
● it was dead, but only its right neighbour was alive
● it was alive, but its immediate neighbours were dead
● it was alive, and only its right neighbour was alive

So, for example, given the following generation:

● The first cell lives, because even though it was dead, its immediate right neighbour was alive.
● The second cell lives because only its immediate right neighbour was alive.
● The third living cell dies (through overcrowding, we surmise!).
● The fourth cell dies.
● The fifth cell lives because, although it was dead, its immediate left neighbour was alive.

So the new generation is:

Write a program that uses a two-dimensional array to chart the progress of the life form. Display the development on the screen as asterisks, as above. Provide a button that allows the user to go on to the next generation.

14.8 Conway's Game of Life In this life form, again, an organism consists of single cells that are on (alive) or off (dead). In this form of life, the organisms exist in a two-dimensional grid world, for example:

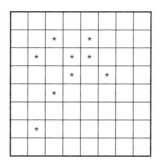

The rules governing this organism are:

1. If a live cell has two or three neighbours, it will survive. Otherwise it will die of isolation or overcrowding.
2. If an empty cell is surrounded by exactly three cells, then a new live cell will be 'born' to fill the space.
3. All 'births' and 'deaths' take place simultaneously.

Write a program to simulate this kind of life. The program should initially allow the user to click on the cells that are to be alive. Provide a button that allows the user to go on to the next generation and display it.

The program needs two arrays – one to represent the current state of life and another to represent the next generation. After a new generation is created, the roles of the two arrays are swapped.

ANSWERS TO SELF-TEST QUESTIONS

14.1 Column 5 is Saturday.
14 computers were sold at shop 3 on Thursday.
This is row 2 and column 3.

14.2   `String[][] board = new String[8][8];`

14.3   `for (int row = 0; row < 8; row++)`
`        for (int col = 0; col < 8; col++)`
`            board[row][col] = "no piece";`

14.4
```
public void output(int[][] array, Graphics g) {
    int x, y;
    y = 10;
    for (int row = 0; row < array.length; row++) {
        x = 10;
        for (int col = 0; col < array[0].length; col++) {
            g.drawString(Integer.toString(array[row][col]),
                                                    x, y);
            x = x + 20;
        }
        y = y + 20;
    }
}


public int[][] multiply(int[][] array, int constant) {
    int[][] newArray = new int[array.length][array[0].length];
    for (int row = 0; row < array.length; row++)
        for (int col = 0; col < array[0].length; col++)
            newArray[row][col] = array[row][col] * constant;
    return newArray;
}
```

14.5
```
public int addRow(int[][] array) {
    int sum = 0;
    int row = 1;
    for (int col = 0; col < array[0].length; col++)
        sum = sum + array[row][col];
    return sum;
}
```

14.6
```
String[][] numbers = {
                        {"one", "two", "three"},
                        {"four", "five", "six"},
                        {"seven", "eight", "nine"},
                    } ;
```

String manipulation

● Introduction

Strings of characters are very important in software. All real-world programming languages have facilities for primitive character manipulation, but Java has a particularly useful collection of methods. In this chapter, we will bring together the string features we have made use of up to now, and extend this by studying the set of string-processing methods.

The main use of strings is in input–output and the user interface. For example, we need to:

- display messages on the screen, which also might involve placing text on command buttons;
- input text from the user. In an applet, this is often from a `TextField` or `TextArea`. In a standalone application, text might also be entered at a keyboard prompt;
- manipulate files. Applets have restrictions on their file-processing capabilities for security reasons, but when we examine files in Chapter 19 we will see that the content of many types of file can be regarded as sequences of strings. Additionally, filenames and directory (folder) names are strings;
- specify and manipulate URLs.

● A note on the `char` type

In this book we are stressing program clarity rather than execution speed. However, sometimes we encounter situations in which we might wish to avoid the extra time penalty of using strings. As an example, consider the case when our strings only hold one character. Java has an additional primitive type called `char`, which stores each item as a 16 bit Unicode character, and a result of this is that char comparison can be done as swiftly as int comparison, whereas the comparison of strings takes longer. Here, we provide examples of its use. We can declare variables and provide an initial value:

```
char initial = 'M';
char marker = '\n';
char letter;
```

Note the use of the single-quote characters. They can only enclose a single character. (The \n, though it looks like two characters, is replaced at compile-time by the single newline (or 'enter') character.)

We can assign values, as in:

```
initial = 'P';
letter = initial;
```

We can compare, as in:

```
if (initial == 's')...
```

and we can make use of the behind-the-scenes number representation of the characters: the digit characters 0 to 9 have successive integer values, so we can use < to mean 'before', and > to mean 'after', as in:

```
if ((initial >= '0')&&(initial <= '9')) //test if digit
```

The characters A to Z and a to z also have the same property, so we can put:

```
if ((initial >= 'A')&&(initial <= 'Z')) //test if upper-case letter
```

The char type is used rarely, but it is efficient in terms of run-time speed. It is vital to note that, along with int, float, boolean, double and long, it is a primitive type. We can compare char values with ==. On the contrary, items of class String are proper objects, not primitive types, and we must use the equals method, as in:

```
String s;
if(s.equals("fred"))...
```

● The String class

As you know from previous examples, we can create strings and arrays of strings. We can also concatenate (join) them, display them and input them from a TextField. What we have not seen up to now is the detailed use of library methods in the class String. The situation is rather complicated in that there are two string classes – String and StringBuffer. We have been discussing 'strings' in general here, with a lower-case 's', and we shall continue to use the term – but to be precise, we mean instances of the class String. For most purposes, this class will suffice, and this is the class we shall describe in detail. The StringBuffer class is appropriate when a program is performing intensive string handling, as in a word processor or compiler. However, it is more intricate.

● Using strings – a recap

Here, we bring together the string facilities that have been shown so far.

We can declare variables and provide an initial value, as in:

```
String x, y;
String myCity;
String myName = "Parr";
String myCountry = new("Japan");
```

In the final line above, we have shown the full way of providing an initial value, because it illustrates that, behind the scenes, the use of new is always involved to allocate space for the string value. However, there is no advantage in using this form – a new is performed whether you explicitly request it or not.

We can assign one string to another, as in:

```
x = "England";
x = "France";
y = x;
x = "";          //a zero-length string
```

This illustrates that the length of a string can vary. Strictly, the old string is destroyed and is replaced with a totally new value. The space that was occupied by the old value will be made available for other data via garbage collection.

We can use the + operator to concatenate strings, as in the familiar:

```
int number = 123;
g.drawString("value is "+ number, 100,100);
```

Take care when using several + operators, as in:

```
g.drawString("value is "+22+33, 100,100);
```

The Java rule is that when one item is a string, the others are converted to strings, so the above displays:

```
value is 2233
```

We can force the numeric addition to be performed first by putting:

```
g.drawString("value is "+(22+33), 100,100);
```

which displays:

```
value is 55
```

A common feature of string processing is to begin with an initially empty string, and to join items onto it as the program runs. We might put:

```
x = x + "something";
```

which adds to the end of x. This is known as 'appending'.

We can compare strings, as in:

```
if (x.equals(y))...
```

We can create arrays of strings (with subscripts starting from 0), as in:

```
String cities[] = new String[10]; //10 components
```

and manipulate elements, as in:

```
cities[1] = "Los Angeles";
```

We can convert strings to `int` and `float`. This is useful when we are presented with strings from a `TextField` (or from a file, as we shall see later). For example, we may put:

```
int intValue = Integer.parseInt(dataString);
```

If the input string does not contain a valid number, this method produces an error indication – an exception. We will study data input in more detail later in the chapter, and in Chapter 16 we shall see how errors can be detected.

This much we have seen. Now we will look at the detail of strings and the available methods.

● The characters within strings

String values are placed between double quote characters – but what if we need to display a double quote on the screen? We could try the following:

```
g.drawString("A "tricky" problem!", 100, 100); //wrong
```

This won't compile, as the second " is taken as the end of the complete string. Instead, we can make use of the 'backslash' character \, which instructs Java to treat the following character as an ordinary character, rather than one with a special meaning. The jargon for \ is the 'escape' character. So, the solution to our quoting problem is:

```
g.drawString("A \"tricky\" problem!", 100,100); //OK
```

which displays:

```
A "tricky" problem!
```

The sequences \n, \t and \u also have a special meaning in Java:

● \n stands for the newline character.
● \t stands for the tab character. Note that the tab settings depend on your computer. Typical settings are at every fourth character position.
● The \u combination is followed by four hexadecimal characters, representing a Unicode international character. We won't use this in our examples.

However, it is important to note that \n and \t do not work when using `drawString`, because this method expects you to use pixel coordinates to control the positioning of text.

● The `String` **class methods**

First, some general points. Each character in a string has an index (or position number). The first character is numbered 0. Furthermore, many of the `string` methods require you to provide index values, and if you accidentally provide a negative index or one that is too large, a message containing the exception name `StringIndexOutOfBoundsException` will be produced.

Here we shall look at the most useful methods of `string`. Because you might want to run applets to confirm your understanding of each method, we will provide a basic `StringDemo` applet with two `TextField` inputs, a 'go' button, and a `TextField` output. When the button is clicked, your choice of string operation will be performed. Figure 15.1 shows the applet running.

To display the results, we have used a `TextField` which can display text via the `setText` method. In addition we have prevented the user from typing over the output by the statement:

```
resultField.setEditable(false);
```

The applet is suitable for use with those methods below which provide an explicit example. Look at the coding below to see where your statements should be inserted.

Though we are using applets as a vehicle for string examples, be aware that, when we come to free-standing programs, the strings might be input directly from files or from a command line. Here is the applet program:

```
import java.awt.*;
import java.applet.*;
import java.util.*;
import java.awt.event.*;


    public class StringDemo extends Applet
        implements ActionListener {
```

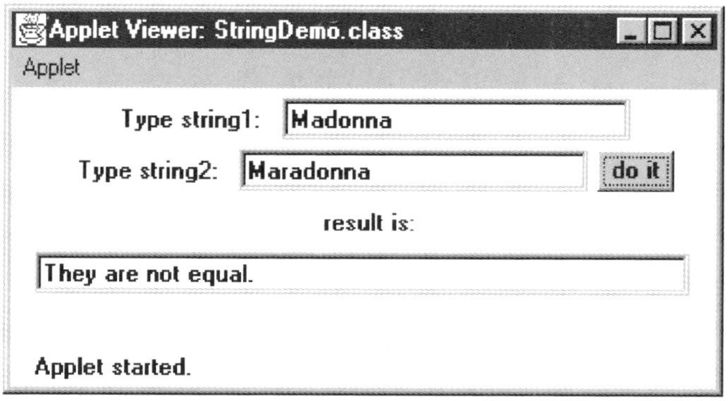

Figure 15.1 Screen for string demo.

```java
    private TextField string1Field, string2Field;
    private TextField resultField;
    Label string1Label, string2Label, resultLabel;
    Button goButton;

public void init() {
    string1Label = new Label("Type string1: ");
    string2Label = new Label("Type string2: ");
    resultLabel = new Label("result is: ");

    goButton = new Button("do it");

    string1Field = new TextField(20);
    string2Field = new TextField(20);
    resultField = new TextField(40);
    resultField.setEditable(false);
    add(string1Label);
    add(string1Field);
    add(string2Label);
    add(string2Field);
    add(goButton);
    goButton.addActionListener(this);
    add(resultLabel);
    add(resultField);
}


public void actionPerformed(ActionEvent event) {
    String result ="";
    if (event.getSource() == goButton) {
        String string1 = string1Field.getText();
        String string2 = string2Field.getText();
        // string example - enter string1 and string2
        //.... insert your code here

        if(string1.equals(string2))
            result="They are equal.";
        else
            result="They are not equal.";

        // end of example
        resultField.setText(result);
    }
}
}
```

● Comparing strings

The most important methods are `equals`, `equalsIgnoreCase` and `compareTo`.

equals

This is used to compare values; we should not use `==` to do this. Here is an example, which can be inserted in the demonstration program:

```
// String example - enter string1 and string2
if (string1.equals(string2))
    result = "They are equal.";
else
    result = "They are not equal.";
// end of example
```

equalsIgnoreCase

This provides a similar facility to `equals`, except the case (upper or lower) of each character is ignored. '`This String`' will be regarded as equal to '`this string`'. To experiment with this, use the above code, but replace the invocation of `equals` by an invocation of `equalsIgnoreCase`.

compareTo

Imagine that we have a number of strings (perhaps holding people's names) which we need to place in alphabetical order. The `compareTo` method allows us to do this. Behind the scenes, the internal integer codes for the characters are used. The only point to be wary of is that lower-case letters have higher codes than upper-case letters. Here are some examples:

ant	is before	bee
and	is before	ant
an	is before	and
ANT	is before	BEE
INSECT	is before	ant
Insect	is before	ant
INSECT	is before	insect

`compareTo` returns an integer result, with the following meaning:

- `0` if the strings are equal;
- a negative value if the string object precedes the parameter;
- a positive value if the string object follows the parameter.

If we put:

```
n = "ant".compareTo("bee");
```

then n will be set to a negative value. You can check this with the following code:

```
//String example - enter string1 and string2
int n = string1.compareTo(string2);
if (n == 0)
    result = "they are equal";
else if (n < 0)
    result = "string1 precedes string2";
else
    result = "string2 precedes string1";
// end of example
```

● Amending strings

Here we look at methods which change a string. Behind the scenes, these methods create a new string rather than changing the original string.

replace

This method replaces one character by another, throughout the string. For example:

```
string1 = "Mississippi".replace('i','a');
```

would place "Massassappa" in string1. You can experiment with the following code. Insert it in the demonstration program.

```
//String example - enter string1
result = string1.replace('a', 'A'); //replace every 'a' by 'A'
// end of example
```

toLowerCase

The toLowerCase method converts any upper-case letters in a string into lower-case letters, as in:

```
string1 = "Version 1.1";
result = string1.toLowerCase();
```

which puts "version 1.1" in result. You can experiment with this by using the following lines of code:

```
//String example - enter string1
result = string1.toLowerCase();
//end of example
```

toUpperCase

The `toUpperCase` method does a similar operation as `toLowerCase`, but changes any lower-case letters into upper-case equivalents. For example:

```
string1 = "Java";
result = string1.toUpperCase();
```

would set `result` to `"JAVA"`.

trim

The `trim` method removes white space from both ends of a string. 'White space' not only means space characters, but also newlines and tabs. If we put:

```
string1 = "        Centre        ";
result = string1.trim();
```

then `string1` becomes `"Centre"`. Here is some code to exercise `trim`:

```
//String example - enter string1
result = string1.trim();
//end of example
```

● Examining strings

These methods allow us to examine a string – for example, to extract a section of it. A section of a string is often called a substring.

length

The `length` method returns the current number of characters in a string, as in:

```
int n = "Java Programming".length();
```

Here, `n` is set to 16. The following code placed within the `StringDemo` applet will display the length of a string that you input:

```
//String example - enter string1
result = "length is " + string1.length();
//end of example
```

Obtaining the length of an array is done differently. For example, the length of an array called `table` is given by `table.length`.

substring

The `substring` method extracts a specified part of a string. The invoker provides the starting position, and the position 1 greater than the last character to be extracted. Take care with this second parameter! In this extract:

```
string1 = "position";
result = string1.substring(2,5);
```

`result` is set to the string `"sit"`. The first position in a string is numbered `0`, and the last character is always at `length()-1`, as you can see from the following diagram:

Index	0	1	2	3	4	5	6	7
Character	p	o	s	i	t	i	o	n

(length is 8)

Here is the code for the example program, which displays its input with the first and last characters removed.

```
//String example - enter string1
result = string1.substring(1, string1.length()-1);
//end of example
```

> **SELF-TEST QUESTION**
>
> **15.1** Explain the effect of the following code:
>
> ```
> String word = "position";
> String s = word.substring(2, word.length() );
> ```

charAt

The `charAt` method returns the character at a specified position. Note that the result is of type `char`, not a string of length 1. In some situations, this will be faster than the use of `substring`. Here is an example:

```
char c1,c2;
string1 = "position";
c1 = string1.charAt(1);        // c1 becomes 'o'
c2 = string1.charAt(4);        // c2 becomes 't'
```

indexOf

This method determines whether a substring is contained within a string. We can provide an offset, specifying where the search is to start. For example:

```
int n = "mississippi".indexOf("is",4);
```

sets n to 4, showing the position of the second `"is"`. (Recall that the first position of a string is numbered 0.)

However, if we put:

```
int n = "mississippi".indexOf("is",5);
```

then n becomes -1, indicating that the string has not been found. (The value 5 indicates a search from the third "s").

Here is some code for the example program, which reports on whether a string contains a substring.

```
//string example - enter string1 and string2
if (string1.indexOf(string2,0) >= 0)
    result = string2+" exists in "+string1;
else
    result = string2+" does not exist in "+string1;
//end of example
```

lastIndexOf

This method is similar in concept to indexOf, but returns the position of the rightmost occurrence of a substring. The value -1 is returned if no match is found. Here is an example:

```
int n = "//a.b.c/directory/file".lastIndexOf("/");
```

The value 17 is returned.

endsWith

This method is used to find out if a string ends with a particular substring. Yes, you *could* use a combination of other methods to accomplish this, but the provided method is less error-prone. The method returns a boolean value. For example:

```
boolean r = "http://path/".endsWith("/");
```

would set r to true.

Here is some code for the example program, which determines whether a substring is present at the end of another string:

```
//string example - enter string1 and string2
if (string1.endsWith(string2))
    result = "string1 ends with " + string2;
else
    result = "string1 does not end with "+string2;
//end of example
```

● **The** StringTokenizer **class**

We have seen that strings can be searched for a substring and, based on the result, can be split into parts. However, when our data contains repeated substrings separated by special characters, the splitting up can be more easily done using the StringTokenizer class. Here are some typical strings that we might want to take apart:

```
January 21  5
4,6  ,7,10,10,12,13,  15,  21,20,19,  8
```

In both of these strings, there is the concept of a *delimiter*, which breaks up the separate items (or tokens). In the first example, representing the hours of sunshine on 21 January, the delimiter is a space, or a series of spaces. In the second example, the delimiter is a comma, but there are also spaces present. The above strings are typical of the kind of data that exists in files. Sometimes such files are created by other Java programs, or they could have been produced by exporting data from a spreadsheet. (For details of file processing, see Chapter 19.)

Here is how we can view the strings token-by-token:

```
String example1 = "January 21 5";
String month, day, hours;
StringTokenizer sunData = new StringTokenizer(example1," ");
month = sunData.nextToken();
day = sunData.nextToken();
hours = sunData.nextToken();
```

What we have done is to create a new instance of the StringTokenizer class, called sunData. In the constructor, we supply the string to be taken apart and a string which contains the delimiter (or delimiters). To deal with the first string, we used " ", with the result that any spaces will be treated as delimiters rather than as data. We then make use of the nextToken method to fetch each item in turn. Depending on the problem, we could choose to convert the strings of digits into int.

For the second string, let us assume that we don't know in advance how many tokens it contains. We can make use of the hasMoreTokens method, which returns true if there is more data for nextToken to fetch. We also supply a delimiter string of " ,", indicating that spaces and/or commas are delimiters. We might put:

```
String example2 = "4,6 ,7,10,10,12,13,  15,  21,20,19,  8";
String item;
StringTokenizer numberList = new StringTokenizer(example2," ,");
while (numberList.hasMoreTokens() ) {
    item = numberList.nextToken();
    // .... process item
}
```

To summarize, the main methods of the class `StringTokenizer` are:

```
nextToken()
hasMoreTokens()
```

● String conversions

Data that we display on the screen or input from the keyboard is in the form of strings – but the internal form that we use may be different. For example, we may need to input a series of digits as a string, and then convert them to an `int` type. Java has a range of 'parse' methods, which convert strings into a variety of types, and many classes in the Java library provide a `toString` method, which produces a string representation of an instance.

However, before looking at the detail of the conversion methods, we need to recall the idea of built-in types versus classes, introduced in Chapter 9. The primitive built-in types (`int`, `float` etc.) are not classes – we don't create instances of them with `new`. However, due to the use of inheritance and polymorphism, many methods are written to work with instances of any class – it is difficult to write software which works with instances of classes *and* built-in types!

To make such a task possible, the Java library provides so-called 'wrapper' classes which act as alternatives to the built-in types, concealing them inside classes. The names of these classes are:

```
Integer
Float
Double
Long
Boolean
Character
Byte
Short
```

Note carefully that the names follow the Java convention of using a capital letter to start the class name. Thus, `float` is the built-in type, and `Float` is its wrapper class.

Let us return to string conversions. Many of the classes in the Java libraries provide a `toString` method which returns a string representation of an object, and the wrapper classes provide `valueOf` methods which:

● can convert a string value into a wrapper type;
● can convert built-in types to wrapper types and vice versa.

Here we will illustrate only those methods needed to do conversion between `string`, `int` and `float`.

To convert an `int` to a `String`:

```
int n = 123;
String s = Integer.toString(n);      //s becomes "123"
```

Note the use of the class name `Integer` before the static method name.

To convert a `float` to a `String`:

```
float f = 12.34f;
String s = Float.toString(f);        //s becomes "12.34"
```

Again, note the use of the class name `Float` (with a capital `F`) before the static method name.

To convert a `String` to an `int`:

```
String s = "1234";
int n = Integer.parseInt(s);
```

The `parseInt` method returns an `int` type.

A common use of this is when a string of digits is obtained from a `TextField`, as in:

```
if (event.getSource() == someTextField) {
    n = Integer.parseInt(someTextField.getText() );
}
```

To convert a String to a float, we can use `parseFloat` as follows:

```
String s = "12.34";
float f = Float.parseFloat(s);
```

When converting user input into numbers, there is always the problem of errors. The user might type:

```
123XY3
```

Here we have assumed that an input error is not dangerous, and in fact our programs which use the above conversion approach will simply not deal with errors. This is not acceptable for serious software, and in Chapter 16 we will see how to detect and handle such errors.

● String parameters

As we have seen in our review of available methods, strings can be passed as parameters and returned as results; their use is reasonably intuitive. However, you may recall that Java has two approaches to the passing of parameters:

● by value for the built-in primitive types;
● by reference for objects (including arrays).

The key difference in these approaches is that when a reference is passed, any changes that we make to the original object (e.g. by using its methods) have an immediate effect within the object referred to. When a value is passed, any changes we make will take place in a local variable, not in the original value. The significance that this has for string parameters is as follows: strings are objects, and are passed by reference. But because changing the value of a string is regarded as creating a totally new string, rather than manipulating an existing value via methods, the change has only a local effect.

In short, you can regard string parameters as behaving like a built-in type (say `int`). Here is an example. We will create a method which doubles a string, thus `"hello"` becomes `"hellohello"`.

```
private String doubleIt(String any) {
    return any + any;
}
```

Here is how we might invoke the method:

```
String s1 = "hello";
s1 = doubleIt(s1);
```

If we try to create a method which can be invoked by:

```
String s1 = "hello";
doubleIt(s1);
```

we have:

```
private void doubleIt(String any) { // doesn't work
    any = any+any;
}
```

This only produces a change in the local `any`, rather than in `s1`.

● An example of string processing

Here we will look at the creation of a string processing method which performs a commonly required function – to examine a string, replacing every occurrence of a given substring by another substring (of potentially different length). Note that the `string` class has a `replace` method, but it can only handle single characters. We will create a method which works with substrings. Here is an example. If we have the string:

```
"to be or not to be"
```

and we replace every occurrence of `"be"` by `"eat"`, we will create:

```
"to eat or not to eat"
```

The basic process is to use `indexOf` to determine the position of a substring – `"be"` here. We then form a new string made up of the left part of the string, the right part, and the replacement string in the centre. We have:

```
"to " + "eat" + " or not to be"
```

The process must then be repeated until there are no more occurrences of `"be"`. There are two problem cases:

- The user of `replace` asks us to replace a value of `""`. We could regard any string as being preceded by an infinite number of such empty strings! Our approach here is to simply return the unchanged original string.
- The replacement string contains the string to be replaced. For example, we might try to change `"be"` to `"beat"`. To prevent an infinite number of replacements taking place, we ensure that we only consider substrings in the right-hand part of the string. We use the variable `startSearch` to keep track of the start of the right-hand part of the string. The full code is:

```
private String replace(String original, String from, String to) {

    String leftBit, rightBit;
    int startSearch = 0;
    int place = original.indexOf(from);
    if (from.length() != 0) {

        while (place >= startSearch) {
            leftBit = original.substring(0, place);
            rightBit = original.substring(place+from.length(),
                                   original.length());

            original = leftBit+to+rightBit;
            startSearch = leftBit.length()+to.length();
            place = original.indexOf(from);

        }
    }
    return original;

}
```

Here is how we might invoke our method:

```
String original = "to be or not to be";
String changed = replace(original, "be", "eat");
```

Obviously, the above extract will not work in isolation, so now we will incorporate it into a program.

● String case study – Frasier

In 1970, Joseph Weizenbaum wrote a program known as ELIZA to simulate a particular style of psychiatrist. It was a simple program, in the sense that it made little attempt to understand the sense of the input that users (patients) typed. For example, if the patient entered:

```
I am feeling sad
```

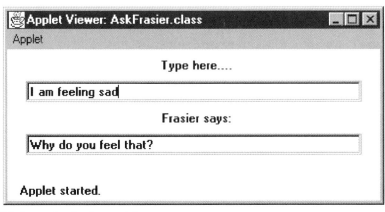

Figure 15.2 Screen for Frasier applet.

then ELIZA might respond with:

```
you are feeling sad - why?
```

Similarly, if the patient typed:

```
I am feeling Java
```

then ELIZA might respond with:

```
You are feeling Java - why?
```

Here we present an even more simplified version, which we will call Frasier, after the US sitcom character.

The approach to the design will be based on the Model–View–Controller, in which the user interface is separated from the string processing. The model class only needs two methods – to accept a question, and to produce a reply. It has the form:

```
class Psychiatrist {
    private String question;
    private String reply;
//etc.
```

and the methods needed are:

```
public void putQuestion(String q)
public String getReply()
```

Now the view and controller. The view is simple to write as we won't use graphics, hence no `paint` or `repaint` is needed. Figure 15.2 shows the program in use. The minimal user interface for such a dialogue program takes the form of two `TextFields`, one to accept user input, and another (uneditable) one to show output from the program. We could have contemplated the use of `drawString` to display the resulting string, but the use of an uneditable `TextField` makes it easier to handle strings of different lengths, and ensures that output does not overwrite any user interface components. Here is the complete applet. Its overall structure is identical to that of the balloon example of Chapter 10.

```java
import java.awt.*;
import java.applet.*;
import java.util.*;
import java.awt.event.*;

public class AskFrasier extends Applet
    implements ActionListener {

    private TextField questionField;
    private TextField replyField;
    private Label questionLabel, psychiatristLabel;
    private Psychiatrist frasier;

    public void init() {
        questionLabel = new Label("Type here.... ");
        psychiatristLabel = new Label("Frasier says: ");
        add(questionLabel);
        questionField = new TextField(40);
        add(questionField);
        questionField.addActionListener(this);
        add(psychiatristLabel);
        replyField = new TextField(40);
        replyField.setEditable(false);
        add(replyField);
        replyField.setText("Go ahead please....");
        frasier = new Psychiatrist();
    }

    public void actionPerformed(ActionEvent event) {
        if (event.getSource() == questionField) {
            String itsValue = questionField.getText();
            frasier.putQuestion(itsValue);
            replyField.setText(frasier.getReply() );
        }
    }
}

class Psychiatrist {

    private String question;
    private String reply;
    private Random randomValue = new Random();
```

```java
    public void putQuestion(String q) {
        question = " " + q + " ";
    }

    public String getReply() {
        int variation = randomValue.nextInt() % 3;
        switch (variation) {
            case 0: reply = transformQuestion(); break;
            case 1: reply = "Why do you feel that?"; break;
            case 2: reply = "please be frank!"; break;
        }
        return reply;
    }

    private String transformQuestion() {
        if (question.indexOf(" I ") >= 0) {
            String tempReply = replace (question," I ", " you ");
            tempReply = replace(tempReply, " am ", " are ");
            return replace(tempReply, " my "," your ") + "-why?";
        }
        else
            if (question.indexOf(" no ") >= 0)
                return "no? that is negative! Please explain....";
            else
                return "\"" + question + "\"-Please re-phrase..";
    }

    private String replace(String original, String from, String to) {
        String leftBit, rightBit;
        int startSearch = 0;
        int place = original.indexOf(from);
        if (from.length() != 0) {

            while (place >= startSearch) {
                leftBit = original.substring(0, place);
                rightBit = original.substring(place + from.length(),
                                        original.length());

                original = leftBit + to + rightBit;
                startSearch = leftBit.length() + to.length();
                place = original.indexOf(from);
            }
        }
        return original;
    }
}
```

Event handling is straightforward – when the user hits 'enter', the question is put to Frasier, and he is then asked for a reply. This is where the real string work gets performed:

```
if (event.getSource() == questionField) {
    String itsValue = questionField.getText();
    frasier.putQuestion(itsValue);
    replyField.setText(frasier.getReply() );
}
```

To make the responses seem more human, we add an element of randomness:

```
int variation = randomValue.nextInt()%3;
switch (variation) {
    case 0: reply = transformQuestion(); break;
    case 1: reply = "Why do you feel that?"; break;
    case 2: reply = "please be frank!"; break;
}
```

The random integer provides three cases. In two of them, we produce a standard reply, but in the other case, we transform the question, by e.g. replacing every " I " by " you ". We add extra spaces at the start and end of the question to assist in detecting whole words. Note that the program has no knowledge of English meanings or grammar. To add this would involve a major programming effort.

Grammar spot

The `String` class methods require us to provide a string to be operated on, as in:

```
String s = "demo";
int n = s.length();
```

Note that we can supply a literal string, or a method invocation which returns a string, as in:

```
n = "another demo".length();
n = s.substring(0, 2).length();
```

Programming pitfalls

● `Strings` are objects, and the `String` class provides methods. The correct usage is, for example:

```
int n = string1.length();
```

rather than:

```
int n = length(string1);
```

- The input of `int` and `float` items uses strings, and is intricate. Follow our examples carefully.
- The final parameter of `substring` needs care. It indicates the position one beyond the item to be extracted.
- A `StringIndexOutOfBounds` exception message will direct you to a line of your program in which one of the index parameters is negative, or attempts to access a character beyond the end of the string.
- The `\n` and `\t` combinations are ignored by `drawString`.

New language elements

- The `char` primitive (built-in) type.
- The `\` as the escape character.

Summary

- Instances of the class `string` contain a sequence of characters. The first character is at position 0.

- `string` instances can be declared and created by e.g.:

      String name = "a sequence of chars";

- The most useful methods for string manipulation are:

Comparing strings
    equals
    equalsIgnoreCase
    compareTo

Amending strings
    replace
    toLowerCase
    toUpperCase
    trim

Examining strings
    length
    substring
    charAt
    indexOf
    lastIndexOf
    endsWith
    StringTokenizer (class)

Conversion

    toString
    parseInt
    parseFloat

(along with the Float and Integer wrapper classes).

15.1 Write a program which inputs two strings from TextFields, and which joins them together. Show the resulting string in an uneditable TextField.

15.2 Write a program which inputs one string and determines whether or not it is a palindrome. A palindrome reads the same backwards and forwards, so 'abba' is a palindrome.

15.3 Write a program to input a string which can be a float or an int. Display the type of the number. Assume that a float contains a decimal point.

15.4 Modify the Frasier program to make it more human, by adding more variation to the replies.

15.5 Write a program which allows input of the form:

    123 + 45
    6783 - 5

(i.e. two integers with + or - between them, spaces separating items) and which displays the result of the calculation.

15.6 Extend Exercise 15.5 so that input of the form:

    12 + 345 - 44 - 23 - 57 + 2345

can be handled. Assume that the user will make no errors. (Hint: the pattern of such input is an initial number, followed by any number of operator/number pairs. Use StringTokenizer. Your program should handle the initial number, then loop to handle the following pairs.)

15.7 Extend Exercise 15.5 so that input can take two forms:

    setm 2 426
    12 + m2

The setm instruction is followed by two numbers. The first one refers to a memory store numbered from 0 to 9, and the second one is a number which is to be stored in the memory. Calculations can now be done using integers as earlier, and also memory names. (Hint: use an `int` array to represent the memory.) Extend your program so that the following forms are processed:

```
m3 = 12 + m5 - 328 - m7
display m3
```

15.8 Write an applet which stores integers as strings, up to a digit length of 50. It should allow the input of two such strings, and provide buttons to select addition or subtraction. (Hint: recall how you were taught to add numbers by hand.) Provide multiply and divide buttons, and implement these features by repeated addition or subtraction.

ANSWER TO SELF-TEST QUESTION

15.1 The value of s becomes `"sition"`.

Exceptions

Introduction

The term 'exception' is used in Java to convey the idea that something has gone wrong – in common parlance, an error has occurred. It is an 'exceptional circumstance'. Note that we mean exception in the sense of unusual, rather than wonderful! As you will be aware from your use of computers, there are a variety of circumstances in which software can go wrong, but good-quality software should cope with predictable problems in a satisfactory way. For example, here are some awkward situations involving a typical word processor, with possible (sometimes unsatisfactory) outcomes:

- The system invites you to type a font size as a number, and you type a name. The system could quit and return you to the operating system, it could ignore your input and leave the font size as it was, or it could display a helpful message and invite you to try again.
- You attempt to load a file which cannot be found on disk. The responses could be similar to the previous case.
- You attempt to print a file, but your printer is out of paper. Again, this can be predicted, and software can be written to take sensible actions. However, this depends on the printer making its current state available to the software. In actual printers, the software can examine various status bits which indicate out-of-paper, on/offline, paper misfeed etc.

SELF-TEST QUESTION

16.1 In the above cases, decide on the best course of action the word processor should take.

Let us look at why we need some form of error notification, and how it might be provided.

When we build software and hardware systems, much of it comes as pre-packaged items, e.g. circuit boards, Java classes and methods. To simplify the design process it is essential to regard these items as encapsulated – we don't want to be bothered with how they work internally, but it is vital that the components which we use can inform our software about error situations. The software can then be set up to detect such notification and to take alternative action. But what action to take? This is the difficult bit! Complex systems consist of a hierarchy of methods – some exceptions can be handled locally in the method in which they occur, but some more serious cases may need to be passed upstairs to higher-level methods. It depends on the nature of the error. In short, there are different categories of error, which may need to be handled in different places.

As we said, things go wrong. But do we need a *special* facility for errors? Surely our `if` statement will do? We could imagine code of this form:

```
if (something wrong)
    handle the problem;
else
    handle the normal situation;
```

Here we have used a mixture of English and Java, to convey the main point. However, if we have a series of method invocations, any of which could go wrong, the logic becomes complex, and can swamp out the normal case. The initially simple flow of:

```
doA();
doB();
doC();
```

would become:

```
doA();
if (doA went wrong)
    handle the doA problem;
else
    doB();
    if (doB went wrong)
        handle the doB problem;
    else
        doC();
        if (doC went wrong)
            handle the doC problem;
        else
    etc.
```

The error cases (which we hope won't happen very often) dominate the logic, and this complexity can make programmers shy away from taking them on. In fact, we will see that the Java exception facilities allow us to stick to the coding for the normal case, and to handle exceptions in a separate area of the program.

The above `if`-based scheme has a further drawback in Java. Recall that methods can have input parameters and can return a single result. What if a method already returns a result as part of its job? It cannot return an additional error indication value easily. We would be forced into returning special values, such as −1 or a zero-length string. Such an approach is not general.

● Exceptions and objects

What kind of item allows the programmer to indicate that an error has happened and allows the error to be detected in another region of the program? For the beginner, it is tempting (but wrong) to assume that this might be done by using `boolean` variables, in the form of:

```
boolean errorCase;

... etc.

if (errorCase == true)
    handle problem...
```

However, this is *not* how errors are indicated in Java. Instead of using variables, we use an object approach. When we want to indicate an exception, we use `new` to create an instance of an appropriate exception class. Another region of the program can then check for its existence. To summarize, an instance of an exception class is created to indicate that an error has happened.

● When to use exceptions

Exceptions provide a kind of control structure – so when should we use them instead of `if` or `while`?

Obviously, if we are using provided classes which have been written to produce exceptions, then we need to handle them. But consider this situation – we have to write a program to add up a series of positive numbers, to be typed in by the user. To indicate the end of the sequence, −1 will be entered. Is the −1 an exception? No – it is expected as part of the normal input. A similar situation occurs when encountering the end-of-file when reading a file. This should not be regarded as an exception. To return to our number problem, the correct solution (in informal English/Java) takes the form:

```
get number;
while (number >= 0) {
    sum = sum + number;
    get number;
}
```

In short, we use the exception-handling facilities for errors rather than predictable normal cases.

● The jargon of exceptions

Java has its own terminology for exceptions. Exceptions are indicated by being *thrown*, and are detected elsewhere by being *caught*. Java has `throws`, `throw`, `try` and `catch` keywords to carry out these tasks. Initially, we will look at the simplest case of catching an exception thrown by a library class.

● A `try-catch` example

Here we present a simple number-doubling applet which invites the user to enter an integer into a `TextField`, and then displays either e.g.:

```
Doubled value is 248
```

or

```
Error in number:retype
```

We shall look at the new features introduced in this particular program, then move on to general cases.

```java
import java.awt.*;
import java.applet.Applet;
import java.util.*;
import java.awt.event.*;

public class ExceptionDemo1 extends Applet
    implements ActionListener {
    private TextField stringField;
    private TextField resultField;
    private Label resultLabel, stringLabel;
    public void init() {
        stringLabel = new Label("Type an integer: ");
        resultLabel = new Label("Answer: ");
        stringField = new TextField(20);
        resultField = new TextField(20);
        resultField.setEditable(false);

        add(stringLabel);
        add(stringField);
        stringField.addActionListener(this);
```

```
                add(resultLabel);
                add(resultField);
        }


        public void actionPerformed(ActionEvent event) {
                if (event.getSource() == stringField) {
                        try{
                                int number = Integer.parseInt(stringField.getText());
                                resultField.setText("Doubled value is "+(2*number));
                        }
                        catch (NumberFormatException e) {
                                resultField.setText("Error in number: retype ");
                        }
                }
        }
}
```

Figures 16.1(*a*) and (*b*) show a run with correct input and a run with the exception handling in use.

The key part of this program is:

```
try {
        int number = Integer.parseInt(stringField.getText());
        resultField.setText("Doubled value is " + (2*number));
}
catch (NumberFormatException e) {
        resultField.setText("Error in number:retype ");
}
```

This is where we say 'if something has gone wrong inside `parseInt`, handle it!'

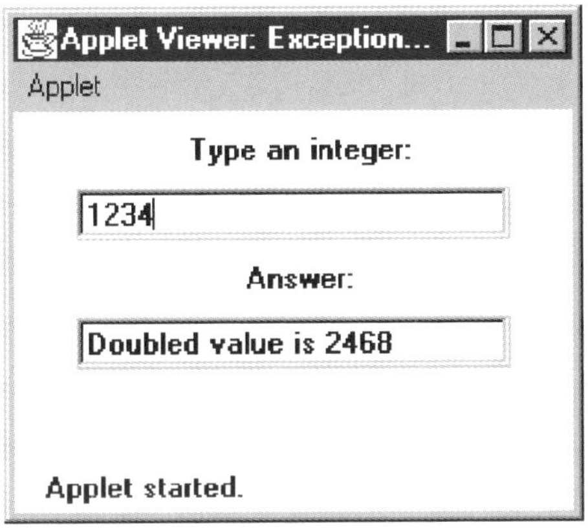

(a) 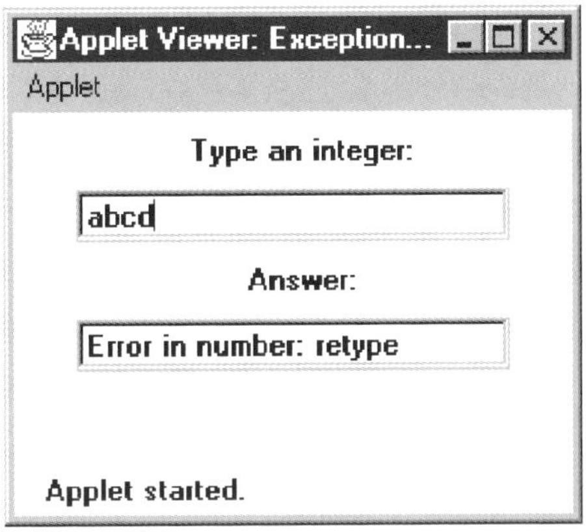   (b)

Figure 16.1 Exception handling.

There is a new statement here, which is basically a control structure. It takes the form:

```
try {
    a series of statements;
}
catch (SomeException e) {
    handle the exception;
}
```

In Java, a group of statements enclosed in { } is known as a 'block'. We talk about the 'try block' and the 'catch block'.

The concept is that we instruct Java to try to execute a block of statements. If it executes without producing an exception, the catch block is ignored, and execution continues beneath the catch block. However, if an exception is produced, we can specify that the catch block executes by stating the class of exception that we wish to catch. In our example, we consulted the library documentation for parseInt, and found that an exception of class NumberFormatException can be produced, i.e. thrown. If another kind of exception occurs, our catch will not be executed, and Java will attempt to find a catch which specifies this exception type. We will describe this process in more detail below. In our example, we have:

```
catch (NumberFormatException e)
```

which is rather like the declaration of a method. Java deposits an object of type NumberFormatException in the parameter, which we chose to name e. We could make use of it if required, by using toString. For example, we could put:

```
catch (NumberFormatException e) {
    resultField.setText("Error: " + e.toString());
}
```

The toString method returns the name of the exception together with a possible additional message clarifying the exception. The above statements produce the message:

```
Error: java.lang.NumberFormatException
```

After the catch block executes, execution continues beneath the catch block. In many cases, because methods deal with one particular task which cannot sensibly continue after an exception related to that task, it is common to return from the method, as in:

```
private void aMethod() {
    try {
    // some code
    }
    catch(Exception e) {
        // handle it
    }
} // return
```

In our example program, this is just what is required – the exception handler displays an error message and ends. The user can then enter a new number into the text field.

● try and scopes

As we stated above, when a try block produces an exception, its execution terminates – it is abandoned. A consequence of this is that any variables declared within it become inaccessible and, in particular, they cannot be used in the catch block, even when it is in the same method. This can be a problem if we want to use those variables to produce a specific error message. For example, we might want to display an offending string if it could not be converted to an integer. Fortunately, the solution is simple: any variables that are required inside the catch block must be declared outside the try block. We must put:

```
private TextField errorField;
... etc

String s;              // available in both the try and the catch
try {
    // code involving s
}
catch (Exception e) {
    errorField.setText("Error: s is "+ s); // correct
}
```

The alternative is the following, which will not compile. The variable s is local to the try block only, not the catch block as well.

```
try {
    String s;
    // code involving s
}
catch (Exception e) {
    errorField.setText("Error: s is "+ s); // will not compile!
}
```

SELF-TEST QUESTION

16.2 Investigate the names of any exceptions that the Integer class might throw.

● The search for a catcher

What if the program doesn't catch a thrown exception? The precise rules for this depend on the class of exception, as we will see later. The basic principle is based on the fact that all programs above a handful of lines are made up of methods. Thus, at run-time, an initial method is invoked, which itself invokes other methods, which in their turn. . . . The run-time method usage is hierarchical (a top-level method invokes lower-level methods etc.) and this pattern of invocations is unpredictable before run-time – because the decision on whether a method is to be invoked or not might be part of an `if`, based on input data.

Imagine that `methodA` invokes `methodB` which invokes `methodC`. If an exception occurs in `methodC`, the search for an appropriate catch begins in `methodC`. If one is not found, the search moves to `methodB`. If `methodB` does not provide a catch, then the search moves up to `methodA`, and if the top-level method does not provide a catch, an exception message is displayed. If the program is an applet, it will continue to run (or limp along) and its results will be unreliable.

● Throwing – an introduction

Let us illustrate the way that many exceptions are thrown. Recall our use of `parseInt` in the first example. You don't need to examine the source code of the libraries – the documentation will suffice – but here is part of its code, from the class `Integer`:

```
public static int parseInt(String s)
                           throws NumberFormatException {
    ...code for the method...

    throw new NumberFormatException();

    ... etc
} // end of parseInt
```

Note the use of `throws` in the header of the method, and the use of `throw` in the body of the method. The `throw` statement is often executed as the result of an `if`: it causes the current method to be abandoned, and starts a search for a matching `catch`. When you set about using provided methods (and you should always search for existing code before writing your own) you will examine a Java library reference manual, whether in book form, in your development environment or on a Web site. The information that such documentation will provide is:

● a short description of the purpose of the method;
● its name, parameter types and return type;
● the classes of any exceptions that it may throw.

Our next step in preparing to use a method is to consider any exceptions it may throw in more detail.

● Exception classes

Here we will explore the varieties of exception classes that are provided in the Java library. Basically, the library provides us with a list of exception class names, but if there is no suitably named exception we can also create our own. We will not cover the process of inventing new exceptions, trusting that you will be able to find a suitably named existing one.

Inheritance is used to classify errors into different types – for example, there are exceptions that are classified as 'big trouble' (such as `OutOfMemoryError`), and exceptions that are less serious (such as `NumberFormatException`). There are around 30 exceptions, but the main ones are shown in Figure 16.2, which shows their inheritance structure, i.e. class hierarchy.

The library documentation tells you the name of any exceptions that a method may throw. To fit it into the above hierarchy you may have to work up the tree, by looking up the parent (i.e. the class that the exception extends) and the parent of the parent. For example, our familiar `parseInt` method, of the `Integer` class, is specified as throwing `NumberFormatException`. From Figure 16.2, we see that this is derived from `IllegalArgumentException`, which is within the unchecked class `RuntimeException`.

From the position of an exception in the class hierarchy, it is possible to figure out how it can be processed. Basically, all exceptions are under the class `Throwable`. There are two main subclasses: `Error` and `Exception`. The `Error` class has exceptions which are serious but difficult to fix up – you will not be concerned with their catching. The class `Exception` is more significant. Most of the exceptions within this class are *checked*,

```
Throwable
     Error (unchecked)
          LinkageError
          VirtualMachineError
               OutofMemoryError
     Exception   (all checked, except for RuntimeException)

          RuntimeException   (unchecked)
               ArithmeticException
               IndexOutofBoundsException
                    ArrayIndexOutofBoundsException
               IllegalArgumentException
                    NumberFormatException

     ┌──────────────────────────────────────────────────┐
     │  IOException   (checked)                          │
     │          FileNotFoundException                   │
     │          MalformedURLException                   │
     │                                                  │
     │  InterruptedException   (checked)                │
     │                                                  │
     │  Other subclasses of Exception, all checked.     │
     └──────────────────────────────────────────────────┘
```

Figure 16.2   Inheritance structure of the main exceptions.

meaning that you *have* to deal with them – your program will not compile if you ignore them. We have put these in the box of Figure 16.2 to show their importance. The odd one out is the class `RuntimeException`, which is unchecked – your program will compile even if you ignore this. We will now examine these concepts in more detail.

● Compilation and checked exceptions

The compiler makes stringent checks on the matching of `throw` and `try-catch` statements. There are three cases:

● A method states that it can throw a class of exception that *must* be acknowledged by the invoker of the method – either by catching it, or stating that it can be thrown – i.e. propagated upwards. If this is omitted, a compilation error will result. In other words, some methods which you use can *force* you to use `try-catch`.
● A method states that it can throw a class of exception that need not be handled. It is your choice whether you use `try-catch` or not. If you don't handle such an exception, the exception is not ignored – it gets passed upward to the method which invoked your method (and then to the method which invoked *that* method etc.), in an attempt to find the first matching `catch`. A match occurs if a `catch` specifies the particular exception, or any class superior to the exception. If no appropriate `catch` exists, an exception message will be displayed by the Java system. If the program is an applet, or it is an application which uses the AWT, execution will continue, but its operation cannot be relied on – for example, incorrect `return` values may have been passed back from methods. If, however, the program is a text-based program with keyboard input–output, its execution will terminate, and you will be returned to your operating system.
● The final case involves the throwing of exceptions which are not stated in a method's header. Here is the reasoning: the use of (for example) integer arithmetic and arrays is widespread throughout the Java library and the code that you will write. Such code can produce errors (e.g. `ArithmeticException` in the case of integer divide-by-zero, and `ArrayIndexOutOfBoundsException` in the class `IndexOutOfBoundsException`, when an array index value is outside the declared range of an array). Both of these are in the `RuntimeException` class. Because many methods can produce these situations, they are not declared, and it is the programmer's decision on whether to use `try-catch` or not.

● Catching – the common cases

We will look at the possible alternatives with three common cases:

● the checked exception `FileNotFoundException`;
● the unchecked exception `NumberFormatException`;
● the unchecked `Runtime` exception `ArrayIndexOutOfBoundsException`.

`FileNotFoundException` (in the class `IOException`) is produced when a program tries to access a file which does not exist – maybe we got the name wrong, or are in the wrong directory, or maybe the wrong disk was inserted. The details of file access are covered in Chapter 19, but all we need to know at present is that, before reading data from a file, we 'open' it with a statement of the form:

```
inFile = new BufferedReader(new FileReader("myfile.txt"));
```

where `myfile.txt` is the name of the file that the program expects to be present. However, the `FileReader` constructor throws a checked exception which we must deal with: we can either use `try-catch`, or specify that the method which contains the above statement can throw the exception. For GUI-based programs which typically allow the user to retype a filename, the first approach is best – we deal with the exception immediately, rather than complicating things for other methods. The approach is basically like our `NumberFormatException` number-doubling example, which uses a `TextField` (named `errorField` here) to display an error message:

```
try {
    inFile = new BufferedReader(new
        FileReader("myfile.txt"));
}
catch (FileNotFoundException e) {
    errorField.setText("missing file-try again!");
}
```

The second approach is to pass the exception up to the invoking method. We create a method, and put:

```
private void openFile() throws IOException {
    inFile = new BufferedReader(new
        FileReader("myfile.txt"));
}
```

With this approach, the invoker of `openFile` must either catch or pass it upwards.

Our second example, involving `NumberFormatException` thrown by `parseInt`, is basically similar; we either catch, or can pass the exception on. The difference from the previous `FileNotFoundException` case is that the compiler does not force us to handle the exception, because `NumberFormatException` (in the class `RuntimeException`) is unchecked.

What options do we have? The simplest option is to intentionally ignore the exception. The compiler will not force us to check it. However, the only time it would be sensible to do this is when we know that the `String` to be converted to an `int` is error-free. (Maybe it has been input from a correct file, or generated internally.) For interactive AWT-based software though, it is essential that we catch potential input errors, and we did this in the number-doubling applet by:

```
try {
    int number = Integer.parseInt(stringField.getText());
    resultField.setText("Doubled value is " +(2*number));
}
catch (NumberFormatException e) {
    resultField.setText("Error in number:retype ");
}
```

As with our file exception we could specify that the method which invokes `parseInt` could throw `NumberFormatException`, hence forcing any invoking methods to catch or explicitly pass it upwards. There is no advantage to doing this, and this approach is not illustrated.

Our final `ArrayIndexOutOfBoundsException` example is not so straightforward. Catching it is fine, but then what? The above examples involved user input, and could be fixed by inviting another attempt. Here is a program fragment with an exception:

```
int a[] = new int[10];         // 0 to 9 inclusive
for(int n = 0; n <= 10; n++) {
    a[n] = 0;
}
```

The `n <= 10` produces a loop from `0` to `10` inclusive, and thus attempts to access `a[10]` – we should have put `n<10`. As with all exceptions in the `RuntimeException` class, it involves a programming mistake, which needs fixing by debugging and recompiling. (Yes, it is true that some advanced software systems provide fail-safe operation by switching to duplicated hardware and/or software when serious errors happen, but most software is not arranged to clean itself up after this kind of error.) So what do we do with `RuntimeExceptions`? In the rare case that we can provide a sensible cleanup we can catch the exception, as in:

```
int b[] = new int[1000];
try {
    // complex code involving b[]
}
catch (ArrayIndexOutOfBoundsException e) {
    // handle the exception
}
```

but in the vast majority of cases, we want the origin of the exception to be indicated, so it can be tracked down and fixed. This is easily done by ignoring the exceptions, which the compiler allows us to do with the `RuntimeException` class, because it is unchecked. The exception is passed upwards to the operating system, applet viewer or browser level, and a message will be displayed, showing the name of the exception followed by a trace of the method invocations, with line numbers relating to the Java source code.

To actually see the display on your particular system, you may need to switch to the Java Console window. An alternative destination for a single line of text is the status bar at the bottom of the applet viewer or browser window, which can be used as in:

```
showStatus("Exception happened: Missing file");
```

but the drawback is that information in the status bar is transient, and might be immediately overwritten by the browser.

We have now covered exceptions in sufficient detail for the beginner, who could sensibly stop here. The following is for the more experienced programmer.

● Using the exception class structure

Figure 16.2 shows the inheritance structure of exceptions. By referring to a parent class, we can catch any exception of that class. For example, we might put

```
try {
     // some code
}
catch (Exception e} {
     // handle it...
}
```

which would catch `RuntimeException`, `IOException`, etc., because `Exception` is their superclass.

If we wanted to treat individual exceptions specially, but still catch all of a particular class, we can put:

```
try {
     // some code
}
catch (IOException e) {
     //handle IO problem
}
catch (Exception e) {
     // handle any others
}
```

The Java compiler requires that you put the more general class at the end. Reversing the order of the above two `catch`es would produce a compilation error.

● `finally`

Consider the case where a program opens a file successfully but encounters an error while reading from the file. A desirable cleanup action is to close the file – effectively, we state that we have finished using the file, and it can be used for other purposes (files are discussed in detail in Chapter 19). Reading a line (a `string`) from a file can produce a checked `IOException`; thus the logic for reading a series of lines is:

```
String line;
try {
    while ((line = myFile.readLine() ) ! = null) {
        // process line
    }
}
catch (IOException e) {
    errorField.setText("Error in file input");
}
finally {
    myFile.close();
}
```

Note that the code to close the file is performed in the normal case *and* in the exception case. The use of `finally` allows us to provide this code in one place, and guarantees that the close code is performed either after an exception, or after correct execution of the `try` block.

Grammar spot

The basic `try-catch` form is:

```
try {
    a series of statements;
}
catch (SomeException e) {
    handle the exception;
}
```

Programming pitfalls

● Failing to acknowledge a checked exception produces a compilation error. You must either catch an exception locally, or specify that your method throws it.
● Allowing an exception to be thrown from a method, when it can sensibly be handled locally.
● Declaring an item in a `try` block and attempting to refer to it in a `catch` block. Such items must be declared above (outside) the `try` block.
● Attempting to catch and process the `RuntimeException` class. In most cases, there is little that can be done. Catching such errors can conceal them, when instead the programmer needs to know about them.

New language elements

● `try`
● `catch`
● `finally`
● the exception hierarchy.

Summary

● An exception is an unusual situation.

● Exceptions are instances of classes, created by `new`.

● When an exceptional situation is detected, an exception is thrown.

● `try-catch` blocks are used. We surround code which could throw an exception by `try { }` and supply a matching `catch` block.

● A checked exception is one which must be acknowledged.

● The inheritance tree of the class `Throwable` (Figure 16.2) is crucial. It shows you the main exceptions you will have to deal with and which class they are in.

● Exceptions within the `RuntimeException` class are difficult to fix up, and in many cases can be intentionally ignored. Any other exceptions underneath the `Exception` class are checked, and must be dealt with.

EXERCISES

16.1 Write an applet which provides two textboxes (a,b) for integer input. Display the result of a/b. Now incorporate exception handling for the textboxes: display a message if non-integer input is used.

16.2 Alter Exercise 16.1 so it handles `float` values instead. (Refer to Chapter 15 for details of `float` input.)

16.3 If you know the length of the three sides of a triangle, the area can be calculated by:

```
area = Math.sqrt(s*(s-a)*(s-b)*(s-c));
```

where

```
s = (a+b+c)/2
```

Write a method for calculating and returning the area. Make it throw an exception when the three lengths cannot form a triangle.
 Write an invoking method which catches your exception.

16.4 Write a program which inputs a string from a text field, representing a date in the form MM/DD/YY (for example, 03/02/01). Use `StringTokenizer` to split it up, and produce an error message if an item is non-numeric, missing completely or specifies an impossible date. Ignore leap years.

16.5 Write a program which calculates compound interest. The user inputs the initial amount, the interest per year as a percentage value (floating point), and the number of years to run. Provide exception handling.

ANSWERS TO SELF-TEST QUESTIONS

16.1 In the first two cases, quitting the program would be a poor course of action. A more useful response is to display some sort of error indication, and allow the user either to have another go or to abandon the selection of the item.

In the third case, the complication is that the printer may run out of paper part-way through a print. The user needs to be informed of this, and may be provided with options to abandon the print request or, assuming that paper has been loaded, continue printing from a particular page.

16.2 A search of the documentation reveals that `NumberFormatException` is the only exception.

Graphical user interfaces

Introduction

The Abstract Window Toolkit (AWT) library contains a comprehensive set of classes and methods for supporting windowing and graphical user interfaces (GUIs). All the programs presented in this book use this approach. We have already introduced a number of the ideas of GUIs at several points in this book. In this chapter we extend these explanations, introducing several new screen components and the idea of layout managers.

Those GUI components that we have met so far are:

- scrollbars – Chapter 6;
- labels – Chapter 6;
- text fields – Chapter 6;
- buttons – Chapter 7;

and these are summarized for reference in Appendix D. We do not repeat a treatment of these features here.

The new ideas presented in this chapter are:

- check boxes;
- group check boxes (radio buttons);
- choice boxes (drop-down lists);
- lists;
- text areas;
- canvasses;
- panels;
- layout managers.

This book concentrates on applets, and this chapter exclusively explains only applet-related features. The discussion of using the AWT in free-standing programs is confined to Chapter 18. Free-standing programs use the idea of *frames*, and if you do not plan to write such a program, you can forget this particular term forever.

● Components – the general approach

Before looking at the detail, let us recall the general approach: components are declared, initialized and added to the screen layout. In addition, our program must state that it implements a class of events, must register with components, and must provide an appropriate method to listen for each event. So, for each component, we will provide details of:

- the implements class
- the declaration and initialization
- the registration
- the event handling.

Note that several components use the same event class: for example, a button-click and a text field 'enter' key both use ActionListener. So, for programs which use both components, our approach is to use an if to detect the source of the event. For completeness, we provide this code as well.

● Check boxes

This is a way in which the user can specify one or more choices by clicking on a box. See Figure 17.1 for an example of three check boxes that allow the user to select food and drink of their choice. The code to set up and display these boxes is as follows:

```
import java.awt.*;
import java.applet.Applet;
import java.awt.event.*;
public class Demo extends Applet
    implements ItemListener {
    private Checkbox cola, burger, fries;

    public void init() {
        cola = new Checkbox("Cola");
        add(cola);
        cola.addItemListener(this);

        burger = new Checkbox("Burger");
        add(burger);
        burger.addItemListener(this);
```

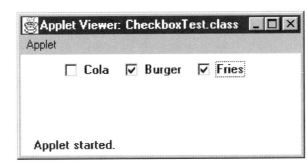

Figure 17.1 Check boxes.

```
        fries = new Checkbox("Fries");
        add(fries);
        fries.addItemListener(this);
    }
```

You can see that (unlike buttons), a check box stays selected on the screen after it has been clicked on.

To handle an event from a check box, the method `itemStateChanged` is used as follows:

```
public void itemStateChanged(ItemEvent e) {
    if(e.getSource() == cola) {
        boolean wantsCola = cola.getState();
    etc...
}
```

An event only tells the program that a box has been changed, not what it has been changed to. You can then invoke `getState` to find out the status of any check box, as shown above. The method returns `true` if the check box has been selected.

Notice how `Checkbox` is spelled – it is one of the few class names that violates the spelling rules.

● Check box groups

A check box group is, not surprisingly, a group of check boxes. The special feature is that only one of the boxes can be selected at once. A check box group is sometimes known as radio buttons, because preselect buttons on early car radios were like this – you could select one station at a time by pushing in one of the buttons. Check box groups are appropriate in some programs, for example to select a colour, as shown in Figure 17.2. When one box is selected, any box already selected is unselected. The code to set up and display these buttons is as follows:

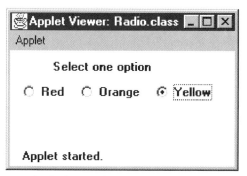

Figure 17.2 Check box group (radio buttons).

```
import java.awt.*;
import java.applet.Applet;
import java.awt.event.*;
public class Demo extends Applet
        implements ItemListener {
    private CheckboxGroup c;
    private Checkbox red, orange, yellow;

    public void init() {
        c = new CheckboxGroup();

        red = new Checkbox("Red", c, false);
        add(red);
        red.addItemListener(this);

        orange = new Checkbox("Orange", c, true);
        add(orange);
        orange.addItemListener(this);

        yellow = new Checkbox("Yellow", c, false);
        add(yellow);
        yellow.addItemListener(this);
    }
```

Notice that you specify the initial state of an individual check box as a boolean parameter when creating the check box.

To handle an event from a check box group, we use a similar approach to the single check box. Note that we do not refer to the group name c. The following code displays the state of each check box on the bottom status bar of the browser or applet viewer:

```
public void itemStateChanged(ItemEvent e) {
    if((e.getSource()==red)|| ( e.getSource()== orange)
                    || ( e.getSource()==yellow) )
        showStatus("CBGroup state= "+red.getState()
            +orange.getState()+yellow.getState());
}
```

In summary, a group of check boxes is just like an ordinary collection of check boxes, except that only one can be selected at a time. To emphasize the difference, they are displayed slightly differently (see Figures 17.1 and 17.2).

● Choice boxes (drop-down lists)

A choice box is a list of options like a menu (Figure 17.3). An item can be chosen from the list by clicking on it. The selected item then appears as the only visible part of the list.
To create a choice:

```
import java.awt.*;
import java.applet.Applet;
import java.awt.event.*;
public class Demo extends Applet
    implements ItemListener {
    private Choice colourChoice;

    public void init() {
        colourChoice = new Choice();

        colourChoice.add("Red");
        colourChoice.add("Yellow");
        colourChoice.add("Blue");
        add(colourChoice);
        colourChoice.addItemListener(this);
    }
```

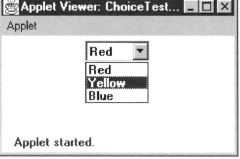

Figure 17.3 A choice box.

To deal with clicking on the required selection, the method `itemStateChanged` is used as follows:

```
public void itemStateChanged(ItemEvent e) {
    if(e.getSource()==colourChoice){
        String aChoice=e.getItem().toString();
}
```

Since menus are not allowed with applets, this is a good way of providing something very similar.

● Lists

A list is a list of text strings, from which one or more items can be selected (see Figure 17.4). A scrollbar is provided to scroll up or down the list. To create a list:

```
List list = new List(3, false);
```

which specifies that only three items in the list will be visible at once. The second para-meter, `false`, signifies that only one item can be selected from the list. Next we add items to the list and then finally add the list to the window: Here is the code:

```
import java.applet.Applet;
import java.awt.event.*;
public class Demo extends Applet
    implements ActionListener {
    private List list;

    public void init() {
        list = new List(3,false);
        list.add("milk");
        list.add("sugar");
        list.add("tea");
        add(list);
        list.addActionListener(this);
    }
```

The event-handling code is slightly different. It involves an implementation of the `ActionListener` class, which responds to list double-clicks. (A single click on a list item involves `ItemListener`, as with check boxes.) When an item is selected from the list by double-clicking on it, an event occurs which must be handled by the method `actionPerformed`. The string value of the selected item can then be obtained using the method `getSelectedItem`:

```
public void actionPerformed(ActionEvent e) {
    if(e.getSource() == list){
        String listSelect = list.getSelectedItem();
}
```

Figure 17.4 A simple list.

If you wish to create a list from which more than one item can be selected, then the second parameter of the constructor method must be true:

```
List list = new List(4, true);
```

Then you must arrange that some other component, like a button, signals that the selection is complete. Then you can use:

```
String[] selection = list.getSelectedItems();
```

to obtain an array of the selected items.

● Text areas

There are two ways of inputting text into a Java program – text fields and text areas. In a text field, a single line of text can be entered. With a text area, a whole series of lines can be entered (see Figure 17.5). A text area is created as follows:

```
TextArea t = new TextArea(10, 40);
```

in which the parameters are the number of rows and the number of columns displayed on the screen. In this case there are 10 lines, each of 40 columns. Further parts of the text can be displayed using the scrollbars which always accompany a text area. Also, if the user continues to input text, the text area automatically scrolls to accommodate it.

There are some very powerful facilities associated with a text area. The user can select an area of text using the mouse (click and drag). Facilities to cut, copy, paste and delete text are all available using the mouse. (In Windows, these are available via the right mouse button.)

After some text has been entered, the usual mechanism is for the user to click on a button to signify that something has happened. The event handler can then input the text using the method getText as follows:

```
public void actionPerformed(ActionEvent event) {
    if (event.getSource() == button)
            String theText = t.getText();
}
```

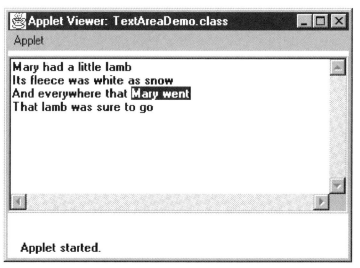

Figure 17.5 A text area.

This input text will usually have new lines embedded in it. These are represented by \n, the usual character for representing new lines in a string.

As additions to the built-in editing facilities, the programmer can create a set of buttons to initiate useful functions. When a button-click event takes place, the program can detect which region of the text has been selected using `getSelectionStart` and `getSelectionEnd`:

- `getSelectionStart` returns the index of the start of the selection.
- `getSelectionEnd` returns the index of the end of the selection plus one.
- `getSelectedText` returns the text of the selection.

As with strings, indexing starts at zero, and a new line counts as a single character.

To insert text into a text area at a particular place, `insert` can be used, as in this example:

```
String newPiece = "I need this";
t.insert(newPiece, int here);
```

To replace text use method `replaceRange`, as in:

```
t.replaceRange("Some replacement text", int fromHere, int toHere);
```

A piece of text can be deleted by replacing it with an empty string, `""`. Finally, text can be inserted at the end of the text area by using `append`.

Using these methods in conjunction with buttons allows all the text editing facilities that are associated with modern GUIs to be implemented. If these facilities are combined with the facility to read and write files, it is easy to write a word processor. But because of the security restrictions on applets, it is only possible to do this with freestanding applications.

● Canvasses

In most of the programs used in this book, graphical objects are drawn directly in the applet window. The drawback with this approach is that they can get in the way of the buttons and other components that are shown in the same window. The programmer has to specify the *x*- and *y*-coordinates of the graphical output very carefully so as to avoid the widgets. The use of a canvas avoids this problem because a canvas is a separate area within a window, suitable for drawing on.

A canvas is created as an object of a class that inherits from the library class `Canvas`. This enables the programmer to write a method `paint` – a method of the created canvas which can be used like the `paint` method in an applet. We can see this at work in an example (see Figure 17.6):

```
import java.awt.*;
import java.applet.*;
public class CanvasDemo extends Applet {
    private MyCanvas canvas = new MyCanvas();

    public void init() {
        canvas.setBackground(Color.gray);
        canvas.setSize(200,100);
        add(canvas);
    }
}

class MyCanvas extends Canvas {
    public void paint(Graphics g) {
        g.drawString("I am in a canvas", 20, 20);
    }
}
```

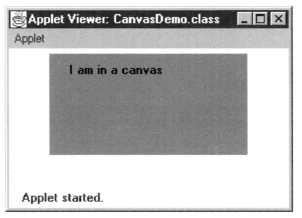

Figure 17.6 A canvas.

The first thing the applet does when it runs is to create an object called `canvas`. This is an instance of the class `MyCanvas`, which is declared as a subclass of `Canvas`. `MyCanvas` only does one thing to subclass `Canvas` – it overrides the method `paint`.

The method `init` sets the size of the canvas (otherwise it would have zero size), colours it grey (so that we can see it distinctly in this demonstration) and adds it to the applet window. When the window is moved or resized, `paint` is invoked to draw the contents of the canvas. Note that the coordinates specified within `paint` are relative to the top-left of the canvas (not the window).

● Panels

A panel is a way of grouping a number of components in a convenient way. A panel does not have a boundary or any other way of being seen on the screen – it is like an invisible boundary. If, say, we want particular buttons at the top of a window and others at the bottom, we can create separate panels for each of the two groups. Then we can specify that one panel goes at the top and the other at the bottom. To create a new panel:

```
Panel p = new Panel();
```

Then components can be added to a panel:

```
Button b1 = new Button("Press Me");
Button b2 = new Button("NO - Press ME");
p.add(b1);
p.add(b2);
```

Finally, the panel can be added to the applet window:

```
add(p);
```

This gives the screen display shown in Figure 17.7. You can see that there is nothing new in this display – panels only become useful when they are combined with different layouts, as we shall see later.

The difference between a panel and a canvas is that a panel is used to group a number of components, whereas a canvas is used to draw text and/or graphics within a rectangular area.

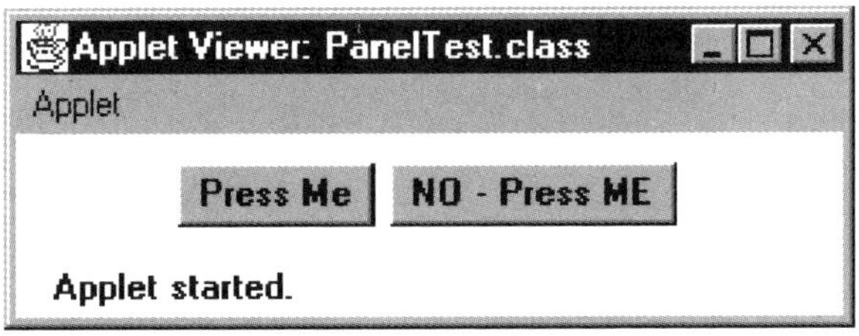

Figure 17.7 A simple panel.

● Layout managers

None of the programs in this book make explicit use of a layout manager. They therefore make use of the default layout manager. This default manager, called *flow layout*, is the one that gets used if you do not ask for anything else.

Flow layout is perfectly acceptable for many programs. However, for particular needs other layouts are available. The commonly used layouts are:

- flow layout – (the default for applets) puts components side-by-side and in rows;
- border layout – (the default for applications) puts components around the sides of the window.

We describe these layouts below.

● Flow layout

The flow layout ensures that the widgets are displayed left-to-right in the order that the program invokes the `add` method, using a new row when necessary. Within each row, the widgets are centred left to right, whatever the width of the window. When a window is resized, the flow manager ensures that these rules are always maintained, so that sometimes extra rows are created when the window width is reduced and vice versa.

This layout is the default for applets – it is what you get if you do not specify a layout.

● Border layout

Border layout divides the area (normally the applet window) into five areas as shown in Figure 17.8. The areas are called North, South, East, West and Center. When the window is drawn, the borders are laid out first. Then the remaining space is occupied by

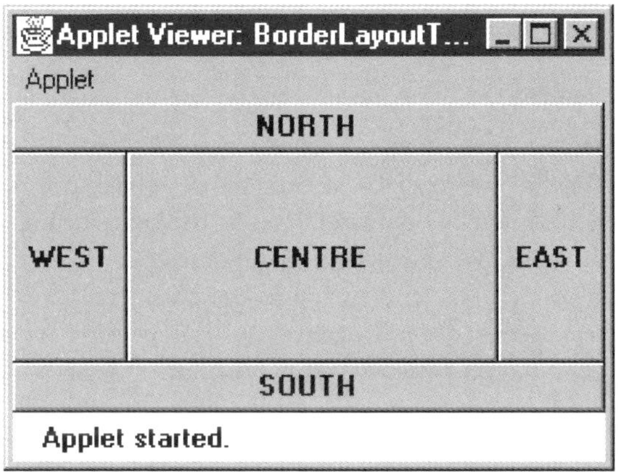

Figure 17.8 Five buttons shown in the border layout, without panels.

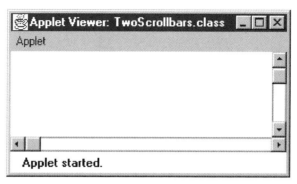

Figure 17.9 Scrollbars stretch automatically to fit the size of the panel.

the centre. When the window is resized, the thickness of the borders remains unchanged, but the size of the centre area changes.

To use this layout, invoke:

```
setLayout(new BorderLayout());
```

Then create widgets as usual:

```
Button north = new Button("NORTH");
Button south = new Button("SOUTH");
Button west = new Button("WEST");
Button east = new Button("EAST");
Button centre = new Button("CENTRE");
```

in which NORTH, SOUTH, etc., are the labels on the buttons. Next we specify which area the buttons will be shown in, as the first parameter to the method `add`. The result is shown in Figure 17.8:

```
add("North", north);
add("South", south);
add("West", west);
add("East", east);
add("Center", centre);
```

This display works OK, but it is not the usual way that buttons look. In Figure 17.8, the buttons are stretched to fill the available area. This drawback can be useful in the case of scrollbars, which (in border layout) stretch to fit the size of the panel (Figure 17.9).

To show buttons as we would normally like to see them, we can use panels. We place the buttons in panels (using `add`), and then add the panels to the window. We will call the panels `top`, `bottom`, `leftSide` and `rightSide`. For brevity, we only give the code for the north panel. The screen display is shown in Figure 17.10.

```
Panel top = new Panel();
top.add(north);
add("North", top);
```

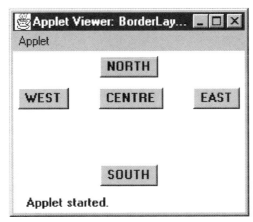

Figure 17.10 Border layout with panels.

The steps involved in this code are:

1. Create a panel.
2. Add the button to the panel.
3. Add the panel to the window.

Border layout is the default layout for applications.

● Designing user interfaces

The design of user interfaces is the subject of whole books in itself. One way to approach design is to sketch out a design on paper before using the computer. Another approach is to use a software tool that can be used to quickly create a mock-up of a screen layout. Some such tools will directly create the Java code from the mock-up. This can save time in reprogramming rejected designs.

There is plenty of scope for alternatives in designing a user interface. First, there are lots of alternative positions on the screen for positioning components. Secondly, some components are alternatives. For example:

● Buttons, check boxes, check box groups and choice boxes can sometimes be used interchangeably.
● Scrollbars and text fields can sometimes be used interchangeably to input numbers.

Finally, sometimes a window is simply too crowded, and the interface should be divided across several windows.

It is often easier to show a prospective user a mock-up of a user interface than it is to describe the interface. The user can then either agree the design or suggest what needs to be changed. This approach is called prototyping.

Summary

● This chapter explained how to use a number of graphical user interface components:

  - check boxes;
  - group check boxes (radio buttons);
  - choice boxes (drop-down lists);
  - lists;
  - text areas;
  - canvasses;
  - panels;
  - layout managers – flow layout and border layout.

● The following graphical user interface elements can only be used by applications, not applets, and are described where indicated:

  - file dialog box (Chapter 19);
  - menus (Chapter 18).

EXERCISES

17.1   Complete the event handler for the check boxes shown in Figure 17.1 to order food and display on the screen the state of an order at any time.

17.2   Create a choice list as in Figure 17.3 and display a chosen item using `drawString`.

17.3   Write an applet that creates a list as in Figure 17.4 and then displays the item that is selected using `drawString`.

17.4   Create a list as in Figure 17.4 from which several items can be selected and display them using `drawString`.

17.5   Write an applet that displays and maintains a shopping list. To enter a new item into the list, the user enters it into a text field and presses a button. To delete an item from the list, the user double-clicks on the item.

17.6   Write a program to display a text area as in Figure 17.5 and experiment with the cut, paste, etc., facilities that are provided.

17.7   Write a program that allows the user to type some text into a text area. Then, when a button is pressed, the program calculates the number of characters and the number of lines in the text.

17.8   Write a program that creates a text area and provides buttons to provide cut, copy and paste operations.

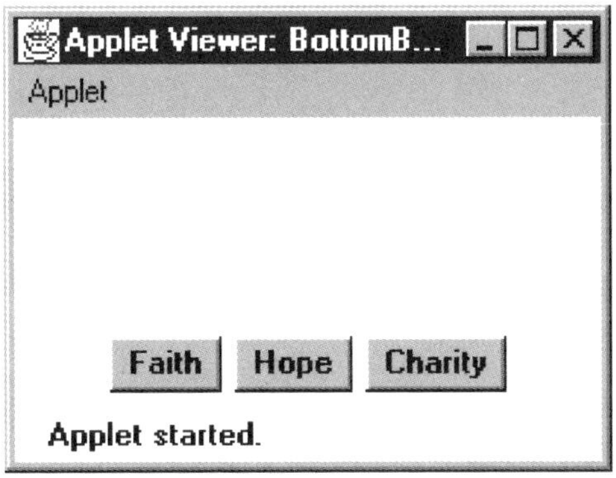

Figure 17.11 A single row of buttons.

17.9 Create horizontal and vertical scrollbars at the left and the bottom of a window as shown in Figure 17.9. Note that you do not need to use panels for this.

17.10 Create some buttons along the bottom of the window as shown in Figure 17.11.

Free-standing programs

Introduction

There are two types of Java program – applets and free-standing programs (called applications). They are written differently (the program structure is different) and they are run differently. An applet is normally invoked from a Web page or, during development, an applet viewer. An application needs no such host and is run as a completely independent program. All operating systems – UNIX, DOS, Windows and MacOS – provide the facility to run such programs. In some operating systems an application can be invoked by clicking on the program icon on the desktop; in some systems they can be invoked by typing the program name in response to the appropriate prompt.

Both types of program can use the GUI facilities of Java – windows, scrollbars, etc. – by employing the same Java library, the AWT (Abstract Window Toolkit). Almost all of the other Java libraries can also be used – but not the applet classes.

Free-standing programs are often regarded as being more trustworthy than applets, because the latter may be downloaded from suspect Web sites. Free-standing programs therefore are invested with freer access to files held on the user's computer. Examples of applications that use files are given in Chapter 19.

In this chapter we see how to construct free-standing programs (applications).

A first program

One of the simplest standalone programs is this:

```
public class Greeting {
    public static void main(String[] args) {
        System.out.println("Hello");
    }
}
```

Notice that it does not need any `import` statements. It has a single method, `main`, which invokes the library method `println` in the library class `System` to display information on the screen. The facilities of the class `System` are described in Chapter 19 on files.

To prepare a free-standing program for execution, it is compiled to byte code using the Java compiler in the usual way. Then the program is invoked directly from the operating system. When you run a free-standing program, you can supply parameters. These are typed after the name of the program. So for example, to run a Java program on UNIX or DOS, you could type:

```
java Hello Doug
```

In this command line, `java` is the name of the Java byte code interpreter. `Hello` is the name of the class, and the string `Doug` is the single parameter. When you run a program, you specify the name of a class. The java system finds the class file with the same name and runs the method called `main` within that class. This method, `main`, must be provided by the programmer and must be declared as `public static void`.

Any parameters (also called arguments) are passed to the program as parameters to the method `main`. As you can see from the header of `main`, the parameters are an array of strings (conventionally called `args`). The first parameter (`Doug` in the above example) is therefore referred to as `args[0]`.

SELF-TEST QUESTION
....

18.1 Write an application which is invoked like this:

```
java Hello Doug
```

and which simply replies hello, followed by the name that is entered as the parameter.

A program can find out how many parameters were passed to it as follows, using the usual way to find the length of an array:

```
int numberOfParameters = args.length;
```

● Running an application

There are two kinds of application:

1. those that use text input and output;
2. those that use windows and widgets.

In programs of the first type, `main` acts as its name suggests and acts as the main or controlling method for the program. It creates new objects and invokes methods as necessary. Only when all the tasks of the program have been completed does `main` end.

The story is different in an application that uses the AWT to do windowing. In such an application, as we shall see below, the `main` method only has a temporary role in initiating objects. This corresponds to the role of the method `init` in an applet, which only serves to set up widget objects before ending.

In any case, the first thing that `main` does is to create a useful object and then invoke a method in it. Conventionally, the object that `main` creates is an instance of the class in which `main` is itself a `static` method. And the method it invokes is another method within the same class. This can look strange at first sight, but is perfectly logical:

```
public class Application {

    public static void main(String[] args) {
        Application a = new Application();
        a.doWhatIsNeeded();
    }

    private void doWhatIsNeeded() {
        // code
    }
}
```

The sequence is:

1. The operating system invokes a static method called `main` within the class `Application`. (Remember that a static method belongs to the class as a whole and not to any object that is instantiated from the class.)
2. `main` creates an instance of the class `Application`.
3. `main` invokes a method of the object.

This, of course, differs from starting an applet. In an applet the first object is automatically created by the Web browser or applet viewer. But in an application, the program has to explicitly create the first object.

● Using the Abstract Window Toolkit with an application

Most modern applications programs use windows, scrollbars and all the features of a graphical user interface. Applications are no different, and to accomplish this they make use of the Abstract Window Toolkit, just as applets do. There are, however, some minor differences.

As an example of how to create a free-standing application, we present the conversion of the balloon applet used widely in this book into a standalone program. We have simply taken the applet code from Chapter 10 and changed it to give the code below and the output shown in Figure 18.1.

Figure 18.1 Screen output for the balloon program as a free-standing application.

```
import java.awt.*;
import java.awt.event.*;

public class PlayBalloon extends Frame implements ActionListener,
              WindowListener {

    private Button grow, shrink;
    private Balloon myBalloon;

    public static void main(String[] args) {
        PlayBalloon f = new PlayBalloon();
        f.setSize(300, 300);
        f.setVisible(true);
    }

    public PlayBalloon() {

        setTitle("Balloon");

        setLayout(new FlowLayout());

        grow = new Button("Grow");
        add(grow);
        grow.addActionListener(this);

        shrink = new Button("Shrink");
        add(shrink);
        shrink.addActionListener(this);
```

```
        myBalloon = new Balloon(20, 50, 50);

        this.addWindowListener(this);

    }
    public void actionPerformed(ActionEvent event) {
        if (event.getSource() == grow)
            myBalloon.changeSize(10);
        if (event.getSource() == shrink)
            myBalloon.changeSize(-10);
        repaint();
    }

    public void windowClosing(WindowEvent event) {
        System.exit(0);
    }

    public void windowIconified(WindowEvent event) {
    }

    public void windowOpened(WindowEvent event) {
    }

    public void windowClosed(WindowEvent event) {
    }

    public void windowDeiconified(WindowEvent event) {
    }

    public void windowActivated(WindowEvent event) {
    }

    public void windowDeactivated(WindowEvent event) {
    }

    public void paint(Graphics g) {
        myBalloon.display(g);
    }
}

class Balloon {

    private int diameter;
    private int xCoord, yCoord;
```

```
public Balloon(int initialDiameter, int initialX, int initialY) {
    diameter = initialDiameter;
    xCoord = initialX;
    yCoord = initialY;
}

public void changeSize(int change) {
    diameter = diameter+change;
}

public void display(Graphics g) {
    g.drawOval(xCoord, yCoord, diameter, diameter);
}
}
```

We now explain how this has been converted into an application from an applet.

If you write an applet by extending the library class Applet, a window area is automatically provided. In contrast, an application that uses windowing needs to explicitly create a window on the screen. Such an area is called a *frame*. The easiest way for an application to create a frame is for it to inherit from (or extend) the library class Frame. So whereas an applet extends Applet, an application extends Frame.

The method main is the first to be invoked when the application runs. In the above program it does:

```
Frame f = new PlayBalloon();
f.setSize(300, 300);
f.setVisible(true);
```

to create the new frame, give it an appropriate size and show it on the screen.

You can see more applications in Chapter 19 on files.

SELF-TEST QUESTION

18.2 Rewrite the program so that it accepts the window size as two parameters and uses them as parameters for the method setSize.

An applet is normally invoked from a Web page, so it has no title bar and no title to the window in which it appears. The applet screen dumps shown in this book have both, but this is because they show the output from an applet viewer rather than a Web browser. (The applet viewer automatically uses the name of the class as the title in the title bar.) To place a title in the title bar of a frame invoke:

```
setTitle("Balloon");
```

giving the required title as the parameter.

Before adding the widgets to the frame (buttons in the above example), a method must be invoked to describe how the widgets are to be arranged in the window. The invocation:

```
setLayout(new FlowLayout());
```

sets up one of the available layouts, which are discussed more fully in Chapter 17. This particular layout (called flow layout) ensures that the widgets are displayed left-to-right in the order that the program invokes the `add` method, using a new row when necessary. Within each row, the widgets are centred left-to-right, whatever the width of the window. This layout is the default for applets and therefore does not need to be specified for an applet. But the default layout for an application is different (and is called border layout).

The next issue to consider is terminating a program. An applet runs from a Web page and therefore terminates when the Web page is no longer accessed. So there is no need for the programmer of the applet to deal with this situation. However, with an application, the program is in complete control and part of its role is to handle its own termination. To do this it must provide a handler for an event called `windowClosing`, as shown in the program above. This event is created when the user clicks on the window close box (which is at the top right of the window in Windows 95, for example). The first step, as usual with any event handling, is to register as a listener to the event. In this case, this is accomplished by:

```
this.addWindowListener(this);
```

The purpose of this statement is to tell the frame object (the `this` on the left) that the object that will handle the events is the current object (the `this` on the right). Thereafter method `windowClosing` handles the event and does so by invoking the library method `System.exit(0)` – which destroys the window and terminates the program. If this handler is omitted, the window close box simply does not work – however many times you click on it. Another way to terminate an application is to provide a button (labelled, say, Exit) which, when clicked, causes `System.exit(0)` to be invoked. You will see that using the interface `WindowListener` carries with it the responsibility of providing a whole set of methods to handle the events with the matching titles. It is mandatory to include them in the program even if, as in this program, they do nothing.

This concludes the list of things that need changing when an applet is converted into an application. You can see that all the changes are concerned with initiating and terminating the execution of the program. In particular, an application must explicitly create the initial object and the window frame. However, most of the program, including the class `Balloon`, is unchanged.

● Converting between applets and applications – summary

For reference, here are the steps to convert a Java application into an applet:

1. Create an HTML page with an `applet` tag to invoke the applet.
2. Delete the `main` method.
3. Alter the class header so that it extends `Applet` rather than `Frame`.
4. Add the `import` for the library class `Applet`.
5. Change the name of the constructor method from the name of the class to `init`.
6. Add an invocation of a method to set the layout of widgets in the applet window. This is typically:

```
setLayout(new BorderLayout());
```

To convert a Java applet to an application:

1. Change the name of the `init` method to the name of the class. This is now the constructor method for the class. Delete the word `void` in the header for this method, since a constructor method has no return type.
2. Alter the class header so that it extends `Frame` rather than `Applet`.
3. Create a new method called `main`, with the header `public static void main(String[] args)`. This method should create a `Frame` object as an instance of the class. So, if the class is called `MyClass`, the `main` method should be:

```
public static void main(String[] args) {
    MyClass f = new MyClass();
    f.setSize(300, 200);
    f.setVisible(true);
}
```

4. Delete the `import` for the class `Applet`, since it is now redundant.
5. Add a method `windowClosing` to handle the event which is the user clicking on the close window button. This also involves adding `implements WindowListener` and `this.addWindowListener(this);` in order to register the event handler.
6. Add an invocation of a method to set the layout of widgets in the frame. This is typically:

```
setLayout(new FlowLayout());
```

Make sure that the applet does not use any of the methods that are special to the `Applet` class – methods including `getAudioClip`, `getCodeBase`, `getDocumentBase`, `getImage`.

● Menus

Applications can set up and use menus, but applets cannot. The reason that applets do not support menus is that a menu normally hangs from a border at the top of a window. But an applet is simply a region within a Web page, often with no discernible boundary. So there is no obvious place for a menu to hang. The following program sets up the menus shown in Figure 18.2.

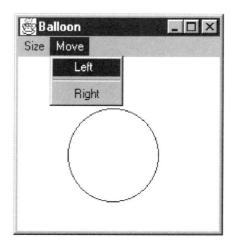

Figure 18.2 Menus.

```java
import java.awt.*;
import java.awt.event.*;


public class MenuBalloon extends Frame implements ActionListener,
                                                  WindowListener {

    private Balloon myBalloon;
    private MenuItem growItem, shrinkItem;
    private MenuItem leftItem, rightItem;

    public static void main(String[] args) {
        Frame f = new MenuBalloon();
        f.setSize(200, 200);
        f.setVisible(true);
    }

    public MenuBalloon() {
        setTitle("Balloon");
        setLayout(new FlowLayout());

        MenuBar menuBar = new MenuBar();

        Menu sizeMenu = new Menu("Size");

        growItem = new MenuItem("Grow");
        sizeMenu.add(growItem);
        growItem.addActionListener(this);
```

```
    shrinkItem = new MenuItem("Shrink");
    sizeMenu.add(shrinkItem);
    shrinkItem.addActionListener(this);


    menuBar.add(sizeMenu);
    Menu moveMenu = new Menu("Move");


    leftItem = new MenuItem("Left");
    moveMenu.add(leftItem);
    leftItem.addActionListener(this);


    moveMenu.addSeparator();


    rightItem = new MenuItem("Right");
    moveMenu.add(rightItem);
    rightItem.addActionListener(this);


    menuBar.add(moveMenu);
    setMenuBar(menuBar);


    this.addWindowListener(this);


    myBalloon = new Balloon(20, 50, 50);
}

public void actionPerformed(ActionEvent event) {
    if (event.getSource() == growItem)
        myBalloon.changeSize(10);
    if (event.getSource() == shrinkItem)
        myBalloon.changeSize(-10);
    if(event.getSource() == leftItem)
        myBalloon.moveLeft();
    if(event.getSource() == rightItem)
        myBalloon.moveRight();
    repaint();
}

public void paint(Graphics g) {
    myBalloon.display(g);
}

public void windowClosing(WindowEvent event) {
    System.exit(0);
}
```

```
    public void windowIconified(WindowEvent event) {
    }

    public void windowOpened(WindowEvent event) {
    }

    public void windowClosed(WindowEvent event) {
    }

    public void windowDeiconified(WindowEvent event) {
    }

    public void windowActivated(WindowEvent event) {
    }

    public void windowDeactivated(WindowEvent event) {
    }
}

class Balloon {

    private int diameter;
    private int xCoord, yCoord;

    Balloon(int initialDiameter, int initialX, int initialY) {
        diameter = initialDiameter;
        xCoord = initialX;
        yCoord = initialY;
    }

    public void changeSize(int change) {
        diameter = diameter + change;
    }

    public void moveLeft() {
        xCoord = xCoord - 10;
    }

    public void moveRight() {
        xCoord = xCoord + 10;
    }

    public void display(Graphics g) {
        g.drawOval(xCoord, yCoord, diameter, diameter);
    }
}
```

The steps in establishing a set of menus are:

1. Create a new menu bar, by instantiating the `MenuBar` class. For example:

```
MenuBar menuBar = new MenuBar();
```

2. Create a new menu, with a title, by instantiating `Menu`. For example:

```
Menu moveMenu = new Menu("Move");
```

3. Create a new menu item by instantiating `MenuItem`. For example:

```
leftItem = new MenuItem("Left");
```

4. Add the menu item to the menu. For example:

```
moveMenu.add(leftItem);
```

5. Register this object as a listener to the menu item events. For example:

```
leftItem.addActionListener(this);
```

6. Add the menu to the menu bar. For example:

```
menuBar.add(moveMenu);
```

7. Repeat steps 2–6 for as many menus as are required.
8. Invoke `setMenuBar`. For example:

```
setMenuBar(menuBar);
```

You will see that each individual menu item is registered separately with the listener, rather like buttons. If desired, a separator can be inserted into a set of menu choices, as is seen between the items Left and Right in Figure 18.2.

The appropriate event handler method for menus is `actionPerformed`, as shown. This is written in the usual manner, using `getSource` to find out which menu selection was clicked on.

Notice that the event handling is written assuming that all the menu selections are unique (for example, the choice Grow only appears once in all the menus). This is not restrictive – merely good user interface design practice.

The handling of the window close button is carried out as described earlier in this chapter.

Summary

Free-standing, or stand-alone programs:

● are invoked directly from the operating system, rather than a browser or applet viewer;

● usually have more privileges than applets, such as access to the local user's files;

● must have a method called `main`;

● cannot use the applet classes, but can use all the other classes, including the AWT (Abstract Window Toolkit). The basic windowing unit is the frame;

● can use menus and file dialog boxes (see Chapter 19).

EXERCISES

18.1 Write an application to display the menus shown in Figures 18.3 and 18.4. When a menu item is selected, display the name of the selected item.

18.2 Choose one of the applets presented in this book and convert it into a free-standing application.

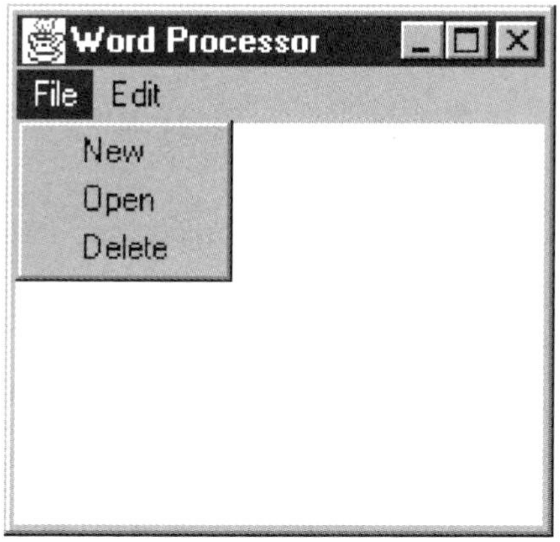

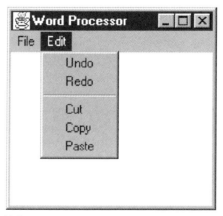

Figure 18.3 See Exercise 18.1.

Figure 18.4 See Exercise 18.1.

● Files, security and applets

As you know, applets can be downloaded from a remote site, and are executed within a browser. However, there is a security issue – the applet may contain bugs, or it might have been written with a malicious intent. One of the key areas which malicious applets might target is the deleting of files. It would be quite possible to write an applet which erased every file on your computer. For this reason, browsers are usually configured to prevent applets accessing files on the machine on which they execute. They can, however, access files on the server from which they were downloaded. The key point is that if you want to write software which accesses files on your computer, you will write applications, not applets. The possible exception to this is the growth of Intranet systems – which use WWW technology but restrict use to within an organization. In this situation, the use of trusted applets may be considered. However, throughout the rest of this chapter we will produce free-standing applications, not applets. The details of constructing applications are provided in Chapter 18.

● File access: stream or random?

Java has over 20 classes for file access, each with its own particular set of methods. But with such a wide choice, which classes should we choose? A major decision involves the choice between stream access and random access. When we use stream access on a file, we must treat the file as a sequence of items which must be processed one after another, starting with the first one. For many tasks, this is completely appropriate. If we use random access, we can skip immediately to a particular byte position in a file. In certain applications (such as databases), this can speed up processing, but is also more intricate to program. In reality, you will be more likely to use a database class library rather than code your own low-level disk access. For this reason, we will focus on streams.

● The essentials of streams

First, let us introduce the jargon, which is similar in most programming languages. If we wish to process the data in an existing file, we must:

1. *Open* the file.
2. *Read* or *input* the data item-by-item into variables.
3. *Close* the file when we have finished with it.

To transfer some data from variables into a file, we must:

1. *Open* the file.
2. *Output* (or *write*) our items in the required sequence.
3. *Close* the file when we have finished with it.

Note that, when reading from a file, all we can do is read the next item in the file. If, for example, we want to examine the last item, we would have to code a loop to read each preceding item in turn, until the required item is reached. For many tasks, it is convenient to visualize a file as a series of lines of text, each made up of a number of characters. Each line is terminated by an end-of-line character. We shall make use of the Java classes that allow us to access a file line-by-line. A benefit of this approach is that it is simple to transfer files between applications. For example, you could create a file by running a Java program, and then load the file into a word processor, text editor, or email package.

● The Java I/O classes

Predictably, the stream classes are organized hierarchically. Here are the most useful input classes:

```
Reader
    BufferedReader
    InputStreamReader
        FileReader


Writer
    PrintWriter
        FileWriter
```

The `Reader` and `Writer` classes are at the top of an inheritance tree, and are extended by a number of character-based classes. For files, we will make use of the `BufferedReader` and `PrintWriter` classes to read and write lines of text, and for non-file input (from keyboard and Web pages) we will also use `InputStreamReader`. As you will see in our examples, programs which use files should import `java.io.*`.

Incidentally, the use of the term 'buffer' means that – behind the scenes – the software reads a large chunk of data from the slow file storage device (e.g. CD-ROM or hard drive), storing it in high-speed RAM. Successive invocations of methods which need to read a small amount of data from the file storage device can swiftly obtain the data from RAM. Thus, a buffer acts as a cushion between the storage device and the program.

● The `BufferedReader` and `PrintWriter` classes

To read and write lines of text, we will use:

● The `readLine` method of `BufferedReader`. This reads a whole line of text into a string. If we need to split the line into separate parts, we can use the `StringTokenizer` class, described in Chapter 15.

● The `PrintWriter` class. This has two main methods: `print` and `println`. Note the lower-case 'l'. These methods write a string to a file, and `println` adds the end-of-line character after the string. If we need to build a line from separate parts, we can use the string operator `+` to join substrings.

● File output

Here, we will present a program which allows you to type in some text, and then save the text in a file. The basic elements of the user interface are:

● a `TextArea` to accept your text (and remember that a `TextArea` allows cut, copy and paste);
● a `TextField` to accept your filename. There is actually an AWT component to allow you to browse and click on a filename, and we will use this later;
● a 'save' button to initiate the transfer of text from the `TextArea` to the file.

Here is the complete application, and Figure 19.1 shows it running. The `Button`, `TextField` and `TextArea` components are not new, so here we will highlight the file usage.

```java
import java.io.*;
import java.awt.*;
import java.awt.event.*;
class FileDemo1 extends Frame
    implements WindowListener, ActionListener {

    private TextArea inputTextArea;
    private Button saveButton;
    private PrintWriter outFile;
```

Figure 19.1 An application to save text in a file.

```java
public static void main(String [] args) {
    FileDemo1 demo = new FileDemo1();
    demo.setSize(300,400);
    demo.makeGui();
    demo.setVisible(true);
}

public void makeGui() {
    saveButton = new Button("save");
    add("North", saveButton);
    saveButton.addActionListener(this);
    inputTextArea = new TextArea(10,50);
    add ("Center", inputTextArea);
    addWindowListener(this);   // for windowClosing
}

public void actionPerformed(ActionEvent evt) {
    if (evt.getSource() == saveButton ) {
        try{
            outFile = new PrintWriter(
                           new FileWriter("testout.txt"), true);
            outFile.print(inputTextArea.getText());
            outFile.close();
        }
        catch (IOException e) {
            System.err.println("File Error: " + e.toString() );
            System.exit(1);
        }
    }
}

public void windowClosing(WindowEvent e) {
    System.exit(0);
}

//empty WindowListener Methods
public void windowIconified(WindowEvent e) {
}
public void windowOpened(WindowEvent e) {
}
public void windowClosed(WindowEvent e) {
}
public void windowDeiconified(WindowEvent e) {
}
```

```
        public void windowActivated(WindowEvent e) {

        }
        public void windowDeactivated(WindowEvent e) {

        }
    }
```

First, we declare:

```
    private PrintWriter outFile;
```

We could have made this local to `actionPerformed`, but, in larger programs, several methods might need file access. Next, we create an instance:

```
    outFile = new PrintWriter(new FileWriter("testout.txt"), true);
```

This seems rather long-winded. Basically, it opens the file known as `testout.txt`. If the file does not exist on your disk, it will be created; if it does exist, it will be over-written and replaced with its new contents. The detail is that we first construct an instance of `FileWriter`, whose constructor allows us to specify a filename as a string. (The `PrintWriter` class has no such constructor.) Then we create an instance of `PrintWriter`, whose constructor can accept two parameters:

● an instance of `FileWriter`
● a boolean value. If we provide a `true` value, the internal buffer will automatically be written ('flushed') to the file whenever a `println` is invoked. We have chosen this so-called 'autoflush' option so that the contents of the file are kept relatively up-to-date. This can assist during debugging. (If we didn't specify this option and your program crashed part-way through, the buffered characters might never reach the file.)

The new instance of `PrintWriter` is then assigned to `outFile`. There are two items, which can be confused initially: one is the name of the file that your operating system uses, and the other is the name of a stream variable within the program – you have free choice of this stream name.

To actually write to the stream, we use `print`, as in:

```
    outFile.print(inputTextArea.getText());
```

Recall that `getText` fetches the entire string from the `TextArea` (which may consist of several lines). We then `print` it to the file. Finally, we close the file:

```
    outFile.close();
```

Creating the output stream with `new` might produce a checked exception, so we surround the code with a `try-catch` block, detecting an `IOException` (or a more specific exception which extends it). In addition, many of the I/O classes can throw exceptions when reading or writing, so we have extended the range of the `try` block to cover the `print` and `close` invocations.

Unfortunately, we are guilty of ignoring a special case here: `PrintWriter` is highly unusual because its potential `print` errors can only be detected by invoking a method known as `checkError`, rather than by catching an exception. We should really put:

```
outFile.print(inputTextArea.getText());
if(outFile.checkError() )       //true if error
    System.err.println("Error during writing to file.");
```

However, because very few exceptions can occur when writing strings to a file (filling the disk is a possibility) we shall intentionally ignore the `PrintWriter/checkError` special case, and emphasize a pattern which fits the overwhelming majority of the I/O classes.

In summary, when the user clicks on the 'save' button, the program:

1. opens the file `"testout.txt"`;
2. obtains a string from the text area;
3. outputs (writes) the string to the file;
4. closes the file.

● File input

Here we will present a program which displays the contents of a file on the screen: a file lister. The basic elements of the user interface are similar to our previous output example:

● a `TextArea` to display the text in the file;
● a `TextField` to accept your filename;
● a 'load' button to initiate the transfer of text from the file to the `TextArea`.

Here is the complete application, and Figure 19.2 shows a run.

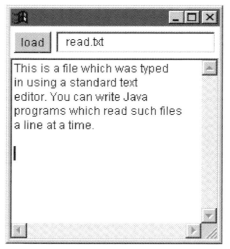

Figure 19.2 An application to display the content of a file.

```java
import java.io.*;
import java.awt.*;
import java.awt.event.*;


class FileDemo2 extends Frame
    implements WindowListener, ActionListener {


    private TextArea inputTextArea;
    private Button loadButton;
    private BufferedReader inFile;
    private TextField nameField;


    public static void main (String [] args) {
        FileDemo2 demo = new FileDemo2();
        demo.setSize(300,400);
        demo.makeGui();
        demo.setVisible(true);
    }


    public void makeGui() {
        Panel top = new Panel();
        loadButton = new Button("load");
        top.add(loadButton);
        loadButton.addActionListener(this);
        nameField = new TextField(20);
        top.add(nameField);
        nameField.addActionListener(this);
        add ("North", top);
        inputTextArea = new TextArea("",10,50);
        add ("Center", inputTextArea);
        addWindowListener(this);
    }


    public void actionPerformed(ActionEvent evt) {
        if (evt.getSource() == loadButton) {
            String fileName;
            fileName = nameField.getText();
            try {
                inFile = new BufferedReader(
                              new FileReader(fileName));
                inputTextArea.setText( "");      // clear the input area
                String line;
```

```
                while( ( line = inFile.readLine() ) != null) {
                    inputTextArea.append(line+"\n");
                }
                inFile.close();
            }

            catch (IOException e) {
                System.err.println("Error in file "
                              + fileName + ": " + e.toString() );
                System.exit(1);
            }
        }
    }

    public void windowClosing(WindowEvent e) {
        System.exit(0);
    }


    // empty WindowListener Methods
    public void windowIconified(WindowEvent e) {
    }
    public void windowOpened(WindowEvent e) {
    }
    public void windowClosed(WindowEvent e) {
    }
    public void windowDeiconified(WindowEvent e) {
    }
    public void windowActivated(WindowEvent e) {
    }
    public void windowDeactivated(WindowEvent e) {
    }
}
```

Now we will focus on the use made of files. First, we declare the instance:

```
    private BufferedReader inFile;
```

Next, we create an instance:

```
    inFile = new BufferedReader(new FileReader(fileName));
```

Then we use `readLine` to input the series of lines in the file, appending each one to our `TextArea`. There is one crucial point here: we don't know how many lines are in the file, so we set up a loop which terminates when there is nothing more to read:

```
while ( ( line = inFile.readLine() ) != null) {
    inputTextArea.append(line+"\n");
}
inFile.close();
```

The `while` condition is rather unusual, but is commonly used. When `readLine` can't find any more data, it returns `null`, and this is assigned to `line`. However, in Java it is possible to make use of the value assigned to a variable directly, and we do this here. The brackets are essential, to ensure that the assignment is performed before the comparison. We could have put:

```
line = inFile.readLine();
while ( ( line != null) {
    inputTextArea.append(line+"\n");
    line = inFile.readLine();
}
inFile.close();
```

but the condensed version (with its roots in the C language) is the idiom which you will see in most published programs.

In summary, when the user clicks on the 'load' button, the program:

1. inputs a file name from the text field;
2. opens a file with this name;
3. inputs lines from the file and appends them to the text area, as long as the end of the file is not reached;
4. closes the file.

● File searching

Searching a file for an item that meets some specified criteria is a classic requirement. Here we will construct a program which searches a file of exam marks, which takes the form:

```
J.Doe, 43 , 67
D.Bell, 87, 99
K.Bush, 54, 32
etc . . .
```

We can create this file by writing and running a Java program, or with a text editor. Each line is split into three areas, separated by commas. However, there may be extra spaces. In data processing, such areas are known as *fields*. The program will allow us to enter a filename, and to enter a student name, which we assume is unique. If the names are not unique, we would have to introduce an extra field to hold a unique identification number for each person. The program will search the file, and display the marks for our chosen student. The code we need to add to our previous file input example is a `while` which terminates when the end of the file is encountered or when the required name is found. We will use a `StringTokenizer` object to fetch each field in turn from the complete line.

Because there are two ways that the loop can terminate, we introduce an additional variable, `found`, to indicate whether the item was found or not. The informal English/Java structure of the search is:

```
boolean found = false;
while ((more lines) && (not found)) {
    get first field;
    if (first field matches name)
        found = true;
        put rest of fields in TextFields;
    }
}
```

We have added a 'search' button, which causes the file to be opened and searched. The user can select any file for searching. We have made the exception handling more specific: a missing filename is indicated, and an error during reading is indicated. The former error can be covered by providing a message suggesting a reinput of the name. An error during reading is difficult to recover from, so we use the `System` class to display a console message and exit to the operating system. Here is the program, which produces the screen of Figure 19.3.

```
import java.io.*;
import java.awt.*;
import java.util.*;          // StringTokenizer
import java.awt.event.*;

class FileSearch extends Frame
    implements ActionListener, WindowListener {
```

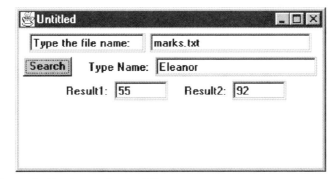

Figure 19.3 An application to search a text file.

```
private BufferedReader inFile;
private Button searchButton;
private TextField result1Field;
private TextField result2Field;
private TextField personField;
private TextField fileNameField;
private TextField errorField;
private String fileName;

public static void main (String [ ] args) {
    FileSearch search = new FileSearch();
    search.setSize(400,400);
    search.makeGui();
    search.setVisible(true);
}

public void makeGui() {
    setLayout(new FlowLayout() );
    errorField= new TextField("Type the File name:");
    errorField.setEditable(false);
    add(errorField);
    fileNameField = new TextField(20);
    fileNameField.setText("");
    add(fileNameField);
    searchButton = new Button("Search");
    add(searchButton);
    searchButton.addActionListener(this);
    add(new Label("Type Name:"));
    personField = new TextField(20);
    personField.setText("");
    add(personField);
    add(new Label("Result1:"));
    result1Field = new TextField(5);
    result1Field.setEditable(false);
    add(result1Field);
    add (new Label("Result2:"));
    result2Field= new TextField(5);
    result2Field.setEditable(false);
    add(result2Field);
    this.addWindowListener(this);
}

public void actionPerformed(ActionEvent evt) {
    if (evt.getSource() == searchButton) {
```

```
                fileName = fileNameField.getText();
                try {
                    inFile = new BufferedReader(
                                  new FileReader(fileName));
                }

                catch (IOException e) {
                    errorField.setText("Can't find file ");
                    return;
                    }
                errorField.setText("Type the file name:");
                // now read the file
                try {
                    String line;
                    boolean found = false;
                    while ((( ( line = inFile.readLine() ) != null)
                          && (! found)) {
                        // tokens split on commas, spaces
                        StringTokenizer tokens = new
                                            StringTokenizer( line, " ,");
                        String nameInFile = tokens.nextToken();
                        if (personField.getText().equals(nameInFile)) {
                            found = true;
                            result1Field.setText(tokens.nextToken() );
                            result2Field.setText(tokens.nextToken() );
                        }
                    }
                    inFile.close();
                }
                catch (IOException e) {
                    System.err.println("Error reading file "+
                                        fileName + ": " + e.toString() );
                    System.exit(1);
                }
            }
        }
    }

    // WindowListener methods - all needed!
    public void windowClosing(WindowEvent e) {
        System.exit(0);
    }

    // empty WindowListener Methods
    public void windowIconified(WindowEvent e) {
    }
```

```
        public void windowOpened(WindowEvent e) {
        }
        public void windowClosed(WindowEvent e) {
        }
        public void windowDeiconified(WindowEvent e) {
        }
        public void windowActivated(WindowEvent e) {
        }
        public void windowDeactivated(WindowEvent e) {
        }
    }
```

SELF-TEST QUESTION

19.1 Modify the `FileSearch` program so that it allows the user to type a substring of the name. Use `indexOf` in the `String` class.

● The `FileDialog` class

When you want to open a file using a GUI-based word processor or editor, you will typically make use of a window which allows you to view selected file types only, and to browse directories. Fortunately, this intricate component is available in the AWT, and is often more convenient than the simple `TextField` we have used up to now. Below we show a simple application which displays a `FileDialog` box when the 'load' button is clicked, and its execution is shown in Figure 19.4. The exact appearance of the box depends on your operating system.

```java
import java.io.*;
import java.awt.*;
import java.awt.event.*;

class FileDialogDemo extends Frame
    implements ActionListener, WindowListener {

    private Button loadButton;
    private FileDialog getNameBox;
    private TextField nameField;

    public static void main(String [] args) {
        FileDialogDemo demo = new FileDialogDemo();
        demo.setSize(500,400);
        demo.makeGui();
        demo.setVisible(true);
    }
```

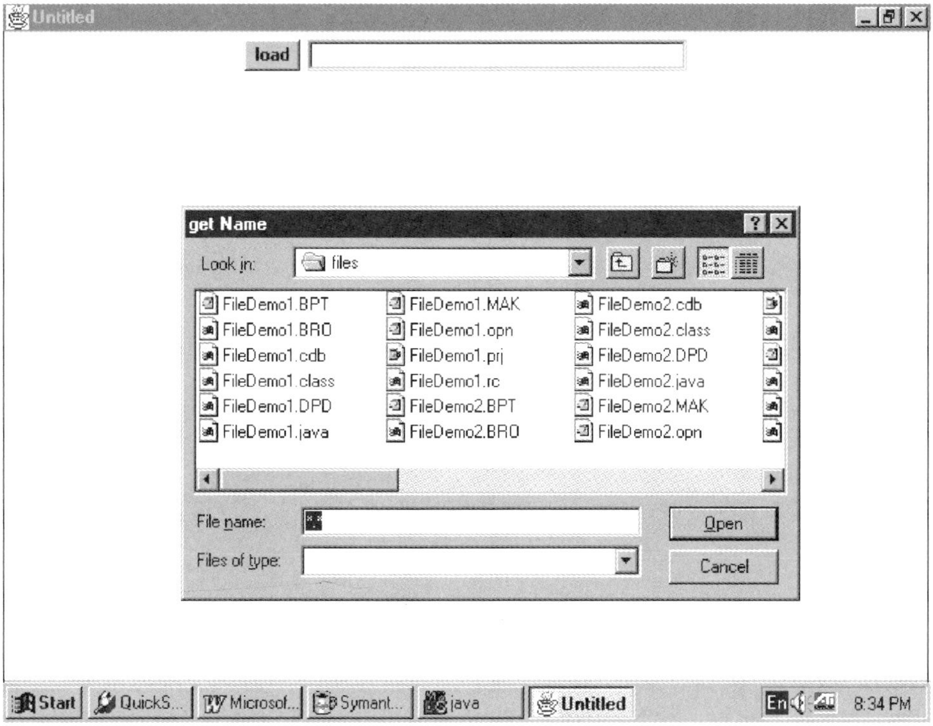

Figure 19.4 Displaying the file dialog.

```
public void makeGui() {
    setLayout(new FlowLayout());
    loadButton = new Button("load");
    add(loadButton);
    loadButton.addActionListener(this);
    nameField = new TextField(30);
    add(nameField);
    addWindowListener(this);    // for windowClosing
}

public void actionPerformed(ActionEvent evt) {
    String fileName;
    if (evt.getSource() == loadButton) {
        getNameBox = new FileDialog(this, "get Name",
        FileDialog.LOAD);
        getNameBox.show();

        // display the name
        fileName = getNameBox.getFile();
```

```
                nameField.setText(fileName);
        }
    }


    public void windowClosing(WindowEvent e) {
        System.exit(0);
    }


    // empty WindowListener Methods
    public void windowIconified(WindowEvent e) {
    }
    public void windowOpened(WindowEvent e) {
    }
    public void windowClosed(WindowEvent e) {
    }
    public void windowDeiconified(WindowEvent e) {
    }
    public void windowActivated(WindowEvent e) {
    }
    public void windowDeactivated(WindowEvent e) {
    }
}
```

Basically, we create a `FileDialog` by declaring it, supplying three parameters to its constructor, then showing it – causing it to be displayed.

```
private FileDialog getNameBox;

getNameBox = new FileDialog(this, "get Name", FileDialog.LOAD);
getNameBox.show();
```

The parameters are:

● the frame (or extension of frame) which creates the box;
● a caption to be used on its title bar;
● a constant – either `FileDialog.LOAD` or `FileDialog.SAVE`.

Finally, we can access the name of the selected file by:

```
String fileName = getNameBox.getFile();
```


● Console I/O

In the history of computing, three styles of user interface have evolved. Initially, the command line approach was used, in which a prompt was displayed on the screen, console or 'terminal' (at the end of a cable) and the user typed data or a command after the prompt. The screen then 'scrolled up', and the next prompt appeared. Input and output was purely textual, and there was just one place that input could occur. The next advance was the use of menus, where users could move a cursor over a menu and use keypresses to enter data or select options. More recently, windowing systems added a mouse as a pointing device, and made it possible to have several applications on screen at once.

In fact, the Java language can be used to write any of these styles of program, and here we will look at the facilities for command line software. But why might we want to create such software? Well, the UNIX operating system is based on this approach, and it has a large collection of utility programs – software tools. Its power comes in part from the capability of building new programs by joining together the existing tools. Typically, each tool is a free-standing application which accepts some textual input, processes it in some way, and passes the modified text on to another tool. Such software need not use the AWT at all. We only need to be able to display messages on the screen and input data or commands. This can be done most simply by a combination of streams and the `System` class.

● The `System` **class**

This class provides three ready-made streams: `System.in`, `System.out` and `System.err`. These streams can be used with a scrolling window known as a 'terminal' or 'console' I/O screen. Even if you are working with the AWT, you will find this class useful for displaying error messages etc.

The `System.in` stream can be used for direct keyboard input, and can also receive text that is piped or redirected into it via an operating system command. However, the methods that are provided with it are so low level as to be unusable to the Java programmer who is used to the convenience of strings. We recommend the following approach to console I/O, which provides us with a `BufferedReader` and the ability to use our familiar `readLine`. To create the stream we can use:

```
    private BufferedReader keyboard;

    keyboard = new BufferedReader(new InputStreamReader(System.in), 1);
```

We have used `BufferedReader` to read from files in our earlier examples. Here we use it again, but with an alternative constructor, one which allows us to specify a buffer size as the second parameter. In the above we have set the buffer size to 1, minimizing the buffering effect.

Here is the explanation for the buffer size: recall that a buffer is an area of RAM used to store a large amount of data. When a program invokes `readLine`, the data can be fetched from RAM, rather than the slower disk. However, this buffering approach is problematic when dealing with interactive keyboard input, because `BufferedReader` might attempt to fill its buffer with several lines of input text. Only then, when its buffer is full, will it send the first of the entered lines to `readLine`. The effect is that the user has to enter several lines before the first line is accessed by the program. This delay in response is totally unacceptable for interactive software! We need to set up the program such that when a line is entered, `readLine` acquires it as soon as the enter key is pressed, and specifying a buffer size of 1 gives the required effect.

Once the stream is created, we read from it by:

```
String line = keyboard.readLine();
```

In the `Finder` and `TinyBrowser` classes below, you will see a method `prompt`, which makes use of keyboard input.

Note that the use of a stream involves a checked exception. This is very unlikely to happen, so we handle it locally, rather than complicating matters for the invokers of `prompt`.

The `System.out` stream provides useful methods already, bearing in mind that Java already allows strings to be joined. We can choose either `print`, which prints a string, or `println`, which prints a string followed by the end-of-line code `\n`. The term 'print' is a legacy from the days of paper printout. Here are some examples:

```
String demo = "some data";
// display: some data being printed
System.out.println(demo + " being printed");
```

Note that the string to be printed might also contain several lines of text. This stream is the direct equivalent of `System.in`, in that its output can be redirected or piped at operating system level. We don't need to create this stream with `new` – it exists already. In the listing below, examine the method `prompt`. It is used by supplying a message to be displayed, and it returns the string that the user typed, for example:

```
String reply = prompt("type your name:");
```

The buffering method for console output is slightly different from that of files. We put:

```
System.out.flush();
```

which ensures that any text sent with `print` will be displayed immediately, rather than when the next `println` occurs. This is useful for displaying prompts, where the user types a response on the same line.

The `System.err` stream can similarly be used with `print` and `println`, but its output cannot be redirected or piped – it won't interfere with the real output of the program. On many systems, error messages will simply appear on the console window. Here is an example:

```
System.err.println("Error... program terminating.");
```

The `System` class also provides a method to terminate applications immediately, known as `System.exit`. We must also supply an integer code, which can be potentially used by the operating system to determine the cause of termination. The convention is that zero means OK, whereas non-zero means something went wrong. You can choose which non-zero error codes to use, and these should be noted in your documentation for the application. Here are some examples:

```
System.exit(0);                      // normal exit

System.err.println("Error in application");
System.exit(3);                      // error exit
```

● Non-AWT applications

Let us make use of the `System` streams to write programs. In Chapter 18, we saw a program which displayed `"Hello"`. Here we will progress to a more useful program: a version of `grep` or `find`, provided by some operating systems, which searches a file to find a particular substring. We shall display every line that contains the requested substring, and, to give us some context, the preceding line and the following line. So, our program has two console inputs – the file to search and the required substring. We could display prompts for both of these and read them from `System.in`. However, sometimes it is more appropriate to supply items as we initiate the program, and we can do this via command line arguments, in a non-interactive manner. If you are running Java from the command line, you can type lines such as:

```
java myprog datafile
```

where the string `datafile` (regarded as command line argument number 0) can be accessed by the program `myprog`. If you are using an integrated development environment, a menu option will allow you to specify any arguments. In our example, we will get the filename from the command line arguments, and get the search string from the `System.in` stream. The `indexOf` method is used to search for a substring – it returns -1 if the substring is not present. The `prompt` method shows keyboard I/O. Here is the program:

```
import java.io.*;
class Finder {

    private String line1, line2, line3;
    private BufferedReader keyboard, inStream;

    public static void main (String [] args) {
        Finder aFind = new Finder();
        aFind.doSearch(args[0]);
    }

    private void doSearch(String fileName) {
        keyboard = new BufferedReader(new InputStreamReader(System.in), 1);
        String wanted = prompt("Type string to find:");
```

```
    line1 = "";
    line2 = "";
    try {
        inStream = new BufferedReader(new
                                FileReader(fileName));

        while ((line3 = inStream.readLine()) != null) {
            if ( line2.indexOf(wanted) >= 0 )
                displayLine();

            // advance to the next group of 3
            line1 = line2;
            line2 = line3;
            // and get new line3 from file...
        }

        // check the last line
        line3 = "";                         // remove null eof value
        if (line2.indexOf(wanted) >= 0)
            displayLine();
        inStream.close();
    }

    catch (IOException e) {
        System.err.println("Error in Finder: "+ e.toString());
        System.exit(1);
    }
}

private void displayLine() {
    System.out.println("<<------------ context:");
    System.out.println(line1);
    System.out.println(line2);
    System.out.println(line3);
    System.out.println("                            ----------->>");
    System.out.println("");
}

private String prompt(String message) {
    String reply = "";
    try {
        System.out.print(message);
        System.out.flush();
        reply = keyboard.readLine();
    }
```

```
            catch (IOException e) {
                System.out.println("Keyboard input "+ e.toString() );
                System.exit(2);
            }
            return reply;
    }


}
```

The program can be run from the command line, and requests a string to find. This is what you would see on your console if you used the file `Finder.java` as input. (The `%` is an operating system prompt.)

```
% java Finder Finder.java
Type string to find:if
<<------------ context:
            while ((line3 = inStream.readLine()) != null) {
                if ( line2.indexOf(wanted) >= 0 )
                    displayLine();
                    ------------>>

<<------------ context:
                line3 = "";
        // remove null eof value
            if (line2.indexOf(wanted) >= 0)
                displayLine();
                    ------------>>
```

● The `File` class

This class provides facilities to manipulate files and directories (folders) as a whole. It is not concerned with accessing the data within files. You can make use of the `File` class without making use of stream I/O, and vice versa. In each case, though, you need to import `java.io.*`.

First, we will make a brief detour into directory structures. As you know, most operating systems provide a hierarchical structure, with a path through such a structure of the form:

```
c:\programming\java\projects\demo.java
```

This is a Windows-style path, on the `c:` drive, with \ used as a separator. On a multi-user UNIX system, the path has additional directories to pass through, and the path might be:

```
/top/staff/MikeParr/programming/java/projects/demo.java
```

If you need to write path-manipulation software that works on any system, you can find out what the file separator is by referring to the string constant `File.separator`.

The above path is absolute – it starts from the very top of the directory and leads you to the file. However, sometimes this is irrelevant: we only need to deal with paths relative to the current directory. For example, if we are currently in the `java` directory, then the path to `demo.java` is `projects/demo.java`. If we are already in the directory `projects`, then the path to the file is simply `demo.java`. The parent of `demo.java` is `projects`.

Now we will provide details of the most useful methods. Initially, we must construct an instance of the class `File` by supplying a string. Once this instance has been created, we can use it.

Here is the instance:

```
File myFile = new
        File("c:\\programming\\java\\projects\\demo.java");
```

Note that the Java escape character \ is coincidentally the same as the Windows file separator. Here, we need to say that the backslash is merely a normal character of the string rather than a special one, so we escape it. Effectively, \\ represents an ordinary \.

In the following examples, we will make the assumption that we are currently in `projects`.

getPath

To find the relative path we put:

```
String relative = myFile.getPath();
```

which returns the result `"demo.java"` – because we are already in the directory.

getAbsolutePath

To find the absolute path, we put:

```
String absolute = myFile.getAbsolutePath();
```

which returns `"c:\programming\java\projects\demo.java"`.

exists

To check that the file exists, we can put:

```
boolean there = myFile.exists();
```

which returns `true` or `false`.

isDirectory

The file might be a directory. We can check this by:

```
boolean checkDirectory = myFile.isDirectory();
```

which returns `true` if the file is a directory, and `false` otherwise.

length

We can find the size of the file in bytes:

```
long myLength = myFile.length();
```

list

We can fill a string array with a list of filenames within a directory:

```
String [] allFiles = myFile.list();
```

In the current example, our `File` object (referring to `"demo.java"`) is not a directory, and `null` would be returned by the method `list`.

● Reading from a remote site

Surprisingly, reading a file on a remote server is no more difficult in Java than reading a local file – this is because of the power of the Java library. Rather than a filename, we need to supply the URL (Uniform Resource Locator) of the file. Below we illustrate a non-AWT application, which prompts the user to enter a URL, and which displays the content of the file on the screen. The program can only handle text files, as you can see from the console view in Figure 19.5.

What about the possibility of creating a program which *writes* to a remote site? The consequences of being able to overwrite any file on the Internet is obviously catastrophic, so the majority of files have protections which will not allow an arbitrary program to write to them.

```
% java TinyBrowser
Type a URL address (e.g. http://java.sun.com/) :http://java.sun.com/
<!DOCTYPE HTML PUBLIC "-//W3C//DTD HTML
3.2//EN"><HTML><HEAD><TITLE><JavaSoft Home Page</TITLE></HEAD><BODY
BGCOLOR="#333399"><!-- begin main page table --><TABLE BORDER=0 CELL-
PADDING=0 CELLSPACING=0> <TR> <TD WIDTH=157 VALIGN=TOP>
```

Figure 19.5 Run of `TinyBrowser`.

```
import java.io.*;
import java.net.*;


class TinyBrowser {

    private BufferedReader inStream, keyboard;

    public static void main (String [] args) {
        TinyBrowser aBrowser = new TinyBrowser();
        aBrowser.fetch();
    }

    private void fetch() {
        String urlString = "";
        String line;
        keyboard = new BufferedReader(new
        InputStreamReader(System.in),1);
        try {
            urlString = prompt
                ("Type a URL address (e.g. http:// java.sun.com/) :");

            // create a link to a URL
            URL urlAddress = new URL(urlString);
            URLConnection link = urlAddress.openConnection();

            inStream = new BufferedReader(new
                        InputStreamReader(link.getInputStream()));

            while ((line = inStream.readLine()) != null) {
                System.out.print(line);
            }
        }
        catch (MalformedURLException e) {
            System.err.println(urlString + e.toString());
            System.exit(2);
        }

        catch (IOException e) {
            System.err.println("Error in accessing URL: "+ e.toString());
            System.exit(1);
        }


    }
```

```
    private String prompt(String message) {
        String reply = "";
        try {
            System.out.print(message);
            System.out.flush();
            reply = keyboard.readLine();
        }
        catch (IOException e) {
            System.out.println("Keyboard input "+ e.toString() );
            System.exit(2);
        }
        return reply;
    }

}
```

Most of the program is concerned with exception handling and console I/O. The essential URL code is:

```
import java.net.*;        // net classes

// create a link to a URL
URL urlAddress = new URL(urlString);
URLConnection link = urlAddress.openConnection();
inStream = new DataInputStream(link.getInputStream());
```

First, we supply a string to the URL class, which performs checks on the syntax – e.g. are the '/' and '.' characters in a correct arrangement? If they are not, a MalformedURLException is thrown. Next, we actually create a connection with the URLConnection class.

As you can see from Figure 19.5, this is a rather primitive browser – it cannot interpret HTML tags (enclosed in < >), or display graphics.

SELF-TEST QUESTION
·····························

19.2 Modify the TinyBrowser program to use the AWT, with a TextField for the URL and a TextArea to display the output.

Grammar spot

In fact, we have seen no new statements or language features, because file facilities are provided by classes rather than being built into the language.

Programming pitfalls

● File access requires us to either use `try-catch` for an `IOException` (which is preferable) or state that our method, which uses streams, `throws` an `IOException`.
● It is not possible to put:

```
myFile = new PrintWriter("demo.txt");
```

Instead we must put:

```
myFile = new PrintWriter(new FileWriter("demo.txt"), true);
```

or, for input:

```
myFile = new BufferedReader(new FileReader("any.txt"));
```

● The `System.exit` method requires an integer parameter.

New language elements

We have introduced these classes:

```
PrintWriter
BufferedReader
URL
URLConnection
File
FileDialog
```

Summary

● Files are opened, then written to (or read from), and finally closed.

● We declare and create file streams by, for example:

```
private FileReader inStream;
private PrintWriter outStream;

outStream = new PrintWriter(new FileWriter("demo.txt"), true);
inStream = new BufferedReader(new FileReader("any.txt"));
```

● The programmer has free choice of the stream variable names. These names become associated with actual operating system filenames.

● The `readLine` method is a convenient method to access input streams.

● The `print` and `println` methods are convenient for output streams.

● The popular idiom to read a file line-by-line is:

```
String Line;
while((line = instream.readLine()) != null) {
    // process line
}
```

● We close streams by, for example:

```
myStream.close();
```

● The `System` class provides ready-created streams: `System.in`, `System.out` and `System.err`.

● The `System.exit(n)` method can be used to abandon an application immediately.

EXERCISES

19.1 Produce an AWT application which allows text to be typed into a `TextArea` and to be written to a file. The filename should be input via a `TextField`.

19.2 Produce an AWT application which can read a file containing lines with three items – a name (with no spaces), and two integers. The items are separated by commas. The application should allow the filename to be selected via a `TextField`, and should provide a 'next' button which causes the next line of the file to be input and displayed in three `TextFields`. Provide the user with an indication of when the end-of-file has been reached.

19.3 Produce an AWT application which is a simple text editor. Initially, use TextFields for file names. It should have:

● a `TextArea` for editing;
● a 'load' button to select and then input a file;
● a 'save as' button to allow the selection of an output file name, followed by the writing of the text to the file;
● a 'save' button to save the text in the name selected by the 'save as' button;
● an 'exit' button.

Finally, modify your editor to use `FileDialog` boxes.

19.4 Produce a non-AWT application which compares two files line-by-line. It should print a message stating that the files are either equal or not equal. Fetch the filenames from the command line. Your application is run by, for example:

```
java FileCompare myfile.txt yourfile.txt
```

19.5 Produce a non-AWT application which replaces one substring by another in a file, writing the new version to another file. The application should use command line arguments for the old and new filenames, and should prompt the user to enter the substring to find and the substring which is to replace it.

19.6 Produce a non-AWT directory lister, which prompts the user for an absolute path and then displays every filename in the directory. If any files are directories, the word "`dir`" should be printed after their name.

19.7 Modify the `TinyBrowser` program so that it repeats its prompt if a `MalformedURLException` is produced. Use a `try–catch` inside a `while`.

19.8 Convert the `TinyBrowser` to an AWT application. It should have a large `TextArea` to display the text, and a single-line `TextArea` for URL entry. Provide a facility to let the user copy a URL address from within the large `TextArea`, and to paste it into the URL entry `TextArea`. (Recall that mouse copy/paste is provided by text areas.)

ANSWERS TO SELF-TEST QUESTIONS

19.1 We modify the following code:

```
if (personField.getText().equals(nameInFile)) {
    found = true;
```

so that it becomes:

```
if (nameInFile.indexOf(personField.getText()) >= 0) {
    found = true;
```

19.2 We base our solution on the previous `FileDemo2` class, which has a 'load' button and a text field suitable for URL input. Adding the main part of the `TinyBrowser` code into `action` gives us the following. Refer to `FileDemo2` for the basic GUI creation.

```
import java.net.*;

class AWTBrowser extends Frame {
    private BufferedReader inStream;

    public static void main (String [] args) {
        AWTBrowser demo = new AWTBrowser();
        demo.setSize(300,400);
        demo.makeGui();
        demo.setVisible(true);
    }

    public void makeGui() {
    // as FileDemo2
    }
```

```
    public void actionPerformed((actionEvent evt) {
        if (evt.getSource() == loadButton) {

            String urlString = nameField.getText();
            String line;
            try {
                // create a link to a URL
                URL urlAddress = new URL(urlString);
                URLConnection link =
                urlAddress.openConnection();
                inStream = new
                    BufferedReader(link.getInputStream());
                while ((line = inStream.readLine()) != null) {
                    inputTextArea.append(line+ "\n");
                }

            }
            // catch as in TinyBrowser...
            }

        }
        return true;
    }
// window shutdown and empty methods, as FileDemo2
```

Graphics and sound

● Introduction

It is common to want to incorporate graphics and sound into the output from a Java program to provide interest and present information in a different way. Graphics and sound information is stored in files. A graphics file can be created using a graphics package, copied from a clip-art file, input to the computer via a scanner, input from a digital camera, clipped from a video recording, captured from a video camera, captured from a TV programme, or fetched from a Web site. An audio file can be recorded from a microphone, copied from a sound effects library, copied from radio, CD or video recording, or fetched from a Web site.

There are a number of different file formats for graphics and for audio. The different formats have evolved historically for different reasons. It is usually the case that graphics and audio software packages will import a variety of file formats and also export different file formats, and so generally it is easy to mix file formats.

A Java program can also directly draw graphical images on the screen using library methods like drawOval, drawRect and drawLine. We have seen how to do this from the earliest chapters in this book.

Two common file formats for graphics are GIF and JPEG. Both are supported by the Java library. GIF stands for Graphics Interchange Format. It was designed as a format for storing pictures that could be used on a variety of systems. It provides for eight bits to represent the colour of each pixel. This is nowadays a very restrictive number of colours, so that GIF is only useful for graphics that need few colours, such as line drawings and cartoons. A GIF file ends with the suffix .gif.

The JPEG (Joint Photographic Experts Group) format provides for 24 bits per pixel to represent colour. This is much more in line with the capabilities of modern displays. It is often necessary to compress files that contain graphics information to save space on disks and to reduce transmission times across networks. JPEG also allows for better compression of graphics information than GIF. A JPEG file usually ends with the suffix `.jpg` (or `.jpeg`).

The Java library supports the following audio file formats: `.au`, `.wav`, `.aif` (or `.aiff`), `.mid` (or `.midi`).

● Displaying graphics

Suppose we have a graphics image that we want to display, contained in a file called `picture.gif` – see Figure 20.1. The essence of what we need to do is to inform the library methods of the name of the file. This is accomplished in two steps. The first task is to inform the library of the filename and to allocate space in memory for the image. This is done using the library method `getImage`. The second step is to load the image from the file into the computer memory and display the graphic on the screen. This is done using the library method `drawImage`. Here is a program to load and display the graphic in the file `picture.gif`:

```java
import java.awt.*;
import java.applet.Applet;

public class Picture extends Applet {
    private Image image;
```

Figure 20.1 Output from the program `Picture`.

```
    public void init() {
        image = getImage(getDocumentBase(), "picture.gif");
    }
    public void paint(Graphics g) {
        g.drawImage(image, 20, 20, 100, 100, this);
    }
}
```

An object of type Image is essentially the space in memory available to hold an image. The method getImage immediately returns an image object, whether or not the image exists in the file.

We must carefully specify where the graphics file is. There are several ways to do this; the first method is illustrated in the program above. In the first method we place the graphics file in the same directory (folder) as the HTML file (Web page) that invokes the applet. Invoking the method getDocumentBase returns the URL of this Web page. This address is presented as the first parameter to the method getImage, which uses this directory name to find the specified graphics file (picture.gif in this example program). This is a convenient way of specifying where the graphics file is.

SELF-TEST QUESTION
....

20.1 Place a graphics file on your disk in the same directory as the above Java program and run the program.

An alternative way of specifying the filename is to use the full Internet address, the URL, as the parameter for drawImage as follows. Such a file could be on your own computer or on someone else's computer somewhere on the Internet. (To do this you need, of course, your computer to be connected to the Internet.)

```
    image = getImage("http://only.an.example/picture.gif");
```

Yet another way of specifying the filename is to place the graphics file in the same directory as the Java program itself. You can then invoke getImage as follows:

```
    image = getImage(getCodeBase(), "picture.gif");
```

in which getCodeBase returns the URL of the program.

It is not until drawImage is invoked that the image is loaded into memory from the file and then drawn. This may take some time, even with a fast computer.

The second and third parameters to drawImage are the *x*- and *y*-coordinates of the top left of the rectangle in which the image will be displayed in the window. The next two parameters are the width and height of this rectangle. The graphical image is scaled (made bigger or smaller) to fit the specified rectangle.

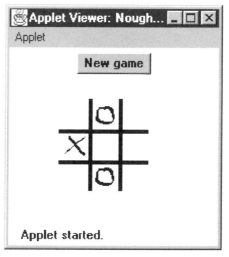

Figure 20.2 Noughts and crosses.

The final parameter of `drawImage` specifies an object that is to be notified when the image has been loaded. Normally we write `this` as the value of this parameter, meaning the current object. Loading a graphics file can take some time, and a more sophisticated program can monitor when the image is loaded. This parameter can assist in the monitoring, and we will not concern ourselves further with this.

SELF-TEST QUESTION
....

20.2 In a game to play Tic Tac Toe (noughts and crosses) it is required to display the graphic for a nought or a cross at different places on the screen (Figure 20.2). Write a method to display a cross within the rectangle defined by x, y, width, height (the same parameters as `drawRect` require.)

● Playing audio clips

Playing an audio clip in Java is very like displaying a graphic. A passage of sound is stored in a file. The most common type of audio file, and the one supported by the Java library, is au. Suppose we have a file called `sound.au` that contains a sound that we want to play. First we have to declare an `AudioClip` object:

```
AudioClip sound;
```

Next we invoke a library method to create an `AudioClip` object. As with graphics, we tell the method where the file is and what its name is:

```
AudioClip sound = getAudioClip(getDocumentBase(), "sound.au");
```

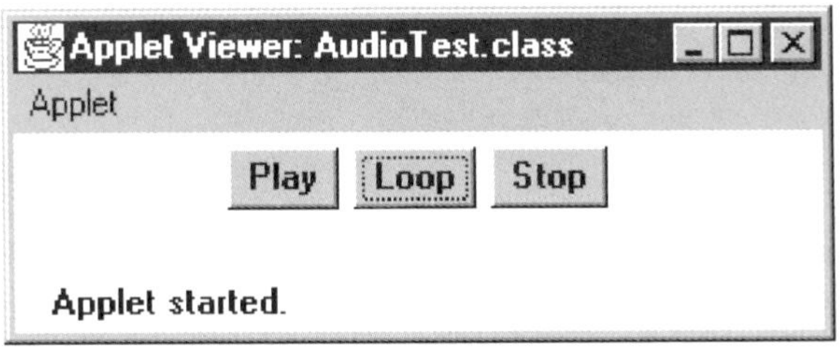

Figure 20.3 The window display for the audio test program.

Next we can play the sound:

```
sound.play();
```

`play` is a method of the class `AudioClip` and therefore a method of any object of the type `AudioClip`, including our object `sound`.

We can do other things with an `AudioClip` object:

```
sound.loop();
```

which plays it repeatedly from the beginning. And:

```
sound.stop();
```

which stops the playing.

It is important to realize that the methods `play` and `loop` only initiate the playing and then immediately return. The program can then carry on and do something else while the clip is playing. It can display text and/or graphics on the screen or display an animation. It can even play several audio clips simultaneously.

As a demonstration of these facilities, here is a program that will play, loop or stop an audio clip. A button is provided to initiate each of these tasks (Figure 20.3). The file called `sound.au` must be in the same directory (folder) as the Java program.

```java
import java.awt.*;
import java.applet.*;
import java.awt.event.*;

class AudioTest extends Applet implements ActionListener {

    private Button play, loop, stop;
    private AudioClip sound;

    public void init() {
        play = new Button("Play");
        add(play);
        play.addActionListener(this);
        loop = new Button("Loop");
```

```
            add(loop);
            loop.addActionListener(this);
            stop = new Button("Stop");
            add(stop);
            stop.addActionListener(this);
            sound = getAudioClip(getDocumentBase(), "sound.au");
        }


    public void actionPerformed(ActionEvent event) {
        if (event.getSource() == play)
            sound.play();
        if (event.getSource() == loop)
            sound.loop();
        if (event.getSource() == stop)
            sound.stop();
        }
    }
```

● Animation

Animation is the name given to movement of graphical images on a computer screen. The images may be text, cartoons or video images. Animation is implemented by displaying a series of images sufficiently quickly that the eye sees continuous movement. This happens when about 30 or more images per second are displayed. If the images are sufficiently simple, they can be drawn and redrawn using methods like `drawOval` and `drawLine`. But if better images are required, current computers cannot draw them sufficiently fast. The images therefore have to be drawn in advance of viewing, and stored in files.

In an early chapter we saw a program that displayed a ball bouncing around the screen. We now return to this example (Figure 20.4). The principle behind the program is to draw the ball, erase it by re-drawing it in the background colour and then to re-draw the ball a small distance away. This is repeated at high speed.

The ball actually travels too fast for the eye to see. We have enhanced the program by slowing down the speed at which the ball travels. This is done by making the program sleep for several milliseconds every time the ball moves. The library method `Thread.sleep` takes as a parameter an integer which is the number of milliseconds that the program will sleep. (A millisecond is 1/1000 of a second.) If the program sleeps for 50 milliseconds then the ball will be moved 20 times per second.

`Thread.sleep` can cause an exception (see Chapter 16 on exceptions), and we must provide exception handling as shown. (This is why we did not use sleeping in the earlier chapter.) This exception will actually never arise in this program because there is only one thread.

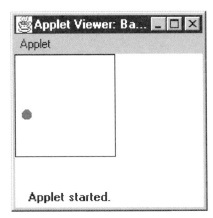

Figure 20.4 The bouncing ball.

```java
import java.awt.*;
import java.applet.Applet;

public class Ball extends Applet {

    private int x = 7, xChange = 7;
    private int y = 2, yChange = 2;
    private int diameter = 10;

    private int rectLeftX = 0, rectRightX = 100;
    private int rectTopY = 0, rectBottomY = 100;

    public void paint (Graphics g) {
        g.drawRect(rectLeftX, rectTopY,
                rectRightX-rectLeftX, rectBottomY-rectTopY);

        for (int n = 1; n< 1000; n++) {
            Color backgroundColour = getBackground();
            g.setColor(backgroundColour);
            g.fillOval (x, y, diameter, diameter);

            if (x + xChange <= rectLeftX)
                xChange = -xChange;
            if(x + xChange + diameter >= rectRightX)
                xChange = -xChange;

            if (y + yChange <= rectTopY)
                yChange = -yChange;
            if(y+ yChange + diameter >= rectBottomY)
                yChange = -yChange;
```

```
            x = x + xChange;
            y = y + yChange;

            g.setColor(Color.red);
            g.fillOval (x, y, diameter, diameter);
            try {
                Thread.sleep(50);
            }
            catch (InterruptedException e) {
                System.err.println("sleep exception");
            }
        }
    }
}
```

The problem with this program is that it completely monopolizes the processor. While it is running, all attempts to use buttons on the screen are ignored. The animation continues until it has completed its 1000 loops. Suppose for example we enhance the program by providing a scrollbar to alter the sleep time. Changing the scrollbar value will be ignored until the animation has ceased. A partial answer is to provide a button to start the animation. But this still means that nothing else can happen during the animation. The ideal solution to this problem is to use multithreading as explained in Chapter 25. In this approach, the program splits into two threads, one to display the animation and the other to handle the user interface. The two threads run at the same time and therefore two activities can be handled simultaneously.

EXERCISES

20.1 Photo album/graphics browser Write a program that inputs the name of a graphics file from a text field and then displays the file. First set up some graphics files in the directory that holds your program. Then, if you are Internet-connected, access some graphics files from the Internet.

20.2 Juke box Write a program that inputs the name of an audio file from a text field. A button allows the audio to be played or stopped. Another button causes the audio to be repeated indefinitely, using the method loop. A third button causes the sound to stop.

Alternatively, set up a number of audio clips in a number of files, and provide buttons to select each of them.

20.3 Text animation Write a program to make some text glide around the screen. Use drawString to display the text of your choice. Make the text bounce when it encounters the boundary of the window. Adjust the speed at which the text moves by altering the time for which the program sleeps. Create a scrollbar that allows the sleep time to be adjusted. Create a text field which allows the user to display the text of their choice.

20.4 Graphics animation Write a program to display an animation. The number of possibilities is limited only by the imagination. One possibility is a lift, represented by a rectangle, that moves up or down under the control of buttons. Use `Thread.sleep` to control the rate at which the animation proceeds. Another possibility is a water drop that falls onto a flat surface, to break into a number of smaller droplets. Use `drawOval` to display the drops. Again use `Thread.sleep` to control the speed.

20.5 Animation Write a program to load and display a sequence of images from a number of different files, with a 100 millisecond wait between the display of each of the images.

20.6 Animation Write a program to make a graphics image, loaded from a file, move around the screen. Use `g.clearRect(int x, int y, int height, int width)` to fill a rectangular area with the background colour – make the image disappear. Use `Thread.sleep` to prevent it moving too fast.
Alternatively, make the image grow in size and then shrink on the screen.

ANSWER TO SELF-TEST QUESTION
....

20.2
```
private void nought(Graphics g, int x, int y, int width, int
                    height) {
    image = getImage(getDocumentBase(), "nought.gif");
    boolean b = g.drawImage(image, x, y, width, height, this);
}


private void cross(Graphics g, int x, int y, int width, int
                   height) {
    image = getImage(getDocumentBase(), "cross.gif");
    boolean b = g.drawImage(image, x, y, width, height, this);
}
```

OO design

● Introduction

You wouldn't start to design a bridge by thinking about the size of the rivets. You would first make major decisions – like whether the bridge is cantilever or suspension. You wouldn't begin to design a building by thinking about the colour of the carpets. You would make major decisions first – like how many floors there are to be and where the lifts should be.

It is the same with programming; most people argue that the programmer should start with the major decisions rather than the detail. The programmer should do design, do it first and do it well. Decisions about detail – like the exact format of a number, or the position of a button – should be postponed. All the stages of programming are crucial, of course, but some are more crucial than others.

When you start out to write programs, you usually spend a lot of time in (sometimes tortuous) trial and error. This is often great fun and very creative. Usually you spend some time wrestling with the programming language. It takes some time to learn good practice and to recognize bad practice. It takes even longer to adopt a systematic design approach to programming. The fun remains, the creativity remains, but the nuisance parts of programming are reduced.

The design process takes as its input the specification of what the program is to do. This is the input into the design process. The end product of the design process is a description of the classes, public variables and methods that the program will employ. This chapter explains how to use one mainstream approach to designing object-oriented programs – object-oriented (OO) design.

We shall use the simple example of the balloon program throughout this chapter to illustrate how to do design. This is an example that has been used several times within this book, and it is probably familiar to the reader. The program simulates a balloon, which is displayed as a simple circle on the screen. The user of the program is provided with buttons that can be clicked on to move the balloon and to change its size. We have seen what this program looks like so we already know the answer to the question of what the design of the program looks like. It consists of two objects – the user interface object and a model of the balloon itself.

We will also introduce a more complex program to use as a design example.

● The principles of object-oriented programming (OOP)

The central ideas of OOP are:

● encapsulation (introduced in Chapter 9);
● inheritance (introduced in Chapter 11);
● polymorphism (discussed in Chapter 28).

If you are new to OOP, you should thoroughly understand encapsulation at an early stage. You need to understand encapsulation to do design. You should think about understanding inheritance before long. It is desirable to understand inheritance in order to undertake design. You can postpone your understanding of polymorphism for a time. But you will eventually need to understand it properly to carry out design well. We now review these three concepts.

Encapsulation

Encapsulation means grouping related information together and protecting it from the outside world. Programs consist of data (variables) and actions (methods); in an object-oriented program these are grouped together appropriately. Such a grouping is an object. The motivation for grouping information into objects is to try to cope with complexity. Computer software is complex – it is hard to design, to test and to debug. Once software is written, it is hard to modify. If variables and methods are scattered haphazardly about a program, the complexity is worsened. Putting related things together makes sense. Once we have grouped things together, a lot of information can be hidden from view – information hiding. Information hiding isn't about privacy or security; it is about avoiding burdening programmers with information they simply don't need to know about – thus reducing complexity. Another word that describes this idea is *abstraction*. It's like using a fridge: you don't need to know how it works in order to use it. Indeed, it is actually difficult to see how a fridge works because you are physically prevented from seeing how it works. We often view a fridge at a high level of abstraction – simply a box that we put things in to make them cool. A lower level of abstraction would see the fridge as consisting of a compressor, pipes, a condenser etc. Information hiding promotes modularity – you can have someone mend the motor in your fridge without interrupting your favourite TV programme.

We have seen earlier in this book how objects are described in Java, how information is grouped together and how information is made publicly accessible or made private. One way of visualizing an object is as a diagram shown in Figure 21.1 in which the

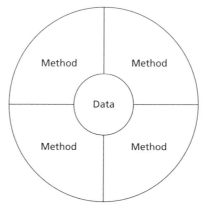

Figure 21.1 Encapsulation in an object.

object consists of a collection of data and methods that are closely related. The data within the object is not usually directly accessible from the outside, but instead any operations on the data are carried out by the methods of the object.

In OOP, classes are important because we know that very often we will want to create distinct items of the same type. For example, it is common to use strings within a program; all the strings are objects of the same type, defined by the same class. Thus classes make for the generalization of objects, promoting simpler programs and the reuse of classes by other programs.

Inheritance

Classes can be used again and again, but inheritance promotes reuse even further. Inheritance means that if we need a new class which is roughly like one that we already have, we can reuse the parts we have and simply define the parts that are new and different. We can do this without touching the class we already have. This ability to build on what we have avoids starting from scratch. It reduces effort and it promotes simplicity. This is dramatically demonstrated by programs that inherit from the java `applet` class, which provides ready-made facilities for window handling which it would otherwise take many months of programming to achieve.

Polymorphism

Suppose that we are writing a program that creates graphical shapes on the screen – circles, ovals, rectangles, etc. The program allows these to be placed on the screen, repositioned and changed in size. We will declare some shapes:

```
Circle circle;
Oval oval;
Rectangle rectangle;
Triangle t;
```

Let us concentrate on changing the size of these shapes and, in particular, making them grow. In the Java code we will invoke a method to make a circle grow like this:

```
circle.grow(change);
```

where the parameter is the percentage change in the size of the object. Similarly, we will, as necessary, invoke similar methods that make the other shapes grow:

```
oval.grow(change);
rectangle.grow(change);
t.grow(change);
```

Each class of object provides a method, named `grow`, that can be invoked to alter the size of object of that type. When the program runs, the Java system ensures that the correct version of `grow` is selected from all the methods with that name. It does this by knowing the type of the object (`Circle`, `Oval`, `Rectangle` etc.). This is polymorphism – the same method name is used for different objects.

It gets even better. We invoke the method that asks any shape to be enlarged:

```
shape.grow(size);
```

where the type of `shape` is any of circle, oval, rectangle, etc. Again the run-time system invokes the version of `grow` that deals with the particular object that is being used at the time. (This assumes that all these shapes are subclasses of a class called, say, `Shape`.)

Polymorphism, then, is the facility for the same method name to be used in conjunction with different objects. Put another way, a method can have multiple implementations, one of which is selected when the program is running depending on the type of the object that is involved. The particular method that is selected is always the method belonging to the class of the object when it was created.

We now leave the challenging topic of polymorphism until Chapter 28 and we do not discuss it further in this chapter.

● The design problem

Identifying the objects

We have seen that an object-oriented program consists of a collection of objects. The problem when starting out to develop a new program is to identify suitable objects. We know that once we have identified the objects we will reap all the benefits of OOP. But the fundamental problem of OOP is how to identify the objects. This is what a design method offers – an approach, a series of steps to identifying the objects. It is just like any other kind of design – you need a method. Knowing the principles of OOP is not enough. By analogy, knowing the laws of physics doesn't mean you can design a space ship; you also have to carry out some design.

Simulation and modelling

One of the principles used in the design of object-oriented programs is to simulate real world situations as objects. You build a software model of things in the real world. Indeed, the first OO language, Simula, was so called because it was intended as a simulation language. Here are some examples:

- If we are developing an office automation system, we set out to simulate users, mail, shared documents and files.
- In a factory automation system, we set out to simulate the different machines, queues of work, orders and deliveries.

The approach is to identify the objects in the problem to be addressed and to model them as objects in the program.

Abstraction plays a role in this process. We need only model sufficient information for the problem to be solved, and we can ignore any irrelevant detail. If we model a balloon, we need to represent its position, its size and its colour. But we need not model the material from which it is made. If we are creating a personnel records system, we would probably model names, addresses and job descriptions but not hobbies and preferred music styles.

The input for the design process is the specification of the required piece of software. The end point is a description of the classes, objects and methods and how they inter-relate (Figure 21.2).

An important distinction between a specification and a design is as follows. A specification says *what* is required and the design says *how* it will be accomplished. The specification is written in natural language (e.g. English); the design is expressed in one of several notations that we will meet later in this chapter.

The model–view–controller architecture

We have seen that a primary task of OO design is to create a model of the application of interest. A model or simulation of an application is not sufficient – it would be deaf,

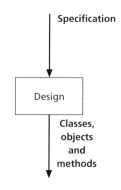

Figure 21.2 The design process.

blind and dumb. Some way of connecting the model to its user is needed. As you will be aware from using a word processor or a text editor, many programs have a major graphical user interface (GUI) component. It is regarded as good design to separate the GUI from the internal workings in order to simplify the task of making changes to such a large complex program. One approach to this separation is the model–view–controller, in which the GUI is regarded as consisting of two parts – the view and the controller. In a word processor, the controller part of the GUI consists typically of buttons and scrollbars to allow the user to input changes such as choosing a new font and scrolling down the document. The view is the representation that the user sees, and often there are a number of views – such as the view of the document as it will appear on the printer and a view more suitable for editing. Obviously, a change that is input via the controller (such as clicking on a button) will usually require the view to be changed, partially or completely.

But the GUI is not the whole story. There is also the inner workings of a program and, for the word processor, this might involve a collection of strings along with the program code to modify them. This section of the program is termed the model, and for programs with a significant GUI it is usually invisible. The model is frequently changed by the controller (for example, when the user inputs some text to the word processor). Alternatively, the model is changed by some internal event (for example, an automatic spell-checker finds a spelling error) and, as a consequence, the model might initiate a change in the view.

In the balloon object, numbers represent its position and size, but these are merely a model consisting of invisible bit patterns inside the computer's memory. We need a way to control a balloon – alter its position and size (the controller) and a way to display it in the window (the view). If we write software to represent a car, we need a model of the engine and its transmission. This model would be invisible. What will be visible are the instruments which tell us what the car is doing (the view) and the controls that enable the user to alter what is going on (the controller).

Thus every object-oriented program consists of:

● the model (e.g. the balloon, the car engine);
● the view (for the balloon, a display of a circle; for the car, the speedometer or the petrol gauge);
● the controller (for the balloon, buttons to change its position and size; for the car, the brake pedal and the steering wheel).

The model itself is usually invisible (except as Java code). The view is visible on the computer screen as a graphical image, dials, graphs etc. The controls are visible as scrollbars, buttons etc. The controller is the inputs to the model and the view is a representation of the outputs from the model.

The model–view–controller is an architecture, a template or a pattern which all OO programs with a significant user interface should follow, in order to separate out the model, the view and the controller parts of the program. The problem for OO design is establishing a structure for the model part of the program, because the structure of the controller and the view parts is usually straightforward.

● Design notations – class diagrams

It is very common in designing software to use diagrams to help describe designs. These diagrams help us think during design and they also document the outcome of a design.

One of the main features of OO programming is the facility to declare a class that inherits something from a superclass. The class diagram illustrates this inheritance. To use an illustration outside computers, we can describe the relationship between different forms of transport in Figure 21.3.

Each class in the diagram inherits qualities from the superclass above it. A superclass possesses attributes that are general. Each class is a specialization of the class above it – it possesses qualities that are special.

The diagram is always a tree, with a single class at the root of the tree. The diagram helps us to see how the different classes relate to each other. In particular, it allows us to see what is above a particular class in the hierarchy, and therefore what classes it is inheriting from. Many development environments have a browser (*not* an Internet browser) that displays the class diagram for all the classes in the library and the ones that make up a particular application. This saves you drawing the diagram. It also helps you to decide where your new class should reside and what it will extend.

For the `Balloon` class described above, remembering that the class `Object` is the superclass of all classes, the class diagram is simply Figure 21.4.

As another example, Figure 21.5 shows a fragment from the class hierarchy within the Java library `java.awt`.

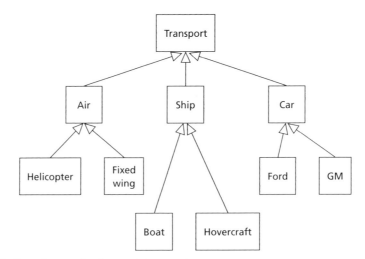

Figure 21.3 Class diagram for forms of transport.

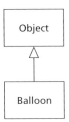

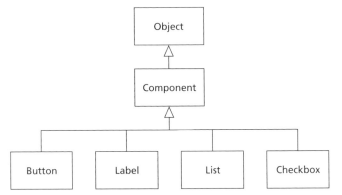

Figure 21.4 Class diagram for the `Balloon` class.

Figure 21.5 Class diagram for some of the graphical user interface components in the Java library.

● The design method – analysing the specification

Now that we have looked at notations for describing a design, we will look at design itself. An effective way to carry out OOD is to use the specification for the software that is to be written. The specification is examined to extract information about the objects and methods.

Here, for example, is the specification for the simple balloon program:

Write a program to represent a balloon. The position of the balloon can be changed and its size can be altered. A balloon can be one of several colours. A balloon should be shown as a circle on the screen.

We look for verbs (doing words) and nouns (things) in the specification. The verbs are methods and the nouns are objects. In the above specification, there is just one significant noun:

`balloon`

So there is one object in this program. The significant verbs in the specification are:

`change` (the position)
`alter` (the size)

and these are the methods associated with the balloon object. The position, colour and size of the balloon are attributes associated with the balloon and so they are data items (variables) within the balloon object.

Now let us review the model–view–controller aspects of this program. The model is the balloon object. Things that can be changed by the user of the program are the size and position of the balloon. These are the controls. Finally the balloon is to be shown as simply a circle. This is the view.

This program needs just one object, the balloon. We generalize the object and design a class named `Balloon`. The particular balloon will be an instance of this class.

To sum up, this program has one class and one instance of the class. The class `Balloon` has private variables:

```
xCoordinate
yCoordinate
radius
colour
```

and public methods:

```
move(int x, int y)
changeSize(int radius)
display()
```

Note that in the spirit of the model–view–controller, we have created a separate `display` method, rather than incorporating graphics statements in methods `move` and `changeSize`.

We have now completed the design – except for connecting the model to the user. To do this, we create a second object (and class) that acts as the user interface. It:

1. creates the buttons on the screen;
2. creates the `balloon` object by instantiating an object from the class `Balloon`;
3. handles the events from mouse clicks on the buttons;
4. provides method `paint`, which is invoked whenever the window needs to be painted.

The design of this program is now fully complete. Design ends at the stage where all of the classes, objects and methods are specified. Design is not concerned with writing (coding) the Java statements that make up these classes and methods.

This example is a simple one – with just one object (and so just one class) for the model. Nonetheless, it illustrates how to extract objects and methods from a specification. We will look at a more complex example in a moment.

To summarize, the design method for identifying objects and methods is:

● Look for nouns in the specification; these are objects.
● Look for verbs in the specification; these are methods.

After identifying objects, the next step is to generalize them by designing classes.

● Case study in design

Here is the specification for a rather larger program, with screen layout shown in Figure 21.6:

The bandit

The program simulates a 'one-armed bandit' slot machine. (These are sometimes called fruit machines.) It costs 25 cents (a quarter) a go, and pays out depending on a combination of three single-digit integers.

The player moves the cursor to the GO button and clicks with the mouse to make the numbers change. This is equivalent to putting a coin in the machine and pulling the handle. This causes the cash in the machine (i.e. the accumulated win) to be increased by 25 cents. The computer randomly chooses three numbers, displayed as shown.

The player wins according to the following scheme:

All 3 are 0	*win 4 quarters*
Any 2 are 0	*win 2 quarters*
Any 1 a 0	*win 1 quarter*
All 3 same	*win 2 quarters*

Any immediate win should be displayed, and the accumulated win recorded by the machine reduced accordingly (because the machine loses!). Initially the accumulated win should be set to zero.

There is a button marked '?' so that the user can query the total amount of money they have won or lost.

Figure 21.6 Window for the bandit program.

Also available is a STOP button to end the program. This stops the program after displaying one of the following three lines:

machine owes player: *(the actual amount)*
player owes machine: *(the actual amount)*
break-even

These are regarded as IOUs (I Owe Yous) to be settled later in cash with the owner of the machine. This ends the specification.

Notice that the user interface to the program is fairly well specified. On reading the specification, you might think that it could be rewritten more clearly or more logically. This is a common reaction to a specification. Part of the job of the programmer is to clarify the specification if necessary, and sometimes this will involve questioning the client.

Now we look for verbs and nouns in the specification. We try to concentrate on the model, rather than the view or the controller. Thus, while we might be intrigued by what the button marked '?' does, it is (only) part of the view, not the model itself. Scanning through the specification, we find the following nouns, which we turn into the names of objects in the model:

```
bandit
accumulatedWin
threeNumbers
winAmount
```

Some of these, expectedly, are mentioned more than once.

We now scan the specification again, this time looking for verbs that we can attach to the above list of objects. We get:

For the object `bandit`:
  (no verbs)
For the object `accumulatedWin`:
   `update`
   `initialize`
   `display`
For the object `threeNumbers`:
   `change`
   `display`
For the object `immediateWin`:
   `calculate`
   `display`

Notice that some of these methods are needed in order to provide a view of the system, rather than for the working of the model itself (for example, the method `display` as part of `accumulatedWin`).

These methods are unusual in not needing any parameters. In general, the methods created during a design need parameters, identified at this same stage of design.

Notice also that we appear not to need any methods associated with the bandit object. This is because it is the central item in the model – it uses, but is not used by, all of the other objects. However, it is used by the view and the controller. If we look again at the specification and check it against the required graphical interface, we see that we need the following interface for the player; these are the methods associated with the bandit object:

go
display (to display the three numbers)
query (to display the accumulated win in response to the ? button)
stop

remembering that stop will involve displaying the final accumulated win. This means we will need an additional method within the accumulatedWin object; we will name this finalTotal.

We now have the full list of objects and the methods associated with each object – we have modelled the bandit. We next need to generalize the objects into classes. We will give them names as follows:

Object	Class
bandit	SlotMachine
immediateWin	Score
accumulatedWin	Total
threeNumbers	Fruit

The next step is to see whether we can reuse any items. Can we generalize any of the classes we have designed so that we can inherit from them? The answer, for this particular program, is no. Can we make use of any classes in the libraries? Yes. The object threeNumbers needs to produce three random numbers and it can do this by making use of one of the random number methods within the library class Random within the package Java.util.

The design of the program is now complete. All that remains is to provide the connection between the model and its user. This is easy – we have shown many examples of this user interface class throughout this book.

To illustrate that the design makes sense, here is the Java coding for the class SlotMachine.

```java
public class SlotMachine {

    private Score immediateWin;
    private Total accumulatedWin;
    private Fruit threeNumbers;

    public SlotMachine() {
        immediateWin = new Score();
        accumulatedWin = new Total();
        threeNumbers = new Fruit();
    }
```

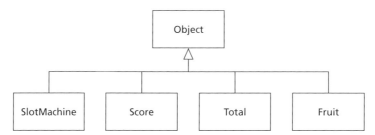

Figure 21.7 Class diagram for the bandit program.

```
public void display(Graphics g) {
    threeNumbers.display(g);
}

public void go() {
    threeNumbers.change();
}

public void query() {
    accumulatedWin.display();
}

public void stop() {
    accumulatedWin.finalTotal();
}
}
```

For the bandit program, the class diagram is shown in Figure 21.7. All the classes are subclasses of the object `Object`.

Finally, we will mention a detail of the implementation. We want the program to display a graphical image of the bandit as shown in Figure 21.6. Chapter 20 on graphics explains how to do this. We create a `.gif` file to hold the graphical image, load it into memory and display it. The methods that accomplish this are part of the class `Applet`. This is the class that is extended by the user interface part of an applet program. So the `bandit` object does not itself display the image – instead, the user interface object handles the graphics.

● Looking for reuse

The final act of design is to check to make sure that we are not reinventing the wheel. One of the main aims of OOP is to promote reuse of software components. Check whether:

- what you need might be in one of the libraries;
- you may have written a class last month that is nearly what you need;
- you may be able to generalize some of the classes you have designed for your program into a more general class that you can inherit from.

One approach to exploring the relationships between classes is to use the 'is-a' and 'has-a' tests described below.

If you find that there is a similar class, use inheritance to customize it to do what you want. In the Java code, the inheriting class begins with the `extends` keyword in its heading.

● Relationships between classes – is-a versus has-a

As we have seen, when we design an object-oriented program, we identify the objects and therefore the classes in the program. The next step is to consider the relationships between the classes. The classes that make up a program collaborate with each other to achieve the required behaviour, but they use each other in different ways. The key objective in studying the classes is to identify any inheritance relationships between the classes. If we can find any such relationships, we can simplify and shorten the program, making good use of reuse.

There are two ways in which classes relate to each other:

1. Inheritance. One class inherits from another. An example is a class that extends the `Applet` class. This is the important relationship to identify.
2. Composition. An object (instantiated from one class) creates objects from another class using `new`. An example is an object that creates a button. Composition is sometimes called aggregation.

The important task of design is to distinguish the first case from the others, so that inheritance can be successfully applied. One way of checking that we have correctly identified the appropriate relationships between classes is to use the 'is-a or has-a' test. The use of the phrase 'is-a' in the description of an object (or class) signifies that it is probably an inheritance relationship. (Another phrase that has the same meaning is 'consists-of'.) The use of the phrase 'has-a' indicates that there is no inheritance relationship.

Let us look at an example to see how inheritance is identified. In the specification for a program to support the transactions in a bank, we find the following sentence:

A bank account describes a person's name, address, account number and current balance. There are two types of account – current and deposit. Borrowers have to give one week's notice to withdraw from a deposit account, but the account accrues interest.

Paraphrasing this specification, we could say 'a current account is a bank account' and 'a deposit account is a bank account'. We see the critical words 'is a' and so recognize that bank account is the superclass of deposit account and current account. Deposit account and current account are each subclasses of account. They will inherit some of the methods from the superclass, for example methods to update the address and to update the balance.

SELF-TEST QUESTION

21.1 Draw the class diagram for a bank account.

As another example, consider the description of an applet window: 'the window has a button and a text field'. This is a 'has-a' relationship, which is not inheritance. The class representing the window simply declares and instantiates `Button` and `TextField` objects and then uses them.

In the bandit program, we saw the need to design four objects (and therefore four classes). The question is: should these inherit from one another in some way? Are there any other classes or superclasses to be identified? If we can identify any such relationships we may well simplify the design of the software by providing reuse. The way to answer the question is to look at a sentence describing the objects. Take the sentence 'a slot machine has a display of three numbers'. The magic words are 'has a', which signal that these are two distinct classes that should not be involved in inheritance. Thus we expect that a slot machine object will use an object that displays three numbers by creating such an object using `new`. If we similarly examine sentences that describe the other classes in the bandit, we come to the same conclusion – they are all distinct classes.

SELF-TEST QUESTION

21.2 Look again at the sentences that describe the components (classes) involved in the bandit program and thereby identify whether the classes are related in a hierarchy that involves inheritance.

In the bandit program we have seen that a slot machine has a display of three numbers. Expressed in a different way, a slot machine uses a `threeNumbers` object or consists of a `threeNumbers` object (among other things). We therefore expect to see the following coding as part of the `slotMachine` class:

```
Fruit threeNumbers = new Fruit();
```

To sum up, the two kinds of relationship between classes are as follows. The most important relationship to identify is the 'is-a' relationship, because this indicates that inheritance can be used.

Relationship between classes	Acid test	Java code involves
Inheritance	is-a	`extends`
Composition	has-a or consists-of	`new`

If you have trouble using the relationships 'is-a' and 'has-a', try using the following equivalents. These simply reverse the classes in the sentences. Thus we might say 'apple is-a fruit', or alternatively, 'fruit can-be-a apple' (which is inheritance). And we might say 'car has-a wheel', or alternatively, 'wheel is-part-of-a car' (which is composition).

SELF-TEST QUESTIONS

21.3 Identify the classes and the relationships between classes in the following description:

> Boeing make four types of aeroplanes. They all have two wings and are passenger planes, but some are bigger than others and the engines are sometimes supplied by different manufacturers.

Draw the class diagram.

21.4 Analyse the relationships between the following groups of classes (are they is-a or has-a?):

1. house, door, roof, dwelling;
2. person, man, woman;
3. car, piston, gearbox, engine;
4. vehicle, car, bus;
5. triangle, rectangle, pentagon, line, polygon, point.

● Guidelines for class design

Use of the design approach that we have described is not guaranteed to lead to the perfect design. It is always worth while checking the design of each class against the following guidelines.

Keep data private

This maintains data hiding, one of the central principles of OOP. If data needs to be accessed or changed, do it via methods provided as part of the class. If a data item is fixed, once initialized, there is no need to provide a method to change it.

Initialize the data

Although Java automatically initializes instance variables (but not local variables) to particular values, it is good practice to initialize them explicitly, either within the data declaration itself or by means of a constructor method.

Avoid large classes

If a class is more than two pages of text, it is a candidate for consideration for division into two or more smaller classes. But this should only be done if there are clearly obvious classes to be formed from the large one. It is counter-productive to split an elegant cohesive class into contrived and ugly classes.

Make the class name and method names meaningful

This will make them easy to use and more appealing for reuse. A common convention is that a method to access data within an object often begins with the word get – as in getTheData. Similarly a method to change some data often begins with the word set – as in setTheData.

Do not contrive inheritance

In the bandit program, classes Score and Total are similar in some respects and therefore are possible candidates for an inherited relationship. But if we consider the requirements of their methods, we see that they are quite distinct. Using inheritance when it is not really appropriate can lead to contrived classes, which are more complex and perhaps longer than they need be.

When using inheritance, put shared methods in the superclass

In the example of the bank account discussed above, all those methods that are common to all bank accounts should be written as part of the superclass so that they can be shared by all the subclasses without duplication. Examples are the methods to update the address and to update the balance.

● Detailed design

Once you have established the design of the overall structure of a program, you need to write the code for the classes and methods. This means taking the specification of each class and method and translating into Java statements. For most small programs this is a simple step. It may be, however, that a particular method needs a lot of work. When a method needs more than say 20 statements, it is probably too long for clarity. It perhaps needs simplifying by rewriting it as a collection of private methods. So the (public) method will invoke one or more private methods within the class to accomplish its task. The process of deciding how an individual method is constructed is called detailed design.

To take a trivial example, suppose that we set out to create a method that provides as a service finding the largest of three integers. The integers are supplied as parameters to the method and the largest value is returned as the value of the method. During the design of the method we realize that we can simplify things if we make use of a supplementary method that finds the largest of just two numbers. Thus we design the public method and a private method:

```
public int largest(int a, int b, int c) {
    return larger(larger(a, b), c);
}


private int larger(int x, int y) {
    if (x > y)
        return x;
    else
        return y;
}
```

● The design approach

We now sum up the approach to OO design advocated in this chapter. The steps are:

1. Study the specification and clarify it if necessary.
2. Derive objects and methods from the specification, so that the design acts as a model of the application.
3. Generalize the objects into classes.
4. Check for reuse of library classes and your own classes, using inheritance as appropriate.
5. If desired, document the classes and objects by drawing class diagrams.

● Event-driven programming

Event-driven programming is the name given to writing programs that must respond to events like mouse clicks. OOP is particularly suitable for event-driven programming. As we have seen, a click on a button is detected by the browser or applet viewer and causes the method `actionPerformed` to be invoked. This method must be provided by the programmer to deal with this and similar events. Other events that can be initiated by the user are typing a number in a text field and pressing the enter key or moving the mouse.

The controller part of an OO program consists of a collection of methods which wait for events. Their whole purpose is to handle these events, and the structure of the software reflects this mission. Some of the events are initiated by the user of the program, using mouse clicks. Other events are those which originate within the program. Invocations of methods within an OO program can be visualized as events. For example, in the balloon program, when the balloon changes its size, an event signals that it must be redrawn. Or if an object needs to display a string on the screen, it invokes a method (in one of the libraries) to carry out the service. This is an event initiated by one object as a request on another. Other events can arise from external sources – devices like disks, printers and communication lines. These events are handled by methods within the operating system.

Thus an event causes a method invocation in an OO program, and the purpose of methods is to handle events.

● Other design approaches

In this chapter we described one very useful approach to OOD. This is one of a number of approaches on offer. The methods differ according to the type of software that they are best suited to. Java is suitable for use in all these application areas, but a different design approach may be needed. These different types can be distinguished as follows:

● Information systems: examples – airline seat reservation system, library catalogue, sales records in a supermarket. These applications are characterized by large volumes of data.
● Real-time systems: examples – fly-by-wire control of an aeroplane, control of a power station, telephone exchange. Such systems must respond to some external event within a very short time. Multithreading is also a feature of such systems.
● Knowledge-based systems (KBS) or artificial intelligence (AI) systems: examples are a chess program, a medical diagnosis system. These systems involve complex data structures and algorithms.
● Parallel or concurrent systems – any computer system that must carry out two or more tasks apparently simultaneously. Java provides the multithreading facility (described in Chapter 25) to support these applications. A simple design approach is suggested in Chapter 25.
● Mathematical or scientific programs, for example, to solve equations. These are characterized by complex processing, with small amounts of data.
● Games. These need good graphics output and fast response times.

In each of these types of system, we have identified the particular feature that is dominant. Thus when we are trying to model the system as an OO program, that same feature will dominate the approach to modelling. So, when modelling an information system, the first step is usually to analyze and model the structure of the data. There are several mainstream techniques for doing this, but these interesting questions are beyond the scope of this book. The design approach that we have explained is a general-purpose method.

Summary

● The principles behind OOP are encapsulation, inheritance and polymorphism.

● The OO design task consists of identifying appropriate objects and classes.

● An OO design is essentially a simulation (a model) of the world of interest.

● A good approach to design is to study the specification of the program to find verbs and nouns. The verbs are methods and the nouns are objects.

● A model is connected to its user via a controller (the inputs to the model) and a view (the outputs from the model).

● Before design is completed, check for classes that can be generalized to promote reuse through inheritance.

● Class diagrams are useful during design and for documenting the end-product.

● 'Is-a and has-a' analysis helps us to distinguish between inheritance and composition.

EXERCISES

21.1 Complete the coding of the bandit program.

21.2 Design the classes for the program with the following specification.

The program simulates a simple desk calculator (Figure 21.8) that acts on integer numbers. It has one button for each of the 10 digits, 0 to 9. It has a button to add and a button to subtract. It has a 'Clear' button, to clear the display, and an equals (=) button to get the answer.

When the clear button is pressed the display is set to zero and the (hidden) total is set to zero.

When a digit button is pressed, the digit is added to the right of those already in the display (if any).

When the + button is pressed, the number in the display is added to the total (and similar, for the − button). The display is set equal to zero.

When the equals button is pressed, the value of the total is displayed.

21.3 Design the classes in the following program.

Battleships is a game normally played by two people using paper and pencil. In this version, a person plays the computer. The computer also records and displays the status of the game. When it is the computer's turn to play, it always plays completely randomly. The game is also slightly simplified.

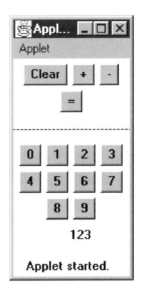

Figure 21.8 The calculator.

Two 10 × 10 grids are shown on the screen. The home grid represents an ocean showing where your battleships are. The enemy grid shows where you have fired a shot, but you cannot see the enemy. You don't know where the computer has placed its ships, and the computer doesn't know where yours are.

Initially you place 10 battleships somewhere on your grid. You do this by clicking the mouse on the squares that you want. The computer also places its own 10 ships somewhere hidden on the target grid. The computer places its ships randomly, but you can, of course, play with a strategy.

The computer determines randomly who goes first. The computer and you then play in turn.

You 'fire' a shot at the enemy (the computer), by clicking on a square on the target grid. The computer displays the position on the grid, so that you can see where you have fired your shots. The computer displays whether or not one of its ships has been sunk.

Then it is the computer's turn to fire at you. Although it holds the data on where your ships are, it does not use this data in choosing (randomly) where to fire at you. But the computer remembers where it has already fired.

Play continues until one player sinks all the enemy ships.

ANSWERS TO SELF-TEST QUESTIONS

21.1

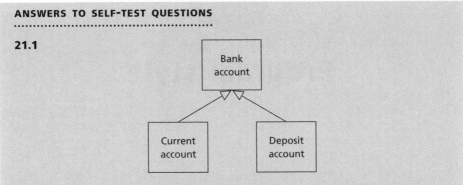

21.2 The answer is given in the text. None of the classes inherit from each other.

21.3 A superclass describes the common properties of the aeroplanes – wings passenger. A subclass for each of the four types inherits from the superclass and describes the individual properties – engine manufacturer, size.

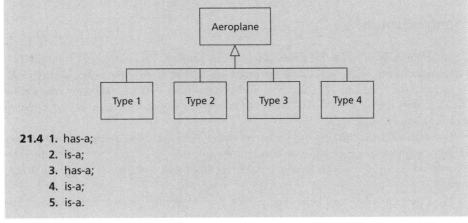

21.4 1. has-a;
   2. is-a;
   3. has-a;
   4. is-a;
   5. is-a.

Program style

● Introduction

Programming is a highly creative and exciting activity. Programmers often get very absorbed in their work and regard the programs that they produce as being very much their personal creations. The stereotypical programmer (man or woman) wears jeans and a T-shirt. He or she drinks 20 cups of coffee in a day and stays up all night just for the fun of programming.

The facts of programming life are often rather different. Most programming is done within commercial organizations. Most programs are worked on by several different people. Many organizations have standards manuals that detail what programs should look like.

Most programs are read by several people – and certainly not just their author. The others are: the people who take on your work when you get promoted or move to another project, the people who will test your program, and the generations of programmers who will look after your program, fixing bugs and making improvements long after you have got another job. So, making your program easy to read is a vital ingredient of programming.

Another aspect of good style is reusability. A program that exhibits style will have classes that can be reused later in another program, written by the same person or someone else.

Unless you are a hobbyist, it's important in practice to know how to produce programs that have good style.

● Objects and classes

Modularity

A Java program is constructed as a collection of objects created from classes. Good design of classes helps to ensure that the program is clear and comprehensible because the program consists of distinct modules. The chapter on object-oriented design (OOD) explained an approach to good design.

Complexity

OOD attempts to design classes that correspond to classes in the problem being solved. These classes are usually present in the specification for the program. A good design will be such that the classes are recognizable as being a model of the specification. The design will reflect the complexity of the problem and no more.

Hiding data

The idea of object-oriented design is to hide or encapsulate data, so that all the interactions between classes take place via the methods rather than by direct access to data. A good class design has a minimum of public variables.

● Program layout

The Java programmer has enormous scope in deciding how to layout a program. The language is free-format – blank lines, spaces and new pages can be used almost anywhere. Comments can be placed on a line by themselves or on the end of a line of code. There's certainly plenty of scope for creativity and individuality.

However, as we have seen, most programs are read by several people other than the original author. So good appearance is vital. We will now look at a set of style guidelines for Java programs. There is always controversy about guidelines like these. No doubt you, the reader, will disagree with some of them.

Names

In Java, the programmer gives names to variables, classes and methods. There's plenty of scope for imagination because:

- names can consist of letters and digits;
- names can be as long as you like;

provided that the name starts with a letter.

The usual advice on names is to make them as meaningful as possible. This rules out cryptic names like `i,j,x,y`, which usually signify that the programmer has some background in maths (but not much imagination for creating meaningful names).

The convention for variables and methods is that they start with a lower-case letter and use an upper-case letter when the name has two or more words glued together. Examples are `myBalloon, theLargestSalary`.

The convention for class names is that they start with an upper-case letter. Examples are `String, Balloon`. This allows the reader to easily distinguish class names from other names in a program without having to search for their declarations. Packages also conventionally begin with a lower-case letter.

Indentation

Indentation emphasizes program structure. There are various styles for indentation, of which just one has been used throughout this book. People also disagree about how many spaces should be used for indentation – four are used in this book.

Blank lines

Blank lines are usually used to visually separate methods. They are also often used within a class to separate the variable declarations from the methods and one method from another.

If there are a lot of variable declarations, different blocks of data can also be separated by blank lines.

New pages

A class is something in itself, distinct from any others. If you can, start each new class at the start of a new page. You may need a tool that allows you to control how programs are printed on paper. If you only ever look at a screen, restrict your classes to one screen.

Perhaps one of the worst crimes in laying out a program is when a method starts on one page of listing but then spills over onto another. The reader's concentration is broken between the end of one page and the start of the new. However, this is unavoidable in a book.

● Comments

There are three ways of putting comments into Java programs:

```
// this is a comment to the end of the line

/* with this kind of comment
you can use as many lines
as you like */

/** this style of comment
is for use in conjunction with a software tool to
produce automatic documentation
*/
```

There is a software tool called javadoc (the Java Documentation Generator) that scans the text of a program and produces an HTML document. This shows for each class: the class inheritance hierarchy and public variables and methods within the class. It also detects and incorporates the above kind of comments (when they are associated with a class, a method or a variable) and uses them in the report. This report can be viewed by a browser.

There is always great controversy about comments in programs. Some people argue that 'the more the better'. However, sometimes you see code like this:

```
// display the hello message
g.drawString("hello", 10, 10);
```

in which the comment merely repeats the code, and is therefore superfluous.

Sometimes code is overwhelmed by suffocating comments which add little to the understanding of the code. It's like a Christmas tree that is overwhelmed with tinsel, baubles and lights – you can't see the tree for the decorations. There is another problem: some studies have shown that, where there are a lot of comments, the reader reads the comments and ignores the code. Thus, if the code is wrong, it will remain so.

Some people argue that comments are needed when the code is complex or difficult to understand in some way. This seems reasonable until you wonder why the code needs to be complex in the first place. Sometimes, perhaps, the code can be simplified so that it is easy to understand without comments. We give examples of such situations below.

Some programmers like to place a comment at the start of every class and, perhaps, the start of a method in order to describe the overall purpose of the class (or method). The Java library classes are documented in this way. Class and method names should, of course, try to describe what they do, so a comment can be redundant.

Our view is that perhaps comments should be used sparingly and judiciously. For example, a complex section of code may need an explanatory comment.

● Using constants

Many programs have values that do not change while the program is running – and don't change very often anyway. Examples are the VAT (value added tax) rate, the age for voting, the threshold for paying tax and mathematical constants. Java provides the facility to declare data items as constants and give them a value. So, for these examples, we can write:

```
final float vatRate = 17.5f;
final int votingAge = 18;
final int taxThreshold = 5000;
final float pi = 3.142f;
```

Variables like this with constant values can only be declared at the top of a class and not as local variables within a method.

Strings and arrays can also be given constant values:

```
final String ourPlanet = "Earth";
final int prices[] = {12, 18, 24};
```

One benefit of using `final` values is that the compiler will detect any attempt (no doubt by mistake!) to change the value of a constant. Thus, for example, given the declaration above:

```
votingAge = 17;
```

would provoke an error message.

Another, more powerful, benefit is that a program that otherwise might be peppered with rather meaningless numbers contains variables (which are constant) with clear, meaningful names. This enhances program clarity, with all its consequent benefits.

Suppose, for example, we need to alter a tax program to reflect a change in regulations. We have a nightmare task if the tax thresholds and tax rates are built into the program as numbers that appear as-and-when throughout the program. Suppose that the old tax threshold is 5000. We could use a text editor to search for all occurrences of 5000. The editor will dutifully tell us where all the occurrences are, but we are left unsure that this number has the same meaning everywhere. What if the number 4999 appears in the program? Is it the tax threshold −1? Or does it have some other completely unrelated meaning? The answer, of course, is to use constants, with good names, and to distinguish carefully between different data items.

Another common use for final values is to specify the sizes of any arrays used in a program, as in:

```
final int arraySize = 10;
```

and thereafter:

```
int myArray[] = new int[arraySize];
```

It is the convention to use upper-case (capital) letters for the names of constants that are provided in the libraries. Thus for example: `PI`, `E`, `HORIZONTAL`. Using upper-case distinguishes these values from others in the program and makes it evident that they are indeed constants. Some programmers use this same convention for the names of any constants.

● Method size

It is possible to get into long and enjoyable arguments about how long a method should be.

One view is that a method should not be longer than the screen or a single page of listing (say 40 lines of text). That way, you do not have to scroll or turn a page to study it as a whole. You can thoroughly study the method in its entirety. It is not so long that you lose track of some parts of it.

Any method that is longer than half a page is a serious candidate for restructuring into smaller methods. However, it depends on what the method does – it may do a single cohesive task, and an attempt to split it up may introduce complications involving parameters and scope. Do not apply any length recommendation blindly.

If you look at programs on the screen, restricting the length of methods to what you can see on the screen at one time can help.

● Classes

Classes are an important building block of OO programs. They are also the unit that facilitates reusability of software components. It is a class that is inherited, or extended. So it is important that classes have good style. Here are some style guidelines.

Class size

If a class is longer than, say, two pages it suggests that it may be too long and complex. Consider dividing it (tenderly) into two or more classes, in such a way as to create viable new classes. It is damaging, however, to divide a coherent class into clumsy incoherent classes.

Method names

We have already emphasized the importance of meaningful method names. When a method has the simple role of obtaining the value of some data item (called, say, `Salary`) it is convention to call it `getSalary`. Similarly, if a method is to be provided to change the value of this same variable, then the conventional name is `setSalary`.

Field order

Remembering that fields are the variables and methods within a class, what order should they appear in? There are both public and private fields to consider. The convention adopted in the Java libraries and in the definitive books on Java is to present them in the following order:

1. variables (public and private);
2. public methods;
3. private methods.

● Consistency

Though people's views on programming style often differ, one thing that they always agree on is that a style should be applied consistently throughout a program. If the style is inconsistent it makes the program hard to read (not to say annoying). It also creates a worry that the original programmer didn't really care about the program and that there is something wrong with it. Throughout this book we have used one consistent style for the layout of programs. It is the style used in the Java libraries and used in the definitive books on Java by James Gosling (the principal designer of Java) and his colleagues.

● Nested `ifs`

Nesting is the term given to the situation in a program when there is a statement within another statement, for example a `while` loop within a `for` loop, or an `if` statement within an `if` statement. Sometimes a nested program is simple and clear. But generally, a high degree of nesting is considered to be bad, and best avoided. It is always avoidable by rewriting the program.

Let's look at nested `ifs`. Consider the problem of finding the largest of three numbers:

```
int a, b, c;
int largest;

if (a > b)
    if (a > c)
        largest = a;
    else
        largest = c;
else
    if (b > c)
        largest = b;
    else
        largest = c;
```

This is certainly a complicated-looking piece of program, and some people might have a little trouble understanding it. People are not always convinced that it works correctly. So, on the evidence, it is difficult to read and understand. Arguably the complexity arises from the nesting of the `ifs`.

An alternative piece of program that avoids the nesting is:

```
int a, b, c;
int largest;

if (a > b && a > c)
    largest = a;
if (b > a && b > c)
    largest = b;
if (c > a && c > b)
    largest = c;
```

which may be clearer to some people. The trouble with this un-nested solution is that the three `if` statements are *always* executed, whereas in the first program only *two* tests are performed. So the second program will run slightly slower. This is true in general – programs with nested `ifs` run faster. Here's another example of nesting. In a program to play a card game, the suit of a card is encoded as an integer (1 to 4). In one part of the program the integer is converted to the string name of the suit as follows.

```
int s;
String suit;

if (s == 1)
    suit = "hearts";
else
    if (s == 2)
        suit = "clubs";
    else
        if (s == 3)
            suit = "spades";
        else
            if (s == 4)
                suit = "diamonds";
```

where there is an `if` within an `if`, within an `if`, etc. This piece of program uses consistent indentation, but perhaps it is not too easy to understand. Some people recommend laying out such a sequence like this:

```
int s;
String suit;

if (s == 1)
    suit = "hearts";
else
    if (s == 2)
        suit = "clubs";
else
    if (s == 3)
        suit = "spades";
else
    if (s == 4)
        suit = "diamonds";
```

which is more compact, but does not show the nesting as clearly.

An alternative is to write the code without nesting, as follows:

```
int s;
String suit;

if (s == 1)
    suit = "hearts";
if (s == 2)
    suit = "clubs";
if (s == 3)
    suit = "spades";
if (s == 4)
    suit = "diamonds";
```

which is arguably much clearer. Again, the penalty is that the clearer program is slower – because all the `if`s are always executed.

No doubt you, the reader, have seen that there is perhaps a resolution to this dilemma. We could recode this piece of program using the `switch` statement as:

```
int s;
String suit;

switch(s)
    {
    case 1 : suit = "hearts"; break;
    case 2 : suit = "clubs"; break;
    case 3 : suit = "spades"; break;
    case 4 : suit = "diamonds"; break;
    }
```

which is both clear and fast. The problem is, however, that the `switch` statement is restricted; you can only use it to switch on the value of an integer or a single character. So, for example, it cannot be used in the program above to find the largest of three numbers. Use of `switch` is not a general solution to the problem of nested `if`s.

The conclusion is this: if you avoid nested `if`s you may suffer a performance penalty. In practice, reduced performance will only matter if the test is carried out inside a loop repeated many times within a program that is time-critical.

Finally, nested `if` statements are not always bad, and there are occasions where nesting simply and clearly describes what needs to be done.

● Nested loops

Let us now look at nesting within loops. Suppose we are writing a program that displays a pattern on the screen as in Figure 22.1, which is a crude graphic of a block of flats. The piece of program could look like this:

```
private void flats(int floors, int flats) {

    int xCoord, yCoord;

    int yCoord = 50;
    for (int floor = 0; floor < floors; floor++) {
        xCoord = 50;
        for (int flat = 0; flat < flats; flat++) {
            g.drawRect(xCoord, yCoord, 20, 20);
            xCoord = xCoord + 25;
        }
    yCoord = yCoord + 25;
    }
}
```

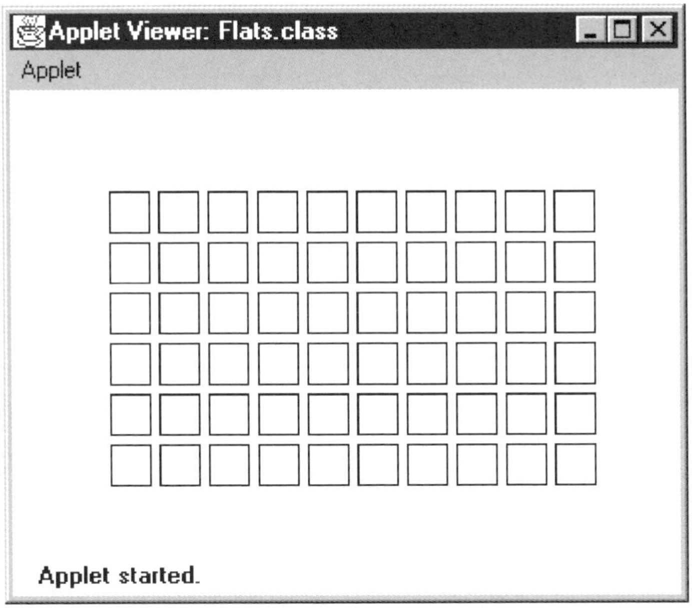

Figure 22.1 Output from a program showing a block of flats.

in which one loop is nested within the other. This is not a particularly complex piece of code, but we can simplify it using another method:

```
private void flats(int floors, int flats) {
    int yCoord = 50;
    for (int floor = 0; floor < floors; floor++) {
        drawFloor(yCoord, flats);
        yCoord = yCoord + 25;
    }
}

private void drawFloor(int yCoord, int flats) {
    int xCoord = 50;
    for (int flat = 0; flat < flats; flat++) {
        g.drawRect(xCoord, yCoord, 20, 20);
        xCoord = xCoord + 25;
    }
}
```

By using an additional method we have eliminated the nesting. We have also expressed explicitly in the coding the fact that the block of flats consists of a number of floors. We have clarified the requirement that there is a change in the y-coordinate for each floor of the block. It is always possible to eliminate nested loops in this manner, and sometimes this results in a simplification of the program.

Research studies have shown that we humans find it difficult to understand programs that use nesting. One researcher has summed this up by saying 'Nesting is for the birds'. But nesting is not *always* bad. Take, for example, the coding to initialize a two-dimensional array:

```
int[][] table = new int[10][10];
for (int row = 0; row < 10; row++)
    for (int col = 0; col < 10; col++)
        table[row][col] = 0;
```

which is clear even with nesting.

● Complex conditions

Complexity in an if, for or while statement can arise when the condition being tested involves one or more 'and's and 'or's. A complex condition can make a program very difficult to understand, debug and get right. As an example, we will look at a program that searches an array of numbers to find a desired number:

```
final int length = 100;
int[] table = new int[length];

int wanted;
int i;

i = 0;
while ( i < length && table[i] != wanted)
    i++;

if (i == 100)
    g.drawString("not found", 10, 10);
else
    g.drawString("found", 10, 10);
```

The problem with this program is that the condition in the while is complex. Even for an experienced programmer it can be difficult to check what has been written and to convince yourself that it is correct. There is an alternative; we will use a flag. It is simply an integer variable, but its value at any time records the status of the search. There are three possible states that the search can be in.

● The program is still searching; the item is not yet found. This is also the initial state of the search. The flag has the value 0.
● The item has been found. The value is 1.
● The search has been completed but without finding the item. The value is 2.

Using this flag, called `searching`, the program becomes:

```
final int length = 100;
int[] table = new int[length];

int wanted;
int i;
int searching;

i = 0;
searching = 0;
while (searching == 0) {
    if (wanted == table[i])
        searching = 1;
    else {
        i++;
        if (i == length)
            searching = 2;
    }
}

if (searching == 2)
    g.drawString("not found", 10, 10);
else
    g.drawString("found", 10, 10);
```

What has been accomplished is that the various tests have been disentangled. The condition in the `while` loop is clear and simple. The other tests are separate and simple. The program overall is arguably simpler.

The moral is that it is often possible to write a piece of program in different ways. Some solutions are simpler and clearer than others. Sometimes it is possible to avoid complexity in a condition by rewriting the program fragment with the use of a flag.

● Documentation

The old saying is just as relevant to programming: 'The job's not done until the paperwork is finished'.

Documentation is the bugbear of the programmer – until, of course, the programmer has to sort out someone else's program! Commercial organizations usually try to encourage programmers to document their programs well. They tell the old and probably fictitious story about the programmer who had a program 95% complete, did no documentation and then went out and got run over by a bus. The colleagues who remained allegedly had a terrible job trying to continue work on the program.

Program documentation typically consists of the following ingredients:

● the program specification;
● the source code, including appropriate comments;
● design information, for example UML diagrams (see Chapter 21 on design);
● the test schedule;
● the test results;
● the modification history;
● the user manual (if needed).

If you ever get asked to take over someone's program, this is what you will need – but don't expect to get it!

Programmers generally find creating documentation a boring chore and tend to skimp on it. They generally leave it to the end of the project, when there's little time available. No wonder it is often not done or done poorly.

The only way to ease the pain is to do the documentation as you go along, mixing it in with the more interesting tasks of programming.

Programming pitfalls

Don't spend hours and hours making your program beautiful only then to find that there is a useful tool available. A pretty-printer, prettifier, beautifier or indenter program will do what its name suggests. Check what prettifiers are available *before* you start to code. Also check whether there are any house standards in your organization before you start to code. You might have to follow them. If you do want to stick to a plan for laying out the program, it's often better to do it from the start, rather than type it in roughly and change it later.

Summary

● Program style is important to promote readability for debugging and maintenance.

● Guidelines for good program layout embrace good names, indentation, blank lines, new pages and comments.

● Java has a useful facility for making selected data items constant.

● Methods should not be too long.

● Nested `ifs`, loops and complex conditions should be used judiciously.

● Good documentation is always worthy.

EXERCISES

22.1 Look at as many programs as you can (including your own) and review their styles. Are they good or bad? Why?

22.2 Discuss the issue of guidelines with colleagues or friends. Does style matter? If so what constitutes good style?

22.3 Investigate what beautifier programs are available.

22.4 Devise a set of style guidelines for Java programs.

22.5 (Optional) Use your style guidelines for evermore.

Testing

● **Introduction**

Programs are complex and it is difficult to make them work correctly. Testing is the set of techniques used to attempt to verify that a program does work correctly. Put another way, testing attempts to reveal the existence of bugs. Such bugs are then subject to debugging (see Chapter 24). As we shall see, testing techniques cannot expose all the bugs in a program, so most large programs have hidden bugs in them. Nonetheless, testing is enormously important. It can typically consume up to one half of the total time spent on developing a program. Microsoft have teams of programmers (who write programs) and teams of testers (who test them). There are as many testers as program-mers. Usually a decision has to be made between continuing the testing or delivering the program to its customers or clients.

In academic circles, the task of trying to ensure that a program does what is expected is called *verification*. The aim is to *verify* that a program meets its specification.

In this chapter we will review different approaches to verification and see what their deficiencies are. We shall see how to go about doing testing systematically.

The techniques we will explain are:

- black box or functional testing;
- white box or structural testing;
- reviews or walkthroughs;
- stepping through code with a debugger;
- formal methods.

A small program that consists only of a single class can usually be tested all at once. A larger program that involves two or more classes may be of such complexity that it must be tested in pieces. In Java the natural size for these pieces is the class, and it is convenient to test a program class by class. This is called *unit testing*. When the complete program is brought together for testing, the task is called *integration* or *system testing*.

We will also look at developing a program bit-by-bit, rather than as a complete program.

● Program specifications

The starting point for any testing is the specification. Time is never wasted in studying and clarifying the specification. This may well necessitate going back to the client or the future user of the program. Take the following specification, for example:

> *Write a program that inputs a series of numbers via a text field. The numbers are terminated by a negative number. The program calculates and displays the sum of the numbers.*

On first reading, this specification may look simple and clear. But, even though it is so short, it contains pitfalls:

● Are the numbers integers or floating point?
● What is the permissible range and precision of the numbers?
● Is the negative number to be included in the sum, or not?

These questions should be clarified before the programmer starts any programming. Indeed it is part of the job of programming to study the specification, discover any omissions or confusions, and gain agreement to a clear specification. After all, it is no use writing a brilliant program if it doesn't do what the client wanted.

Here now is a clearer version of the specification, which we will use as a case study in looking at testing methods:

> *Write a program that inputs a series of integers via a text field. The integers are in the range 0 to 10 000. The series of numbers is terminated when a button labelled 'End of Data' is pressed. The program calculates and displays the sum of the numbers.*

You can see that this specification is very precise – for example, it stipulates very clearly the permissible range of input values.

SELF-TEST QUESTION

23.1 Can you see any remaining deficiencies in the specification that need clarification?

● Exhaustive testing

One approach to testing would be to test a program with all possible data values as input.

Consider the program to input and sum a series of numbers. There could be one, two or 10 000 numbers. Each number has an enormously large range of possible values and could be entered in many different orders. All-in-all, the number of possible combinations of numbers is fantastic. All the different values would have to be keyed in and the program run repetitively. The human time taken to assemble the test data would be years. Even the time that the computer (fast as they are) needs would be days. Finally, checking that the computer had got the answers correct would drive someone mad.

Thus exhaustive testing – even for a small and simple program – is not feasible. It is important to recognize that perfect testing, for all but the smallest program, is impossible. Therefore we have to adopt some other approach.

● Black box (functional) testing

Knowing that exhaustive testing is infeasible, the 'black box' approach to testing is to devise sample data that is representative of all possible data. Then we run the program, input the data and see what happens.

Black box testing is so called because no knowledge of the workings of the program is used as part of the testing – we only consider inputs and outputs. The program is thought of as being invisible within a black box. Black box testing is also known as functional testing because it uses only a knowledge of the function of the program.

For the program to add up the series of numbers, we need some representative data. Being bold, we might argue that any integer is typical of any other integer. Also, two pieces of data are representative of any number of pieces of data. Thus we choose one set of test data:

   8   12   end of data button

and the testing is complete!

Cautiously, we might worry that this is too limited. We might argue that to have no numbers is special and that therefore we should also test the program with no data, simply pressing the:

   end of data button

Still slightly concerned that this testing is inadequate, we might argue that the number zero as a piece of input data is special and that therefore we should also test the program with:

   8   0   12   end of data button

which completes the testing of this program according to the black box approach.

We reasoned that we needed three sets of test data. These three sets, together with a statement of the expected outcomes from the testing, constitute a *test specification.* We run the program with the three sets of data and note any discrepancies between prediction and outcomes.

Test number	Data	Expected result
1	8 12 end of data	20
2	end of data	0
3	8 0 12 end of data	20

This approach to devising test data for black box testing is to use *equivalence partitioning.* This means looking at the nature of the input data to identify common features. Such a common feature is called a partition. In the program to add up integer numbers, all the integers are similar in the sense of being equally valid as data for this program. To emphasize the idea of partitions, a good idea is to sketch the nature of the data and the partitions within it. The permissible data for our program is integers in the range 0 to 10 000, which we can diagram like this:

0	10 000

in which all the integers are visualized as being in a single partition, with the limits of the numbers at each end. We then take the step of asserting that every number within this partition is equivalent to any other, for the purpose of this program. Hence the term equivalence partitioning. So any number chosen from within the partition is representative of (or equivalent to) any other. Thus the pair of numbers, 8 and 12, chosen above, are representative of all the others.

As another example, consider the case of a program that inputs someone's age and decides whether or not they can vote. Suppose that the voting age is 18. We draw the diagram of the partitions:

0	17	18	infinity

There are two partitions, one including the age range 0 to 17 and the other partition with numbers 18 to infinity. A number like 12 is equivalent to any other in the first partition and the number 21 is equivalent to any number in the second. So we devise two tests:

Test number	Data	Outcome
1	12	Cannot vote
2	21	Can vote

Unfortunately we can see that these tests have not investigated the important distinction between someone aged 17 and someone aged 18. Anyone who has ever written a program knows that carrying out comparisons using `if` statements is error prone. So it would be advisable to investigate this particular region of the data. This is the same as recognizing that data values at the edges of the partitions are worthy of inclusion into the testing. Therefore we create two additional tests:

Test number	Data	Outcome
3	17	Cannot vote
4	18	Can vote

In summary, the rules for selecting test data for black box testing using equivalence partitioning are:

1. Partition all possible input data values.
2. Select representative data from each partition (equivalent data).
3. Select data at the boundaries of partitions.

SELF-TEST QUESTIONS

23.2 A program's function is to input three integer numbers and find the largest. Devise black box test data for this program.

23.3 In a program to play the game of chess, the player specifies the destination for a move as a pair of subscripts, the row and column number. The program checks that the destination square is valid; that is, not outside the board. Devise black box test data to check that this part of the program is working correctly.

● White box (structural) testing

White box testing makes use of a knowledge of how a program works – it uses the listing of the program code. The knowledge of how the program works, its structure, is used as the basis of devising test data. Ideally, you write down the expected outcome of the test, a test specification. Then you run the program, input the data and see what happens.

Here is the code for the essence of the program we are using as a case study:

```
public class Sum {
    private int total;

    public Sum() {
        total = 0;
    }
```

```
public void nextNumber(int n) {
    total = total + n;
}

public void endData(){
    repaint();
}

public void display(g) {
    g.drawString("sum of numbers is" + total, 50, 50);
}

}
```

The principle of white box testing is that every statement in the program should be executed at some time during the testing.

Using the test data:

8   0   12   end of data button

will make sure that every statement is executed. So we only need one set of data to test this program in a white box fashion. (Black box testing needed three sets, one of which coincided.) In our example program, it is obvious how to choose white box test data, but in large complex programs it may not be as easy.

SELF-TEST QUESTIONS
....

23.4 A program's function is to find the largest of three numbers. Devise white box test data for this section of the program.

The code is:

```
int a, b, c;
int largest;

if (a > b)
    if (a > c)
        largest = a;
    else
        largest = c;
else
    if (b > c)
        largest = b;
    else
        largest = c;
```

> **23.5** In a program to play the game of chess, the player specifies the destination for a move as a pair of integer subscripts, the row and column number. The program checks that the destination square is valid; that is, not outside the board. Devise white box test data to check that this part of the program is working correctly.
>
> The code for this part of the program is:
>
> ```
> if ((row > 8) || (row < 1))
>     g.drawString ("error", 10, 10);
> if ((col > 8) || (col < 1))
>     g.drawString ("error", 10, 10);
> ```

● Inspections and walkthroughs

An approach that doesn't make use of a computer at all in trying to eradicate faults in a program is called inspection or a walkthrough. In an inspection, someone simply studies the program listing (along with the specification) in order to try to see bugs. It works better if the person doing the inspecting is not the person who wrote the program. This is because people tend to be blind to their own errors. So get a friend or a colleague to inspect your program. It is extraordinary to witness how quickly someone else sees an error that has been defeating you for hours.

To inspect a program you need:

- the specification;
- the text of the program on paper.

In carrying out an inspection, one approach is to study it a method at a time. Some of the checks are fairly mechanical:

- variables initialized;
- loops correctly initialized and terminated;
- method invocations have the correct parameters.

Another check depends on the logic of the particular program. Pretend to execute the method as if you were a computer, avoiding following any method invocations into other methods. (This is why a walkthrough is so-called.) Check that:

- the logic of the method achieves its desired purpose.

During inspection, you can also check that:

- variable and method names are meaningful;
- indentation is consistent;
- the logic is clear and correct.

Although the prime goal of an inspection is not to check for style, a weakness in any of these areas may point to a bug.

The evidence from controlled experiments suggests that inspections are a very effective way of finding errors. In fact, inspections are at least as good a way of identifying bugs as actually running the program (doing testing).

● Stepping through code

Some debuggers allow you to step through a program, executing just one instruction at a time. This is sometimes called single-shotting. Each time you execute one instruction you can see which path of execution has been taken. You can also see (or watch) the values of variables. It is rather like an automated structured walkthrough.

In this form of testing, you concentrate on the variables and closely check their values as they are changed by the program to verify that they have been changed correctly.

A debugger is usually used for debugging (locating a bug); here it is used for testing (establishing the existence of a bug).

● Formal verification

Formal methods employ the precision and power of mathematics in attempting to verify that a program meets its specification. They then place emphasis on the precision of the specification, which must first be rewritten in a formal mathematical notation. Currently the two specification languages in use are called Z and VDM. Once the formal specification for a program has been written, there are two alternative approaches:

1. Write the program and then verify that it conforms to the specification. This requires considerable time and skill.
2. Derive the program from the specification by means of a series of transformations, each of which preserves the correctness of the product. This is currently the favoured approach.

Formal verification is very appealing because of its potential for rigorously verifying a program's correctness beyond all possible doubt. However, it must be remembered that these methods are carried out by fallible human beings who make mistakes. So they are not a cure-all.

Formal verification is still in its infancy and is not widely used in industry and commerce, except in a few safety-critical applications. Further discussion of this approach is beyond the scope of this book.

● Unit testing and integration (system) testing

Even the most experienced programmer cannot write a program and get it working properly straight away. A long period of debugging and testing is the norm in programming. This can be very frustrating for novices. If a program is small – say a single class – then it can be tested all at once. But if a small-to-medium sized program is written, compiled and run all together, then it is difficult to test and difficult to debug.

One approach to writing a program is to write the whole program, key it in and try to compile it. The key word here is 'try' – because most programmers find that their friendly compiler will find lots of errors on the first compilation of their program. It can be very disheartening – particularly for novices – to see so many error messages arising from a program that was the result of so much effort. Once the compilation errors have been banished, the program will usually exhibit strange behaviours during the (sometimes lengthy) period of debugging and testing. A useful technique for helping to avoid these frustrations is to do things bit by bit. The usual technique is to test the program in small pieces – one class at a time. This is called *unit testing*. Once the individual classes have been tested, the complete program is tested. This is called *integration* or *system testing*.

Unit testing is carried out using black box testing, white box testing, inspection, stepping or a combination of methods. Integration testing is usually carried out using black box testing.

How can an individual class be tested in isolation from the rest of a program? Inspection and stepping (using a debugger) present no problems, but white box testing and black box testing require the class to be executed under controlled conditions. We now describe a method that allows a class to be tested in isolation. Suppose as an example we are writing a computer game program. One of the objects is a total score which is an instance of a class named Total. This class provides methods to carry out:

● initialization of a total to zero;
● increase the total by an amount;
● reduce the total by an amount;
● return the current total.

The Java code for the class is given below. You can see that is has an additional method called main, which has been added to the class purely for testing purposes:

```java
public class Total {
    private int amount;

    public Total() {
        amount = 0;
    }

    public void win(int change) {
        amount = amount + change;
    }

    public void lose(int change) {
        amount = amount - change;
    }
```

```
public int getTotal() {
    return amount;
}


public void display(Graphics g) {
    g.drawString("value is " + amount, 10, 10);
}


public void main(String[] args) {
    Total score = new Total();
    Graphics g = this.getGraphics();

    g.drawString(score.getTotal(), 10, 10);
    score.win(50);
    g.drawString (score.getTotal(), 10, 30);
    score.lose(50);
    //etc
}
}
```

We test the class Total by invoking its methods with special code constructed solely for the purpose of testing. Such code is called a *test bed*. The name derives from a physical test bed to which something like a jet engine is bolted for testing. We can conveniently write this test code as part of the class itself as the additional method main. When testing is complete, there is no need to delete this code; it will do no harm and can remain in case of later need. For testing purposes the class can be run as a free-standing application. When invoked in this way main is executed first.

To carry out its duty, this test method main should, as shown:

● create one or more objects of the class;
● invoke each of the methods;
● display information using drawString.

Finally here are some details of using this approach. The graphics content object, g, can be obtained by invoking the method getGraphics as shown. The method main has to have parameters (arguments) as shown, but these can be ignored.

● Incremental development

It is common practice to unit test a program and then test the complete program. But if all the units are brought together at once in integration testing, it can be difficult to locate any errors. An alternative to this big-bang testing is piece-by-piece programming – usually called *incremental* programming. The steps are:

1. Write a small piece of the program.
2. Key it in, compile it, run it and debug it.
3. Add a new small piece of the program.
4. Repeat from step 2 until the program is complete.

The trick is to identify which piece of program to start with and which order to do things in. Let us review the structure of an OO program. An OO program consists of a collection of objects, created from classes. Objects are self-contained and modular, and are therefore natural candidates to be tested one at a time. One object uses another by invoking the methods in it. So, if an object A uses an object B, we should first test B. Once B is trustworthy we should test A. (On the other hand, if we try to test A first, we would not know whether an error was caused by A or B.) This approach is called *bottom-up testing* because we are testing the objects at the bottom of the invocation hierarchy first. In the above example of unit testing, the class `Total` does not use any other classes (other than library classes) and therefore should be coded and tested first.

In incremental testing, either black box or white box testing (or both) are applied to an individual class, then to a class that uses the class, and so on. The part of the program under test is tested against its specification. This specification may not exist on paper but it notionally exists just the same. (In big software systems, specifications for subsystems are normally documented.)

● Conclusion

There is no foolproof testing method that will ensure that programs are free of errors. The best approach would be to use a combination of testing methods – black box and white box – together with inspection. To use all three methods would, however, be very time-consuming. So you need to exercise considerable judgement and skill to decide what sort of testing to do and how much testing to do. A systematic approach is vital.

Incremental testing avoids looking for a needle in a haystack, since a newly discovered error is probably in the newly incorporated class.

Testing is a frustrating business – because we know that, however patient and systematic we are, we can never be sure that we have done enough. Testing requires massive patience, attention to detail and organization.

Summary

- Testing is a technique that tries to ensure that a program is free from errors.

- Testing cannot be exhaustive because there are too many cases.

- Black box testing uses only the specification to choose test data.

- White box testing uses a knowledge of how the program works in order to choose test data.

● Inspection simply means studying the program listing in order to find errors.

● Stepping through code using a debugger can be a valuable way of testing a program.

● Unit testing means testing a program piece-by-piece, one class at a time.

● Integration or system testing means testing a complete program (usually after unit testing).

● Incremental development can avoid the complexities of developing large programs.

EXERCISES

23.1 Devise black box and white box test data to test the following program. The program specification is:

The program inputs a series of integers from the keyboard using a text field. The program finds the largest of the numbers. The numbers are terminated when a button labelled Start Again is pressed.

Try not to look at the text of the program, given below, until you have completed the design of the black box data.
    The program involves the following class:

```
class Biggest {
    private int largest;

    public Biggest() {
        largest = 0;
    }

    public void nextNumber(int n) {
        if (n > largest)
            largest = n;
    }

    public void display(Graphics g) {
        g.drawString(" largest so far is" + largest, 50, 50);
    }

    public void startAgain() {
        largest = 0;
    }
}
```

23.2 Devise black box and white box test data to test the following program. The program specification is:

The program is to determine insurance premiums for a holiday, based upon the age and gender (male or female) of the client.

For a female of age >=18 and <=30 the premium is £5. A female aged >=31 pays £3.50. A male of age >=18 and <=35 pays £6. A male aged >=36 pays £5.50. People aged 50 or more pay half premium. Any other ages or genders are an error, which is signalled as a premium of zero.

The code for this program is:

```java
public float calcPremium(float age, String gender) {
    float premium;

    if (gender.equals("female"))
        if ((age >= 18) && (age <= 30))
            premium = 5.0f;
        else
            if (age >= 31)
                premium = 3.50f;
            else
                premium = 0.0f;
    else
        if (gender.equals("male"))
            if ((age >= 18) && (age <= 35))
                premium = 6.0f;
            else
                if (age >= 36)
                    premium = 5.5f;
                else
                    premium = 0.0f;
        else
            premium = 0.0f;

    if (age >= 50)
        premium = premium * 0.5f;

    return premium;
}
```

ANSWERS TO SELF-TEST QUESTIONS
....

23.1 The specification does not say what is to happen if something goes wrong. There are several possibilities. The first situation is if the user enters data which is not a valid integer – for example, a letter is entered instead of a number. The next situation is if the user enters a number greater than 10 000. The final eventuality that might arise is if the sum of the numbers exceeds the size of number that can be accommodated by the computer. If integers are represented as `long` values in the program, this limit is huge (see Chapter 12), but it could arise.

23.2 The specification does not stipulate any limits on the size of the integers, so we assume the maximum range possible.

Each of the data values can take values from minus a large number to plus a large number. We partition the range of each data value into negative, zero and positive. We then choose a representative value from each:

First number:	−9	0	+34
Second number:	−56	0	+4
Third number:	−2	0	+123

So the black box test data is all combinations of these values:

Test no.	Data		
1	−9	−56	−2
2	−9	−56	0
3	−9	−56	123
4	−9	0	−2
5	−9	0	0

etc.

Any one of the three data values could be the largest, so we check that we have tested for all three cases (we have).

Finally, we realize that the specification does not stipulate what happens if two or more of the inputs are equal. So either we query the specification with the client, or we make a reasonable assumption. Suppose we assume that if two or more values are equal, the program should display the largest value. Test data for this is:

Test no.	Data		
1	4	4	2
2	2	5	5
3	6	4	6
4	3	3	3

23.3 A row number is in three partitions:

within the range 1 to 8 (say 3)
less than 1 (say −3)
greater than 8 (say 11)

If we choose one representative value in each partition and similar values for the column numbers (5 − 2 and 34), the test data will be:

Test no.	Data	
1	3	5
2	−3	5
3	11	5
4	3	−2
5	−3	−2
6	11	−2
7	3	34
8	−3	34
9	11	34

We might consider that data near the boundary of the partitions is important and therefore add to the test data for each partition so that it becomes:

within the range 1 to 8 (say 3)
less than 1 (say −3)
greater than 8 (say 11)
1
8
0
9

which now gives many more combinations to use as test data.

23.4 There are four paths through the program, which can be exercised by the following test data:

Test no.	Data		
1	3	2	1
2	3	2	5
3	2	3	1
4	2	3	5

23.5 There are three paths through the program extract, including the path where neither of the conditions in the `if` statements is true. But each of the error messages can be triggered by two conditions. Suitable test data is therefore:

Test no.	Row	Column
1	5	6
2	0	4
3	9	4
4	5	9
5	5	0

Debugging

Introduction

Debugging is the name given to the job of finding out where the bugs are in a program and then fixing the problem. A bug is an error in a program and, because we are all human, all programs tend to have bugs in them when they are first written. Let us trace what happens to a program as it is being developed:

1. **Compilation**
   After you have keyed in a program, you usually have to spend some time getting rid of the compilation errors. A common example is a semicolon missing. The Java compiler carries out a comprehensive series of checks on a program, thus exposing many errors that might otherwise persist. Eventually the program compiles 'cleanly'. Once a program is free of compilation errors, it usually does something visible – even though it may not be exactly what you want.

2. **Linking**
   All programs make use of library methods and some make use of programmer-written classes. These classes are linked only when the class is invoked, while the program is running. But when the program is compiled, checks are carried out that all the methods that are invoked do exist and that the parameters match in number and type.

3. **Running**
   A program runs, but it is most unusual for it to work as expected. In fact it is usual for the program to fail in some way or behave in a way other than was intended. Some errors are detected automatically and the programmer is notified – like an attempt to access a part of an array that does not exist (a subscript error). Others are more subtle and simply give rise to unexpected behaviour. You have a bug in the program – or more likely many bugs! So you have to carry out some debugging.

Later on in this chapter we give examples of common errors that arise in Java programming.

The term bug originated in the days of valve computers, when (the story goes) a large insect became lodged in the circuitry of an early computer, causing it to malfunction. Hence the term 'bug' and the term 'debugging'.

The problem with debugging is that the symptoms of a bug are usually very uninformative. So we have to resort to detective work to find the cause. It's like being a doctor: there is a symptom, you have to find the cause and then you have to fix the problem.

Once the more obvious faults in a program have been eliminated, it is usual to start carrying out some systematic testing. Testing is the repeated running of a program with a variety of data as input. It is discussed in Chapter 23. The aim of testing is to convince the world that the program works properly. But normally testing reveals the existence of more bugs. Then it's time to do some debugging. So testing and debugging go hand-in-hand.

SELF-TEST QUESTION
....

24.1 What is the difference between debugging and testing?

Many programmers like debugging; they see it as exciting – like watching a mystery thriller in which the villain is revealed only at the last moment. Certainly, along with testing, debugging often takes a long time. Do not be worried that debugging takes you some time – this is normal!

● Debugging

A program runs but behaves unexpectedly. How do we find the source of the problem? Most programs display something on the screen, but otherwise what they do is invisible. We need something like X-ray specs to gain some insight into how the program is behaving. This is the key to successful debugging – getting additional information about the running program.

One way to obtain additional information is to insert extra output statements in the program so that it displays information as it is running. One useful way is to invoke the `println` library method, which displays a string on the screen:

```
System.out.println("xCoord =" + xCoord);
```

`println` (short for print line) is a legacy from the days when the output from a program was printed on paper rather than displayed on the screen, but now it is useful for debugging. The joy of this method is that it will work with any type of object as its parameter – it is a truly general purpose method. The `toString` method associated with the object (if it exists) is automatically invoked to convert the object to a string. Most of the classes in the library provide a `toString` method for this purpose. It is good practice for any class that you write to provide such a method. For example, take the `Balloon` class that was used in Chapter 10:

```
class Balloon {
    private int diameter;
    private int xCoord, yCoord;

    public Balloon(int newDiameter, int newX, int newY) {
        diameter = newDiameter;
        xCoord = newX;
        yCoord = newY;
    }

    public void move(int xChange, int yChange) {
        xCoord = xCoord + xChange;
        yCoord = yCoord + yChange;
    }

    public void changeSize(int change) {
        diameter = diameter + change;
    }
}
```

We will write the additional method `toString`, which will be useful in debugging:

```
public String toString() {
    return "x = " + xCoord +
           " y = " + yCoord +
           " diameter = " + diameter;
}
```

This method could be used as follows:

```
System.out.println(myBalloon.toString());
```

We can leave the method `toString` in the program forever, just in case it is needed. It is like scaffolding that was used to help construct a building, but is left for evermore to help maintain it.

The values displayed by `println` appear somewhere, but exactly where depends on the particular operating system and browser (or applet viewer). For example, with a Java-enabled Netscape browser, the output can be viewed by selecting the Options menu and then the Show Java Console option. The output appears in a scrollable window.

The trick is to choose the best points in the program to put the `println` statements. Generally, good points to choose are:

● just before a method is invoked (to check that the parameters are OK) or right at the start of the method;

● just after a method is invoked (to check that the method has done its work correctly) or right at the end of the method.

You can use `println` to display information about the object that the `println` is actually in, by using the word `this`:

```
System.out.println(this);
```

which causes `println` to invoke the `toString` method of the current class, displaying whatever information the programmer has thoughtfully provided. (Remember that `this` is the name for the current object, the one within which instructions are currently being executed.)

We saw in Chapter 23 on testing how to test a class in isolation. This complements the above approach to debugging.

● Using a debugger

The Java system that you are using probably has a *debugger*. A debugger is a program that helps you debug your program. It runs alongside your program, allowing the progress of the program to be inspected. It will provide several facilities. Unfortunately, debuggers are not standardized – they are all different and therefore we can't explain all the different facilities in detail. Some of the debuggers that are available are rather primitive. For example, the jdb (java debugger) is text-based and command-line oriented, with UNIX ancestry. There are also good debuggers available, which are part of an integrated development environment.

We will explain the principles of using a good interactive, integrated debugger. Imagine three windows on the screen, all visible at once. The first is the usual display created by the running program. The second displays the source code of the Java program. The third displays the names of selected variables together with their current values.

Using a debugger, the programmer places a *breakpoint* in the program. A breakpoint is a place in the program where execution stops. A breakpoint is inserted by pointing to a line in the text of the program with the cursor and selecting a menu option. Then the program is set running. When a breakpoint is reached, the program freezes, a pointer highlights the position of the breakpoint in the program text and the debugger displays the values of variables as they are at the moment in the program's execution. Any discrepancy between what they actually are and what they should be provides valuable information for debugging.

A debugger will also let you execute a program one line at a time; this is called *single-shotting* or *stepping*. The option is provided to execute any method at normal speed. It can safely be assumed that library methods are free from errors, so it is reasonable to go at full speed when library methods are used.

It is easy to have a lot of fun with a debugger, but the down-side can be that it uses a lot of time. A productive way to use a debugger is as follows:

1. From the symptoms of the bug, make a deduction about where the bug lies. You may be able to predict that the error lies within any of two or three methods.
2. Place breakpoints at the entry and exit of the methods under suspicion.
3. Run the program. When the program stops at the entry to a method, inspect the values of the parameters. At the exit, inspect the value of the return value and the values of significant instance variables. Thus identify the method within which the bug lies.
4. Run the program again, stopping at the entry to the erroneous method. Single step through this method until you see the discrepancy between expectation and reality. You have found the bug.

● Common errors

Certain errors are commonly made by Java programmers. We list some of them below. It's worthwhile checking any suspect program for these errors.

Compilation errors

The Java compiler carries out a lot of checking on a program as it compiles it to byte code. This is part of trying to ensure that Java programs are robust. An error caught at compile-time is easily fixed, but if it is left undetected until run-time it may take a lot of debugging. So although compile-time errors can be annoying, they are good value.

Method invocation

If a method named `doIt` takes no parameters, it is easy to write a method invocation like:

```
object.doIt; rather than object.doIt();
```

The former is regarded as an attempt to access a variable named `doIt` within the object.

`if` *statements*

It is easy to forget that `if` statements need brackets surrounding the condition:

```
if (a == b) etc
```

Brackets

A common error is to omit a curly bracket { or } or have one in the wrong place. Good and consistent indentation can help you to see and correct this problem.

Semicolons

This is the most common compilation error: leaving out semicolons. The compiler will usually flag the statement after the one in error.

Linking errors

When a program is compiled, the compiler checks all method invocations – including the use of methods in other classes. A common error is a method name spelled wrongly. Another error is to get the number of parameters wrong, or the type of a parameter wrong.

When the program refers to a method in another class, other errors that can arise are:

● An `import` statement is missing or specifies the wrong package.
● The class heading omits the word `extends`, followed by the relevant class name.

Run-time errors

Run-time errors are errors that occur as the program is running, but are caught by the run-time system. Again this is part of the measures designed to ensure that programs are robust – a program that has gone wrong may act like a bull in a china shop. Run-time errors lead to an error message being displayed and the program being stopped (if it is an application).

Array indices

If an array is declared as:

```
int table[] = new int[10];
```

then the following `for` loop will incorrectly try to use the 11th element of the array:

```
for (int s = 0; s <= 10; s++)
    table[s] = 0;
```

When this happens the program is stopped and an `ArrayIndexOutOfBoundsException` exception is thrown.

Arithmetic exceptions

If a program attempts to divide an integer by zero the program will stop and an error message is displayed. It is fairly easy to let this happen inadvertently, for example in a program that contains this fragment:

```
int a, b, c, d;
c = d;
a = b/(c-d);
```

Floating-point arithmetic does not give rise to exceptions like this; instead the program continues and the result of the calculation is infinity (see Chapter 12).

Null pointer exception

If you declare an object like this:

```
Button button;
```

and then use it without creating an instance of the object (using `new`):

```
add(button);
```

you will get a `NullPointerException` to say that you are trying to use an object that has not been created.

Logical errors

Logical errors are the hardest to find, because they depend on the way that the individual program works. Therefore there is no automatic detection of such errors. Some specific errors are, however, common.

Initialization
It is easy to fail to initialize a variable appropriately. In Java, all variables are automatically initialized to some definite value – for example, integers are initialized to zero automatically – but this may not be the intended value. Some compilers flag variables that are used without being initialized. Arrays are initially full of garbage, unless they are initialized in some way.

Events
Failing to provide handling for an event (a mouse click, for example), or alternatively handling an event that you currently want to ignore.

Forgetting to invoke `repaint` when something changes that needs to be redisplayed.

Misuse of the language

If the programmer does not fully understand how to use Java properly, perfectly healthy looking programs will not work as expected. Here are some common cases.

Compound statements
```
if (a > b)
      x = x + a;
      y = y + b;
  z = z + c;
```

will work as the language determines rather than as the indentation suggests. To make it work as the indentation suggests, insert brackets as follows:

```
if (a > b) {
      x = x + a;
      y = y + b;
  }
  z = z + c;
```

Equality

It is tempting to write statements such as:

```
if (s == "abc") ...
```

where s is a string. This will compile correctly, but if the programmer wants to test to see whether s is equal to "abc", it will not work as intended. To achieve this end, the following test is required:

```
if (s.equals("abc")) ...
```

which uses the method equals on objects of type String.

The first if statement is meaningful, but tests whether the string s and the literal "abc" are actually the same object – which they are not. The string s is an object which the program has created using new:

```
String s = new String();
```

whereas the string "abc" is a completely distinct string, created automatically by the compiler. So these two strings are not, and can never be, the same object. (Their values could be the same, but they are not the same object.)

This example uses strings, but the same idea applies when any two objects are being compared for equality – the operator == is almost certainly wrong and instead the equals method of the object should be used.

Infinite loops

It is easy to make a slip and place a semicolon immediately after a while statement such as:

```
int a;
while (a == 0);
```

This error is not detected by the compiler and may cause the program to loop forever.

Summary

- Debugging is finding errors (bugs) in a program and fixing them.

- Java development systems provide a debugger program that can assist.

- A breakpoint is a place where the program temporarily stops to permit inspection of the values of variables.

- Single-shotting is watching the execution flow through the program.

ANSWER TO SELF-TEST QUESTION

24.1 Testing is attempting to demonstrate that a program is free of bugs. Knowing that a bug exists (as a result of testing), debugging is trying to locate the bug.

Threads

Introduction

If you use a personal computer you can usually ask it to do several things at once: print a file, edit a different file, display the time, receive email. In reality, a single computer can only do one thing at a time, but because a computer works so quickly, it can share its time between a number of activities. It does this so fast that it gives the impression that it is doing them all at once.

When a Java program does several things at once it is called *multithreading*. (Some other terms that are used for multithreading are *parallelism* and *concurrency*.) Such a program can do several things seemingly at once: display several animations, play sounds, allow the user to interact. Any one of the activities that it is performing is called a *thread*. This chapter is about writing threads in Java.

We have seen that a program is a series of instructions to the computer, which the computer normally obeys in sequence. The sequence is diverted by method invocations, loops and selection (`if`) statements, but it is still a single path that moves through the program. We could use a pencil to simulate the execution of a program, following the path through the program. In multithreading, two or more paths are set in motion. To follow the paths of execution now needs several pencils. Remembering that a computer is only capable of doing one thing at once, we realize that it is dividing its available time between the different threads so as to give the impression that they are all executing at the same time.

Multithreading

Our first example is a real, human one – a group of people shopping for a meal. Suppose that three students share a house. They decide to have a meal and to split up the work of shopping:

● one buys the meat (they are not vegetarians);
● one buys the vegetables;
● one buys the lager;

and these things they do concurrently. This way the whole shopping job gets done quicker. But notice that at some time they must synchronize their activities in order that the meal gets prepared and that they all sit down to eat it at the same time. This may just involve waiting until the last person has returned from the shops.

A group of musicians in an orchestra play different instruments simultaneously, reading their different parts from a musical score. The score tells each of them what to do and helps them synchronize their notes.

Our next example is a time-sharing computer system, where a single computer shares its processor time among a number of users, all of whom believe that they are doing things in parallel. The users have their own terminals and, provided that the computer is sufficiently powerful, they all believe that they have exclusive use of the machine. In fact, of course, the operating system of the computer shares the time among the users.

Next, the process of controlling a plant. In a biscuit factory controlled by a computer, which has ovens, weighing machines, valves and pumps, the computer must ensure that each of a number of separate activities is carried out. There may be several different concurrent activities within the plant to be controlled.

The next example is a personal computer, which may have several things going on at once:

● displaying a clock;
● printing a file;
● carrying out editing of a file;
● receiving electronic mail;

and all of these are to be carried out as if the processor is devoting its time exclusively to one of the threads.

● Independent threads

Back in an early chapter we saw a program that made a ball bounce around a rectangle on the screen (Figure 25.1). Here is the text of the animation program.

```
import java.awt.*;
import java.applet.Applet;
import java.awt.event.*;


public class Bouncer extends Applet implements ActionListener {

    private Button start;
```

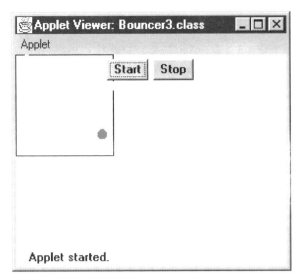

Figure 25.1 The bouncing ball screen.

```
public void init() {
    start = new Button("Start");
    add(start);
    start.addActionListener(this);
}

public void actionPerformed(ActionEvent event) {
    if (event.getSource() == start) {
        Graphics g = getGraphics();
        Ball ball = new Ball(g);
        ball.display();
    }
}
}

class Ball {

    private Graphics g;
    private int x = 7, xChange = 7;
    private int y = 0, yChange = 2;
    private int diameter = 10;
    private int rectLeftX = 0, rectRightX = 100;
    private int rectTopY = 0, rectBottomY = 100;
```

```java
public Ball(Graphics graphics) {
    g = graphics;
}
public void display() {
    g.drawRect(rectLeftX, rectTopY,
            rectRightX - rectLeftX, rectBottomY - rectTopY);

    for (int n = 1; n < 1000; n++) {
        g.setColor(Color.white);
        g.fillOval (x, y, diameter, diameter);

        if (x + xChange <= rectLeftX)
            xChange = -xChange;
        if (x + xChange >= rectRightX)
            xChange = -xChange;

        if (y + yChange <= rectTopY)
            yChange = -yChange;
        if (y + yChange >= rectBottomY)
            yChange = -yChange;

        x = x + xChange;
        y = y + yChange;
        g.setColor(Color.red);
        g.fillOval (x, y, diameter, diameter);

        try {
            Thread.sleep(50);
        }
        catch (InterruptedException e) {
            System.err.println("sleep exception");
        }
    }
}
}
```

The program uses one object to handle the user input and another object to represent the ball object. The program provides a button labelled 'Start' to start the ball bouncing. There is a delay in the program so that the ball does not go too fast. To do this the program invokes library method sleep. The parameter passed to sleep is the time in milliseconds that the program wants to sleep. To use this method it must be provided with an exception handler as shown. (The explanation for the cause of an InterruptedException is given later in this chapter, and this particular exception can be safely ignored.) The other feature of this program is that the graphics context, g, is passed from the user interface object to the ball object when the ball object is created with its constructor function.

The trouble with this program is that while the ball is bouncing around, nothing else can happen. The program is in control of the computer. If we provided a button labelled 'Stop', it would not work. In fact, none of the buttons on the screen will work. The program is completely monopolizing the computer until the loop is ended. The solution is to create two threads – one to handle the user interface (buttons etc.) and the other to draw the animation.

● Initiating threads

To prevent the bouncing ball program from monopolizing the computer we want to create two threads running at once. One thread is, as usual, the user interface object. It has the job of creating any other objects and then lying in wait for any events, which it will then handle. The other thread draws the bouncing ball. The first object, the user interface object, creates the second thread. Thereafter, the two run together, sharing the processor. The bouncing ball thread periodically goes to sleep for 50 milliseconds. This importantly allows the user interface thread to get some time running on the processor. We shall see more and more of this kind of cooperation between threads.

The user interface class (and thread) is, as usual, an extension of the library `Applet` class. The other class (thread) is an extension of the library class `Thread`. The only requirement of this class is that it must provide a method named `run`. It is this method that the Java system invokes to set the thread running. But the act of creating the thread is done by the user interface object. First it creates the new object, just as any other object is created, with:

```
Ball ball = new Ball(g);
```

Then it asks the Java system to run the thread, using the library method `start`:

```
ball.start();
```

The original program structure with one thread is shown in Figure 25.2. It shows how the bouncing ball object monopolizes the machine to the exclusion of anything else. The new program structure with two threads is shown in Figure 25.3. The user interface thread initiates the bouncing ball thread. The two threads then run together.

```
import java.awt.*;
import java.applet.Applet;
import java.awt.event.*;


public class Bouncer2 extends Applet implements ActionListener {

    private Button start;
```

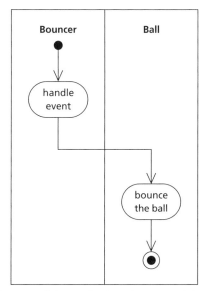

Figure 25.2 UML activity diagram of the single-thread version of the bouncing ball program.

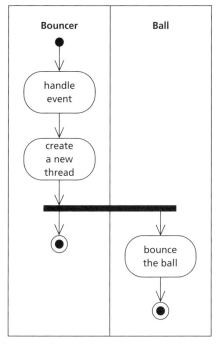

Figure 25.3 UML activity diagram of the two-thread version of the bouncing ball program.

```
    public void init() {
        start = new Button("Start");
        add(start);
        start.addActionListener(this);
    }

    public void actionPerformed(ActionEvent event) {
        if (event.getSource() == start) {
            Graphics g = getGraphics();
            Ball ball = new Ball(g);
            ball.start();
        }
    }
}

class Ball extends Thread {
    private Graphics g;
    private int x = 7, xChange = 7;
    private int y = 0, yChange = 2;
    private int diameter = 10;
    private int rectLeftX = 0, rectRightX = 100;
    private int rectTopY = 0, rectBottomY = 100;

    public Ball(Graphics graphics) {
        g = graphics;
    }

    public void run() {
        g.drawRect(rectLeftX, rectTopY,
                    rectRightX - rectLeftX, rectBottomY - rectTopY);

        for (int n = 1; n < 1000; n++) {
            g.setColor(Color.white);
            g.fillOval (x, y, diameter, diameter);
            if (x + xChange <= rectLeftX)
                xChange = -xChange;
            if (x + xChange >= rectRightX)
                xChange = -xChange;

            if (y + yChange <= rectTopY)
                yChange = -yChange;
            if (y + yChange >= rectBottomY)
                yChange = -yChange;
```

```
        x = x + xChange;
        y = y + yChange;

        g.setColor(Color.red);
        g.fillOval (x, y, diameter, diameter);

        try {
            Thread.sleep(50);
        }
        catch (InterruptedException e) {
                System.err.println("sleep exception");
        }
    }
  }
}
```

Now comes the exciting part. You can test to see that the application, the ball, no longer greedily uses the processor by clicking on the start button while a ball is already bouncing. An additional ball is created which bounces around the rectangle along with the existing ball. You can create new balls indefinitely. This is a graphic illustration of the responsiveness of the user interface thread while the application thread is running. It also shows dramatically how new objects are created using new. (Incidentally, when a new Ball object is created, it is assigned to the value of the single variable, ball. Thus the program loses all references to any balls created earlier. They therefore become candidates for destruction by the automatic garbage collection mechanism. However, as you will see if you run the program, it is not for some time that the garbage collection system notices these objects, and destroys them.)

SELF-TEST QUESTION

25.1 Alter the program so that it creates two rectangles at different places on the screen, with a ball bouncing around in each. You need one thread for each ball. The user interface object is a third thread. Make maximum reuse of the existing classes.

You now have all you need to write programs that do lots of things simultaneously. You can display a clock, display an animation, play a game, edit some text – all at the same time. You need to create a thread for each of these parallel activities as shown above.

We have seen how to create threads that run in parallel, sharing the processor. A key feature of these threads is that they do not interact or communicate with each other. Once created, they are independent threads. This is a common and very useful scenario in multithreading. An alternative scenario is where the threads interact with each other as they are running. This introduces complications, as we shall see later in this chapter.

● Dying and killing

The program as written makes the ball bounce for a limited time (1000 repetitions), controlled by the `for` loop. When the thread `ball` has finished looping, it exits the method `run` and dies. This is the normal way in which a thread dies.

We want to improve the bouncing ball program so that a ball keeps bouncing until we stop it, by pressing a button. In the user interface thread, we provide a new button, labelled 'Stop', in the usual way:

```
Button stop = new Button("Stop");
add(stop);
```

A good way to terminate the bouncing ball thread is to set up a boolean flag named `keepGoing`. This is initially made `true` when the object is created, but is set `false` when the user presses the stop button. The loop in the ball object is:

```
while (keepGoing) {
    // etc.
}
```

The part of the event handler now needed to handle the button labelled stop is:

```
if (event.getSource() == stop)
    ball.pleaseStop();
```

and the method in the class `Ball` is:

```
public void pleaseStop() {
    keepGoing = false;
}
```

So now the improved program is:

```
import java.awt.*;
import java.awt.applet.Applet;
import java.awt.event.*;


public class Bouncer3 extends Applet implements ActionListener {

    private Button start, stop;
    private Ball ball;

    public void init() {
        start = new Button("Start");
        add(start);
        start.addActionListener(this);
```

```
        stop = new Button("Stop");
        add(stop);
        stop.addActionListener(this);
    }

    public void actionPerformed(ActionEvent event) {
        if (event.getSource() == start) {
            Graphics g = getGraphics();
            ball = new Ball(g);
            ball.start();
        }
        if (event.getSource() == stop)
            ball.pleaseStop();
    }
}

class Ball extends Thread {
    private boolean keepGoing;
    private Graphics g;
    private int x = 7, xChange = 7;
    private int y = 0, yChange = 2;
    private int diameter = 10;
    private int rectLeftX = 0, rectRightX = 100;
    private int rectTopY = 0, rectBottomY = 100;

    public Ball(Graphics graphics) {
        g = graphics;
        keepGoing = true;
    }

    public void pleaseStop() {
        keepGoing = false;
    }

    public void run() {
        g.drawRect(rectLeftX, rectTopY,
                    rectRightX - rectLeftX, rectBottomY - rectTopY);

        while (keepGoing) {
            g.setColor(Color.white);
            g.fillOval (x, y, diameter, diameter);

            if (x + xChange <= rectLeftX)
                xChange = -xChange;
```

```
            if (x + xChange >= rectRightX)
                xChange = -xChange;

            if (y + yChange <= rectTopY)
                yChange = -yChange;
            if (y + yChange >= rectBottomY)
                yChange = -yChange;

            x = x + xChange;
            y = y + yChange;

            g.setColor(Color.red);
            g.fillOval (x, y, diameter, diameter);

            try {
                Thread.sleep(50);
            }
            catch (InterruptedException e) {
                System.err.println("sleep exception");

            }
        }
    }
}
```

This program now works very nicely. When you press the start button, a ball is created and bounces around the rectangle until you press the stop button. Pressing start again creates a new ball and so on. The user interface thread is always responsive to user actions (clicking on a button) and the application thread (the ball object) no longer hogs the processor.

Another thing you might want to do is to make a thread wait until another has died. This is done with the method join, as in:

```
ball.join()
```

which causes the thread that invokes join to wait until thread ball has died.

SELF-TEST QUESTION

25.2 Write a program that consists of two threads – the user interface thread and one other (which could be a thread that displays the time in minutes and seconds for two minutes). The first thread initiates the second, using start. It then waits (using join) until the second has terminated. It should then display a message to say that it has terminated.

● The state of a thread

It is useful to understand the idea of the states of a thread. A thread can be in any one of these states:

- New It has just been created with the new operator, just like any other object, but it has not yet been set runnable by means of the start method.
- Running It is actually running on the computer, executing instructions.
- Runnable It would like to run, is able to run, but some other thread is currently running.
- Blocked For some reason the thread cannot proceed until something happens. A typical example would be that the thread has invoked sleep and is suspended for a number of milliseconds.
- Dead The run method has exited normally.

One thread can find out the state of another thread by invoking the library method isAlive. It returns true if the thread is runnable or blocked. It returns false if the thread is new or dead. For example:

```
if (ball.isAlive())
    g.drawString("The ball is alive", 20, 20);
```

SELF-TEST QUESTION

25.3 Use isAlive in the user interface object to test the status of the ball object in the bouncing ball program.

● Scheduling, thread priorities and yield

The Java system has the job of sharing the single (or sometimes multi-) processor among the threads in a program. It is often the case that there are several threads that are runnable – they are ready and able to run when the processor becomes available. The scheduler must choose between them. Different schedulers on different machines and Java systems may work differently. There is no guarantee that any particular scheduling is provided. The programmer must be careful not to make any assumptions about when a particular thread will be selected to run.

By default, the Java system gives all the threads that are created the same priority. Thereafter the Java system will share the processor equitably among the active threads. Even so, it is easy for a thread to hog the processor, shutting out other threads. Therefore any thread with a social conscience should invoke the method yield like this:

```
yield();
```

at such times as it may otherwise be too greedy. If no other threads are runnable, the thread continues.

● Mutual exclusion and synchronized

We now turn to the more complex situation where two or more threads interact as they are running. (Thus far we have considered only independent threads.) Suppose that two threads are each incrementing the value of a shared integer maintained within a separate object:

```java
import java.applet.Applet;
import java.awt.*;

public class TwoCounters extends Applet {

    public void init() {
        TextArea display = new TextArea(2, 50);
        add(display);
        SharedNumber count = new SharedNumber(display);

        Counter1 counter1 = new Counter1(count);
        Counter2 counter2 = new Counter2(count);
        counter1.start();
        counter2.start();
    }
}

class Counter1 extends Thread {
    private SharedNumber count;

    public Counter1(SharedNumber count) {
        this.count = count;
    }

    public void run() {
        for (int i = 1; i <= 10; i++)
            count.increment();
    }
}

class Counter2 extends Thread {
    private SharedNumber count;

    public Counter2(SharedNumber count) {
        this.count = count;
    }
```

```
      public void run() {
          for (int i = 1; i <= 10; i++)
              count.increment();
      }
   }

   class SharedNumber {

      private int n = 0;

      private TextArea display;

      public SharedNumber(TextArea display) {
          this.display = display;
      }

      public void increment() {
          n = n + 1;
          display.append(n + ", ");
      }
   }
```

This is a simplified version of the sort of activity that occurs very often in multithreading. It could be that the threads are adding to the score in a computer game. It could be that the threads are keeping a log of the number of visits to a Web site.

What will happen if the above two threads are set running in parallel? Taking an obvious view, each will increment the shared variable, which will take on the values 1, 2, . . . up to 20, as in Figure 25.4. You could run this program a thousand times and this is exactly what will happen. But although this will almost always happen, occasionally the outcome will be unpredictable, and sometimes very strange indeed. The outcome depends on when the scheduler chooses to suspend one thread and resume the execution of the other. The scheduler does not know what the intent of the two threads is, and

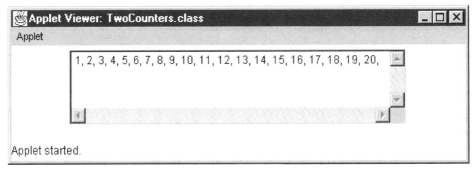

Figure 25.4 Screen output from the two counters program.

might suspend either one of the two threads at any time. Indeed, the interval between successive suspensions may be random – hence the non-determinacy. To see what *might* happen and therefore *will* happen eventually, consider the following sequence of events:

1. The thread `counter1` starts to increment the counter. It loads the value into a temporary storage area. Suppose the value happens to be 5.
2. Thread `counter1` is suspended by the scheduler. The thread `counter2` resumes execution. It loads the value of the counter (still equal to 5) into a temporary storage area.
3. Thread `counter2` is suspended. Thread `counter1` resumes. It increments the value, so that the value 5 becomes 6. It stores the value back in the variable.
4. Thread `counter2` is suspended. `counter1` resumes. It increments the value that it is holding in temporary storage (which is 5) to become 6, and stores it back into the variable.

The outcome is that the value of the variable has become 6, when it should have become 7. Now you might argue that this is a rather bizarre sequence of events. You might argue that this particular sequence will happen once in a blue moon. The fact remains that it might happen and therefore we must avoid it happening.

To solve this problem, we need to ensure that the shared variable is accessed by one thread at once. We control the access so that one thread can carry out its business properly and to its conclusion. Only then do we allow any other thread access. The problem to be solved is to allow only one thread access to something (e.g. a shared data item) at a time. While one thread has access, the other should be excluded and vice versa. This requirement is known as *mutual exclusion*.

The way to ensure mutual exclusion is to specify any methods which share variables as `synchronized` in their headers. These methods must also be within the same class. The Java system ensures that within a particular object, only one of the synchronized methods can only be entered by a thread at a time. Any thread trying to enter any synchronized method in the object while any of them is in use is blocked until such time as the first has exited from the method. Thus:

```
class SharedNumber {

    private int n = 0;

    private TextArea display;

    public SharedNumber(TextArea display) {
        this.display = display;
    }

    public synchronized void increment() {
        n = n + 1;
        display.append(n + ", ");
    }
}
```

Commonly, threads exhibit this general structure:

```
while (true) {
    doSomething();
    accessSomeSharedResource();
    doSomethingElse();
}
```

The thread is an infinite loop. In the body of the loop, the thread carries out some action. Then it needs access to some shared resource – a variable, a file, the screen, a communication link. Finally, the thread does something else. The part of the program where it accesses a shared resource is known as a *critical region.*

In summary, when some data is accessed by two or more threads, there is a need for mutual exclusion. This is achieved by placing the data in its own object and providing access (as usual) via methods. These methods must be declared as synchronized so that only one thread can enter one method at a time, excluding any others.

● Thread interaction – wait and notify

Our next problem also involves mutual exclusion, but rather than the shared resource of an integer counter, the resource will be the screen. Suppose that two threads want to display something in a text area. Suppose they are poets and they each want to display a poem that they have written. Here is the code for the two threads:

```
import java.applet.Applet;
import java.awt.*;

public class Poets extends Applet {

    public void init() {
        TextArea display =
            new TextArea("", 10, 30, TextArea.SCROLLBARS_VERTICAL_ONLY);
        add(display);
        Nursery nursery = new Nursery(display);
        Revolutionary revolutionary = new Revolutionary(display);
        nursery.start();
```

```
                revolutionary.start();
        }
}

class Nursery extends Thread {
    private TextArea display;

    public Nursery(TextArea display) {
        this.display = display;
    }

    public void run() {
        while (true) {
            display.append("Mary had a little lamb\n");
            display.append("Its fleece was white as snow\n\n");
            try {
                Thread.sleep(5000);
            }
            catch (InterruptedException e) {
                display.append ("sleep exception - design fault\n");
            }
        }
    }
}

class Revolutionary extends Thread {
    private TextArea display;

    public Revolutionary(TextArea display) {
        this.display = display;
    }

    public void run() {
        while (true) {
            display.append("Praise Marx\n");
            display.append("and pass the ammunition\n\n");
            try {
                Thread.sleep(5000);
            }
            catch (InterruptedException e) {
                display.append("sleep exception - design fault\n");
            }
        }
    }
}
```

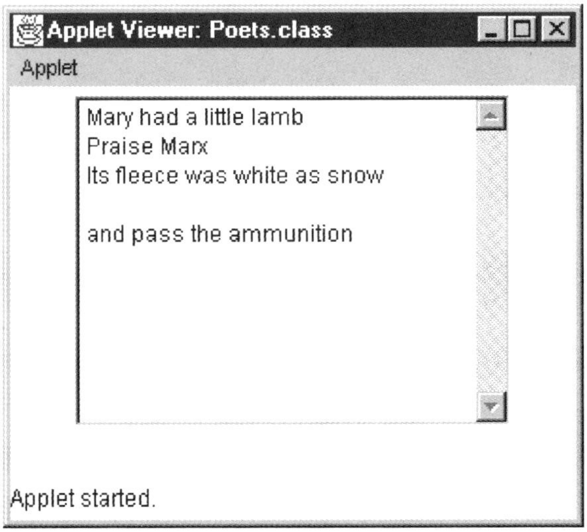

Figure 25.5 Output from the poets.

What would we see in the window when the two poet threads are running? You can see that they are both trying to display their message in the same text area. Because their output is in the same place, it could look like Figure 25.5, in which the poems are inter-leaved and therefore confused. We need to control the situation so that one thread has exclusive access to the text area for an appropriate length of time. But how do we con-trol and coordinate the outputs from the poets? We *could* attempt to use `synchronized`, as in the previous counter example, but this would be overkill – too restrictive. The structure of many threads is:

```
do some non-shared activities
access some shared resource
do some non-shared activities
etc.
```

We want a means of switching on a mutual exclusion around a critical region – a section of code which accesses a shared resource – just as traffic lights enclose the critical region at a road intersection.

Returning to the poets, we do not want to curb the poets' passion too much, but we will insist as part of the design of the program that each of them issues a request (invokes a method) to use the screen before starting output. Then, after they have finished, they should issue a notification to say so. A poet thread now looks like this:

```
class Revolutionary extends Thread {
    private TextArea display;
    private ScreenController screen;
```

```
    public Revolutionary(TextArea display, ScreenController screen) {
        this.display = display;
        this.screen = screen;
    }

    public void run() {
        while (true) {
            screen.askFor();
            display.append("Praise Marx\n");
            display.append("and pass the ammunition\n\n");
            screen.relinquish();
            try {
                Thread.sleep(5000);
            }
            catch (InterruptedException e) {
                display.append ("sleep exception - design fault\n");
            }
        }
    }
}
```

We create a guardian object called screen for the text area. Its mission is to ensure that
only one client is using the text area at once. It accepts requests to use the text area
and notifications that users have finished using it. It maintains a boolean variable called
inUse, which is set true when some thread has been granted access to the text area,
and false otherwise. (Initially the value is false.) The boolean variable is accessed only
by methods that are synchronized. We saw earlier why any shared variable needs protection of this kind. The object enforces the discipline that, once any thread has issued
a request to use the text area, any other threads must wait until the first has completed
its use. We are using synchronized access to a shared variable to control access to a
shared resource – the text area.

To make a thread wait if the text area is already in use, it invokes the wait method.
This is a library method that causes the thread to wait until another thread invokes a
notify method. (When using wait, it must supply an exception handler to handle a
possible InterruptedException. We shall see later how this might arise, but this particular exception can be safely ignored.) As soon as a waiting thread is released by a
notify, it is free to run. If several threads are waiting, only the longest-waiting thread
is released from its wait.

```
  public class ScreenController {
      private boolean inUse = false;

      public synchronized void askFor() {
          while (inUse)
              try {
```

```
                    wait();
              }
              catch (InterruptedException e) {
                    System.err.println("Exception");
              }
         inUse=true;
     }


     public synchronized void relinquish() {
         inUse = false;
         notify();
     }

 }
```

Now each poet can display their poem, free of interference, and then wait for five seconds. We have controlled access by competing threads to a shared resource (the text area). When a poet invokes `askFor`, the value of the boolean `inUse` is tested. If it is `false`, `inUse` is set to `true`, signifying that the resource is now in use. If the value of `inUse` is `false`, the thread that invoked `askFor` invokes the `wait` method. This suspends the poet thread until a `notify` is invoked by some other thread. This happens when another poet finishes using the text area, and invokes `relinquish`. When method `askFor` is released from its wait, it sets the boolean variable to `true`, signifying that the resource is in use.

The interaction between the threads is encapsulated within the object `screen` (an instance of `ScreenController`). Methods within this object are protected using the description `synchronized`. Any use of `wait` and `notify` within this object, `screen`, refers to this object, and only this object. (There may be a number of threads within a particular program that invoke `notify`, but only an invocation of `notify` within the object `screen` can affect any thread waiting within this object.)

You might think that it is more appropriate to use an `if` statement rather than a `while`, as follows, omitting the `try` clause for clarity:

```
 if (inUse)
      wait();
```

It is very tempting to write the program in this way, because it seems clear that the thread only has to wait if `inUse` is true. However, this is an unsafe way to write programs of this kind. It might work sometimes, but it is much better to write a `while` loop. The reason is as follows. Once it is released from waiting, a thread should and must go back to check again that the data has the desired value – in case some other thread has changed it. This is most neatly accomplished using a `while` loop as shown above.

Let us now summarize what `wait` and `notify` do:

`wait`: suspends the thread that invokes it until such time as some other thread invokes `notify` within this same object;

`notify`: releases just one of any threads that are waiting within the object. If no thread is waiting, `notify` does nothing.

To complete this topic, and to illustrate that mutual exclusion is no minor problem, let us consider two real computer systems.

A bank maintains records of customers' accounts on a computer with many terminals. One bank clerk at one terminal enters a transaction to credit a particular account by £1000. Another clerk simultaneously enters a transaction to debit the same account by £1000. What can go wrong?

An airline maintains records of bookings on a computer with many terminals. One travel agent interrogates the system to find out whether seats are available on a particular flight. On finding that two seats are available, he turns round to the client to ask whether she wants the seats. While they are conversing, someone at another terminal books the seats.

To summarize, sometimes two or more threads require intermittent access to some shared data. Uncontrolled access can cause strange things to happen. Mutual exclusion is the term used to describe controlling the access so that only one thread has access at once. It can be implemented by describing any methods that access the shared resource (object) as `synchronized`. This handles short-term access to a shared variable.

For resources like the screen or a file, which are shared, a guardian object needs to be designed. It maintains a boolean variable to control access. Waiting to use the resource is accomplished using the `wait` method. Another thread ends the waiting by executing `notify`. This handles long-term access to a shared resource.

One of the great strengths of objects is encapsulation of shared data. This is further exploited when different threads access shared variables. All that is needed is to add the one word `synchronized` to the method header.

● The producer–consumer problem

In mutual exclusion and in the examples we have looked at so far, threads tend to compete with each other. Now, in contrast, we look at situations where two or more threads collaborate in carrying out some work. The scenario is this: one thread (a producer) will create some information which it passes on to a second thread (a consumer) which deals with the information.

The clock

This program acts as a digital clock, displaying the hour, minutes and seconds (Figure 25.6). Each of these is maintained by a distinct thread. The user interface thread creates and starts the threads:

```
public class Clock extends Applet {

    public void init() {
        TextField showSeconds = new TextField(20);
        add(showSeconds);
        TextField showMinutes = new TextField(20);
        add(showMinutes);
```

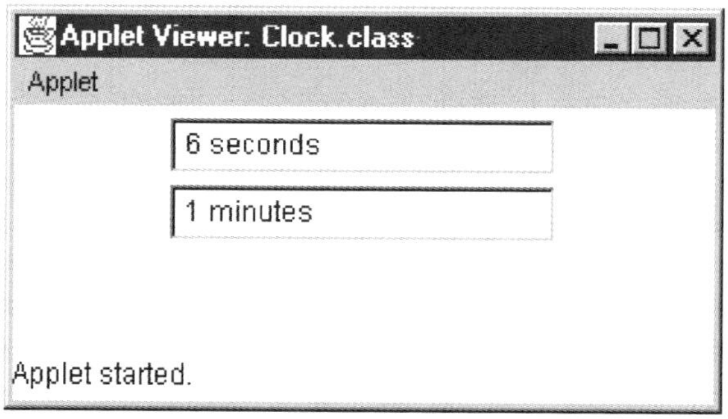

Applet Viewer: Clock.class

Applet

6 seconds

1 minutes

Applet started.

Figure 25.6 The clock.

```
        TickTock minuteTick = new TickTock();

        Minute minute = new Minute(showMinutes, minuteTick);
        minute.start();

        Second second = new Second(showSeconds, minuteTick);
        second.start();
    }
}
```

The two other threads – `minute` and `second` – act like a production line (Figure 25.7). Thread `second` is the first in the chain. It goes to sleep for 1000 milliseconds (1 second) by invoking `sleep(1000)`. When a second has elapsed it updates its count of the number of seconds. Meanwhile, thread `minute` is asleep, waiting to be woken up by thread `second` when 60 seconds have elapsed.

We have already seen the way that threads sleep and get woken up. To sleep, a thread executes method `wait`. This suspends the thread until an event occurs. The event

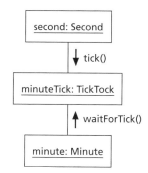

Figure 25.7 Structure of the clock program.

happens when some other thread executes the method notify. Both these methods must be used within synchronized methods, which in turn are within an object.

Here is the code for class Second. It sleeps for a second. Then it updates its count of the number of seconds. If a minute has elapsed, it invokes method tick in object minuteTick to wake up thread minute.

```java
class Second extends Thread {

    private int seconds = 0;

    private TextField showSeconds;
    private TickTock minuteTick;

    public Second(TextField showSeconds, TickTock minuteTick) {
        this.showSeconds = showSeconds;
        this.minuteTick = minuteTick;
    }

    public void run() {
        while(true) {
            try {
                Thread.sleep(1000);
            }
            catch (InterruptedException e) {
                System.err.println("Exception");
            }
            if(seconds == 59) {
                minuteTick.tick();
                seconds = 0;
            }
            else seconds++;
            showSeconds.setText(seconds + " seconds");
        }
    }
}
```

The class for thread minute is given below. It invokes method waitForTick in object minuteTick to suspend itself until a minute has elapsed. When it continues, it updates its count of the number of minutes.

```java
class Minute extends Thread {

    private int minutes = 0;
    private TextField showMinutes;
    private TickTock minuteTick;
```

```
public Minute(TextField showMinutes, TickTock minuteTick) {
    this.showMinutes = showMinutes;
    this.minuteTick = minuteTick;
}

public void run() {
    while(true) {
        minuteTick.waitForTick();
        if (minutes == 59) {
            minutes = 0;
        }
        else
            minutes++;
        showMinutes.setText(minutes + " minutes");
    }
}
}
```

The object that handles the interaction between the threads `second` and `minute` contains two `synchronized` methods. Method `waitForTick` causes its user to wait. Method `tick` signals that the other can continue by invoking `notify`.

```
public class TickTock {

    private boolean tickHappens = false;

    public synchronized void waitForTick() {
        while (!tickHappens)
            try {
                wait();
            }
            catch (InterruptedException e) {
                System.err.println("Exception");
            }
        tickHappens=false;
    }

    public synchronized void tick() {
        tickHappens = true;
        notify();
    }
}
```

The above clock program is an example of two threads that cooperate with each other in a very simple way. From time to time the first thread needs to alert the other to the fact that something has happened. The second thread waits for this event and, when it happens, takes some action. This is an example of a very simple producer–consumer pair in which no information is passed from one thread to the other. We now look at a more complex example where information is passed from one thread to another.

The café

As the next example, consider a computer system for a café (Figure 25.8). This program could be used in a real café to keep track of orders. Alternatively it could act as a simulation of a café. In this program actual information is passed from one thread to another. An order is entered into the computer by pressing a button. The buttons available are burger, fries and cola. An order is displayed on the screen and then entered into a queue. The queue is displayed on the screen. The chef takes orders from the queue on a first-come, first-served basis. The chef can only work on one order at a time, which is displayed on the screen. When the chef has completed the order, he or she presses a button labelled 'Complete' to remove the order from the screen.

You can see that there is a chain of people involved in the café. These correspond to the different threads (Figure 25.9). We need three threads for this program:

1. the user interface;
2. the waiter – to accept an order, display it and enter it into the queue;
3. the chef – to remove an item from the queue, display it, and wait until it is cooked. If there is no order in the queue, the chef waits.

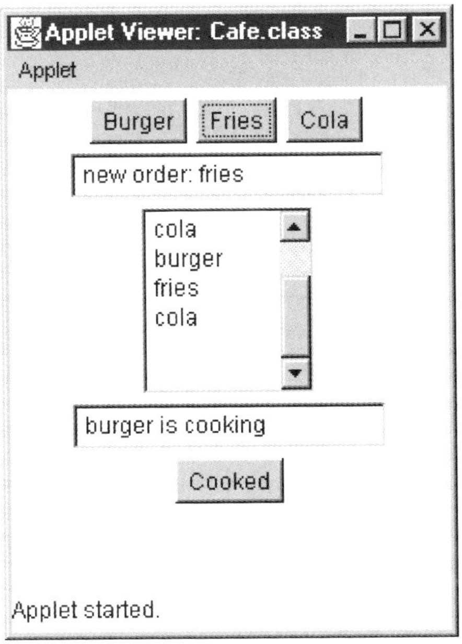

Figure 25.8 The café.

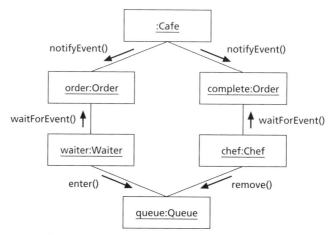

Figure 25.9 Structure of the café program.

In addition to the three thread objects are two other objects (`order` and `complete`) which handle the interaction between the threads.

First we will look at the code for the user interface, class `Cafe`. There is nothing new here. The two other threads (`waiter` and `chef`) are created and set running. These threads are passed the objects that they need to communicate and also the graphics context, `g`. The user interface thread also handles the events when the buttons are pressed. An order is passed to the `waiter` thread by invoking method `notifyEvent` of the `order` object. The information that cooking is complete is passed to the `chef` thread by invoking method `notifyEvent` of object `complete`.

```
public class Cafe extends Applet implements ActionListener {

    private Button burger, fries, cola, cooked;
    private TextField newOrder =
        new TextField("awaiting order", 20);
    private TextArea queueDisplay =
        new TextArea("QUEUE\n", 5, 10,
                        TextArea.SCROLLBARS_VERTICAL_ONLY);
    private TextField cooking =
        new TextField("nothing is cooking", 20);
    private Order order, complete;

    public void init() {
        burger = new Button("Burger");
        add (burger);
        burger.addActionListener(this);
        fries = new Button("Fries");
        add (fries);
```

```
        fries.addActionListener(this);
        cola = new Button("Cola");
        add (cola);
        cola.addActionListener(this);

        add(newOrder);

        add(queueDisplay);

        add(cooking);

        cooked = new Button("Cooked");
        add (cooked);
        cooked.addActionListener(this);

        order = new Order();
        Queue queue = new Queue(queueDisplay);
        complete = new Order();

        Waiter waiter = new Waiter(newOrder, order, queue);
        waiter.start();

        Chef chef = new Chef(cooking, complete, queue);
        chef.start();
    }

    public void actionPerformed (ActionEvent event) {
        if (event.getSource() == burger)
            order.notifyEvent("burger");
        if (event.getSource() == fries)
            order.notifyEvent("fries");
        if (event.getSource() == cola)
            order.notifyEvent("cola");
        if (event.getSource() == cooked)
            complete.notifyEvent("cooked");
    }
}
```

The waiter thread loops forever and does the following:

1. Waits for an order by invoking method waitForEvent of object order.
2. When an order is entered (by pressing a choice from one of the three buttons), the user interface thread notifies the waiter that there is an order.
3. Collects the order, displays it, waits for 5 seconds.
4. Enters the order into the queue.
5. Notifies the chef thread that something has been put in the queue.

Here is the code:

```
class Waiter extends Thread {

    private Order order;
    private TextField display;
    private Queue queue;

    public Waiter(TextField display, Order order, Queue queue) {
        this.order = order;
        this.display = display;
        this.queue = queue;
    }

    public void run() {
        while (true) {
            String newOrder = order.waitForEvent();
            display.setText("new order: " + newOrder);
            try {
                Thread.sleep(5000);
            }
            catch (InterruptedException e) {
                System.err.println("Exception");
            }
            display.setText("awaiting order");
            queue.enter(newOrder);
        }
    }
}
```

The interaction between the user interface thread and the waiter takes place via an object named order. This object holds the order itself, together with the methods that ensure that it is handled properly. Remember that any data that is accessed by two or more threads has to be enclosed in an object and that the methods that access the data must be declared synchronized. When the waiter is collecting an order, it has first to wait for one to be entered via the buttons. When the user interface is placing an order, it must notify that it has done so. The code for an order is:

```
public class Order {

    private String order = "";

    public synchronized void notifyEvent(String newOrder) {
        order = newOrder;
        notify();
    }
}
```

```
public synchronized String waitForEvent() {
    while (order.equals(""))
        try {
            wait();
        }
        catch (InterruptedException e) {
            System.err.println("Exception");
        }
    String newOrder = order;
    order = "";
    return newOrder;
    }

}
```

Now let us turn our attention to the queue. The queue allows us to decouple the waiter and the chef, allowing them – when possible – to work at their own pace. We will represent the queue as an array of strings:

```
String[] queue = new String[5];
```

Associated with the queue is a counter, named count, that describes how many orders are in the queue. Putting something in the queue involves:

```
queue[count] = item;
count++;
```

Taking something out of the queue is a little more difficult because we have to move everything up to fill the gap left when the first item is removed:

```
item = queue[0];
count--;
for (c=0; c < count; c++)
    queue[c] = queue[c+1];
```

Now we know that if two threads are to access the same data, then there has to be mutual exclusion. As before, we will create an object that looks after this shared data, the queue. It accepts requests to add an item to the queue:

```
queue.enter(item);
```

and requests to remove an item from the queue:

```
queue.remove(item);
```

and these methods must be described as synchronized.

Finally, if there is nothing in the queue, the chef must wait until there is something to cook. And when the waiter puts something in the queue, it must notify the chef that there is an order to work on. If the waiter places, say, three items in the queue, it will execute notify three times. The enter method counts up these three notifys. The remove method waits for at least one notify, then extracts an item, and decrements the count. Thus remove can be invoked three times. The fourth time we invoke it (on an empty queue) its wait will be executed.

Here is the text of the Queue class:

```
class Queue {
    private TextArea display;
    private String[] queue = new String[5];
    private int count = 0;

    public Queue(TextArea display) {
        this.display = display;
    }

    public synchronized void enter(String item) {
        queue[count] = item;
        count++;
        display();
        notify();
    }

    public synchronized String remove() {
        while (count == 0)
            try {
                wait();
            }
            catch (InterruptedException e) {
                System.err.println("Exception");
            }
        String item = queue[0];
        count--;
        for (int c = 0; c < count; c++)
            queue[c] = queue[c+1];
        display();
        return item;
    }

    private void display() {
        display.setText("QUEUE\n");
        for (int c = 0; c < count; c++)
            display.append(queue[c] + "\n");
    }
}
```

Now this program is not the simplest you may ever have seen, and sometimes it helps to check that it is OK with the following sort of reasoning.

Let us first consider what happens to the variable count. The variable count simply counts how many items there are in the queue:

- Initially there are 0 items in the queue.
- Method enter increments count.
- Method remove decrements count.

Now let us turn our attention to the methods. As far as method remove is concerned:

- If there is something in the queue, that is if count is greater than 0, it simply goes ahead and removes the item.
- If the queue is empty, that is if count is equal to 0, it must wait (using method wait) until such time as method enter releases it from the wait by doing a notify.

Note that wait and notify have no effect on the value of count. The relationship between wait and notify is that if one thread is waiting, notify wakes it up. If no thread is waiting, notify has no effect.

This completes our reasoning about the program, convincing ourselves that it works correctly. This helps because thread programs are notoriously difficult to debug and it is well worthwhile spending more time on checking.

As in an earlier program, you might think that it is more appropriate to use an if statement rather than a while, as follows (omitting the try clause for clarity):

```
if (count == 0)
    wait();
```

It is very tempting to write the program in this way, because the thread only has to wait if count == 0. However, this is an unsafe way to write programs of this kind. It might work sometimes, but it is much better to write a while loop. We will repeat the argument as follows. Suppose that there are a number of consumer threads rather than just one. In this case there are not, but it is better to write programs of this type on the assumption that there might be other threads around. Then at any time there might be several threads waiting for something to be placed in the empty array. They all have invoked wait and are suspended. Suppose that a thread is released from its wait and simply tries to remove a string from the array. It might just be that some other thread has intervened and removed the data. So it is better for a thread, once released, to check again that the data is available, using a while loop.

If using wait and notify seems difficult, you are right! You are not alone. Everyone finds it hard to get to grips with these methods and everyone has to think very hard and very clearly to use them properly.

We have now completed most of the café program. One thing that remains is the object (called complete) that handles the interaction between the user interface thread and the chef. We reuse the class Order for this purpose. The class Order acts as an intermediary between two threads, one of which passes a string to the other. We reuse it instead simply to pass the information that the meal is complete.

The chef thread loops forever and does the following:

1. removes an order from the queue (or waits until there is an order in the queue);
2. displays the order;
3. waits until the complete button is pressed;
4. erases the display of the order.

The coding for the Chef class is:

```
class Chef extends Thread{

    private TextField display;
    private Order complete;
    private Queue queue;

    public Chef(TextField display, Order complete, Queue queue) {
        this.display = display;
        this.complete = complete;
        this.queue = queue;
    }

    public void run() {
        display.setText("nothing is cooking");
        while (true) {
            String order = queue.remove();
            display.setText(order + " is cooking");
            String cookedInfo = complete.waitForEvent();
            display.setText("nothing is cooking");
        }
    }
}
```

We still have one matter to resolve. If there are a lot of orders the queue will become full. If the space available for the queue is very long, this will not happen very often, but we still have to cater for it. As the program is written, the method enter will simply try to place an order beyond the end of the queue array (which will result in an error). We can prevent this by providing a method as part of the Queue class that allows a user to ask whether the queue is full or not:

```
public synchronized boolean isFull(); {
    return count == queue.length;
}
```

and use this in the waiter thread:

```
if (!queue.isFull())
    queue.enter(newOrder);
```

Clearly, we will need to display a message to tell the user that this has happened. To sum up, the café consists of several threads that collaborate. Each thread produces some information, which it passes on to another thread. The interaction between threads is encapsulated within objects. Because these objects are accessing shared data items, the methods are marked as `synchronized`. If a thread has to wait for an order it invokes `wait`. If a thread needs to tell another that something has happened it invokes `notify`.

This producer–consumer scenario is very common in computer systems. Another example is a computer that controls a jukebox in a pub. The computer controls the record player and inputs requests from consoles distributed about the pub. The computer queues up requests from the consoles in a first-come, first-served manner in a software queue. Information is passed from a producer thread (that receives and queues up requests) to a consumer thread (that plays the records).

Because the producer–consumer scenario is so widely used, and because it is complicated and error-prone to program it using `wait` and `notify`, it is likely that higher-level methods for sending messages between threads will be available.

To summarize, a common situation in multithreading is where two or more threads collaborate to carry out some task. One thread creates some information to be passed onto a second. There is a need to communicate information and synchronize actions. This is entitled the producer–consumer situation. It can be programmed using an object that handles the communication between the threads. This object maintains the information that is passed from producer to consumer. It provides `synchronized` methods for the producer and the consumer to access the data. It causes the consumer to `wait` when there is no information and it causes the consumer to `notify` when it provides new information.

● Interruptions

Use of some of the methods associated with threads, `sleep` and `wait`, must provide an exception handler to deal with a possible `InterruptedException`. This exception will not arise unless deliberately programmed and so it can safely be ignored. An interruption is the situation where one thread wants to interrupt what another thread is doing. This could arise in the café program when an order is cancelled or it is the end of the day and time to shut the whole system down. A controlled closedown is desirable. To achieve this, one thread can interrupt another by invoking the method `interrupt`, for example:

```
chef.interrupt();
```

This has no effect on the thread, unless it is in the process of a `wait` or a `sleep`. But a thread can check to see whether it has been interrupted using the method `interrupted`. For example, a typical style of usage would be:

```
while (!interrupted()) {
    // continue
}
```

If a thread is in the course of performing a `wait` or a `sleep` and some other thread causes an interrupt, then an exception is created, and this can be handled by providing an exception handler in the usual way.

● Deadlock

In the early days of computers, some systems occasionally just 'seized up' – they seemed in a way to be running normally, but no actual work was being done. The only remedy was to switch the machine off and boot up again – not a very satisfactory solution. The cause was a mystery. Only later was it realized that the cause was deadlock.

One way of seeing how deadlock arises is to consider the famous dining philosophers problem. Figure 25.10 shows five philosophers seated at a table eating. Between each pair of philosophers is a single fork. Each philosopher alternately eats and thinks (forever). In order to eat, a philosopher needs to use both of the forks on either side of the plate. Normally this will be OK, but occasionally someone will have to wait for a fork that is being used by their neighbour.

But what happens when all the philosophers pick up their left fork? They all now have one fork and need the other. And they are all stuck. This is deadlock.

In a program, suppose that two threads each require intermittent access to the same two resources. The resources could be a file, the screen or whatever. Suppose that the sequences are:

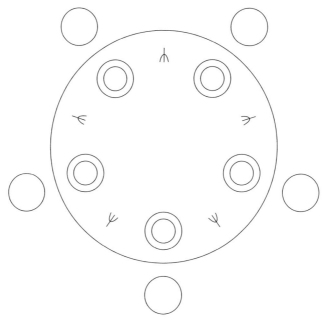

Figure 25.10 Dining philosophers.

Thread 1	Thread 2
`acquireResourceA();`	`acquireResourceB();`
`acquireResourceB();`	`acquireResourceA();`
`etc`	`etc`

Then if it should so happen that thread 1 is suspended just after it acquires resource A, and thread 2 is suspended just after it acquires resource B, then each thread will then have something that the other needs in order to proceed. Each will be held up forever; we have deadlock. (And it may not happen very often, but if it does it is a catastrophe.)

To sum up, we now have a new problem that may arise in multithreaded systems when threads interact or share resources.

We can't just ignore deadlock and hope it will never happen. The Java system does not help, unfortunately. It does not detect deadlock (and so it certainly does not solve the problem). The programmer has to ensure that it will not happen. There are several possible strategies. We will discuss only one – prevention.

In prevention, we design the system in such a way that we can guarantee that deadlock will never occur. One way to do this is to recognize that deadlock arises, not because of sharing but because of the *order* in which threads require resources. If all threads request the resources *in the same sequence*, deadlock cannot occur. So in the dining philosophers, if we number the forks from 1 to 5, and insist that philosophers only ever try to pick up forks according to that ordering, deadlock will never occur. We could put up a notice above the table, telling the philosophers to behave in this way. In a computer system, similarly, we could ensure during design that all threads access resources in the same sequence.

To summarize, deadlock is where two threads are stuck, each waiting for something that the other is holding.

● Designing multithreaded programs

There is one simple and pragmatic approach to designing programs that need multiple threads:

1. Use the design method described in Chapter 21 in order to identify classes and objects.
2. Analyse the application to see which activities need to be carried out in parallel.
3. Identify those objects that need to be threads.
4. Identify the nature of the interaction between the threads (independent, mutual exclusion, producer–consumer) and adopt the programming pattern appropriate to the situation.

So the overall approach is to model the application as objects and then to decide which of them are threads. Then handle any interaction between the threads.

This is a perfectly viable approach for small and medium programs. More elaborate methods are also available in the literature (beyond the scope of this book).

Programming principles

The main motivation for multithreading is the need to do two or more things at once. So a program is split up into parts that execute concurrently.

Concurrency is very common, both in real life and in computer systems. A parallel activity inside a computer is called a thread, task or sometimes a process. (Java uses the first term.) The code of each individual thread looks like a normal sequential program. The Java system shares out the processor time among the threads in such a way that it seems like they are all executing in parallel. This is sometimes called *apparent concurrency*. If two people are collaborating over a meal, or if a computer system consists of a number of processors, then there is *real concurrency*. Some computer scientists call apparent concurrency 'parallelism' and real concurrency simply 'concurrency'. Whatever the terminology we adopt, an essential characteristic of the situation is that the parallelism is explicitly in the hands of the programmer.

We can categorize the various common cases in which threads interact as follows:

● threads ignore each other, e.g. the bouncing balls;
● threads share data held in main memory, e.g. the counting threads;
● threads collaborate in a task, e.g. the café;
● threads compete for access to a resource, e.g. poets competing to use the screen.

Programming with threads requires care. We have considered a number of examples in this chapter. The general design principles are these:

1. If the threads do not interfere with each other, there is no problem.
2. If two or more threads access shared data (variables) in memory, place the data in an object. (You would probably do that anyway.) Label the methods within the object as `synchronized`. This will ensure that the data is properly maintained.
3. If threads need to coordinate their activities (as in the common producer–consumer scenario), use `wait` and `notify`, again within an object. These methods must be invoked from within methods that are `synchronized`. Invoking `wait` causes the thread to be suspended until some other thread executes a `notify` within the same object.

    `wait` and `notify` are almost always used in a standard pattern as follows. The thread that is waiting for some condition executes code that looks like this:

    ```
    synchronized void waitThenDo() {
        while (!condition)
            wait();
        // carry out the required task
    }
    ```

where `condition` is the condition that is awaited. The execution of `wait` causes this thread to be suspended. Another thread can then enter the same object, using one of the `synchronized` methods. This might be another thread that has to wait, or a thread that releases a waiting thread. The thread that notifies this thread that something has happened simply executes:

```
synchronized void tellTheOther() {
    notify();
}
```

If a number of threads are waiting within the same object, then only one thread is released from its wait. This is the thread that has been waiting longest.

Summary

- It is common in Java programs for two or more threads to run in parallel. Each thread looks like a normal sequential program. The scheduler shares the processor time among the threads that are ready to execute. The `start` method is used to set a new thread running. A thread object must be declared as extending class `Thread`, and must provide a method `run` that is executed when the thread is started.

- Strange, non-deterministic things can happen if two or more threads have un-controlled access to some shared variables. There is therefore a need for mutual exclusion, the situation where only one thread is permitted access at any one time. Mutual exclusion can be enforced by creating an object to look after the resource. This object accepts requests from client threads as method invocations that are labelled `synchronized`. Once a `synchronized` method is being used, no other thread can use it or any other `synchronized` method within the object. This ensures the correct behaviour of the threads.

- A second major scenario in parallel programming is where several threads col-laborate in some goal, passing information from one to another, like an assembly line. Each pair of threads is called a producer–consumer pair. An intermediary object between each pair facilitates the communication, by providing the necessary storage for messages. The intermediary object provides `synchronized` methods for entering information and for removing items. The client threads have to wait when necessary. The library method `wait` causes a thread to wait until some other thread executes an invocation of method `notify`.

- If care is not exercised during design, deadlock can occur in parallel programs. It can occur if two threads each acquire a resource which the other then requests.

EXERCISES

25.1 Clocks Write a program to show two clocks. One is an analogue clock, with an hour hand, minute hand and second hand. Draw the clock simply as a circle with simple lines for the hands. The other clock is a digital clock, showing hours, minutes and seconds as digits. Create a thread for each of the clocks. Each clock should sleep for 100 milliseconds, which is 1/10 second. The program can get the time by invoking library method currentTimeMillis(), which returns the current time in milliseconds as a long. (A millisecond is one thousandth of a second.) The time is measured from 1 January 1970 (the so-called epoch). It is called UTC (Coordinated Universal Time) and is essentially the same as Greenwich Mean Time (GMT).

25.2 Stopwatch Write a program that displays two buttons, labelled start and stop. When start is pressed, the program records the time. When stop is pressed, it displays the time that has elapsed since the start button was pressed. Display the time in seconds and tenths of a second. Use the library method currentTimeMillis (see Exercise 25.1) to get the time.

25.3 Reaction timer A program displays two buttons, labelled 'Start again' and 'Now'. When you press 'Start again', the program waits for a random time in the range 5 to 20 seconds. When a message 'Press Now' is displayed, you press 'Now' as quickly as you can. The program displays how long you took, in seconds and tenths of a second. A reaction time of 1/10 second is about as fast as you can ever hope to be. Use the library method currentTimeMillis (see Exercise 25.1) to get the time.

25.4 Breakout Breakout is a game shown in Figure 25.11. You can move the paddle left and right under the control of the mouse. A ball bounces off the paddle towards a wall of bricks. When the ball hits a brick it bounces off the brick, but

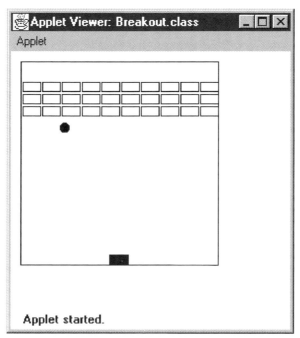

Figure 25.11 Screen layout for the Breakout game.

the brick is destroyed. When the ball breaks a hole in the wall, it can escape, or break out. In this case, you win. If you miss the ball with the paddle, it is lost. You get five balls. If you lose them all before breaking out, you lose.

A button labelled 'New Game' allows you to start again.

One thread is the ball. Another thread is the paddle. The third thread is the user interface.

25.5 The car park A car park has two entrances and two exits, each controlled by barriers. A transducer at the entrance detects the presence of a vehicle and tells the computer. If there is space in the car park it raises the barrier, issues a numbered ticket and records the time of arrival. On exit an attendant keys in the ticket number, notifying the computer that the car is leaving. The computer calculates the cost, displays it and raises the barrier. The computer also controls an illuminated sign on the entrance which displays 'FULL' or 'SPACES'.

Write a program that simulates the behaviour of a car park. Create four buttons that correspond to cars entering and leaving at the two entrances and two exits. Start by assuming that the car park can accommodate any number of cars. Then alter it so that the car park can only deal with 10 cars.

25.6 The clock Complete the coding of the clock program described in the text.

25.7 The café Suppose that the café described in the text has not one but two cooks. How do the threads need to be modified in order to cope? (Do not write any new code. Just work out what changes are necessary and, of course, make maximum reuse of existing classes.)

ANSWERS TO SELF-TEST QUESTIONS
····································

25.1 Extend the class that represents the ball and create an additional constructor method so that the position and size of the rectangle can be specified as parameters. Here is the new additional class:

```
class FlexiBall extends Ball {

    public FlexiBall(Graphics g,
            int rectLeftX, int rectRightX, int rectTopY,
                                    int rectBottomY) {
        this.g = g;
        this.rectLeftX = rectLeftX;
        this.rectRightX = rectRightX;
        this.rectTopY = rectTopY;
        this.rectBottomY = rectBottomY;
    }

}
```

Then rewrite the user interface class to create the two bouncing balls as follows:

```
import java.awt.*;
import java.applet.Applet;

public class TwoBouncers extends Applet {

    public void init() {
        Graphics g = getGraphics();

        Ball ball1 = new Ball(g);
        ball1.start();

        FlexiBall ball2 = new FlexiBall(g, 200, 300, 0, 100);
        ball2.start();
    }
}
```

25.2

```
import java.awt.*;
import java.applet.Applet;

public class Waiting extends Applet {
    public void init() {
        Graphics g = getGraphics();
        Clock clock = new Clock(g);
        clock.start();

        clock.join();
        g.drawString("All over", 40, 20);
    }
}

class Clock extends Thread {

    public void run() {

        for (int timeElapsed = 0; timeElapsed < 120;

timeElapsed++) {
            try {
                Thread.sleep(1000);
            }
            catch (InterruptedException e) {
                System.err.println("sleep exception");
            }
```

```
                        g.drawString(toString(timeElapsed), 20, 20);
                }
        }
}
```

25.3 We will add an additional button called status to the user interface, which can be pressed to give a status report on the ball thread. When this button is clicked, the following code within method action displays the appropriate message:

```
if (event.getSource() == status) {
    Graphics g = getGraphics();
    if (ball.isAlive())
        g.drawString("The ball is alive", 300, 20);
    else
        g.drawString("The ball is dead", 300, 20);
}
```

25.4
```
public void synchronized decrement() {
    n = n - 1;
}

public int synchronized getValue() {
    return n;
}

public void synchronized display() {
    g.drawString(n + ", ", x*20, 30);
    x++;
}
```

Programming in the large – packages

Introduction

Most of the programs shown in this book consist of only a few classes – five at most. In addition the programs use library classes. These are fairly small programs. With programs that consist of 20 to 30 classes or more, it is important to place the classes in groups. These groups are called *packages* (for the obvious reason that they are a package of classes). The library classes are already grouped into packages, for example `java.applet`, `java.awt` and `java.util`.

Packages are useful because they help cope with the complexity of a large program. This complexity is encountered when such a program is designed, when it is coded, when it is tested, when it is debugged and when it is altered after it has been in use. A package contains a group of classes that are related in some way. For example, a package could contain all the GUI parts of a program. Another package might contain the file-handling parts of the program. Finally, a third package might contain the classes that model the essence of the application that is being programmed. As an example of a library package, the package `java.awt` contains classes that provide methods to display buttons and draw graphical images and a wide range of facilities associated with displays on the screen.

If a program is sufficiently large that it must be written by a group of different programmers, packages provide the natural unit for dividing up the work.

Just as a class encapsulates related data and methods, so a package encapsulates a group of related classes. A class provides controlled access by other classes to its components and similarly a package provides selective access to its components.

● Packages and files

As we saw in an earlier chapter, it is usual practice in Java to place the source code of each class in a separate file. The filename should have a name derived from the class name. So if for example a class is called `Whizz`, it is stored in a file called `Whizz.java`. (When this file is compiled, a byte code file is created called `Whizz.class`.)

Each package is given a (meaningful) name by the programmer. The name of a package follows the same rules for names as variables, classes and methods. Remember that class names start with a capital letter, while variable and method names start with a lower-case letter. By convention, package names start with a lower-case letter.

The classes that make up a package are placed together in their own directory (folder). The directory name should be the same as the package name. The name of the package is given at the beginning of all the classes in a `package` statement. So, for example, if a package is called `useful`, all the classes that make up the package must be in a directory called `useful` and the statement:

```
package useful;
```

must appear as the first statement in each of the classes in the package.

SELF-TEST QUESTION
....

26.1 Classes called `Monday`, `Tuesday`, `Wednesday`, `Thursday`, `Friday`, `Saturday` and `Sunday` are grouped into a package called `week`. Name the files and the directory that are needed. Write down the `package` statements that are needed.

Most small programs, including all those shown in this book, do not use packages (other than the library packages). If a class has no `package` statement at its head, it is regarded as being in an *anonymous* package. For a small program, all the classes are usually written like this, with no `package` statements. The class files for such a program can either be stored together in a single file, or stored one per file in the same directory.

● Using packages and `import`

If another class wants to use a class called `Whizz` which is within a package called `useful`, it needs an `import` statement at its head:

```
import useful.Whizz;
```

Then the using class can invoke a static method called `doIt` within class `Whizz` like this:

```
Whizz.doIt();
```

If a class needs to use *all* the classes within `useful`, a shorthand declaration can be made:

```
import useful.*;
```

in which the * means *every* class within the package useful.

Remember that the package statement must appear first in the coding of a class. So a typical structure for the first few lines of a class to be placed in a package is:

```
package useful;
import java.awt.*;
import java.applet.Applet;
class Whizz {
    // contents of class Whizz

}
```

SELF-TEST QUESTION
....

26.2 Classes called Monday, Tuesday, Wednesday, Thursday, Friday, Saturday and Sunday are grouped in a package called week. Write down the import statement that will be needed to use the class Friday. Write the statement to create an object friday of the class Friday. Write down the import statement that will be needed to use all the classes in the package.

In general, a set of packages can be held in a number of directories (folders) in a tree-structured filing system such as is provided by UNIX and by Microsoft operating systems. For example, we could store useful within a directory called secret, which is in turn within a directory called projects. The name of the file containing the class Whizz is:

/projects/secret/useful/whizz.class on a UNIX system

or:

projects\secret\useful\whizz.class on a Microsoft system

and we would need a corresponding import statement to use class Whizz like this:

import projects.secret.useful.whizz;

This is the same on *any* system, because the slashes have been replaced by periods to ensure that the import statement is independent of the convention for directory (folder) names. The period notation also makes for a uniformity of naming that is consistent with the period in method invocation – objectName.methodName.

The names of all the Java library packages begin with the word java, for example the package java.applet. A library class can be used provided the appropriate import statement is used; for example, the class Applet can be used after the declaration:

import java.applet.Applet;

For convenience the particular library package java.lang is always automatically imported into every class, so no import is needed for it. This is because it contains classes vital to nearly every program, such as string handling and multithreading.

The `import` statement is a useful shorthand, and is, in fact, unnecessary. A class can always use the full name of a method or variable, instead of using a `package` statement. For example, the class `Date` in the package `java.util` can be used like this:

```
java.util.Date today = new java.util.Date();
int date = today.java.util.getDate();
```

which are quite cumbersome. Alternatively an `import` is normally used, which then allows the use of an abbreviated name for the class:

```
import java.util.Date;

...

Date today = new Date();
int date = today.getDate();
```

● Identifying packages

Grouping classes into packages is a task that should ideally be carried out at the design stage of programming. We have seen in Chapter 21 one approach to identifying the classes that are needed in a program. During design, it will be recognized that one class uses other classes. These in turn may use other classes. Such a group of classes are potential candidates for inclusion into their own package.

Often also during design it will be recognized that some classes are used by a number of different classes within the program. Such classes are like library classes, utility classes that have widespread application. They also are good candidates for inclusion into a distinct package. Remembering that reuse is central to OOP, it is recommended practice to design such utility packages not just for the immediate program, but for more general applicability for use in future programs.

There are no rules for how many classes to have in a package, but it would be usual to have between 2 and 12 classes per package. (Each class might in turn contain between 2 and 12 `public` methods.)

● Scope (visibility) rules for packages

Not only do packages allow classes to be logically grouped into convenient units, they also provide for closer control over accessibility to the class fields (usually methods). We have already met the descriptions `public` and `private` for methods and variables. We now introduce additional descriptions. Suppose that a class is in a particular package. Ranging from most to least accessible, the options for access to a variable or a method are:

1. `public` – accessible from anywhere;
2. `protected` – accessible from any class within this package and also from subclasses in other packages;
3. default (no description) – accessible from any class in this package;
4. `private` – accessible only from within this class.

As we have seen, in nearly all programs variables are declared as `private` and only methods are given the other labels. Occasionally a variable might be designated as having the default access, if it was extensively used by the classes within the package. For example, in a word processing program, the position of the cursor on the screen (the *x*- and *y*-coordinates) might be described as providing the default access in order to allow classes fast and convenient access to the values.

Summary

- A package is a grouping of related classes.

- A package is given a name. The rules for names are the same as for classes, methods and variables. A `package` statement at the head of a class names the package it belongs to.

- All the classes that make up a package are placed in the same directory (folder), but in different files. The directory name should be the same as the package name. Just as a class is in a file by itself (with a filename the same as the class), a package is in a directory by itself (with the same name as the package).

- An individual class within a package can be used by writing an `import package Name.Classname;` statement at the top of the using class.

- All the classes within a package can be used by writing an `import packageName.*;` statement at the top of the using class.

- The accessibility of variables and methods within the classes of a package can be controlled using the descriptor `protected` (the field is accessible from any class within this package and also from subclasses in other packages) and the default description (the field is accessible from any class in this package).

- The purpose of packages is to support writing medium-to-large programs. The library classes are in packages for this same reason.

EXERCISE

26.1 You will be unlikely to create your own packages unless you write programs that are larger than those given or suggested as exercises in this book. However, the library classes are grouped into packages. If you have a browser, browse the libraries. Alternatively consult Appendix B to see how library classes are arranged into packages.

ANSWERS TO SELF-TEST QUESTIONS

26.1 The files that are needed are:

```
Monday.java, Tuesday.java, Wednesday.java etc.
```

The compiled class files should be placed in a directory (folder) called week. The first line in each of the files should be:

```
package week;
```

26.2 To use the class Friday, we put:

```
import week.Friday;
```

To create an object of the class Friday, known as Friday, we put:

```
Friday Friday = new Friday();
```

To use all the classes in the package, we put:

```
import week.*;
```

Advanced object-oriented programming – abstract classes and interfaces

● Introduction

The design approach presented in Chapter 21 is a useful approach to identifying the classes and methods for a small-to-medium sized program. In this chapter we explore Java facilities that help simplify the design of programs – usually of medium to large size.

Advanced OOD is more concerned with identifying class structures and inheritances. So the goal of advanced design is to identify commonalities between classes that can be exploited by creating class hierarchies with inheritance. The overwhelming advantage of accomplishing this successfully is smaller programs. There are also valuable by-products like ease of reuse and maintainability.

This chapter is not for novices and presumes a good understanding of objects, classes and inheritance.

Two new Java facilities are described in this chapter – interfaces and abstract classes.

We have already seen – in most of the programs in this book – how interfaces are used by very simple programs as part of the mechanism for handling events from GUI components such as buttons, scrollbars and text boxes. It just so happens that interfaces are the neatest way for programs to deal with events. But we have postponed a full explanation of how interfaces work until a very late point in this book, because interfaces are normally regarded as a fairly advanced feature of programming.

● Abstract classes

There is a particular feature of Java which facilitates designing classes for reuse. This is the *abstract* class facility. Here is an example of an abstract class:

```
public abstract class Shape {

    protected int x, y, width, height;

    public void setX(int newX) {
        x = newX;
    }

    public void setY(int newY) {
        y = newY;
    }

    public void setWidth(int newWidth) {
        width = newWidth;
    }

    public void setHeight(int newHeight) {
        height = newHeight;
    }

    public abstract float getArea();
}
```

This class is part of a program that manipulates two-dimensional graphical objects on the screen. This program will manipulate a variety of graphical objects – including, for example, circles and rectangles. We can identify properties that all the shapes have in common – for example, the *x*- and *y*-coordinates of the top left of a rectangle that contains the shape, and the height and width of that rectangle. The class Shape describes these properties common to all of the shapes.

Some of the methods of the class are given in full – setX and setY. These are general-purpose methods that will be inherited and used by classes that represent all the shapes. The method getArea, however, will be peculiar to the particular shape because, for example, the area of a circle is calculated differently from the area of a rectangle. So the method getArea is not given in full. In fact only the heading of the method is given, preceded by the word abstract. This signifies that any class that inherits from this class must provide a proper implementation of a method getArea. The crime for disobeying this rule is simply that no object of the class Shape can be instantiated. Also, no object of a subclass can be created unless this abstract method is provided. To further confirm the situation, if a class contains a method declared as abstract the class itself must be declared as abstract.

A suitable use of the above abstract class is as follows. The class Rectangle inherits from the class Shape, overriding the method getArea:

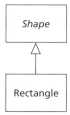

Figure 27.1 Class diagram showing an abstract class.

```
public class Rectangle extends Shape {

    public float getArea() {
        return height * width;
    }
}
```

In a UML class diagram, an abstract class is shown in the same way as any other class, except that its name is written in italics. Figure 27.1 shows the relationship between the classes Rectangle and Shape.

Declaring a class as **abstract** forces the programmer who is using the class (by inheritance) to provide the missing methods. This is a way, therefore, by which the designer of a class can enforce a particular design. The term 'abstract' is used for the following reason. As we look higher and higher up a class hierarchy, the classes become more and more general or abstract. In the example above, the class Shape is more abstract and less concrete than a Rectangle. The superclass abstracts features – like the position and size in this example – that are common between its subclasses. It is common in large OO programs to find that the top few levels of the class hierarchies consist of abstract methods. Similarly in biology, abstraction is used with classes like mammals, which do not exist (in themselves), but serve as abstract superclasses to a diverse set of subclasses. Thus we have never seen a mammal object, but we have seen a cow, which is an instance of a subclass of mammal.

SELF-TEST QUESTIONS

27.1 Write a class that extends (subclasses) class Shape to represent a circle.

27.2 Design a class hierarchy for three-dimensional shapes (cubes, spheres etc.). Make appropriate use of abstract classes.

27.3 Design an abstract class that describes the elements common to various different types of bank account. A checking account can go overdrawn, but no interest accumulates. Money can either be deposited or withdrawn from any type of account. An account is set up with an account number and a name.

● Interfaces

We have already seen (in many of the programs in this book) the use of interfaces, which can be recognized by the use of the word `implements` in a class heading. Now we complete the explanation of the interface mechanism. Java provides a notation for describing designs, called *interfaces*. An interface is just like the description of a class but with the bodies of the methods omitted. Do not confuse this use of the word 'interface' with the same word in GUI; here we are talking about the list of public methods provided by a class. An interface for the class `Balloon` is:

```
public interface Balloon {
    public void changeSize(int newDiameter);
    public void move(int newX, int newY);
    public void display(Graphics g);
}
```

Notice that the word `class` is omitted in an interface.

Only the method names and their parameters are described in an interface; the bodies of the methods are omitted. An interface describes a class, but does not say how the methods and the data items are implemented. It thus describes only the services provided by the class; it represents the outward appearance of a class as seen by users of the class (or an object instantiated from it). By implication it also says what the person who implements the class must provide.

An interface can be compiled along with any other classes, but clearly cannot be executed. But someone who is planning to use a class can compile the program along with the interface and thereby check that it is being used correctly. Anyone who has written a Java program knows that the compiler is extremely vigilant in finding errors that otherwise might cause mischievous problems when the program executes. So any checking that can be done at compile-time is most worthwhile.

A person who is implementing an interface class can specify in the heading of the class that a particular interface class is being implemented. So, for the above example, they can write the following as the heading for the class:

```
public class Spheroid implements Balloon
```

and the compiler will then check that this class has been implemented to comply with the interface declaration – that is, it provides the methods `changeSize`, `move` and `display`.

This is what happens when interfaces are used in event handling. For example, an applet that uses a button typically begins with the heading:

```
public class Elephant extends Applet implements ActionListener
```

which describes the commitment that this class will comply with the requirements of the interface `ActionListener` – for example, by providing a method `actionPerformed`, to be invoked when a button is pressed.

An interface is used to describe the external appearance of a class, its methods and parameters without describing the implementation of the class. The innards of such a class are absent. So an interface is merely a skeletal view of some class that is yet to be separately implemented. For example, the interface for a bank account class names an interface, the methods and their parameters, but it says nothing about how the class will be implemented. It provides a statement of what the class will provide as a service to its users, without saying how it will be provided. It also states what the class that implements the interface must provide.

SELF-TEST QUESTION
....

27.4 Write an interface to describe a class that will maintain information about a bank account. The constructor method for the class has two parameters – the account number and the account name. Other methods are `deposit`, which requires a single integer parameter, and a `withdraw` method, which requires a single integer. Finally, the method `getBalance` returns an integer.

So interfaces provide what is truly an interface between the users of a class and the provider of that class. Notice once more that the word `class` does not appear in an interface declaration.

Interfaces can easily be used to describe an inheritance structure. For example, suppose we wanted to describe an interface for a `Ball` type that is a subclass of the interface `Balloon` described above. We can write:

```
public interface Ball extends Balloon {
    public void setColour(Color c);
}
```

which extends the interface `Balloon` so that the interface `Ball` has an additional method to set the colour of an object. This now describes a new interface, called `Ball`. We could similarly describe a whole tree structure of classes as interfaces, describing purely their outward appearance and their subclass/superclass relationships.

In summary, interfaces can be used to describe:

● the classes in a program;
● the inheritance structure in a program, the is-a relationships.

What interfaces *cannot* describe are:

● the implementations of methods (this is the whole point of interfaces);
● which classes use which other classes, the has-a relationships (this needs some other notation).

One way to use interfaces is to carry out the design and write the interfaces for all the classes in a program before beginning the coding of implementation of the classes. Interfaces complement class diagrams (Chapter 21) as the documentation of a program's design.

Interfaces are useful for the design of small programs, but become particularly useful in medium-sized and large programs that make use of more than a few classes. In large programs that involve teams of programmers, their use is almost vital as a way of facilitating communication amongst the team members.

● Multiple inheritance and interfaces

Java is primarily a language that provides single inheritance – a class can inherit from (or be the subclass of) only one class. The class structure is a tree, with the root at the top, in which a class can have many subclasses but only one superclass. Figure 27.2 shows illustrative classes `Balloon` and `Game` as subclasses of superclass `Applet`, and classes `Animation` and `Banner` as subclasses of `Thread`. Each class appears only within a single tree and each class has only a single superclass. Sometimes we would like a class to inherit from more than one superclass, as described in the following class header and shown in Figure 27.3.

```
public class Game extends Applet, Thread // error
```

But this heading is wrong because it attempts to extend two classes. This would be called *multiple inheritance*. Some languages, such as C++, permit multiple inheritance, but Java does not. Multiple inheritance allows a class to inherit sets of methods from a number of classes, and it is therefore potentially very powerful.

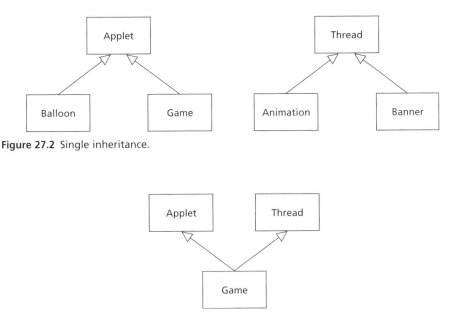

Figure 27.2 Single inheritance.

Figure 27.3 Multiple inheritance.

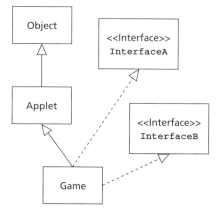

Figure 27.4 Multiple inheritance using interfaces.

If we think about classification systems in science and nature, it is often the case that objects belong to more than one class. We humans, for example, belong to one gender class, but also to a class that likes a particular type of music. So we all belong in one inheritance tree for gender, another for musical taste, another for mother tongue and so on.

Java was designed to be a simple (but powerful) language and so permits only single inheritance – a class can only inherit from one superclass. This avoids several of the confusions of multiple inheritance, which we will not discuss here.

There is, however, a way of emulating a facility similar to multiple inheritance in Java by using interfaces. Earlier in this chapter we explained the use of interfaces as a way of describing a design. In addition to their role in documenting a program, interfaces can also be used to provide a form of multiple inheritance. This is because, while a class can only extend a single class, it can implement any number of classes.

This is illustrated in Figure 27.4, in which interfaces are headed by <<interface>>. A dotted (or dashed) line means 'implements'. This is coded as follows:

```
class Game extends Applet implements InterfaceA, InterfaceB
```

If `Game` was inheriting from `InterfaceA` and `InterfaceB`, it would inherit a set of methods from `InterfaceA` and `InterfaceB`. But instead `Game` is implementing interfaces `InterfaceA` and `InterfaceB`. And `InterfaceA` and `InterfaceB` have no methods on offer. What it does mean is that class `Game` agrees to provide the interfaces described in `InterfaceA` and `InterfaceB`. This means that `Game` has agreed to conform to certain behaviour. The code for implementing `InterfaceA` and `InterfaceB` has to be written as part of the class `Game`.

As an example, we will consider the software to run all the devices in a modern household – the TV, stereo, kitchen equipment and so on. We will first create some classes that describe the different types of equipment. We will group them into the classes `Entertainment`, `Cleaning` and `Cooking`. As usual in a design of any size, these will be abstract classes that specify the implementation of some of the methods and specify only the existence of some other methods. Here, for example, is the class `Entertainment`:

```
abstract class Entertainment {
    protected int volume;
    private boolean on;

    public void switchOn() {
        on = true;
    }

    public void switchOff() {
        on = false;
    }

    public abstract void changeVolume(int amount);

    public abstract void display(Graphics g);
}
```

Methods `switchOn` and `switchOff` are implemented. Any class that extends `Entertainment` need not implement them (but may override them). However, methods `changeVolume` and `display` *must* be implemented by any extending class. For example, we could declare a class `TV` as follows:

```
class TV extends Entertainment {

    private int channel;

    public void changeVolume(int amount) {
        volume = volume + amount;
    }

    public void display(Graphics g) {
        g.fillRect(10, 10, 10, volume);
    }
}
```

This is clearly a simplification because we need, at least, a method to change the TV channel. But it illustrates what we are about to explain.

SELF-TEST QUESTION
....

27.5 Write a method as part of the class `TV` to enable the channel number to be changed.

The other abstract classes `Cleaning` and `Cooking` can be written in a similar manner, and classes `Vacuum`, `Toaster`, `Oven` etc., written as subclasses. This is an excellent structure for the program.

Suppose now that we want to write a class called `ElectricityManager` and an instance of this called `electricityManager`. This object has the responsibility of maintaining a record of how much electricity is consumed in the household. Now some of the devices in the household will be electrical, and some will use other power sources – like gas or batteries. This is a case where an appliance is a member of a class `Entertainment`, `Cleaning` and `Cooking`, but is also potentially an instance of another class – `Electricity` or `Gas`. We can resolve this problem using interfaces. We make sure that any appliance that uses electricity provides certain methods that can be used by the `electricityManager` to carry out its calculations. These methods are:

● `setTimeInUse`, to initialize the time for which the appliance is switched on to some value (usually zero);
● `getTimeInUse`, to obtain the total time that the appliance has been in use;
● `getPower`, to return the power consumption of the device, for example 100 watts.

We can specify these requirements as an interface that any electrical device class must provide:

```
interface ElectricalDevice {
    public void setTimeInUse(int time);
    public int getTimeInUse();
    public int getPower();
}
```

And now we must go back and enhance the heading of class `TV`:

```
class TV extends EntertainmentDevice implements ElectricalDevice
```

Having made this declaration, we must actually provide implementations of the methods `setTimeInUse`, `getTimeInUse` and `getPower` within the class `TV`. These are:

```
public void setTimeInUse(int time) {
    this.time = time;
}

public int getTimeInUse() {
    return time;
}

public int getPower() {
    return 100;
}
```

and we need also to alter `switchOn` and `switchOff` to maintain a count, `time`, of the time that the TV is switched on.

Now let us see how `electricityManager` is used:

```
electricityManager.calcPower(tv1);
electricityManager.calcPower(stereo);
electricityManager.calcPower(tv2);
```

The object `electricityManager` has a method `calcPower` that calculates the power consumed by the object passed to it as its parameter. The `electricityManager` adds this consumption to its total electricity consumption. Here is an outline of part of the `ElectricityManager` class:

```
class ElectricityManager {

    private int totalPower;

    public void calcPower(ElectricalDevice device) {
        int power = device.getTimeInUse() * device.getPower();
        totalPower = totalPower + power;
        device.setTimeInUse(0);
    }

}
```

Notice that the type of the parameter that can be passed to `calcPower` is `Electrical-Device`, the name of the interface. This stipulates that this parameter must be an object that accords with this interface – any such object must provide the methods `getTime-InUse`, `getPower` and `setTimeInUse`. This restricts the type of object that can be passed to this method – as is always the case when using parameters. Moreover, as usual, the compiler can check that the method is being used correctly.

To sum up, this example illustrates how an interface can be used to specify a particular behaviour of a class (object). It then allows objects with this behaviour to be used as parameters for appropriate methods.

This mechanism is used for Java event handling, as illustrated by nearly all the example programs in this book. Suppose, for example, that a program uses a button. In this case the object that handles the event must be declared as:

```
class ButtonProgram implements ActionListener
```

so as to comply with the interface `ActionListener`. This means it must include a method called `actionPerformed`. The program creates the button object:

```
Button button = new Button("caption");
```

and then passes the current object, `this`, to the button object as a parameter:

```
button.addActionListener(this);
```

The button object now knows which object to invoke when a button event occurs and it can confidently invoke method `actionPerformed` within the object.

There is a final useful feature of interfaces – a variable can be declared to be of an interface type. For example:

```
ElectricalDevice e;
```

And we can assign any object that is an instance of a class that implements the interface `ElectricalDevice` to this variable. For example, we have already discussed a class `TV` which implements `ElectricalDevice`:

```
class TV extends EntertainmentDevice implements ElectricalDevice
```

So if we create an instance `tv1` of class `TV`:

```
TV tv1 = new TV();
```

we can then assign this object to an object of type `ElectricalDevice`:

```
ElectricalDevice e = tv1;
```

and invoke the methods specified in the interface. For example:

```
e.setTimeInUse();
```

This mechanism is used with audio clips as described in Chapter 20. The library component `AudioClip` is an interface. But we can declare a variable of this type, create an object and assign a value to it:

```
AudioClip sound = getAudioClip(getDocumentBase(), "sound.au");
```

and then invoke a method of the object:

```
sound.play();
```

We will now consider a second example of using an interface. Suppose that we want to write a method `largest` that finds the largest item in an array. This is a simple enough task. But we are ambitious because we want the method to work on an array that contains any type of data – integers, strings or any type of object. (This is a classic test of how well a programming language can demonstrate its power.)

The way to succeed in writing this method is to advertise the fact that it will work with data of any type, provided that the data conforms to a specified behaviour. The required behaviour is that the data type (the class that supports the type) provides a method called `greaterThan` to allow values to be compared. This method is to be invoked like this:

```
x.greaterThan(y)
```

and returns a boolean value. Now, the way to ensure that a class provides a particular method is to insist that it conforms to a particular interface. The way to do this is to declare an interface called (say) `Sortable`:

```
interface Sortable {
    public boolean greaterThan(Sortable y);
}
```

and legislate that any data that is supplied to the method `largest` must implement this interface. If we now assume that this method is always available, we can write method `largest` to find the largest value in the array:

```
public Sortable largest(Sortable[] array) {
    Sortable biggest = array[0];
    for(int s = 1; s < array.length; s++)
        if(array[s].greaterThan(biggest)) biggest = array[s];
    return biggest;
}
```

Note how this method makes use of the method `greaterThan` to compare values of the objects. Note also how it only accepts data of the type `Sortable`.

Finally, any user of this method must ensure that the objects in the array provide the method `greaterThan`. So if we declare, for example, a class `BankAccount`, and we want to make use of method `largest`, we must ensure that it implements `Sortable`:

```
public class BankAccount implements Sortable {

    public boolean greaterThan(Sortable y) {
        // code to implement this method
    }

    // other methods of the class BankAccount

}
```

Thus we have used an interface to force compliance to a particular behaviour. The same class, `BankAccount`, could be made to conform to other interfaces, so that it can use other general-purpose classes and methods. Thus a kind of multiple inheritance is at work.

● Interfaces versus abstract classes

Interfaces and abstract classes can be confusingly similar. The differences are as follows:

1. An abstract class can provide an implementation of one or more methods. An interface provides *no* implementation.
2. A class can implement *more than one* interface, but only extend (inherit from) *one* abstract class.
3. An interface is something that is used by the compiler at *compile-time* to perform checking. By contrast, an abstract class implies inheritance, which involves linking of the appropriate method at *run-time*.
4. An abstract class implies that its abstract methods will be fleshed out by classes that extend it; inheritance is expected. But an interface simply specifies the skeleton for a class, without any implication that it will be used for inheritance. (However, an interface can specify inheritance.)

Programming pitfalls

Remember that:

● A class can only extend one other class, including an `abstract` class.
● A class can implement any number of interfaces.

New language elements

● `interface` – the description of the external interface to a class which may not yet be written;
● `implements` – used in the header of a class to specify that the class implements a named interface;
● `abstract` – a class that contains at least one `abstract` method, i.e. a method that is not implemented in the class, but which must be implemented by any subclass.

Summary

● Interfaces can be used to describe the services provided by classes and the inheritance structure of classes. Interfaces are useful for describing designs and have the advantage of being checkable by the Java compiler.

● Abstract classes encourage the use of class hierarchies and inheritance by enabling the description of the structure of superclasses that extract the common features of a number of subclasses.

● Interfaces can also provide a kind of multiple inheritance feature, which allows general-purpose methods and classes to be written.

● Together with packages (described in Chapter 26), the abstract class and interface features of Java provide all the necessary facilities to carry out the construction of large-scale object-oriented programs.

EXERCISES

Interfaces as design descriptions

27.1 Use interfaces to describe the design of the following program. The program displays a spaceship as a graphical image on the screen. The spaceship can be moved using buttons to move it left, right, up and down. The program consists of two classes. The first is the user interface that provides the usual applet methods `init` and `paint`, together with the event handling method `action`.

The second class represents a spaceship object and provides methods to create an object, display it and move it 20 pixels in each direction.

27.2 Use interfaces to describe the bandit program, designed in Chapter 21.

27.3 Use interfaces to describe one of the more complex programs given in this book, for example the café program presented in Chapter 25.

Abstract classes

27.4 Write an abstract class to describe two-dimensional graphical objects (square, circle, rectangle, triangle etc.) which have the following properties. All such objects share integer variables that specify the x- and y-coordinates of the top-left of a bounding rectangle, the height and the width. All the objects share the same methods setX and setY to set the values of these coordinates. All the objects share methods setWidth and setHeight to set the values of the width and height of the object. All the objects have a method getArea which returns the area of the object and a method display which displays it , but these methods are different depending on the particular object.

27.5 All bank accounts have a constructor method that has as parameters the name and account number. All accounts permit deposit and withdrawal of money and a method to get the current balance. Deposit accounts do not allow overdrafts, but current accounts do. For current accounts, provide a method to set the overdraft limit. Deposit accounts provide a method to calculate the interest due at a particular date. Write an abstract class to describe both types of bank account.

27.6 A three-dimensional drawing package supports three kinds of objects – cube, sphere and cone. All have a position in space, defined by x-, y- and z-coordinates. Each has a size, defined by a height, width and depth. Every object provides a method to move the object from the origin to a position in space. Every object provides a method to rotate it around the x-, y- and then z-axes. All the objects provide a method to display themselves. Write an abstract class to describe these three-dimensional objects.

Interfaces as a kind of multiple inheritance

27.7 Complete the coding of the household management system, with appliances tv1, tv2, stereo and toaster.

ANSWERS TO SELF-TEST QUESTIONS

27.1
```
public class Circle extends Shape {

    public float getArea() {
        return (Math.PI * width * width);
    }

    public void setHeight(int newHeight) {
        width = newHeight;
    }
}
```

27.2
```
public abstract class ThreeD {

    protected int x, y, z, width, height, depth;

    public void setX(int newX) {
        x = newX;
    }

    public void setY(int newY) {
        x = newY;
    }

    public void setZ(int newZ) {
        z = newZ;
    }

    public void setWidth(int newWidth) {
        width = newWidth;
    }

    public void setHeight(int newHeight) {
        height = newHeight;
    }

    public void setDepth(int newDepth) {
        depth = newDepth;
    }

    public abstract float getVolume();
}
public class Cuboid extends ThreeD {
```

```
            public float getVolume {
                return height * width * depth;
            }
        }
27.3    public abstract class Account {

            protected int balance, interest;
            protected String name;
            protected int number;

            public void setName(String newName) {
                name = newName;
            }

            public void setNumber(int newNumber) {
                number = newNumber;
            }

            public int getBalance() {
                return balance;
            }

            public void deposit(int amount) {
                balance = balance + amount;
            }
        }
27.4    public interface Account {
            public Account(int number, String name);
            public void deposit(int amount);
            public void withdraw(int amount);
            public int getBalance();
        }
27.5    public void changeChannel(int newChannel) {
            channel = newChannel;
        }
```

Polymorphism

Introduction

Polymorphism is the third of the three fundamental pillars of OOP. (The other two are encapsulation and inheritance.) But before we look at polymorphism we first need to understand the idea of casting. We also need to look more closely at the nature of objects.

Casting is all about assigning an object of one class to a variable declared as an object of another class. This sounds like changing an object from one class to another – but, as we shall see, it isn't.

As examples to illustrate casting and polymorphism, here are several classes that we will use in this chapter. There is a superclass `Animal` and three subclasses of `Animal` – `Cow`, `Pig` and `Snake`.

```
class Animal {
    private int weight = 0;

    public void setWeight(int initWeight) {
        weight = initWeight;
    }

    public int getWeight() {
        return weight;
    }

    public String says() {
        return "Animals can't talk!";
    }
}
```

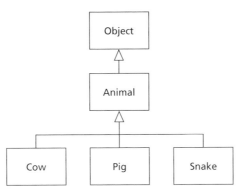

Figure 28.1 Class diagram for the various animal classes

```
class Cow extends Animal {
    public String says() {
        return "Moo";
    }
}

class Pig extends Animal {
    public String says() {
        return "Grunt";
    }
}

class Snake extends Animal {
}
```

We will use the class diagram in Figure 28.1 to illustrate the relationships between the classes. The diagram reminds us that `Object` is implicitly the superclass of any class that does not say it extends something.

● Casting the built-in types

Some types of data are built into the Java language. These types are `byte`, `short`, `int`, `long`, `float`, `double` and `boolean`. The language provides these data types as readymade building blocks for the programmer to use. The programmer can also group together variables of these types to create objects as necessary. Variables of the built-in types are not objects and they are not created with the `new` keyword. Casting is concerned with converting data into a different type and we have already met the idea much earlier in this book. For example, consider converting an `int` variable into a `float` variable. To do this we need to be aware that the numeric built-in types vary in size as follows:

double	64 bit floating point number
float	32 bit floating point number
long	64 bit integer
int	32 bit integer
short	16 bit integer
byte	8 bit integer

If we do this:

```
byte x;
int y = x;
```

we are asking Java to put something smaller (8 bits) into something larger (32 bits). There is plenty of space and therefore there is no problem. However if, for example, we need to place a `double` into an `int`, we are placing something bigger (64 bits) into something smaller (32 bits). Java makes us spell out that we are aware that something might go wrong:

```
double d = 123.456;
int i = (int) d;
```

This is termed 'casting' and the casting operator is the type of the destination type written in brackets.

Casting the built-in types of Java is different from casting objects; built-in data is *changed* by casting. In the above example, the value of the variable i becomes 123, converted from the value 123.456. In contrast, as we shall shortly see, when casting is used with objects, something very different happens.

● References

When an object is created using `new`, space is allocated to it in memory. For example, take the statement:

```
Cow daisy = new Cow();
```

As we have seen, this creates an instance of the class `Cow` and assigns it to the variable `daisy`. A variable, such as `daisy` doesn't actually contain an object – instead it holds a pointer to the object. This pointer is known as a *reference*. So, in this example, the variable `daisy` contains a reference to a `Cow` object. Most of the time when we discuss these ideas, we can be less long-winded and simply say that the variable contains the object. Sometimes, however, we need to be more aware about what actually goes on.

One way of visualizing a reference is as a memory address. Remember that when an object is created, space is created in the computer memory to hold information about the object, including most importantly the values of the variables within the object. We can think of a reference as being the numerical address of the region in memory where the object is held.

Notice that there is only ever one unique copy of an object, though there may be several references to it. This helps understand why an object always retains its original identity. For example, suppose we do this:

```
Cow daisy = new Cow();
```

and then:

```
Cow alice = daisy;
```

What does this second assignment mean? We now know that a variable holds a reference to an object (which can be thought of as a pointer to the object). So the assignment statement copies the reference (pointer). Thus after the assignments, `daisy` and `alice` both contain a reference to the same object. Note the difference from built-in types. If we copy an integer, for example, the value of the integer itself is copied into the destination variable.

SELF-TEST QUESTION
....

28.1 Decide which cow is heavier after the following sequence of instructions:

```
Cow daisy = new Cow();
Cow betty = daisy;
daisy.setWeight(800);
betty.setWeight(900);
```

Finally, what does it mean to test for the equality of two objects, as in the following statement:

```
if (betty == daisy) …
```

The `==` operator tests whether the two references are equal, that is whether they refer to the same object.

SELF-TEST QUESTION
....

28.2 What happens to the value of the variable `same` in the following sequence of instructions?

```
boolean same = false;
Cow daisy = new Cow();
Cow betty = new Cow();
if (betty == daisy)
    same = true;
daisy = betty;
if (betty == daisy)
    same = true;
```

● Casting objects

What happens if you try to assign an object of one class to a variable of another class? It isn't immediately obvious that this is either necessary or legal. Java is, after all, a *strongly-typed* language in which data of different types has to be carefully declared. Each object, derived from a particular class, can only be used for specific purposes – those declared as part of the class description. Moreover the compiler keeps a vigilant eye on what the programmer does. For example if we declare:

```
Button button = new Button();
```

we can't use a method of some other class, for example:

```
button.setWeight(100); // is illegal
```

and the compiler will signal it as an error. However, there are occasional, but vital, programming situations where it is necessary to assign an object of one class to a variable of another class. For example, using the animal classes declared above, we can write:

```
Cow daisy = new Cow();
Animal animal = daisy;
```

in which an object `daisy` of the class `Cow` is assigned to a variable `animal` belonging to the class `Animal`. Looking at the class diagram makes it obvious that this assignment moves the object `daisy` *up* the hierarchy. As we will see shortly, this is valid and will work.

However, the general advice on doing this kind of thing (assigning an object to a variable of a different class) is:

1. If you do it, think carefully about why are you doing it.
2. If you do it, be careful.

Changing the class of an object is on a par with a human being changing their genes. Your genes are fundamental, and you can never change them. But you can change your name – although you might not do it very often and it is not something to be undertaken lightly. But sometimes you need to do it.

In OO programming there is a fundamental rule that, whatever happens to it, an object always retains the identity of the class from which it was created. Using the human analogy, even if you change your name, you remain the same person – your genes do not change. So there is always a valid set of methods that can be applied to a particular object, and this set of methods is determined at the time when the object is created from a particular class using `new`.

The rules for assigning objects are:

1. You cannot move something *across* the class hierarchy.
2. You can move something *up* the tree without problems.
3. You can move something *down* the tree, but you must be explicit and use *casting*.

In brief, here are the respective reasons for these rules:

1. If you consider the (illegal) act of moving across the tree, then the methods associated with the destination class are almost certainly not valid or may be absent. In the above example you can't assign an object of class `Cow` to a variable of class `Snake`. This makes sense because there are fundamental differences between these two classes – a cow can talk, but a snake cannot talk. A `Cow` is not a `Snake`.
2. If you move something up the tree, the methods provided by the superclass are valid. In the example, every `Cow` object (say `daisy`) is an `Animal`.
3. If you move from a superclass to a subclass, down the tree, you are moving to an arena where there may be additional methods – which might not be valid for the object. In the example, every `Animal` object (say `animal`) is not a `Pig` – though some are. So you have to be careful when you do this – and Java forces us to be careful by making us use casting.

Let us examine each of these in more detail. First, moving an object across the class hierarchy would be an attempt to move an object into a variable of a different class, which may have different methods from the original class. This is contrary to the spirit of strong typing, which is a feature of Java. Strong typing means that when an object is declared it has a precise type, defined by its class. Further, only the methods defined by that class (or its superclasses) are valid for use with the object.

Next we will look at moving up the tree. It is valid to assign a reference to an instance of a subclass to a variable which has the type of any of its superclasses higher up the inheritance tree. For example:

```
Animal animal = daisy;
```

(The class diagram helps us see that class `Cow` is a subclass of `Animal`.) The object `daisy` is an instance of the class `Cow`, but now it is assigned to a variable of class `Animal`. The variable `animal` now refers to a `Cow` object – but remember also that `daisy` remains a `Cow`. The terminology is a little misleading – a superclass has less functionality than a subclass. Remember that a subclass *extends* some class, providing additional variables and methods. So when you assign an object reference to a variable of a superclass, all the methods of the superclass are guaranteed to work Nothing can go wrong.

The opposite is not true; an instance of a superclass cannot be assigned to a variable that has the type of a subclass. This is demotion down the inheritance tree, assigning an object of a class higher up the tree to a variable of a class lower down the tree. Thus the following is wrong and is flagged as an error by the compiler:

```
Cow daisy = animal; // not allowed
```

The reason for this restriction is as follows. A subclass usually provides methods additional to those in its superclass. (This is, after all, the purpose of extending a class.) These methods simply are not applicable to an object of the superclass. If such a method in the subclass were to be invoked, a catastrophic error might occur. Luckily, the compiler helps the programmer to avoid this occurrence. For example, suppose class `Snake` has an additional method:

```
class Snake extends Animal {

    public String shedSkin() {
        return "shedding skin";
    }
}
```

Then the sequence:

```
Animal animal = new Animal();
Snake snake = animal;
String text = snake.shedSkin();
```

would probably not be what was intended, because it implies that it is valid for all animals (cows, pigs, etc.) to shed their skin. And, in fact, the compiler would find fault with the second statement in this sequence.

One of the features of Java is that it helps write robust programs. This is one case where the compiler detects that the programmer may be trying to do something that is unsafe.

It is however possible to move objects down the class hierarchy, provided that the programmer does it deliberately and explicitly using *casting*. The name of the destination class is put in brackets like this:

```
Pig piggy = (Pig) animal;
```

Remember that when this happens, the object `animal` is not converted to a `Pig`. Instead, the reference to `animal` is copied into the variable `piggy`. Casting means explicitly changing the type of the variable in which a reference to an object is stored. It forces the programmer to be explicit about what he or she is doing. But the programmer should only do it when they know for certain that the destination is valid.

Remember that this operation will only be valid, and allowed by the compiler, provided that object `animal` belongs to a class which is the superclass of `Pig`. This is another example of how the Java language helps the programmer to avoid making mistakes.

SELF-TEST QUESTION
....

28.3 Write code to assign the object `animal` of type `Animal` to a variable of type `Snake`.

In summary, an object (once created) retains its fundamental identity, whatever is done to it. An analogy is, if you are born English, you stay English even if you go to live in the USA. If you place an object in a variable of a different type, the object can only be assigned to a variable whose class is a superclass of the object or a subclass of the object.

In other words, things are kept strictly in the family. But to move something down the tree, you must use explicit casting. Casting of objects is not a common thing to do, but when it is needed, it is vital. (Very few of the programs in this book use it.)

Java is a strongly-typed language, which means that checks are carried out at every opportunity to ensure that data is used properly. However, Java is also a strongly *statically* typed language, which means that many checks are carried out at compile time. The Java compiler will always detect the following errors:

● assignment across the inheritance tree;
● assignment down the inheritance tree without proper casting;
● invoking a method that is not valid for the named class.

At *run time*, the following checking is carried out:

● assignment down the inheritance tree, when the object is not an instance of the destination class. This produces a `ClassCastException` when the program is running.

Casting is only necessary in special circumstances because, as we shall shortly see, polymorphism can usually be relied upon to make sure that the method appropriate to the object is always invoked. The only occasion on which casting is necessary is when it is necessary to invoke a method that is unique to the subclass. For example:

```
Snake snake = (Snake) animal;
String text = snake.shedSkin();
```

Since the method `shedSkin` is unique to the class `Snake`.

● instanceof **and casting**

The Java keyword `instanceof` allows a program using an object to find out which class the object belongs to. For example, the GUI event handler method `actionPerformed` is invoked both when button events occur and when the enter key is pressed in a text field. Suppose that we want to write a method `handleButtons` that handles all the button events and a method `handleTextFields` to handle text field events. Luckily the library method `getSource` returns an object of type `Object` that caused the event. Then we can use the Java keyword `instanceof` to distinguish between the two sets of events:

```
public void actionPerformed(ActionEvent event) {
    if (event.getSource() instanceof TextField)
        handleTextFields(event);
    if (event.getSource() instanceof Button)
        handleButtons(event);
}
```

Here is a second example. In a program that manipulates graphical objects, it might be necessary to test to see which particular object is in use at a particular time. Suppose that the program is using a variable `shape` to hold the object currently in use. Then we can write

```
if (shape instanceof Triangle) ...
if (shape instanceof Circle) ...
```

to ascertain what kind of object is in use – and process it appropriately.

As a final example, the `instanceof` operator can be used to check whether a cast will be valid. When a running program carries out a casting operation, the Java system checks that the cast is valid. The class of the receiving variable must match the class of the object. If they do not match, the run-time error `ClassCastException` is created and the program is terminated. To avoid this disastrous situation we can write:

```
if (animal instanceof Snake) {
    Snake sid = (Snake) animal;
    String text = sid.shedSkin();
}
```

Here we have checked that the animal object is indeed a snake before casting it.

Thus the operator `instanceof`, a Java keyword, allows a program to test to see which class an object belongs to.

Note the spelling of the word `instanceof`, which breaks the normal rule for naming in Java. (Usually the second word starts with a capital letter.)

● Polymorphism

We will now use the animal classes again, this time constructing a complete small program that uses them. We will create an instance of `Cow` named `daisy` and an instance of `Pig` named `wilber`. We will also declare a variable named `animal` of type `Animal`.

```
import java.awt.*;
import java.applet.Applet;

public class Farmyard extends Applet {
    public void init() {
            Pig wilber = new Pig();
            Cow daisy = new Cow();

            Animal animal;
            String talk;

            animal = daisy;
            talk = animal.says();
            add(new Label(talk));

            animal = wilber;
            talk = animal.says();
            add(new Label(talk));
    }
}
```

Figure 28.2 Output from the Farmyard program.

Running this program gives the output shown in Figure 28.2. You can see that the two identical invocations of `says`:

```
animal.says();
```

give two different outputs. This is not necessarily what you might expect, but it is entirely correct. Two different outputs are displayed because the Java system automatically selects the version of `says` associated with the class of the object (not the class of the variable that refers to it). The class of an object is determined when the object is created using `new`, and stays the same whatever happens to the object. When method `says` is first invoked, the variable `animal` contains the object `daisy` and so the version of `says` in the class `Cow` is invoked. The corresponding thing happens with `wilber`.

This feature is called *polymorphism*, which is a big term for an obvious idea. When you invoke a method, polymorphism makes sure that the appropriate version of the method is automatically selected. Most of the time when you program in Java you are not aware that the Java system is selecting the correct method to invoke. It is all automatic and invisible.

The rule is that the method that is invoked on an object is always the method belonging to the class of the object. Remember that the class of the object is determined when the object is created using `new`. Whatever you do to an object in a program, it always retains the properties it had when it was created. In the family analogy, you retain your identity and your relationship with your ancestors whether you get married, change your name, move to another country or whatever. This seems common sense, and indeed it is.

Polymorphism allows us to write a single statement such as:

```
animal.says();
```

instead of a series of `if` statements like this:

```
if(animal == daisy)
    talk = daisy.says();
if(animal == wilber)
    talk = wilber.says();
```

which is clumsy and long-winded. If there were a significant number of animals, there would be a correspondingly large number of `if` statements. This demonstrates how powerful and concise polymorphism is.

As we have seen in this small example, polymorphism often makes a segment of program smaller and neater through the elimination of a series of if statements. But this achievement is much more significant than it may seem. It means that a statement like:

```
animal.says();
```

knows nothing about the possible variety of objects that may be used as the value of animal. So information hiding (already present in large measure in an OO program) is extended. We can check this out by assessing how much we would need to change this segment of program to accommodate some new type of animal (some additional subclass of Animal), say a cat; the answer is that we would not need to modify it at all. Thus polymorphism enhances modularity, reusability and maintainability.

To summarize, the rules for polymorphism are:

1. An object always retains the identity of the class from which it was created. (An object can never be converted into an object of another class.)
2. When a method is invoked on an object, the method associated with the class of the object is always used.

An object can be assigned to a variable of another class and passed around the program as a parameter, but it never loses its true identity. 'Once a pig, always a pig' might be an appropriate slogan. So, as we have seen, in the above program fragment, the appropriate method is always selected. When this happens:

```
animal.says();
```

the version of the method says that matches the actual object is selected. This can only be decided when the program is running, immediately before the method is invoked. This is termed *late binding, dynamic linking* or *delayed binding*. It is an essential feature of a language that supports polymorphism.

You can pass an object around a program (either by assigning it to other variables or by passing it as a parameter) but you can only invoke methods that are valid for the object. The vigilant type checking of the Java compiler polices this. Thus obvious errors like:

```
String text = daisy.shedSkin();
```

are flagged because the class Cow from which daisy is created does not have a method shedSkin.

There are, however, more subtle pitfalls. Suppose we write an additional method milk for the class Cow:

```
public String milk() {
    return "milking in progress";
}
```

Then we write:

```
Cow daisy = new Cow();
Animal animal = daisy;
String text = animal.milk();
```

The first statement creates an object, daisy. The second assigns the object daisy up the inheritance tree to the variable animal. So far, nothing is wrong. But the third statement will not compile, because the class Animal does not possess a method named milk. The compiler, vigilant as ever, will not allow a method invocation on what appears to be an object of a class that does not support the method.

The remedy is to provide an abstract method milk as part of the class Animal:

```
public abstract String milk();
```

(Abstract methods were introduced in Chapter 27.) Clearly, this method does very little. But writing it as part of the class Animal serves to ensure that the compiler knows that the operation milk is available on an object of class Animal. Then when the program is run, polymorphism goes into action, selecting the correct method. So the abstract method is never actually used. An abstract method simply says that a method with this name is declared somewhere in a subclass.

Another example of the Java compiler's vigilance is the use of the graphics object, usually given the name g. This object is commonly passed around a Java program as a parameter and used in conjunction with methods such as drawString and drawOval. But you can only use these methods provided that you declare this object as being of the class Graphics. When you do so, the compiler can look up in the library to check what methods are associated with class Graphics (or its superclasses). This compile-time checking prevents illegal methods being invoked on objects – it ensures that objects are always used properly.

SELF-TEST QUESTION
·····························

28.4 Which of these statements will create compile-time errors?

```
public void paint(Graphics g) {
    g.drawString("try me", 10, 10);
    Object graphics = g;
    graphics.drawString("for size", 10, 40);
    Graphics newG = graphics;
    newG.drawString("and again", 10, 70);
}
```

The vigilance of the compiler means that when you write a Java program you often get lots of error messages – and it can take some time to locate and fix them. But, once the compile-time errors have been eradicated, a program usually runs and does something useful, even if it is not exactly what you intend. This vigilance usually saves programming time, because bugs left until run-time often take considerably longer to fix. Moreover, a program that has been thoroughly checked at compile-time is likely to be more reliable and robust for the whole of its working life.

But the use of casting requires care. Don't cast something unless you are certain (from your understanding of the logic of the program) that the cast will be successful – otherwise you will postpone an error until run time, when it is harder to find and fix.

Polymorphism case study: shape display program

This example is a program that displays graphical shapes on the screen – squares, circles and similar. The program uses a general-purpose class called Shape, which describes all the shared attributes of these shapes, including where they are on the screen:

```
class Shape {

    int x, y;
    int size = 20;

    public void draw(Graphics g) {
        g.drawString("no drawing available" x, y);
    }
}
```

Each shape is described by its own class, a subclass of class Shape. For example:

```
class Circle extends Shape {

    Circle(int initialX, int initialY) {
        x = initialX;
        y = initialY;
    }

    public void draw(Graphics g) {
        g.fillOval(x, y, size, size);
    }
}

class Square extends Shape {

    Square(int initialX, int initialY) {
        x = initialX;
        y = initialY;
    }

    public void draw(Graphics g) {
        g.fillRect(x, y, size, size);
    }
}
```

Here is a program that illustrates using these classes to create two shapes, storing them in an array and displaying them. The output is shown in Figure 28.3.

```
import java.awt.*;
import java.applet.Applet;
```

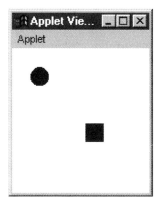

Figure 28.3 Output from the shape display program.

```
public class Shapes extends Applet {

    public void paint(Graphics g) {
        Circle circle = new Circle(20, 20);
        Square square = new Square(80, 80);
        Shape[] collection = new Shape[100];

        collection[0] = circle;
        collection[1] = square;


        for (int s = 0; s < collection.length; s++) {
            collection[s].draw(g);
        }
    }
}
```

Again, polymorphism is in use. In this program the method draw is invoked on two occasions with different results according to which object is in use.

Polymorphism case study: bank accounts

This example is a simple information system that holds information about people's bank accounts. A bank offers its customers two kinds of account – a regular account and a gold account. The two types of account provide some shared facilities but they also offer distinctive features. The common facilities are:

● recording name, address, etc.;
● opening an account with an initial balance;
● maintaining and displaying a record of the current balance.

A regular account can be checked to see if the account is overdrawn. A gold account holder can overdraw indefinitely. A regular account has interest calculated as 5% per year of the amount. A gold account has interest at 6% per year, less a fixed charge of $100 per year.

Because the accounts support some common features, we can declare a class that describes these common features:

```
class Account {

    int amount;
    private String person;

    public void open(int initialAmount, String person) {
        amount = initialAmount;
        this.person = person;
    }

    public String getPerson() {
        return person;
    }

    public String checkOverdrawn() {
        return "no overdraft checking done";
    }

    public int calculateInterest() {
        return 0;
    }

}
```

We can now describe each of the two distinctive types of bank account as subclasses of this general class:

```
class Regular extends Account {

    public String checkOverdrawn() {
        if (amount < 0)
            return "account is overdrawn";
        else
            return "overdraft is OK";
    }

    public int calculateInterest() {
        return (amount * 5 / 100);
    }
}
```

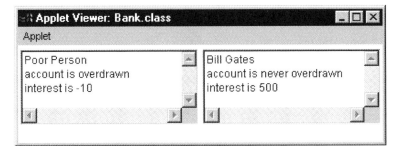

Figure 28.4 Output from the bank program.

```
class Gold extends Account {

    public String checkOverdrawn() {
        return "account is never overdrawn";
    }

    public int calculateInterest() {
        return (amount * 6 / 100) - 100;
    }
}
```

We will now construct a program to use these classes – the output is shown in Figure 28.4. This program creates two bank accounts – one a regular account, and the other a gold account. Each is created with a person's name and some initial amount of money. A method named `displayAccount` is invoked to display the name, overdrawn status and interest of each account. This method exploits polymorphism by invoking the method `calculateInterest`, for example, on the object passed to it as a parameter. Whichever object is passed, polymorphism ensures that the matching method is invoked.

```
import java.applet.*;
import java.awt.*;
import java.awt.event.*;

public class Bank extends Applet {

    private TextArea display1 = new TextArea(4, 25);
    private TextArea display2 = new TextArea(4, 25);

    private Regular account1 = new Regular();
    private Gold account2 = new Gold();
```

```
        public void init(){
            add(display1);
            add(display2);


            account1.open(-200, "Poor Person");
            account2.open(10000, "Bill Gates");


            displayAccount(account1, display1);
            displayAccount(account2, display2);
        }


        public void displayAccount(Account account, TextArea display) {
            display.setText(account.getPerson() + "\n");
            display.append(account.checkOverdrawn()+ "\n");
            display.append("interest is " + account.calculateInterest());
        }
    }
```

Within the method `displayAccount`, methods `checkOverdrawn` and `calculateInterest` are invoked. But whichever account is used, the matching method is automatically selected and executed, using the mechanism of polymorphism.

Programming principles

Polymorphism represents the third major element of OOP. The complete set of three are:

1. Encapsulation means that objects can be made highly modular.
2. Inheritance means that desirable features in an existing class can be reused in other classes, without affecting the integrity of the original class.
3. Polymorphism means designing code that can easily manipulate objects of different classes. Differences between similar objects can be processed transparently.

Novice programmers normally start out by using encapsulation, later move on to inheritance and subsequently use polymorphism.

This chapter has presented three examples of the use of polymorphism:

● a toy system – the farm
● a graphics system – the shape display program
● an information system – the bank

The toy system of farm animals is introduced purely for illustration of the principles of polymorphism. But the other two programs are embryonic real programs.

Each of these case studies exhibits a diversity of objects that have common factors incorporated into a superclass. Now we know that the facility of inheritance helps describe the similarity of groups of objects in an economical fashion. The other side of the coin is using objects, and this is where polymorphism helps us to use objects in a concise uniform way. The diversity is handled not by a proliferation of `if` statements, but instead by a single method invocation. So, should you see code that looks like this:

```
if (objectX // is of type A
    actionA();
if (objectX // is of type B
    actionB();
```

you should instead think of using polymorphism. If actionA and actionB represent a similar concept, then make this concept a method of a superclass and re-write the code as:

```
objectX.action();
```

so making use of polymorphism to select the appropriate method.

Thus polymorphism helps construct programs that are:

● concise (shorter than they might otherwise be);
● modular (unrelated parts are kept separate);
● easy to change and adapt (for example, introducing new objects).

Polymorphism is often used in conjunction with data structures. In Chapter 13, we saw how a number of objects could be collected and held together in a data structure such as an array or an array list. Such a structure could hold:

● all the animal objects in the farmyard;
● all the graphical objects currently displayed on the screen;
● all the bank accounts maintained by the bank.

In the graphics example, when the screen needs to be redrawn, each object in the structure is retrieved one by one and asked to draw itself. Suppose that the structure containing these graphical objects is called `screen` and that a method `getNextObject` is provided to retrieve an object. Suppose also that the object `screen` provides a `moreObjects` method to allow the user to test whether there are any further objects in the structure. Then provided that we have written a `draw` method within each class of object, we can simply use the polymorphism mechanism to draw all the objects as follows:

```
while (screen.moreObjects()) {
    Shape shape = screen.getNextObject();
    shape.draw();
}
```

This is a typical scenario in which polymorphism is invaluable.

In general, the approach to exploiting polymorphism within a particular program is as follows:

1. Identify any similarities (common methods and variables) between any objects or classes in the program.
2. Design a superclass that embodies the common features of the classes.
3. Design the subclasses that describe the distinctive features of each of the classes, while inheriting the common features from the superclass.
4. Identify any place in the program where the same operation must be applied to any of the similar objects. It may be tempting to use `if` statements at this location. Instead, this is the place to use polymorphism.
5. Make sure that the superclass contains an abstract method corresponding to every method that is to be used polymorphically.

Programming pitfalls

If you write a casting operation, you must be completely certain that the destination class is the same as (or is a superclass of) the class of the object. The penalty is a run-time error called a `ClassCastException`.

If you are exploiting polymorphism, and grouping a number of classes under a single superclass, you must ensure that the superclass describes all the methods that will be invoked on any instance of the superclass. Sometimes this will require abstract methods in the superclass that serve no purpose other than enabling the program to compile.

New language elements

● A variable contains a reference to an object, not the object itself.
● A reference to an object can be placed in a variable whose class is higher up in the class hierarchy.
● Casting allows a reference to an object to be placed in a variable whose class is lower in the hierachy. The casting operator is the name of the destination class, enclosed in brackets.
● `instanceof` allows a program to test which class an object belongs to.

Summary

The rules for assigning objects are:

1. You cannot move something *across* the class hierarchy.
2. You can move something *up* the tree without problems.
3. You can move something *down* the tree, but you must be explicit and use *casting*.

A casting operator is simply the name of the required target class enclosed in brackets.

The principles of polymorphism are:

1. An object always retains the identity of the class from which it was created. (An object can never be converted into an object of another class.)
2. When a method is invoked on an object, the method associated with the class of the object is always used.

Polymorphism enhances information hiding and reusability by helping to make pieces of code widely applicable.

EXERCISES

28.1 Within the farm program, create a new class of animal called `Cat`. It makes the noise 'mew'. Change the class diagram to describe the new class. Enhance the program so that a particular instance of a cat says something.

28.2 In the shapes program add a new shape – a straight line – to the collection of available shapes. Use the library method `drawLine` to actually draw the line object. Add code to create a line object, add it to the list of objects (in the array) and display it along with the other shapes.

28.3 Enhance the shapes program into a full-blown drawing package that allows shapes to be selected from a menu and placed in a desired location on the screen. Either enter the position and size of an object using the text fields or alternatively write the program so that users can specify the position with a mouse click. (To get a mouse click position see Chapter 13 and Appendix D.)

28.4 Within the bank program, create a new type of bank account called `Platinum` which is similar to the other types of bank account. Draw a class diagram to illustrate all the types of bank account. `Platinum` accounts pay interest at 10%, with no charges and no penalty for overdrafts. Enhance the program to test that it uses polymorphism properly with this new type of account.

28.5 Within the bank program, add new capabilities to the bank accounts – methods to deposit and withdraw an amount of money. These facilities are common to all types of bank account. Enhance the bank program to test these methods.

ANSWERS TO SELF-TEST QUESTIONS

28.1 1. An instance of class `Cow` is created and a reference to the object is placed in the variable called `daisy`.
2. The reference in `daisy` is copied into `betty`. (So both variables now contain references to the same object.)
3. The weight of the object referenced by `daisy` is set to 800.
4. The weight of the object referenced by `betty` is set to 900.

But both variables hold references to the same object. So there is only a single weight, 900.

28.2 After the first if, `same` is `false`.
After the second if, `same` is `true`.

28.3   `Snake sid = (Snake) animal;`

28.4 `graphics.drawString("for size", 10, 10);`
will cause a compile-time error because the class `Object` does not support a method `drawString`.
`Graphics newG = graphics;`
will cause a compile-time error because a cast is necessary.

The Swing GUI components

29

● Introduction

This chapter is concerned with the Swing graphical user interface components. So far, we have used the AWT – the Abstract Window Toolkit. Basically, the Swing GUI components are a much-improved and enhanced alternative to the AWT components. The Swing components are part of the Java Foundation Classes (JFC) which also includes classes for advanced two-dimensional graphics, and drag-and-drop functionality. To get the most out of this chapter, we suggest that you need to be familiar with the AWT components, and that you browse through Chapter 17 to remind yourself of how each component is used.

What is wrong with the AWT? In Java's early days, it was the only package available to construct a GUI, and had the great benefit of being portable. For example, a GUI program would run on a Microsoft Windows system and on a Macintosh system, with similar (though not identical) results.

However, in order to get portability, Java's designers took the approach of the lowest common denominator, choosing a simplified subset of components which could be run on any operating system. For example, the AWT does not allow a picture on a button, and the amount of text allowed in an AWT text area is too little for serious text-editing. The Swing components overcome such drawbacks.

But how does Swing differ from the AWT? We can answer this from three viewpoints – the technical view, the user view and the programmer view.

To answer this question from a technical view, we need to look in more detail at the inner workings of the AWT. Not only did the creators of the AWT select the lowest common denominator of components, but they left most of the work involved in administering a component to the particular operating system – a so-called 'peer' component, which the AWT accessed. In the Swing component set, however, the components are written in Java, with the operating system doing much less work. To emphasize this, consider a button – basically a rectangle that can be clicked, causing an event. The button dims temporarily to give feedback to the user. In the AWT button, the above tasks are mainly done by the operating system, but if you investigate the source code for the Swing button, you can actually see the Java instructions which draw rectangles, alter the shade when clicked, etc. Minimal use is made of the operating system. The AWT components are often termed 'heavyweight' components, and the Java-coded Swing components are termed 'lightweight' because of their reduced dependence on the native operating system.

From the user's point of view, how is Swing better? Many of the Swing components are higher-level than AWT ones – we are freed from the lowest common denominator effect. For example, we have a table class, which allows us to manipulate information on the screen in rows and columns. In the AWT, we would need to build this component from an array of text fields. In addition, the look and feel (the appearance and operation) of the GUI can be made totally consistent across different platforms.

But what about the programmer view? Well, it depends. You can use simple Swing components in a basically similar way to AWT components: you add them to your layout, and register with them for event-handling. Apart from minor changes to class names and methods, there is no extra difficulty. However, if you want to create a superior user interface (which you can't do anyway with the AWT) you will have to become familiar with a much larger set of classes and their methods. Finally, the advanced programmer can create new components, written entirely in Java.

The drawback is that Java is an interpreted language with a slower execution speed than traditional compiled languages such as C and C++, which are often used to write GUI components.

● Swing applets and applications

In this single chapter, we do not attempt to cover the whole range of Swing. Instead, we will look at the basic use of familiar components as covered in Chapter 17, and also describe the more powerful components. Figure 29.1 and Appendix J show the code and appearance of an applet with most of the simple components included, and Figure 29.4 and Appendix J show an application. We will make frequent reference to them. Note the required imports. For each component there exists a Swing class starting with 'J', indicating that the component is written in Java.

Each component is discussed, and the code used to manipulate it is extracted from the large examples. Note that the top-level containing windows `JFrame` and `JApplet` are not lightweight – their look and feel is fixed by your operating system, and cannot be changed. In addition, we cannot add components directly to them – instead we add to their content pane, which is obtained via the method `getContentPane`. Again, note the imports that we use in the examples.

The use of layout managers is the same as in the AWT, the main change being that the default AWT layout for applets was flow layout, but in Swing applets it is border layout. In our applet of Figure 29.1, we explicitly set flow layout by:

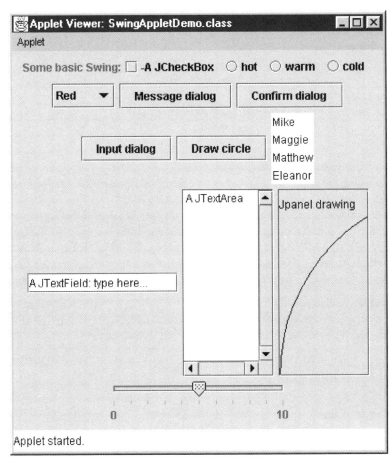

Figure 29.1 Output from the Swing applet.

```
// in init()
Container c = getContentPane();
c.setLayout(new FlowLayout() );
```

The default layout for an application is still border layout as in the AWT.

The Swing button

The Swing button is provided by the JButton class. We add it to the current layout and pick up events in the same way as an AWT button – Appendix J shows the code and Figure 29.1 shows the appearance. The coding from our applet is:

```
// declaration
private JButton button1, button2, button3, button4;
```

```
// creation, layout, event registering-in init()
button1 = new JButton("Message dialog");
c.add(button1);
button1.addActionListener(this);


// handling the event
public void actionPerformed(ActionEvent e) {
    if (e.getSource() == button1) {
        // etc...
```

In order to show that the button is responding to an event, we display a message on the screen using the JOptionPane dialog box described below. The dialog box is a new and useful feature of Swing.

Swing also allows us to put an image on a button. Because the image must exist in a separate file it is simpler for us to show this in an application. Basically, we create a GIF or JPEG image in a file (perhaps with a paint program) and place the file in the same folder as the class file of the application. Our image in the example was 20 by 20 pixels. The appearance is shown in Figure 29.4, and here is the extract from Appendix J:

```
// ovalimage.jpg is 20 by 20 pixels
Icon ovalIcon = new ImageIcon("ovalimage.jpg");
flipButton = new JButton("Flip the GUI", ovalIcon);
```

In an applet, the code would be more complicated because we have to explicitly write code to download the image from the server. This is not shown.

The Swing tool tip

A tool tip is a text message that pops up when you hold the mouse over a component. Conventionally it provides help, such as explaining what a button is for. It is particularly useful in a GUI containing lots of components, as it occupies no permanent screen area. A tool tip is not a class in itself, but every component inherits a setToolTipText method. The following code from our applet shows how to attach one to a button.

```
button1 = new JButton("Message dialog");
c.add(button1);
button1.setToolTipText("click to see a message dialog");
button1.addActionListener(this);
```

The Swing dialog box

A dialog is a pop-up window, which is 'modal'; activity in other windows is prevented until the user deals with it, for example by clicking 'OK'. We use it in our applet as a simple way of displaying results to the user, but in serious software a dialog is used to force the user to take note of a message, or to enter essential data. From a user-interface

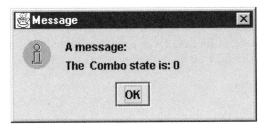

Figure 29.2 a JOptionPane dialog.

point of view, dialogs should be used with care, as they can disrupt the user's flow of work. A dialog box is provided by the Swing JOptionPane class. There are four variations on the dialog.

To simply display a message, we can put:

```
JOptionPane.showMessageDialog(null, "Hi There!");
```

Note that we invoke a static method of the JOptionPane class. No new is needed.

The first parameter states the component on which the dialog is to be centred. Passing null centres it in the middle of the screen. The second parameter is a string expression which, as usual, can involve several strings joined with the + operator. Figure 29.2 shows the message dialog, as produced by the code in our applet.

The second form of the dialog provides a confirm request, with 'Yes', 'No' and 'Cancel' buttons. Here is the coding from our applet:

```
int userResponse = JOptionPane.showConfirmDialog(null, "Delete files?");
```

We can process the reply using some provided constants from the JOptionPane class:

```
if (userResponse == JOptionPane.NO_OPTION)
    // user clicked 'No'
else if (userResponse == JOptionPane.YES_OPTION)
    // user clicked 'yes'
else if (userResponse == JOptionPane.CANCEL_OPTION)
    // user clicked 'Cancel'
else if (userResponse == JOptionPane.CLOSED_OPTION)
    // user closed the dialog - could treat as 'Cancel'
```

The third form is an input dialog, allowing the user to enter a string, or to cancel the dialog:

```
String bookTitle = JOptionPane.showInputDialog(null, "Enter book title");
if (bookTitle == null)
    // user cancelled
else
    // process bookTitle string
```

The fourth style, not shown here, allows us to pass an array of components (e.g. text areas, radio buttons) to be displayed in the dialog. We have also omitted details of other constants of JOptionPane, which can be passed as parameters to produce various symbols on the dialogs, for example a large exclamation mark to indicate a warning.

The Swing label

The Swing label is very similar to the AWT version, but with more possibilities. For example, you can add an image to the label, in the same way that we added an image to a button in the application example of Figure 29.4. The code from our applet is:

```
// declaration
private JLabel label1;


// adding to the layout-in init()
label1= new JLabel("Some basic Swing:");
c.add(label1);
```

The Swing check box

The JCheckBox class provides a single box which can be checked (ticked) or not. Its spelling now conforms to the Java convention, with JCheckBox, rather than the AWT's Checkbox. The code from our applet is:

```
// declaration
private JCheckBox checkBox1;


// creation, layout, event registering-in init()
checkBox1= new JCheckBox("-A JCheckBox");
c.add(checkBox1);
checkBox1.addItemListener(this);


// handling the event
public void itemStateChanged(ItemEvent e) {
    if (e.getSource() == checkBox1)
        JOptionPane.showMessageDialog(null,
                "checkBox changed to: " + checkBox1.isSelected());
// etc...
```

We provide an itemStateChanged method to handle the event, and make use of the boolean method isSelected to access the component.

The Swing radio button

The Swing JRadioButton class provides a group of choices, only one of which can be selected. In the AWT they were referred to as a CheckboxGroup. The code from our applet is:

```
// declaration
private ButtonGroup radioButtons;
private JRadioButton hotRadio, warmRadio, coldRadio;

// creation, layout, event registering-in init()
hotRadio = new JRadioButton("hot",false);
c.add(hotRadio);
hotRadio.addItemListener(this);

warmRadio = new JRadioButton("warm",false);
c.add(warmRadio);
warmRadio.addItemListener(this);

coldRadio = new JRadioButton("cold",false);
c.add(coldRadio);
coldRadio.addItemListener(this);

radioButtons = new ButtonGroup();
radioButtons.add(hotRadio);
radioButtons.add(warmRadio);
radioButtons.add(coldRadio);

// handling the event
public void actionPerformed(ActionEvent e) {
    if (e.getSource() == hotRadio)
        JOptionPane.showMessageDialog(null, " hot clicked");
// etc...
```

Note that we can set the initial state of the choices as we create them. As with all the Swing components which allow choices, we can detect their change of state as it happens via its event, but it is often better – especially when the user is making several related choices – to give the user an 'OK' button, indicating that all the choices have been made. The current state of the component can then be accessed. This is an issue in the design of the user interface.

In the above event code, the itemStateChanged method will be invoked twice, because changing the state of the radio buttons involves setting the old selection to false, and setting the new selection true (even though the user only clicks once). If you wish to find the state of a radio button without detecting the event, you can put:

```
if (coldRadio.isSelected() ) // boolean result
    // yes, it was
```

The Swing combo box

The combo box provides a drop-down list of options, rather like a menu. Only one item can be selected. In the AWT it was referred to as a `Choice`. Here is some typical code from our applet:

```
// declaration
private JComboBox combo1;

// creation, layout, event registering-in init()
combo1= new JComboBox();
combo1.addItem("Red");
combo1.addItem("Yellow");
combo1.addItem("Blue");
combo1.addActionListener(this);
c.add(combo1);

// handling the event
public void actionPerformed(ActionEvent e) {
    if(e.getSource() == combo1){
        int n=combo1.getSelectedIndex();
// etc...
```

Often we choose not to detect a combo event; instead, we obtain the selection after a button-click, accessing either the index number of the selection (from zero upwards) or access the selected object that was stored in the item. In our case we used strings, so here we cast the returned object to a string.

```
int n = combo1.getSelectedIndex();    // or :-
String s = (String) combo1.getSelectedItem();
```

Other facilities exist – for example we could make a combo box editable so the user can either click on a pre-set choice, or can type in a string. We can also add image icons to the choices.

The Swing list

Swing provides us with a `JList` class, similar in principle (though not in detail) to the AWT `List` class. Unlike the combo box, there is no 'drop-down' facility, so a list occupies more screen space. Here, we will show the essential code from our applet, for a list in which only one item can be selected. Note that behind the scenes, Swing components are designed with an MVC approach, as explained in Chapter 10. When using a `JList`, we have to make explicit use of a supporting `DefaultListModel` class:

```
// declaration
private JList list1;
private DefaultListModel listModel;
private JTextField textField1;
```

```
// creation, layout, event registering-in init()
listModel = new DefaultListModel();
listModel.addElement("Mike");
listModel.addElement("Maggie");
listModel.addElement("Matthew");
listModel.addElement("Eleanor");

list1 = new JList(listModel);
list1.setSelectionMode(ListSelectionModel.SINGLE_SELECTION);
c.add(list1);
list1.addListSelectionListener(this);

// handling the event
public void valueChanged(ListSelectionEvent e) {
    if(e.getSource() == list1)
        JOptionPane.showMessageDialog(null,
        "Chose list item number:"+list1.getSelectedIndex());
}
//etc...
```

Because we restricted our example to a single-selection list, it is possible to obtain the number of the chosen item by:

```
int n = list1.getSelectedIndex();
```

The full capabilities of JList include the use of items other than strings, the selection of several items at once, and the adding of a list to a JScrollPane to provide scrollbars.

The Swing text field

The JTextField class is equivalent to the AWT TextField, allowing the user to enter a single item, and complete the entry by hitting the enter key. Here is the basic code:

```
// declaration
private JTextField textField1;

// creation, layout, event registering
textField1 = new JTextField(15);
textField1.setText("A JTextField: type here...");
c.add(textField1);
textField1.addActionListener(this);

// handling the event
public void actionPerformed(ActionEvent e) {
    if (e.getSource() == textField1)
        JOptionPane.showMessageDialog(null,"You hit enter " +
            "on textfield. Text is:\n"+ textField1.getText());
//etc...
```

There is also a `JPasswordField` class, which prevents typed characters being seen by an observer.

The Swing slider

The Swing `JSlider` class lets the user drag a knob to select a position. Though there is still a `JScrollBar` class in Swing, the slider is more convenient in 'stand-alone' cases. (The `JScrollPane` class comes with built-in scrollbars for scrolling items that are added to the pane. The `JTextArea` below shows this style.) The slider code from our applet is:

```
// declaration
private JSlider slider1;


// creation, layout, event registering-in init()
// give it 'ticks' from 0 to 10
slider1 = new JSlider(JSlider.HORIZONTAL, 0, 10, 5);
slider1.setMajorTickSpacing(10);
slider1.addChangeListener(this);
slider1.setMinorTickSpacing(1);
slider1.setPaintTicks(true);
slider1.setPaintLabels(true);
c.add(slider1);


// handling the event
public void stateChanged(ChangeEvent e) {
    if (e.getSource() == slider1)
        textArea1.append("\nslider1 is: " + slider1.getValue());
//etc...
```

This code detects a movement in the slider, and obtains the new value. The event code will be invoked several times as the user operates the slider, but the final time it is invoked, the value will be the one that the user has settled on. There are other methods for customizing a slider, such as providing text labels and icons alongside.

The Swing text area

The `JTextArea` class provides an editable area for text, which must be all in the same font. (There are other Swing components, including `JTextPane` which allow text in a mixture of fonts, together with images.)

In the AWT, scrollbars were built in to the `TextArea` class, but in Swing, we add the `JTextArea` to a `JScrollPane` container. In our applet code, we have requested scrollbars to be always present, rather than appearing when the amount of text warrants them.

```
// declaration
private JTextArea textArea1;


// creation, layout
// a text area in a scroll pane
textArea1 = new JTextArea(" A JTextArea");
textArea1.setLineWrap(true);
JScrollPane areaScrollPane = new JScrollPane(textArea1);
c.add(areaScrollPane);
```

There is no event-handling for text areas, but Swing supports the same methods that we described in Chapter 17.

The Swing file chooser

The `JFileChooser` class lets the user navigate through folders and select a file name. It is similar in nature to the AWT `FileDialog` class. The appearance is shown in Figure 29.3, and the code to manipulate it appears below. Remember that normally applets don't access files.

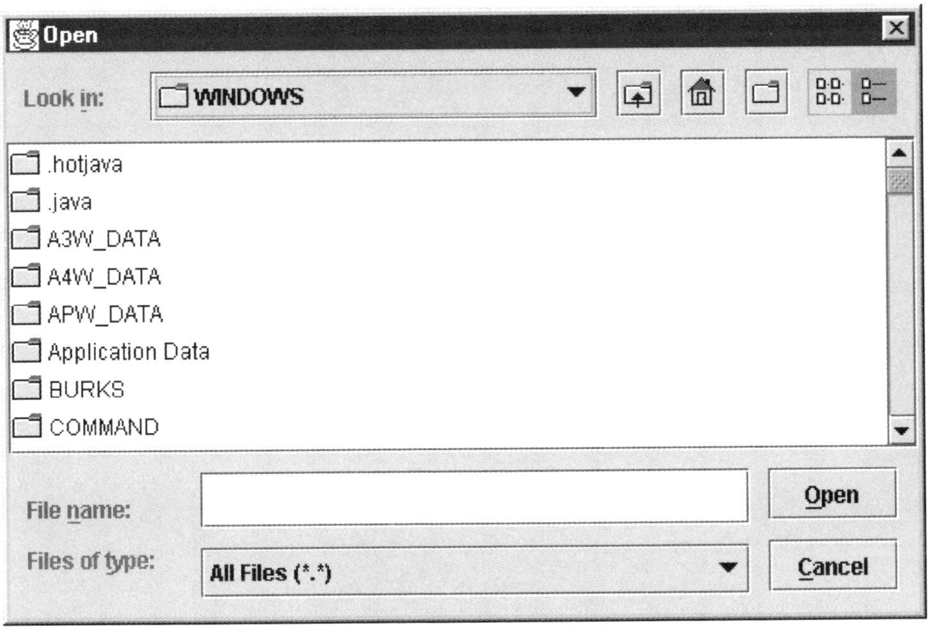

Figure 29.3 A file chooser.

```
JFileChooser fileChooser = new JFileChooser();
int userResponse = fileChooser.showOpenDialog(this);
if (userResponse == JFileChooser.CANCEL_OPTION )
    JOptionPane.showMessageDialog(null, "User cancelled.");
else
    JOptionPane.showMessageDialog(null, "User chose" +
                            fileChooser.getSelectedFile());
```

The chooser returns an integer, which we compare against provided constants to see if the user cancelled the dialog. We can then access the selected file, which is an instance of the `File` class, as in Chapter 19. In our example, the file chooser appears when we click the 'open' menu item, and we simply display the chosen file name as a string.

We can also use a 'save' of the file chooser, with:

```
int userResponse = JFileChooser.showSaveDialog();
```

The Swing menu

Swing menus are provided by the `JMenu`, `JMenuBar`, and `JMenuItem` classes. Their creation follows the same logic as the AWT menu system. We create a top-level menu bar, create an individual menu, then add menu items to the menu. When the menu is complete, we add it to the menu bar. Repeat for each menu. Figure 29.4 shows the creation of a menu system consisting of a 'File' menu with 'open' and 'save' menu items, and an 'Edit' menu with 'copy' and 'paste' items. In the extract below, we only show the creation of the 'open' and 'copy' items, though the full code is given in Appendix J.

```
// declaration
JMenuBar wholeMenuBar;
JMenu fileMenu, editMenu;
JMenuItem openItem, saveItem, copyItem, pasteItem;
```

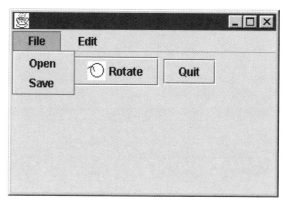

Figure 29.4 Output from the Swing application (Java metal look and feel).

```
// creation, layout, event registering
setJMenuBar(wholeMenuBar );

// file menu, with Open, save
fileMenu = new JMenu("File");

openItem = new JMenuItem("Open");
fileMenu.add(openItem);
openItem.addActionListener(this);

saveItem = new JMenuItem("Save");
fileMenu.add(saveItem);
saveItem.addActionListener(this);

wholeMenuBar.add(fileMenu);

// handling the event
public void actionPerformed(ActionEvent e) {
    if (e.getSource() == openItem) {
//etc...
```

As in the AWT menu, we can add sub-menus and separators. With Swing, we can add accelerator keys, image icons, and other controls (such as radio buttons) to menu items.

● Other Swing components

Here, we briefly review Swing containers, and the `JTree` and `JTable` classes.

The range of Swing containers is a major advance in functionality over the AWT. Earlier, we looked at the top-level `JApplet` and the `JFrame` classes, which always have the look and feel of the local operating system. (These heavyweight components cannot be avoided at the *outer* level of the GUI.) Here, we look at the more flexible Swing lightweight containers.

Containers can have components added to them, and will lay out their components based on the chosen (or default) layout scheme for the container. The flow layout, grid layout, border layout and card layouts are as described in Chapter 17, and in addition we have `BoxLayout`, which is similar in effect to a flow layout.

A full description of the containers would be rather lengthy, so here we will provide an overview.

The `JScrollPane` provides scrolling facilities for suitable components that are added to it. The applet shows a scrollable pane in use, providing scrolling for a text area. Here is a code extract:

```
// a text area in a scroll pane
textArea1 = new JTextArea(" A JTextArea");
textArea1.setLineWrap(true);
JScrollPane areaScrollPane = new JScrollPane(textArea1);
areaScrollPane.setVerticalScrollBarPolicy(
                    JScrollPane.VERTICAL_SCROLLBAR_ALWAYS);
areaScrollPane.setHorizontalScrollBarPolicy(
                    JScrollPane.HORIZONTAL_SCROLLBAR_ALWAYS);
areaScrollPane.setPreferredSize(new Dimension(100,200));
c.add(areaScrollPane);
```

The `JPanel` class can contain other controls, in a similar manner to the AWT `Panel` class. For example, you might add a series of buttons to a panel, and then add the panel as a whole to another component – maybe to the 'north' edge of a `BorderLayout`. The `JPanel` can also be used for drawing, as shown in our applet example:

```
// a panel in a scroll pane
paper = new Paper();
JScrollPane paperScrollPane = new JScrollPane(paper);
paperScrollPane.setPreferredSize(new Dimension(100,200));
c.add(paperScrollPane);
```

The `JSplitPane` provides a rectangular area split into two parts. Components can be added to each part. The user can change the area allocated to each part by dragging the splitting line with the mouse. This component is not shown.

The `JTabbedPane` provides a set of overlapped screens. The non-visible screens can be brought to the front by clicking on their 'tab' which projects from their top or bottom. You often see this style used in collections of spreadsheets, or in configuration tools for large software packages, with a tabbed pane for each separate area of configuration. This component is not shown.

The `JToolBar` provides a container for other components, typically buttons. It looks initially similar to a panel, but allows the user to drag it around the screen and place it at the edge of a component, or even outside a component entirely. This component is not shown.

The `JTree` and `JTable` classes

The `JTree` class provides a hierarchical view of data – you may be familiar with this from your use of a file browser, in which you can open up folders to an appropriate depth. The `JTree` class lets the programmer store information in a tree structure, and provides a GUI which allows the user to expand and contract branches of the tree.

The `JTable` class provides for the displaying and manipulating of tabular data. Visually, it appears in the familiar row/column form of a spreadsheet. Each cell can contain textual items, and also images. The class lets you set up the contents of cells, and respond to events from the user, such as the selection of a particular cell. Though it looks like a spreadsheet, no calculation facility exists – this would have to be programmed. This component is not shown here.

● Changing the look and feel

The appearance of a GUI is termed its 'look and feel'. Different platforms, although they have similar components such as buttons and menus, normally have a slightly different appearance and usage. For example, the size of a button might vary, or the clickable area of a checkbox might be white or grey. The default look and feel for Swing software is called 'metal', and it is unique – different from the style of GUI on any other platform. Figures 29.1 and 29.4 show the Java metal look and feel.

Swing provides the surprising feature of allowing the look and feel to be changed, with the so-called 'pluggable look and feel'. The look and feel can be set either by reconfiguring the Java system, or dynamically as a program executes.

Though it might sound attractive to (for example) use a Mac look and feel on a Microsoft Windows system, this is prohibited for copyright reasons, even though it is technically feasible. In fact, Microsoft systems cannot be switched to Mac look and feel, and Mac systems cannot be switched to Microsoft look and feel. Of course, Java metal can be used on any system.

So, if an identical look and feel is important to you, go for metal. But you might also allow your software to be switched to the look and feel of its platform.

● Converting from AWT to Swing

If you are using this text to learn Java, it is unlikely you will wish to convert an existing applet or application to Swing. Rather, you will choose Swing or AWT in advance.

If however you do wish to convert, there are several major factors to consider before beginning to recode.

- Are you dealing with a real applet which will be run in a browser (as opposed to the applet viewer)? If so, it is best to avoid Swing; it is not yet implemented by all browsers. The 'Java plug-in' is available to allow browsers to handle Swing, but not all users have this.
- Are you doing a line-by-line conversion, or will you redesign the GUI, making use of the higher-level Swing components (such as tables)? You may end up with a better product if the GUI is re-designed.
- If your current program does complex multithreading, beware. Swing components are not regarded as 'thread-safe', and you may have to do some replanning. This advanced topic is not covered here.

Here we will assume that you will do a line-by-line conversion, and suggest some high-level steps to follow:

1. Sun's Java Web site suggests starting by temporarily removing the

   ```
   import java.awt.*;
   ```

   thus causing the compiler to indicate AWT classes being used. Once these lines have been amended, the import needs to be replaced because there are some AWT classes still required, such as layout managers.

2. Insert the required Swing imports as used in our example, and recompile to check for any incorrect method names.
3. Make changes to the GUI creation. Recall that the Swing applet default layout is border and that, for applets and applications, you add to a content pane, not directly to the top-level frame. Below you will see the conversion of an AWT applet used in a previous chapter.

Swing and paint

Conversion of code which doesn't make use of graphics (`drawOval` etc.) is basically straight-forward. However, code which uses `paint` requires recoding. Recall that `paint` is used to refresh the screen either when the program amends the display or when the user manipulates (for example resizes) the window. The problem is that Swing uses a `paintComponent` method which is not equivalent to `paint`. One solution (in certain cases) might be to avoid the use of `paint` totally, using `getGraphics` instead. But this is tedious in some cases.

The preferred solution is to use the `paintComponent` method in a separate class. If you have adopted our object-oriented style, the changes are localized, but if you have created monolithic code, you will have to do a major rewrite, looking closely at the scopes of variables. Our applet example of this chapter shows the approach, and below we provide the Swing equivalent of our balloon applet used throughout Chapter 9.

Our original applet uses the same area of the screen both to contain buttons and display graphics. This makes for a short program but is rather undisciplined compared to most windows applications. Swing makes us use separate areas for these separate tasks. We have adopted the approach of using a panel to contain the two buttons, adding it to the north of a border layout. Though this requires extra code, this code is not complex. Here is the conversion:

```java
import java.awt.*;
import java.awt.event.*;
import javax.swing.*;
import javax.swing.event.*;

public class SwingPlayBalloon extends
    implements ActionListener {

    private JButton grow, shrink;
    private Balloon myBalloon;

    public void init() {
        Container c = getContentPane(); //border layout - default

        JPanel buttonPanel = new JPanel();

        grow = new JButton("Grow");
        buttonPanel.add(grow);
        grow.addActionListener(this);
```

```
        shrink = new JButton("Shrink");
        buttonPanel.add(shrink);
        shrink.addActionListener(this);

        c.add(buttonPanel, BorderLayout.NORTH);

        myBalloon = new Balloon(20, 50, 50);
        c.add(myBalloon, BorderLayout.CENTER);
    }

    public void actionPerformed(ActionEvent event) {
        if (event.getSource() == grow)
            myBalloon.changeSize(10);
        if (event.getSource() == shrink)
            myBalloon.changeSize(-10);
        myBalloon.display();
    }
}

class Balloon extends JPanel {
    private int diameter;
    private int xCoord, yCoord;

    public Balloon(int initialDiameter, int initialX, int initialY) {
        diameter = initialDiameter;
        xCoord = initialX;
        yCoord = initialY;
    }

    public void changeSize(int change) {
        diameter = diameter + change;
    }

    public void paintComponent(Graphics g) {
        super.paintComponent(g); //essential
        // now, our balloon:
        g.drawOval(xCoord, yCoord, diameter, diameter);
    }

    public void display() {
        repaint();
    }
}
```

Programming pitfalls

● Many Web browsers do not support Swing applets. Check the current situation carefully before starting to design and code.
● Swing components in certain types of multithreaded programs are not safe (without intricate programming).
● It is tempting to think in AWT terms, thus for example forgetting to add components to a content pane, or forgetting that the default layout in Swing applets is border layout (in AWT it is flow layout).

Summary

● Swing is a GUI component set which is coded in Java.

● Swing produces an identical look and feel on any system.

● Swing has a much wider variety of components than the AWT.

● The look and feel of a Swing GUI can be changed.

EXERCISES

29.1 Investigate the current availability of Swing within current major browsers.

29.2 Convert the 'little and large' applet of Chapter 7 into Swing. (Consider creating a new Circle class).

29.3 Write a file-processing program, using Swing, which reads in a Java program line-by-line, and converts every declaration of an AWT component to its Swing equivalent. The modified code should be written to an output file. (Make use of the `replace` method which can be found in our coverage of strings – Chapter 15.)

Java – in context

30

Introduction

In this chapter we explain how Java relates to the computing and Internet scene. In addition, Java is constantly being updated by new class libraries, tools and technologies. We provide a survey of the current scope. We begin by reviewing the main features of Java as summarized in a paper, called the 'White Paper', from Sun Microsystems that launched the language. The features were identified as:

- simple;
- object-oriented;
- network-savvy;
- interpreted;
- robust;
- secure;
- architecture neutral;
- portable;
- high-performance;
- multithreaded;
- dynamic.

Simple

Java was partly conceived as a reaction to a perceived complexity in other mainstream languages – primarily C++. Some see C++ as a large and unwieldy language, difficult to learn, displaying inconsistent concepts and prone to accidental misuse. Java, by contrast, is small and beautiful. For example, while C++ has multiple inheritance, Java has the simpler single inheritance. In C++ the programmer can directly manipulate pointers to objects in memory, but this highly dangerous practice is unavailable to the Java programmer.

Simplicity means ease of learning, mastery of the language by its users and fewer errors. Java was designed as a small language, with the hope that it will be widely and completely understood, implemented and adopted. Most languages, as they have evolved, have got bigger and it may be that the same will happen to Java. As the designers of Java say: '. . . realizing that the system will only get larger in later releases we have elected to start small'. Let us hope that their original design vision prevails.

● Object-oriented

Java is an object-oriented (OO) language. This book has explained that this means that a program is constructed from objects, in turn created from classes. This promotes program modularity. Classes can inherit variables and methods from superclasses. This is enormously powerful in supporting the reuse of software. In consequence, OO programs are generally much smaller than equivalent programs that are not OO. There is also the bonus of increased reliability obtained by using tried-and-tested software, rather than starting from scratch.

The OO paradigm currently dominates computing, not only in programming but in analysis, in design and in databases.

● Platform independence (portability)

How much work is involved in moving (porting) a program onto a different platform? In essence, this is the issue of portability. Java was designed as a language that can be ported easily to any computer and operating system. It currently runs on all the major computers and operating systems. Portability is achieved by compiling Java to a machine-independent code named *byte code*. This is code for a 'pretend' computer – one that can be simulated in software. The simulation software is named the *Java Virtual Machine* (JVM). A JVM is needed for every type of computer that runs Java and a JVM has been written for nearly all computers. A JVM is in fact a comparatively small program – about 256 kbyte – and is fairly easy to write. The JVM is available to run on a whole number of processors, not just Intel processors. Neither is the JVM locked into any one operating system, like Windows or UNIX. Thus a Java program can be distributed (as byte code) and run on any of a large range of machines.

When a Java program is compiled, information about which library methods and variables are used is retained in the file of byte code. Traditionally the next phase is linking, combining the byte code of the program with the byte code of the libraries that have been used. In Java the linking to libraries is postponed until the program is actually run. This dynamic linking has several advantages. First it means that Java byte code can be transmitted more rapidly around the network, free of the encumbrance of library software.

This improves speed. Second, when the Java code arrives at a site and begins execution, it is linked with the Java library that is specific to that site. This improves portability. Finally, when any of the libraries are updated, the Java program picks up the very latest version automatically. This enormously assists in maintaining and updating software.

Many of the Java libraries run unchanged on any machine, but some must be tailored to work with the host operating system. For example, the AWT methods that carry out windowing activities must use the facilities of the host windowing system. This means that the AWT classes must interface with the particular operating system and are therefore special. The consequence is that while Java programs running on different machines have the same look and feel, the details of the scrollbars and window control icons are different on different operating systems.

Another feature of Java that contributes to portability is the fact that data types are defined to have sizes that are independent of an individual machine. Thus, for example, an integer is always 32 bits, irrespective of the machine. This means that the programmer can be confident about the behaviour of a program, wherever it is executed. This very simple standardization is not the case in other languages, notably C and C++, where the size of data types changes from one machine to another.

● Performance

Transmission of Java programs around the Internet or within an intranet is fast, because Java code is compact. Moreover the library software is not transmitted with the program, but is linked at the time of execution on the target machine. Any performance problems with Java arise at execution time. Java programs are interpreted by the Java virtual machine (JVM) and therefore they run slower than similar programs that directly use the machine instructions of the computer. For example, programs written in C or C++ are compiled directly to machine code and run about 10 times faster than a similar Java program. (The C or C++ program is not, of course, portable.) For many purposes, the running speed is not important. However, for certain types of application – some embedded systems or real-time systems – performance is crucial. Java is running faster due to improved JVM construction and faster machines – but choose it with care for certain problem domains.

● Security

If you access (visit) a remote Internet site, retrieve a program and bring it (download) for execution on your own machine, you are taking a risk. An unknown program might:

● crash your machine;
● delete files;
● access and transmit private information to another machine;
● fill up your disk space;
● introduce a virus.

Such damage may be the result of malice or accident – the result is the same. Worries about such damage restrict the use of the Internet and users need to protect themselves. Java provides the necessary mechanisms for users to protect themselves from rogue programs. Indeed, this was one of the major design aims of Java. Java does this by means of a whole series of devices which we will now describe.

The Java language itself

Unlike some other languages, Java does not allow the use of pointers. In some languages the programmer is allowed to set up pointers, normally to data structures. But once given the access to a pointer, the programmer can by accident or design then access anything in memory. For example (if it was allowed), a program could access private data within an object. So the banning of pointers in Java is itself a security measure.

Java is strongly typed. This means that if you declare a variable as, say, an integer, the compiler ensures that it is consistently used as an integer and not, for example, as a character. If the programmer wants to convert a piece of data from one type to another, it has to be done explicitly. (This is called casting.) Compile-time checking like this is cheap and effective compared with detecting and eradicating bugs that become evident only when the program is running.

The Java language is completely object-oriented, and one major aspect of this is encapsulation. Variables and methods within an object that are declared private cannot be accessed from outside the object. So there is clear and explicit control over access to data and actions.

The Java language prevents a programmer from accessing a variable that has not been initialized. Some other languages allow access to a variable that has not been initialized. This is an error by the programmer in assuming either that they have done it explicitly or that the system does it for them implicitly.

The Verifier

When a new piece of Java byte code arrives for execution the Verifier checks it to ensure that it is safe. This is to minimize any risk that the code was damaged in transit or that unsafe code has been created using a tool other than the regular Java compiler. The checks ensure that:

- the code does not create dangerous pointers;
- access to private variables and methods is valid;
- methods are invoked with parameters of the correct type;
- no illegal data conversions are done.

The class loader

One way that a villain could penetrate Java's defences is to supply some classes that pretend to be standard Java classes. If such classes were mistakenly loaded instead of the proper classes, any amount of damage could be done. To prevent this, the class loader carefully distinguishes between different packages and particularly between local built-in classes and any others.

The Java Virtual Machine (JVM)

Once checked, byte code is not directly executed on the machine but is interpreted. This means that the program is prevented from accessing the raw machine instructions – with all the power and danger that would imply. It is by this mechanism that a whole series of facilities are denied to the program:

● access to areas of memory that contain operating system information;
● access to files and to the Internet;
● the capacity to modify another program or the program itself;
● the use of other programs running on the system.

Thus a Java program runs in a box or a cage (sometimes called a sandbox), and everything it does is constrained.

Arrays

One potential way in which a rogue program could do damage is to declare an array and then access elements of the array that don't actually exist – elements with a subscript that is greater than the size of the array. This is prevented in Java because the JVM checks that a subscript is within the defined bounds.

Garbage collection

When an object in a Java program is no longer used, the system automatically releases the memory that was allocated to it. This is called automatic garbage collection. In languages like C++ it is the responsibility of the programmer to explicitly invoke the operating system informing it that a piece of memory is free. The following errors can and do occur in such languages:

● failing to free memory when it is no longer needed, causing the program to accumulate ever increasing regions of memory;
● freeing the same piece of memory twice, causing subtle memory corruption bugs that can be difficult to find;
● freeing memory but continuing to use it, causing similar problems.

These problems are completely avoided because Java provides automatic garbage collection.

The filing system

The person invoking a Java applet can control that applet's access to files by specifying an option to the browser. The user can assess the reliability of the applet and decide (for example) that it can read from a local file, but not write to a local file.

Summary

Java provides several mechanisms for protection:

- the language and the compiler – e.g. absence of pointers;
- verification of byte code;
- the class loader;
- the filing system and network access.

Java's security measures are comprehensive and wide-ranging. There is, however, no cast-iron guarantee that a malicious programmer cannot penetrate the defences.

● Netcentric

Java is a language intimately connected with the Internet and intranets. (An intranet is a network supported within an organization that uses Internet technology.) It is a language that allows many Internet-related activities to be performed easily. We saw in Chapter 19 on files that a program can read data from any file on the Internet (provided that it has appropriate security privileges). This means that the Internet is seen as one huge global filing system. Information anywhere can be accessed by a Java program, just as easily as if it is on a local disk. Textual, graphical, animation and audio information can be retrieved and displayed. Orders for products can be placed by adding information to a remote file (security provisions allowing).

Java is a world language in a different sense. It uses the Unicode standard for representing and manipulating characters. This is a recent international standard that provides 16 bits for the representation of a character, in contrast to earlier standards like ASCII which provide only eight bits. This means that Java programs can manipulate characters of all the languages of the world, including (for example) Mandarin, Urdu and Japanese. This also means that programmers can use their own language for names of variables, methods and classes.

Last, but certainly not least, parts of a Java program can reside in different places on the Internet, to be retrieved and run as necessary. As we have seen, Java programs are constructed from classes. The Java system uses dynamic linking. This means that a class is only loaded and linked with the object that uses it when it is first referred to. This first reference is usually the creation of an instance of the class using `new` and the constructor method of the class. The different classes from which a program is made can be stored on different computers across the Internet. When a class is needed, it can be retrieved, loaded, linked and finally executed. It is not always that there is a need to use this facility, but as we shall see it can be very useful.

● Thin clients

It is common these days for organizations to use large numbers of PCs connected via a network. Users run programs that are stored on their PCs. The data that is processed may be held locally on the hard disk of the PC, but sometimes it is stored on a fast, large central server (a powerful computer with plentiful disk storage). The typical modern PC is powerful, has a large local storage capacity and is relatively expensive. In part, Java grew out of an alternative vision. If network capacity is high, central servers can be used to store all the programs and data. When the user needs to run a program it is downloaded from a server across the network. Thus the PC no longer needs its own hard disk and filing system software. Finally, the computer does not need a large and complex operating system – like Windows. All-in-all this computer can be simpler and cheaper. This minimal computer is called a network computer (NC) – sometimes also called a thin client or a slim client.

There is a second and perhaps more compelling reason for using thin clients – support and maintenance. Organizations typically have hundreds of PCs. These, of course, cost money to buy, but they often cost more to run. Time and money need to be spent on installing software, updating software, and backing up files on each individual machine. A thin client eliminates all these costs, which can amount to twice as much as the initial purchase price of a PC. Any software updates only need to be carried out once – on the server. The server also provides automatic backup for files. Thus massive savings can potentially be made by replacing PCs with thin clients.

How does this relate to Java? The answer is that Java was designed for constructing exactly this type of software because it strongly supports networking. In addition Java software provided on a server can be downloaded for use on any of a variety of platforms – PCs, Apple computers and UNIX/LINUX boxes. This vision extends to the operating system itself. The most widely used operating system, Microsoft Windows, is very greedy in its use of RAM and hard disk space. Thus any thin client built using Windows needs a hard disk and plenty of RAM, which hardly makes it thin! As an alternative, a network computer could run a minimal operating system that is little more than a Web browser, the Java run-time system, and the JVM.

The reality is different from the vision – network computers have been launched several times, but have never (yet) taken off. The reason may be the market strength of Microsoft.

● Microsoft versus the world

Microsoft Windows operating systems currently account for around 90% of the world market for personal computer operating systems. This has been seen as a massive near-monopoly. Microsoft operating systems run on Intel processors and this powerful combination is sometimes known as Wintel. The other companies in the computer industry are jealous of this power and would like to break the alleged monopoly. They see Microsoft as dominating the market, weakening their market share and eventually forcing them out of business. Java has become a weapon in this battle. Led by Sun Microsystems, the opponents of Microsoft have promoted Java as a means of creating portable software that will run on any machine and under any operating system.

Microsoft has responded by (allegedly) tailoring its Java compiler and libraries to the architecture of Intel machines and Windows operating systems, thus trying to lock users into the Wintel monopoly. Sun's lawsuit against Microsoft remains unsettled at the time of writing.

Of course, software is an immense and lucrative business, and we do not take the view that Microsoft is the only company that wishes to dominate the market. However, in 2000, a US federal court decided that Microsoft had too much of the market and was acting to stifle competition. The ruling was that Microsoft had to split into two parts – operating systems and applications. Microsoft has appealed against the ruling. How this affects Java is unclear, but it seems that Microsoft is producing competitive products. In 2000, it published details of Visual Studio.Net, a large package containing (among other things) a fully object-oriented version of their popular Visual Basic system, and secondly a new language named C# ('C sharp') which is object-oriented, based on C++, highly Web-oriented, and allowing rapid development.

● The versions of Java

In the beginning there was version 1.0. Significant changes were introduced (especially in event-handling) resulting in version 1.1. Version 1.2 quickly progressed to Java 2, the current one and the one we use in this book.

But the situation is not quite so simple! In recognition of the range of devices which might contain processors (e.g. cookers, phones, etc.) Sun has provided three editions:

1. Standard. Probably the version you are using on a PC.
2. Enterprise, for (potentially large) organizations requiring major server software, distributed databases, Internet sales, etc.
3. Micro. This edition is capable of running in a very small amount of memory, and it is aimed at embedding code in such devices as mobile phones, pagers and set-top boxes.

There is also an application environment known as Personal Java for non-desktop computers (such as handhelds, PDAs, etc.), which have a limited GUI. This is based on Java 1.1 at the time of writing.

● Java capabilities

Enhancements to Java can arise through the addition of new libraries (helped by Java's object orientation), and also through software which allows Java to be used in new ways (for example Remote Method Invocation). Here we survey the most significant capabilities provided by Sun, in the form of libraries and technologies. However, note that many other companies also create Java software.

● Java libraries

Java is a small language and much of the power of Java programs arises from the facilities provided by the large (and sometimes complex) libraries. There has been much effort made to add to these libraries to promote the usage of Java. The following is a selection from the complete list:

● Java Language and Utilities. These provide the facilities (described in this book) for windowing and file input–output. They also support networking – writing programs that communicate with programs on another computer.
● Java Electronic Commerce Framework. The race is on to commercialize the Internet and this library should help. This library consists of facilities to send credit card information or electronic money securely across the Internet.
● Java Security. This provides facilities for digital signatures and authentication.
● Java Media Framework. Comprehensive facilities for media playback.
● Java Collections Framework. Data structures such as sets, linked lists, and maps.
● Java 3D. Classes for creating and displaying 3D worlds.

● Internationalization

There are hundreds of human languages in the world and, ideally, software should be able to adapt itself to any one of these. Internationalization is the process of giving software this quality. Let us look at some of the problems:

● Different languages have different character sets. For example, Spanish has accented letters, and uses inverted question-marks at the start of questions. And then there are non-European languages, such as Chinese.
● Dates and times. The UK uses day/month/year format, whilst the USA uses month/day/year format. Other countries have other conventions – and of course there are different names for the months and days of the week!
● Currency format. Different countries have different currency symbols: sometimes the symbol comes before the amount, and sometimes after.

The internationalization of a program might involve all these issues, together with the obvious issue of the translation of all the text that the user sees. Captions of buttons, labels, error messages, and help screens are all to be changed. Basically, full internationalization is difficult to achieve!

Java doesn't provide for full internationalization automatically. But it has classes which help, and it also works with the Unicode character standard:

1. Classes: there is the concept of a *locale* – an area with its own language. A Java program can find out its locale, and then make use of classes which do the appropriate formatting of currency, date and time.
2. The use of Unicode: this is a 16-bit agreed coding of the characters used by most of the world's languages, and it is built into Java. In fact, the classes we used for file I/O will work with Unicode files. You could use such files to contain the text to be displayed on (for example) buttons, rather than fix it in the code. It is then possible to supply a new file when a different language is required.

To summarize, you still have to plan how you are going to do your internationalization, but Java provides significant help via its classes and Unicode.

● Databases – JDBC

Databases are big business. Without a database, banks, manufacturing companies, airlines, supermarkets, etc. could not function. Aside from the use of word processors, spreadsheets and email, the database can be regarded as the most vital software component of businesses.

As an example, a shop which sells computers would use a database to hold stock levels, customer and supplier addresses, mailshot and invoice production, and staff salaries.

Currently, most databases are termed 'relational'. The data is held in tables which can be related to each other. Most databases can be accessed locally by either menu commands or typed-in queries, in a standard language known as SQL (Structured Query Language).

In larger organizations, there is often a central database with a large number of people accessing it, often from different countries and using different types of computer. This is where the portability of Java pays off. The JDBC (Java Database Connectivity) classes allow a Java applet running on (for example) a desktop machine to pass SQL queries to a database on another computer. The results are then passed back.

Of course, other software exists which can do this, but Java proponents stress the portability of the Java approach.

To summarize, JDBC allows access to SQL-compatible databases.

● RMI – Remote Method Invocation

A few years ago, the owner of a home PC was never exposed to the possibility of interaction between several computers. Now, with the tremendous increase in Internet use, the idea of interacting with programs on other machines is mainstream. In the corporate computing area as well, networks are the norm.

In certain application areas, it can be beneficial to distribute the processing power over several computers, which will then interact with each other when required. Let us imagine a multinational corporation. It will certainly have a large database, and could use the JDBC library to access this. However, if the application area is rather non-standard, then a database might not fit. What if the corporation want to provide software for a group of participants in different countries to cooperate in building up a design? This might require a window on to which anyone could type or draw. Every participant can see everyone else's work. One possible arrangement is for each participant to have a program on their computer to handle the local drawing, and to have a program on a central server to broadcast any new input. Software such as this can be developed more easily if an individual's computer can invoke methods on a server. In Java, this is known as RMI (Remote Method Invocation).

There is already a standard approach to this kind of distributed software, known as CORBA (Common Object Request Broker Architecture) which is not tied to any single company or programming language, and Microsoft has a similar system known as DCOM (Distributed Component Object Model). At the time of writing, it is uncertain whether one approach will dominate.

So, what does RMI let you do? Basically, you (or someone else) can set up Java software on a server. You can then write Java software on another machine which can invoke methods on the server. In addition, parameters can be passed as in normal method invocation, and part of the power of RMI comes from the fact that parameters of *any* type can be passed, not just simple numbers or strings.

RMI has a great deal of potential, as it is simpler than its competitors, but market forces rather than technical issues are likely to determine the winner in the world of distributed computing.

● Java beans

Sun states that a bean is 'a reusable software component that can be manipulated visually in a builder tool'. Before explaining the significance of this, let us examine the consumer electronics industry. There are agreed standards which ensure that, for example, your new CD player will work properly with any amplifier that has CD input facilities. The standard is at the level of plug sizes, and at the level of voltage. The result of this is that it is simple to create a new hi-fi system by plugging together a set of modules.

Back to software. Imagine that you are writing a text editor in Java, and you wanted to build in a spellchecker. What if you could open up your favourite word-processor and drag its spellcheck button into your text editor? (You can't actually do this at the moment, but it is a nice idea!)

The beans concept is rather similar. A programmer can write beans, which are Java classes written in a particular style. A bean might provide a sophisticated GUI for the programmer (for example, a spreadsheet bean) or its significant feature might be in the concealed code and data (for example, a spellchecker bean). In either case, the bean provides an icon at design-time, so that the programmer can visually incorporate and manipulate it. Here is the bean process, in rather more detail:

- A bean is either designed and coded, or purchased elsewhere. Coding a bean is similar to the coding of any Java class, but the programmer has to follow particular naming and style conventions.
- The software into which the bean is to be placed is written in such a way as to allow the bean to be incorporated. In some simple cases, no coding is needed.
- To incorporate the bean into the application, we use a special beans development environment; there are several available, including BDK (Beans Development Kit) from Sun. The environment allows beans to be selected graphically, and either dropped into an application, or connected to other beans.

So, beans are Java classes written in a particular way. They can easily be incorporated in beans-ready software. Those of you who have used Microsoft's Visual Basic may be familiar with 'custom controls' which can be used in a similar manner. In fact, beans are closest to Microsoft's Active X technology, which similarly allows the downloading of controls to Web pages. The future of beans is potentially huge, but this is based on the assumption that a large number of beans will be produced and will be available for purchase in an 'off the shelf' manner. Currently, the clear leader in this form of reuse is Microsoft's Visual Basic.

● Java servlets

Web interaction is enabled by programs on a server computer interacting with software (typically a browser) on a client computer. For example, a user might enter a name into a field in a Web page, and this data is passed to a program on the server, which might use this name to access a database. There are a number of ways to create server-side software, the most common one being the use of the HTTP/HTML Common Gateway Interface (CGI) facility, which is typically dealt with by a Perl program on the server, though CGI programs can be written in almost any language, including C, C++, and Java.

An alternative to CGI is to use Java servlets on the server. A servlet is a Java program coded according to certain conventions, with useful utility classes (for example, for accessing data from the client). Many servers (such as Apache and Microsoft IIS) allow servlets to be executed.

The benefits of servlets are:

● each time the Web page is used, and data is sent to the server, the single servlet creates a new thread. In the CGI approach, it is often the case that a fresh copy of the CGI program is created and executed. This is regarded as inefficient;
● a servlet can be run in a sandbox, providing better security;
● a servlet is platform-independent (assuming that the existing server software allows servlets to be incorporated).

● JavaScript

JavaScript is a scripting language for use in conjunction with Web pages. It has no language features in common with Java, although (as a language) it has concepts similar to some of those in Java.

A JavaScript program is embedded within a Web page and is introduced by a special HTML tag. The language provides:

● variables of type boolean, numeric and string;
● arrays of these data types;
● calculations;
● the usual control structures – sequences, loops and selection;

- methods (known as functions);
- a limited library of built-in functions;
- event handling for mouse-click events;
- output to the screen and input from the keyboard.

JavaScript is not an object-oriented language; classes and inheritance are not supported. There is no large library, such as is provided with Java.

Although JavaScript lacks the power and flexibility of Java, it does allow certain types of program to be constructed. These typically display information for the user, input data from the user via text boxes, check (verify) the data, and transmit the data to a remote server. JavaScript brings some life to Web pages through user interaction and the facility to present changing text and graphics.

The similarities between JavaScript and a Java applet are:

- the name;
- invoked from a Web page;
- runs on the client, not the server;
- subject to security restrictions, such as not accessing local files;
- runs on nearly every computer.

The main differences between JavaScript and Java are:

- different languages;
- Java is a general-purpose programming language; JavaScript is a specialized language for use with Web pages;
- Java is object-oriented; JavaScript is not;
- Java is used by programmers; JavaScript is used by Web authors;
- Java is compiled, then interpreted; JavaScript is directly interpreted.

In summary, Java and JavaScript are different languages that complement each other.

● Conclusion

Several trends are apparent in the computer industry:

- a tremendous growth of Internet use;
- the importance of Web interaction;
- use of intranets (an intranet is a local network, usually within a corporation, that uses Internet technology);
- reduction in the cost of networking;
- the fusion of the computer and telecommunications industries;
- the incorporation (embedding) of computers within consumer products;
- interest in multimedia;
- the realization of the vital need for secure computing across networks;
- a fight against the dominance of Microsoft (Windows operating system) and Intel (PCs).

Java has been born out of the need to create new technologies to deal with these trends. Java is no 'silver bullet' that solves problems as if by magic. There is no 'killer application' that makes it indispensable in the way that the VisiCalc spreadsheet made the Apple II computer a success. Instead, Java combines the best of current technologies in a very elegant synthesis to provide a 'Swiss Army knife' of facilities for computing into the new millennium.

Summary

Many of the above topics could fill a book individually, and there are also the areas of security and networking which we have not covered. New Java products are coming out rapidly, and are often significant. Check out Sun's Web site frequently, for new products and downloads. They are at:

```
http://java.sun.com/
```

EXERCISES

30.1 'Java is just another programming language'. Bill Gates. Discuss.

30.2 The performance overheads of Java programs make it impracticable for many applications. Discuss.

30.3 A fully object-oriented Visual Basic will kill off Java. Discuss.

30.4 Suggest the future for Java.

Appendix A

Java and C++ – the differences

This appendix is aimed at two kinds of people:

- those who know C++ and want to know how Java is different;
- those who know Java and want to know how C++ is different.

This comparison is intended as an introduction to the differences between the two languages, rather than an in-depth analysis.

Java owes a lot to C++ and therefore they have a lot in common. They both:

- are general-purpose programming languages;
- are textual;
- incorporate object-oriented ideas.

A note on terminology: in C++, methods are called functions.

Language size

Java is smaller than C++ – it has fewer facilities. This is not necessarily a bad thing – as Lenin said, in a different context, 'make smaller to make better'. Most of the features of high-level programming languages that are not absolutely vital have been left out of Java. The advantages, generally, of a smaller language are:

- easier to learn;
- easier to understand, test, debug and maintain a program;
- concentration on essentials.

Arguably C++, which was derived from C, is large and complex. (Take a look at many C++ texts, which are long.) So Java is perhaps a welcome return to basics.

The bottom line is that C++ has a number of features which are not present in Java. Examples are: operator overloading, header files, a preprocessor, pointers, structures, unions, templates and implicit type conversion. Some of these are arguably useful and others are superfluous.

● Object-oriented programming

Both Java and C++ support object-oriented programming. However, Java is object-oriented from the ground up – it was explicitly designed from the start to be object-oriented. C++ was derived from C (not an object-oriented language) and the object-oriented features are add-ons to a smaller language. It is easy to write a non-object-oriented program in C++, but not so easy in Java.

● Inheritance

Java supports only *single inheritance*. This means that a class can only inherit from one other class. There are major arguments in object-oriented circles about inheritance – what is useful and what is desirable. Some languages, including C++, support *multiple inheritance*, where a class can inherit from more than one other class. The designers of Java thought that this was complicated and unnecessary.

● Compilation and interpretation

Both Java and C++ are compiled, but whereas C++ is usually compiled to machine code, Java is compiled to a machine-independent low-level code called byte code. This byte code is then interpreted by the Java Virtual Machine running on the particular machine that is apparently running the Java program. This gives the Java code platform independence – the same byte code can be run on any of a huge variety of machines, with different operating systems. The cost is the slowing down of run-time speed – up to a factor of 20.

● Machine independence

We have already seen how, because of Java byte code, Java programs can be run on any of a variety of machines. This machine independence goes further, however. In C++, for example, there is uncertainty about how big a variable declared as an integer can be. Depending on the architecture of the target machine, a C++ integer can be 16, 32 or 64 bits long. Thus the way that a program behaves will be different from one machine to another. Such ambiguity is removed in Java, because an integer is defined to be 32 bits long and a long integer is defined to be 64 bits long – whatever the architecture of the machine it is running on.

Java is so machine-independent that porting a Java program to another machine does not even require recompilation. (This contrasts with C++.)

● Robustness and security

Java programs run on a virtual machine, rather than a real machine (like C++). This means that the Java Virtual Machine can carry out a number of checks that a program is running properly. For example, references to arrays are checked to ensure that the subscript is within the array bounds. When something goes wrong – for example, the program attempts to access an illegal region of memory – the program does not crash (as with C++), but instead the virtual machine performs an orderly handling of the situation.

Similarly, the virtual machine can check for viruses within Java byte code.

● Multithreading (concurrency)

Concurrency is sometimes called multithreading or parallelism. It is the ability to do two or more things at once. Now, while it is true that a single-processor computer can only execute one instruction at once, a computer is sufficiently fast to switch between a number of tasks that are apparently being carried out simultaneously. This switching is called multithreading, multitasking or concurrency. If you want to write a Java program to get two people to dance on the screen simultaneously, you need multithreading.

Java was designed from the start to provide concurrency (as part of the libraries). C++ does not support concurrency in such an integrated way.

● Garbage collection

When a C++ program requests memory to use as workspace, it must keep track of it and return it to the operating system when it ceases to use it. This requires extra programming and extra care. It is a common source of errors in C++ programs. This task of garbage collection is carried out automatically in Java – an object that is no longer used is automatically destroyed and the memory released.

On the other hand, the explicit release of resources (as is carried out in a C++ destructor function) is useful for releasing such resources as files and windows.

● Pointers

C++ has pointers but Java does not. Pointers are a way of referring to the actual memory address of a variable or a function. Programming with pointers has long been a touchstone of the real hard-bitten programmer. But programming with pointers is extremely error-prone and, because of the dangerous nature of machine addresses, can lead to subtle bugs and sometimes errors that defy removal.

In C++, parameters can be passed to functions either as values or references (pointers). In Java, any parameter that is a built-in type is passed to methods by value. This creates a degree of safety, because a method cannot change the value of the parameter back in the invoking method. If a value is to be returned to the user (invoker) of a method, it is returned as the value of the method (function). In computer science, this style of programming is regarded as being very pure. It corresponds to a mechanism provided in *functional* programming languages. However, in Java all objects (including arrays and strings) are passed as reference parameters (pointers) to methods. So this safety feature does not extend to objects.

In C++, pointers can be used to access an element of an array, but in Java array accesses are restricted to indices.

Java does use pointers, but they are invisible and inaccessible to the programmer. For example, when an object is created by a program as it executes, the Java system creates a pointer to the object.

● Libraries

Like C++, Java programs make extensive use of functions (methods) from libraries. This tends to make the language itself smaller as many actions are carried out by library functions rather than the language itself. An example is input–output facilities.

● Strings

In C++, strings are represented and manipulated as arrays of characters. Although there are plenty of library functions to help, it is not always convenient, it is not conceptually simple and it can be error-prone. In Java, a string is not the same as an array of characters; it is simpler in concept and is more easily manipulated. For example, rather than terminating a string of characters with a special character (as in C++), strings in Java have their length stored alongside them. Both C++ and Java provide a comprehensive set of library functions (methods) to manipulate strings.

● Data structures

Both Java and C++ support one-dimensional arrays. C++ directly supports multi-dimensional arrays, but this is done in Java by using the concept that a component of an array can itself be an array. The effect is therefore very much as if multidimensional arrays are directly supported.

We have already seen that Java does not support pointers that can be manipulated by the program. At first sight this is disappointing for programmers who like to build linked lists. But Java does use pointers – though they are invisible and inaccessible to the programmer. In a real sense, Java provides a higher level view of data structures than C++, a view in which pointers are at a lower level, invisible and managed by the system.

A classic case in programming in C++ with pointers is a linked list. Each item in such a list consists of some data together with a pointer to the next item in the list. So long as the program knows where the first item in the list is (a pointer to it), the chain of pointers can be followed to any position within the list. (There is also a special pointer value that denotes the end of the list.) Linked structures like this have the advantage that items can be added or removed from any position in the list. Also, the length of the list can be extended indefinitely.

To implement this in C++ requires the explicit use of pointers. In Java, however, the way that it can be implemented is to regard every item in the list (an object) as consisting of the data item accompanied by another object – the remainder of the list.

The Java code looks like this. The particular example is where the data item in each item of the list is a single integer. The code is given for creating a new list and for inserting a new item into a list.

```java
public class Item {
    private Item next;
    private int data;

    public Item(int integer) {
        this.next = null;
        this.data = integer;
    }

    public void insert(int i) {
        Item temp = new Item(i);
        temp.next = this.next;
        this.next = temp;
    }

}
```

● Exception handling

Exceptions are unusual situations that arise as a program is running. Some can be anticipated by the programmer (for example, when a program is asked to calculate the square root of a negative number); others are less easily foreseen (for example, the program attempts to access a protected area of memory). Some programming languages, including C++ and Java, provide language mechanisms, called exception handlers, for dealing with exceptions.

● Templates

One of the more popular object-oriented features of C++ is templates. Templates allow the programmer to create a set of functions (methods) – that is, a class – which act on a type that is not defined. The type of the data is defined when the class is used. This powerful facility allows the programmer to write a reusable, general-purpose class.

Java does not support templates.

● Names and packages

One problem with large C++ programs is that there can be a clash between different classes with the same name. This can be a particular problem with large software, written by a number of people and perhaps using library classes from a number of sources.

Java helps to solve this problem by providing a package concept. A number of classes can be grouped into a package. Two classes with the same name but in different packages are regarded as unique. C++ has a facility called namespaces which solves this same problem.

Appendix B

Java libraries

This appendix describes selected methods and data from the Java libraries. All Java programs use some library classes to accomplish their task. Java itself is a small language and the libraries provide most of the functionality. Java provides a host of library methods that are grouped into classes and in turn organized into several libraries listed below.

For each item in the libraries, we give the full heading, for example:

```
public void paint(Graphics g)
```

so that all the information on how to use them is available. Inspection of the full heading allows us to see what parameters are needed (or empty brackets if there are none) and what return value is returned (or void if no value is returned).

Here is a commentary on the libraries (remembering that a field is either a variable or a method):

- Nearly all the available fields of the libraries are methods – there are very few variables. This reflects the design principle of information hiding, whereby access to variables is usually via method invocations.
- All the fields are labelled public, because it is only public items that can be used.
- Fields labelled final cannot be overridden in a subclass. They are fixed and unchangeable.
- Fields labelled static belong to a class as a whole and not to individual objects instantiated from the class. Thus they are invoked by writing a statement of the form:

  ```
  Classname.methodName();
  ```

- Constructor methods such as TextField, Label and Date have no return type.

Here are the Java libraries with an outline of their contents.

java.lang

Contains the classes that support the main features of the languages like objects, strings, numbers, exceptions and threads.

java.util

These are useful utility classes such as `Random` and `ArrayList`.

java.io

Text input and output streams for characters and numbers.

java.net

Classes that carry out networking functions, interacting with the Internet.

java.awt

`awt` stands for Abstract Window Toolkit. These are the facilities for providing windows, buttons, text fields, pull-down menus and scrollbars. The graphics methods, such as `drawString`, are also in here.

java.applet

These classes provide support for Java applets (programs run from a Web browser).

● import

The `import` statement is a way of allowing the programmer to abbreviate the name of a method, rather than give its full package name. For each class we explain which `import` statement, if any, is required to use the class in a convenient way. The `java.lang` package is automatically imported into every Java program, because it provides vital methods which are used by nearly every Java program.

● java.applet.Applet

```
import java.applet.Applet;
```
  See also `java.applet.AudioClip`

`public AudioClip getAudioClip(URL url)`	Returns the audio clip object from the site specified by the `url`.
`public AudioClip getAudioClip(URL url, String name)`	Returns the audio clip object from the site specified by the `url` and the name.

`public URL getCodeBase()`	Returns the url of the applet code (the class file).
`public URL getDocumentBase()`	Returns the url of the HTML page that invoked the applet.
`public Image getImage(URL url)`	Returns the image object from the location specified by the url.
`public Image getImage(URL url, String name)`	Returns the image object from the location specified by the url and the name relative to the url.
`public void init ()`	Invoked by the browser or applet viewer when the applet program is ready to run. This method is usually overridden by the programmer to carry out the initialization necessary for the program.
`public void play(URL url)`	Plays the audio clip at the url, without first loading the audio clip (see getAudioClip above). See also the method **play** of java.applet.AudioClip.
`public void play(URL url, String name)`	Plays the audio clip at the url and the name relative to the url, without first loading the audio clip (see getAudioClip above). See also the method **play** of java.applet.AudioClip.
`public void setSize (int width, int height)`	Requests that the size of the available area on the screen be changed to the new size.

● java.applet.AudioClip

`import java.applet.AudioClip;`

`public abstract void loop()`	Plays a sound clip repeatedly.
`public abstract void play()`	Plays a sound clip from the beginning.
`public abstract void stop()`	Stops the playing of the sound clip.

● java.awt.BorderLayout

`import java.awt.Borderlayout;` or `import java.awt.*`

`public BorderLayout(String label)`	Creates a new border layout manager.

See also method **add** in java.awt.Container

● `java.awt.Button`

`import java.awt.Button;` or `import java.awt.*;`

public **Button**(String label)	Creates a button with the label.
public String **getLabel**()	Returns the label on this button.

See also method **add** in `java.awt.Container`

● `java.awt.Canvas`

`import java.awt.Canvas;` or `import java.awt.*;`

public **Canvas**()	Creates a canvas.
public void **paint**(Graphics g)	Repaints this canvas. This method is usually overridden by the programmer.

See also methods **add** and **setSize** in `java.awt.Container`

● `java.awt.Checkbox`

`import java.awt.Checkbox;` or `import java.awt.*;`

public **Checkbox**(String s)	Create a check box with the label s.
public **Checkbox**(String s, CheckboxGroup g, boolean state)	Create a check box with the label s, within the check box group g and with initial state.
public boolean **getState**()	Returns the state of the check box.

● `java.awt.CheckboxGroup`

`import java.awt.CheckboxGroup;` or `import java.awt.*;`

public **CheckboxGroup**()	Creates a new check box group to which check boxes can be added.

● `java.awt.Choice`

`import java.awt.Choice;` or `import java.awt.*;`

public **Choice**()	Creates a new choice box group to which choices can be added.
public void **addItem**(String item)	Add an item to this choice box.
Public String **getSelectedItem**()	Returns the item selected.

● java.awt.Component

import java.awt.Component; or import java.awt.*;

public Color **getBackground**()	Returns the background colour.
public Graphics **getGraphics**()	Returns the graphics context, usually called g.
public void **paint** (Graphics g)	Overridden by the programmer to paint the window. g is the graphics context.
public void **repaint**()	Invoked by the programmer when the screen display needs to be repainted. Results in paint being invoked.
public void **setSize**(int width, int height)	Resizes the component to the specified size on the screen.
public void **setVisible**(boolean visible)	Make the component visible (or not) on the screen.

● java.awt.Container

import java.awt.Container or import java.awt.*;

public Component **add**(Component comp)	Adds the component to the end of the container.
public void **remove**(Component comp)	Removes the component from the container.
public void **setSize**(int width, int height)	Resizes this component to the specified size.
public void **setLayout**(LayoutManager m)	Sets the layout manager. Options are: FlowLayout(), GridLayout(), BorderLayout().

Example:

```
Button b = new Button("Hello");
add(b);
```

● java.awt.FileDialog

import java.awt.FileDialog; or import java.awt.*;

public **FileDialog**(Frame parent, String title, int mode)	Creates a file dialog window. The parent is the frame that creates the window.

The title is the title of the window. The mode is either `FileDialog.LOAD` or `FileDialog.SAVE`.

`public String getFile()`   Returns the name of the file that has been selected, or null if none has been selected.

Note that `show()` (from the `Dialog` class) is used to display the dialog.

● java.awt.FlowLayout

`import java.awt.FlowLayout;` or `import java.awt.*;`

`public FlowLayout()`   Creates a new flow layout manager.

● java.awt.Frame

`import java.awt.Frame;` or `import java.awt.*;`

This class is for use with a free-standing application only – not an applet.

`public Frame()`   Creates a frame.

`public void setTitle(String s)`   Sets the title of the frame to the string `s`.

● java.awt.Graphics

`import java.awt.Graphics;` or `import java.awt.*;`

This group of methods provides facilities to display strings and graphical objects on the screen.

An object is drawn in the current colour, which can be changed using method `setColor`. The available colours are: black, blue, cyan, darkGray, gray, green, lightGray, magenta, orange, pink, red, white, yellow. For example, to change the colour to red, invoke:

```
setColor(red);
```

Coordinates of objects are expressed as *x* and *y* pixel coordinates. *x* is measured across the screen from the left. *y* is measured down the screen, with 0 at the top.

Many of the graphical objects are considered to be drawn inside an invisible (containing) rectangle whose top left pixel coordinates are *x,y*. The height and width of the rectangle, measured in pixels, are the two other parameters.

`public abstract void clearRect (int x, int y, int width, int height)`   Clears the specified rectangle by filling it with the background colour.

`public void` **`draw3DRect`**`(int x,`
`int y,int width, int height,`
`boolean raised);`
	Draws a highlighted 3D rectangle.
	If raised is true, the rectangle appears
	raised.

`public void` **`drawArc`**`(int x, int y,`
`int width, int height, int`
`startAngle, int arcAngle);`
	Draws a circular or elliptical arc.
	The arc is drawn from `startAngle` to
	`startAngle+arcAngle`.
	Angles are measured in degrees.
	An angle of 0 is the 3 o'clock position.
	A positive `arcAngle` means
	counterclockwise.

`public abstract boolean`
`drawImage``(Image image, int x,`
`int y, int width, int height,`
`ImageObserver observer)`
	Draws the image inside the rectangle
	specified, scaling the image if necessary.
	An object must be specified as the last
	parameter. This object is notified if the
	image is not yet completely loaded.
	Normally this parameter is simply **`this`**.
	See also method **`getImage`** in
	`java.applet.Applet`.

`public void` **`drawLine`**`(int x1,` `int y1, int x2, int y2);`	Draws a line from coordinates x1, y1 to x2, y2.
`public void` **`drawOval`**`(int x,` `int y, int width, int height)`	Draws an ellipse or a circle (if width and height are the same).

`public void` **`drawPolygon`**`(int`
`xPoints[], int yPoints[],`
`int nPoints);`
	Draws a closed polygon using the pairs of
	coordinates in the two arrays.
	A line is drawn from the first point to the
	last point.

`public void` **`drawRect`**`(int x,` `int y, int width, int height);`	Draws a rectangle using the current colour.

`public void` **`drawRoundRect`**`(int x,`
`int y, int width, int height,`
`int arcWidth, int arcHeight);`
	Draws a rectangle with rounded corners
	in the current colour.
	`arcWidth` is the horizontal diameter of
	the arc at the four corners, and
	`arcHeight` is the vertical diameter.

`public void` **`drawString`**`(String s,` `int x, int y);`	Draws a string. The baseline of the first character is at coordinate x, y. The characters are in the current font and current colour.

`public void` **`fillArc`**`(int x, int y,`
`int width, int height,`
`int startAngle, int arcAngle);`
	Draws a pie shape using the current
	colour. See **`drawArc`** for the meanings
	of the parameters.

`public void` **`fillOval`**`(int x, int y,` `int width, int height);`	Draws a filled ellipse or circle.

`public void fillPolygon(int xPoints[], int yPoints[], int nPoints);`	Fills a polygon with the current colour. See `drawPolygon` for the meaning of the parameters.
`public void fillRect(int x, int y, int width, int height);`	Fills the rectangle with the current colour.
`public void fillRoundRect(int x, int y, int width, int height, int arcWidth, int arcHeight);`	Fills a rounded rectangle with the current colour. See `drawRoundRect` for the meaning of the parameters.
`public void setColor(Color c);`	Sets the current colour. The available colours are listed at the top of this table.

● java.awt.Label

`import java.awt.Scrollbar;` or `import java.awt.*;`

`public Label(String label)`	Creates a new label.

See also method **add** in `java.awt.Container`

● java.awt.List

`import java.awt.List;` or `import java.awt.*;`

`public List(int r, boolean many)`	Creates a new list with `r` rows visible. If `many` is true, then multiple items can be selected. If `many` is false, then only one item can be selected.
`public void add(String item)`	Adds item to list.
`public void add(String item, int index)`	Adds item at index.
`public String getSelectedItem()`	Returns a string, the name of the selected item, or `null` if no item selected (list allows only one item to be selected).
`public String[] getSelectedItems()`	Returns a string array of the selected items (list allows several items to be selected).
`public void remove(int index)`	Removes item at index.
`public void remove(String item)`	Removes first occurrence of item.

See also method **add** in `java.awt.Container`.

● java.awt.Menu

import java.awt.Menu; or import java.awt.*;

public MenuItem **add**(MenuItem mi)	Adds a menu item to a menu.
public void **addSeparator**()	Adds a separator to a menu.
public **Menu**(String string)	Creates a menu with the string as its name.

● java.awt.MenuBar

import java.awt.MenuBar; or import java.awt.*;

public Menu **add**(Menu m)	Adds a menu to a menu bar.
public **Menubar**()	Creates a menu bar.

● java.awt.MenuItem

import java.awt.MenuItem; or import java.awt.*;

public **MenuItem**(String string)	Creates a menu item with the string as the label.

● java.awt.Panel

import java.awt.Panel; or import java.awt.*;

public **Panel**()	Creates a new panel.

● java.awt.Scrollbar

import java.awt.Scrollbar; or import java.awt.*;

public **Scrollbar**(int orientation, int value, int visible, int minimum, int maximum)	Creates a new scrollbar. See Appendix D.
public int **getValue**()	Returns the integer value.

See also method **add** in java.awt.Container.

● `java.awt.TextArea`

`import java.awt.TextArea;` or `import java.awt.*;`

`public TextArea(int rows, int cols)`	Creates a new text area of size `rows` by `cols`.

`public TextArea(String text, int rows, int cols, int vis)`	Creates a new text area, initialized with the string.
	`vis` specifies which scroll bars to display by giving one of:
	`SCROLLBARS_BOTH`
	`SCROLLBARS_HORIZONTAL_ONLY`
	`SCROLLBARS_VERTICAL_ONLY`
	`SCROLLBARS_NONE`

`public void append(String s)`	Appends the string `s` to the end of the current text.
`public void insert(String s, int here)`	Inserts the string at index `here`.

See also class `TextComponent` for useful methods and also method `add` in `java.awt.Container`.

● `java.awt.TextComponent`

This is the superclass of the classes `TextArea` and `TextField` and provides useful methods that enhance those in `TextArea` and `TextField`.

`import java.awt.TextComponent;` or `import java.awt.*;`

`public String getSelectedText()`	Returns the text selected by the user.
`public int getSelectionEnd()`	Returns the index to the first character selected by the user.
`public int getSelectionStart()`	Returns the index to the last character selected by the user.
`public String getText()`	Returns the complete text.
`public void setText(String s)`	Sets the entire text to string `s`.
`public void setEditable(boolean b)`	if `b` is true, the component becomes editable.

● `java.awt.TextField`

`import java.awt.TextField;` or `import java.awt.*;`

`public TextField(int cols)`	Creates a new text field, `cols` characters wide.

See also class `TextComponent` for useful methods and method `add` in `java.awt.Container`.

● `java.io.BufferedReader`

`import java.io.BufferedReader;` or `import java.io.*;`

`public BufferedReader(String Name)`	Creates a new `BufferedReader`.
`public BufferedReader(String name, int buffSize)`	Create with a buffer size.
`public final String readLine()`	Reads the next line of text from the data stream.

● `java.io.File`

`import java.io.File;`

`public File(String name)`	Creates an instance of class `File`, with the filename given as the parameter.
`public boolean exists()`	Returns `true` if the file specified by the object exists, or `false` otherwise.
`public String getAbsolutePath()`	Returns the full pathname of the file specified by this object.
`public String getPath()`	Returns the pathname of the file specified by this object.
`public boolean isDirectory()`	Returns `true` if this file exists and it is a directory, or `false` otherwise.
`public long length()`	Returns the length of the file in bytes, or zero if the file does not exist.
`public String[] list()`	Returns an array of filenames in the directory specified by the file object.
`public final static String separator`	This data field holds the value of the path separator character, which is specific to the particular operating system.

● `java.io.FileReader`

`import java.io.FileReader;` or `import java.io.*;`

`public FileReader(String name)`	Creates a file reader from a file with the specified name.
`public void close()`	Closes the stream.

See also class `java.io.BufferedReader`

● java.io.FileWriter

import java.io.FileWriter; or import java.io.*;

public **FileWriter**(String name, boolean flush)	Creates an output file writer from a file with the specified name.

See also java.io.PrintWriter

● java.io.PrintWriter

import java.io.PrintWriter; or import java.io.*;

public **PrintWriter**(OutputStream out)	Creates an instance of a print stream that sends its output to the output stream out.
public void **close**()	Closes the print stream.
public void **flush**()	Flushes this print stream. Any buffered output is written to the stream.
public void **print**(item)	Print the item. The item can be a character, double, float, int, long or String.
public void **println**(item)	Print the item, followed by a new line character.

● java.lang.Double

No import required.

public static double **doubleValue**()	Converts a Double to a double.
public static String **toString**(double d)	Converts the double into the equivalent string.
public static double **parseDouble**(String s)	Converts a string into a floating-point double.

Examples:

```
double d = Double.parseDouble("0.1234");
String s = Double.toString(d);
```

● java.lang.Float

No import required.

`public float floatValue()`	Converts a `Float` to a `float`.
`public static String` `toString(float f)`	Converts the `float` into the equivalent `String`.
`public static float` `parseFloat(String s)`	Converts a string into a float. A `NumberFormatException` is created if the string does not contain valid characters.

Examples:

```
float d = Float.parseFloat("0.1234");
String s = Float.toString(d);
```

● java.lang.Integer

No import required.

`public static int` `parseInt(String s)`	Converts a string of decimal digits into an integer. The digits may be preceded by a minus sign. A `NumberFormatException` is created if the string does not contain valid characters.
`public static String` `toString(int i)`	Converts the integer into the equivalent string.

Examples:

```
int i = Integer.parseInt(aString);

String s = Integer.toString(i);
```

● java.lang.Long

No import required.

`public static long` `parseLong(String s)`	Converts a string of decimal digits into a long integer. The digits may be preceded by a minus sign. A `NumberFormatException` is created if the string does not contain valid characters.
`public static String` `toString(long i)`	Converts the integer into the equivalent string.

Examples:

```
long i = Long.parseLong(aString);
String s = Long.toString(i);
```

● `java.lang.Math`

No `import` is required.

This class provides mathematical methods and two constants.
All angles are expressed in radians.

`public final static double E`	Value of e
`public final static double PI`	Value of π
`public static int abs(int a)`	
`public static long abs(long a)`	
`public static float abs(float a)`	
`public static double abs(double a)`	
`public static double acos(double a)`	
`public static double asin(double a)`	
`public static double atan(double a)`	
`public static double ceil(double a)`	Returns the nearest integer (as a double) that is greater than or equal to `a`.
`public static double cos(double a)`	
`public static double exp(double a)`	e^a
`public static double floor(double a)`	Returns the nearest integer (as a double) that is less than or equal to `a`.
`public static double log(double a)`	Natural log, to base e
`public static int max(int a, int b)`	
`public static long max(long a, long b)`	
`public static float max(float a, float b)`	
`public static double max(double a, double b)`	
`public static int min(int a, int b)`	
`public static long min(long a, long b)`	
`public static float min(float a, float b)`	

```
public static double min(double a,
double b)
```

```
public static double pow(double a,
double b)                               aᵇ
```

```
public static synchronized double
random()
```
Returns a pseudo-random number in the range 0.0 up to but not including 1.0.

See also class `java.util.Random`

```
public static double
rint(double a)
```
Returns the nearest integer to `a`, expressed as a double. If `a` is midway between two integers, it returns the even number.

```
public static int round(float a)
```
Returns the nearest integer to `a`, expressed as an integer.

```
public static long round(double a)
```
Returns the long that is closest to `a`.

```
public static double sin(double a)
```

```
public static double sqrt(double a)
```

```
public static double tan(double a)
```

Example:

```
y = Math.sqrt(x)
```

● java.lang.String

No `import` is required.
   Note that the + operator can be used to concatenate (join) strings.

```
public char charAt(int index)
```
Returns the character at the specified position.

```
public int
compareTo(String string)
```
Returns 0 if the strings are equal.
Returns a negative value if the string object precedes the parameter.
Returns a positive value if the string object follows the parameter.

```
public boolean endsWith(String
substring)
```
Returns `true` if a string ends with a particular substring.

```
public boolean equals(Object
object)
```
Returns `true` if the string has the same value as the parameter.

```
public boolean
equalsIgnoreCase(String string)
```
Returns `true` if the string is the same as the parameter, ignoring cases.

`public int indexOf(String string, int index)`	Returns the index of the first location of the substring in the string, starting from the position of the second parameter. Returns –1 if the substring is not present.
`public int lastIndexOf(String string)`	Returns the index of the rightmost location of the substring in the string. Returns –1 if the substring is not present.
`public int length()`	Returns the length of the string.
`public String replace(char oldChar, char newChar)`	Returns the string with all occurrences of `oldChar` replaced by `newChar`.
`public String()`	Create a new string.
`public String substring(int startIndex, int endIndex)`	Returns a specified part of a string. The first parameter is the starting position. The second parameter is the position one greater than the last character to be extracted (note the lower-case *s*).
`public String toLowerCase()`	Returns the string converted to lower-case.
`public String toUpperCase()`	Returns the string converted to upper-case.
`public String trim()`	Returns the string, but with white space removed from both ends. White space means space characters, newlines and tabs.
`public static String valueOf(param)`	Converts the parameter to a string. The parameter can be of type `Object`, `char[]`, `boolean`, `char`, `int`, `long`, `float`, `double`.

See also class `java.util.StringTokenizer`

● `java.lang.System`

No `import` is required.

This contains some miscellaneous, but useful, methods and also three convenient streams.

`public static long currentTimeMillis()`	Gets the current time in milliseconds. A millisecond is 1/1000 second. The time is measured from 1 January 1970.

`public static PrintStream` **`err`**	The standard error stream. This stream is already open and ready to accept output data. By convention, this stream is used to display error messages that should come to the immediate attention of the user.
`public static InputStream` **`in`**	The standard input stream. This stream is already open and ready to supply input data. Typically this is keyboard input.
`public static PrintStream` **`out`**	The standard output stream. This stream is already open and ready to accept output data.
`public static void` **`exit`**`(int status)`	Terminates the application and closes the window. The status should be 0 for a normal exit.

● `java.lang.Thread`

No `import` is required.

This class provides the methods for multithreading.

`public void` **`interrupt`**`()`	Interrupts the named thread.
`public static boolean` **`interrupted`**`()`	Returns `true` if the current thread has been the subject of an interrupt by some other thread.
`public boolean` **`isAlive`**`()`	Returns `true` if the thread is running or blocked, `false` if the thread is new or dead.
`public final` **`join`**`()`	Wait until the named thread has terminated.
`public void` **`notify`**`()`	Wakes up a thread that is suspended on a wait operation.
`public void` **`run`**`()`	Overridden by a thread. This method constitutes the code of a thread that is initiated by the `start` method.
`public static void` **`sleep`**`(int m)`	The thread is suspended for `m` milliseconds. There is no guarantee that the thread will be woken up after exactly the required number of milliseconds. This method must provide an exception handler for an `InterruptedException`.

`public void` **`start`**`()`	Initiates the running of a thread.
`public void` **`yield`**`()`	Suspends this thread temporarily and allows some other thread some processor time.
`public void` **`wait`**`()`	Causes the thread to be suspended until a notify operation is performed on the same object. This method must provide an exception handler for an `InterruptedException`.

● java.net.URL

`import java.net.URL;` or `import java.net.*;`

`public` **`URL`**`(String url)`	Creates a URL object from the string `url`. If the string does not conform to the syntax rules for a URL, a `MalformedURLException` is thrown.
`public URLConnection` **`openConnection`**`()`	Returns a `URLConnection` object that represents a connection to the remote object referred to by the URL.

See also class `java.net.URLConnection`

● java.net.URLConnection

`import java.net.URLConnection;` or `import java.net.*;`

`public` **`URLConnection`**`(URL url)`	Creates a URL connection object to the specified URL.
`public InputStream` **`getInputStream`**`()`	Returns an input stream that reads from this connection.

● java.util.ArrayList

`import java.util.*;`

`public` **`ArrayList`**`()`	Creates a new empty array list.
`public void` **`add`**`(Object object)`	Adds the new element to the end of the array list. The size of the array list is increased by 1.

`public Object get(int index)`	Returns the element at index. The object is not removed.
`public void add(int index, Object object)`	Inserts the object at position index. The element that was at this position and all elements with index greater than index are moved up one position.
`public boolean isEmpty()`	Returns true if the array list is empty, otherwise false.
`public void clear()`	Removes all the elements in an array list. The size becomes 0.
`public void remove(int index)`	Removes the item at position index. All elements with an index greater than index are moved down.
`public Object set(int index, Object object)`	Replaces the element at position index. Returns the original object.
`public int size()`	Returns the number of items in the array list.

● java.util.Date

```
import java.util.Date;
```

`public int getDate()`	Returns the day of the month.
`public int getDay()`	Returns the day of the week. 0 is Sunday.
`public int getHours()`	Returns the hour of the day, between 0 and 23, in the 24 hour clock system. 0 is midnight.
`public int getMinutes()`	Returns the number of minutes past the hour.
`public int getMonth()`	Returns the month. 0 is January.
`public int getSeconds()`	Returns the number of seconds past the minute.
`public int getTime()`	Returns the number of milliseconds since 1 January 1970, 0 hours, 0 minutes, 0 seconds.

See also `currentTimeMillis` in class `java.lang.System`

Sample code:

```
Date date = new Date();
int day = date.getDate();
g.drawString("date is " + day, 50, 50);
```

● java.util.Random

```
import java.util.Random;
```
These methods return what are apparently random numbers. In fact they are only pseudo-random, because one is calculated from the next. To ensure that they appear random, the first value is derived from a seed, which is normally based on the current time. (The milliseconds part of the current time always appears to be random.) To explicitly give the seed a value (when testing, for example) use setSeed.

See also method random in Java.lang.Math

public **nextFloat**()	Returns the next pseudo-random number, uniformly distributed from 0.0 to 0.999 . . .
public **nextDouble**()	Returns the next pseudo-random number, uniformly distributed from 0.0 to 0.999 . . .
public **nextInt**()	Returns the next pseudo-random number, uniformly distributed in the range of int.
public **nextLong**()	Returns the next pseudo-random number, uniformly distributed in the range of Long.
public void **setSeed**(long seed)	Sets the seed of the random number generator.

Sample code:

```
Random r = new Random();
float f = r.nextFloat();
g.drawString("random is "+ f, 50, 50);
```

● java.util.StringTokenizer

```
import java.util.StringTokenizer;
```

public **StringTokenizer**(String s, String delim)	Constructs a string tokenizer for the string s. The characters in the parameter delim are the delimiters for separating tokens.
public boolean **hasMoreTokens**()	Returns true if there are more tokens in the string, or false otherwise.
public String **nextToken**()	Returns the next token from this string tokenizer.

Appendix C

HTML summary

● Introduction

HyperText Markup Language (HTML) is the language used for creating Web pages. It describes the formatting that a document needs when it is displayed using a Web browser like Netscape Navigator or Microsoft Internet Explorer. Normally when you use a Web browser you just see the text and graphics displayed as its creator intended. Behind this are HTML commands specifying the layout. Similarly, when you create Web pages you use an editor that puts all the HTML commands in automatically. So most of the time you never see the HTML. Here is a small example of some text with HTML commands embedded in it:

```
<TITLE> Interesting Page </TITLE>
<H1> The nature of oppression </H1>
<P> That was only a prelude.
<P> Those who burn books will in the end burn men.
<P> Heinrich Heine
```

You will see that the formatting information appears inside the pointed brackets < and >. These are called tags. These tags can be in either upper-case or lower-case – we show them here in upper-case for emphasis.

This appendix describes the HTML commands that provide:

- headings, paragraphs and lists;
- links to other documents;
- graphics, sounds and animations;
- Java applets.

To view a Web page, you need a Web browser, such as Netscape Navigator or Microsoft Internet Explorer.

To create a Web page, you need either:

- an HTML editor, which usually allows you to create Web pages in a WYSIWYG (What You See Is What You Get) style. This is the preferred way of creating Web pages and it avoids the need to understand HTML; or
- an ordinary editor, in which case you insert all the formatting instructions (tags) explicitly. With this approach you need to know about HTML commands.

● Headings, paragraphs and lists

An HTML document should start with a line like:

```
<TITLE>this is the title</TITLE>
```

The browser takes this to be the name of the document and displays it as part of the header, rather than as part of the document. This is also the title that is saved as a bookmark.

Normal headings in the text start with `<H1>` and end with `</H1>`. This is a major heading; smaller headings can be enclosed between `<H2>` and `</H2>` and so on.

A browser will take no notice of new lines in the text, but instead decide itself where to put new lines. If you want to say where new lines go, then put `<BR>` at the appropriate place in the text. Similar is `<P>`, which gives a new paragraph, usually with a blank line between the paragraphs. These two tags are unusual because they appear alone – all the others come in pairs, with a start tag and an end tag bracketing the text to be formatted.

If you want a piece of text to be in bold, sandwich it between `<B>` and `</B>`. Italic is `<I>...</I>`.

Numbered lists can be described as shown in the following example:

```
<OL>
<LI>edit
<LI>compile
<LI>run
</OL>
```

which would produce:

1. edit
2. compile
3. run

when displayed.

If you want bulleted rather than numbered items, use `<UL>` instead of `<OL>`. For example:

```
Java is:
<UL>
<LI>small
<LI>robust
<LI>fun
</UL>
```

● Links to other Web pages

If you have ever surfed the Web, you will know that one of the central features of browsing is the ability to click the mouse on a link to another place in the same document or else to a completely different document (Web page). The browser usually highlights words or phrases that are links by showing them in a different colour from the rest of the text and underlining them. (Graphics objects can also act as links – see later.)

Suppose we want to create a link in our current document that looks like this:

For more information click: <u>here</u>

to another of our own files called:

more/info/stats.html

The HTML version of the link looks like:

```
For more information click: <A HREF = "more/info/stats.html">here</A>
```

The tag begins with the letter A (anchor). This is followed by an HTML parameter, introduced by HREF=. The parameter is the name of the file, enclosed in double quotes. Next comes the text that is to act as the user's visual link. Finally comes the closing </A> tag.

To refer to a file in the folder above our current file, we put:

```
<A HREF = "../demo.html">here</A>
```

If you want to specify a file somewhere else on the World-Wide Web, it is necessary to give the uniform resource locator (URL) of the desired file. This is the only difference in linking to a Web file rather than your own. For example:

```
For the LA Times click:
<A HREF="http://www.latimes.com/"> here </A>
```

● Graphics, animation and sound

A graphical image is stored in a computer in a file. An image can be created by a program, downloaded from a digital camera, scanned in from a scanner or extracted from a video image. Different graphics packages use different file formats, and as usual the suffix at the end of the name distinguishes the type. Examples are GIF, X Bitmap (XBM) and JPEG. Remember that it takes longer to transmit graphics files (because they are bigger than text files) and therefore you generally have to wait for graphics to be displayed. Remember also that the browser has to support viewing of the file type you are using.

If you want to display a graphical object, you place a tag like this in your HTML file:

```
<IMG SRC="name">
```

where the name in quotes after the parameter `SRC=` is the URL or the address of the graphics file.

If you want a graphical image to act as a link to another file, the command is the same as we saw in the case of a text link:

```
<A HREF="new file name"><IMGSRC="name"></A>
```

Sound and animation work in exactly the same way. A piece of sound or a piece of animation is held in a file. Sound files usually have the suffix `AU`; graphics files are typically `MOV` or `MPEG`. You usually would not want to include them directly in an HTML document, because playing them would be out of the user's control. Instead you would want to click on some text or on some (usually small) graphic to start the sound or the animation. To do this, you just use the same tag as for invoking a link to any other file:

```
<A HREF="name of sound or animation file"> click here for the biz </A>
```

● Java applets

To run a Java applet from an HTML document, insert the following tag at the place in the document where you want the applet to run:

```
<APPLET CODE="file name or URL of Java program"
WIDTH=300 HEIGHT=80></APPLET>
```

The two parameters are the width and height (in pixels) that the applet will use on the screen in pixels.

● The future of HTML

Like any computer language, HTML has progressed trough standards, the current one being 4.0, though Netscape and Internet Explorer vary on their interpretation of some advanced features. One of the strengths of HTML is that, if a browser does not understand some feature, like the Java Applet tag – `<APPLET` – then it ignores it. So the browser never crashes or gets into trouble – the worst that can happen is that something you might expect to happen doesn't.

In the long term, XML (Extensible Markup language) will be increasingly important. XML has tags too, but unlike HTML, these tags describe *content*. For example, we might choose to tag the word 'Washington' as <city> rather than <surname>.

XSL (Extensible Stylesheet Language) can then be used to instruct a Web browser to display cities in a different format to surnames.

From the Java point of view, applets provide the possibility of downloading an XML document along with the code to display it.

● Reference summary

` `	new line
`<P>`	new paragraph
`<TITLE>...</TITLE>`	Title to be used by browser
`<H1>...</H1>`	major heading
`<H2>...</H2>`	minor heading, etc.
`<I>...</I>`	italic
`<B>...</B>`	bold

```
<OL>
<LI>...
<LI>...          numbered list
<LI>...
</OL>
```

```
<UL>
<LI>...
<LI>...          bulleted list
<LI>...
</UL>
```

`<A HREF="file or URL">...</A>`   link to another document

```
<APPLET CODE="file or URL of Java program"
WIDTH=.. HEIGHT=...></APPLET>          run a Java applet
```

● Bibliography

NCSA's Beginner's guide to HTML is at:

http://www.ncsa.uiuc.edu/General/Internet/WWW/HTMLPrimer.html

Appendix D

Widgets and event handling

● Introduction

This appendix collects together, for reference, all the information on creating and handling a few, selected GUI (Graphical user Interface) widgets (windowing gadgets).

To create and handle events, a number of things are written in the program:

1. The following `import` is written at the top of the program:

```
import java.awt.event.*;
```

2. The class that handles the event declares that it `implements` a particular interface.
3. The widget is created, using the constructor method of the desired widget class.
4. The widget is added to the window.
5. The object that is to handle the event is registered with the appropriate listener.
6. A method is provided to react to the event.

● Scrollbars

		example
implements	AdjustmentListener	
constructor	Scrollbar(params)	
register listener using	void addAdjustmentListener(Object o)	`bar.addAdjustment Listener(this)`
event handler method(s)	void adjustmentValueChanged(AdjustmentEvent event)	
useful methods	int getValue()	`event.getValue()`

The parameters for the method `Scrollbar` to create a new scrollbar are:

1. the orientation, which must be either `Scrollbar.HORIZONTAL` or `Scrollbar.VERTICAL`;
2. the initial value (an integer) of the scrollbar;
3. the visible amount. This is used when a scrollbar is employed to view an image (text or graphics) that is larger than the available viewing area. The visible amount specifies the amount of the image that is visible and the size of the scroll box (the sliding rectangle in the middle of the scrollbar). For example, if the scroll box is half the size of the scrollbar, then half the image is visible;
4. the minimum value (an integer);
5. the maximum value (an integer).

The user of a scrollbar can change its value in the following ways:

1. Click on the arrow at one end of the bar. This changes the value by 1.
2. Click and drag on the scroll box. This changes the value by an amount corresponding to the distance dragged.
3. Click in the area between the scroll box and the end of the range. This changes the value by the page size.

● Labels

```
Label toms = new Label("Tom:");
add(toms);
tom = new Scrollbar(Scrollbar.HORIZONTAL, 0, 1, 0, 100);
add(tom);
```

When a label is created as shown in the above example, it is placed alongside the widget that is created next (the scrollbar in the above example). Labels do not need any event handling.

● Buttons

		example
implements	ActionListener	
constructor	Button(String s)	
register listener using	void addActionListener(Object o)	`button.addActionListener(this)`
event handler method(s)	void actionPerformed(ActionEvent event)	
useful methods	Object getSource()	`event.getSource()`
	String getActionCommand()	`button.getActionCommand()`

● Text fields

A text field is a box into which the user can type any number of characters. The user can change the characters using the delete key. When the user presses the return key, an event is caused which is usually handled by the method `actionPerformed` as shown below. The string that is returned by `getText` does not include the return key. If multi-line input is required, then a text area is the appropriate widget. A text field can also be used to display (output) text using the `setText` method.

		example
implements	ActionListener	
constructor	TextField(int width)	
register listener using	void addActionListener(object o)	`field.addActionListener` `(this)`
event handler method(s)	void actionPerformed(ActionEvent event)	
useful methods	Object getSource()	`event.getSource()`
	String textField.getText()	`textField.getText()`
	void setText(String s)	`textField.setText("hello")`

When a text field is created, it can optionally be given a width parameter, an integer number of characters, like this.

```
inputData = new TextField(10);
```

If a number is being input via a text field, it can be converted to an integer using `Integer.parseInt` or `Long.parseLong`. If the number to be input is a floating-point number, it can be converted to the internal representation using `Float.parseFloat` or `Double.parseDouble`. If an illegal character is present in the string, an exception is thrown by these library methods. If no exception handler is provided, an error message is produced.

● Mouse events

Events are divided into two sets:

1. those describing the status of the mouse (use interface `MouseListener`);
2. those describing movements of the mouse (use interface `MouseMotionListener`).

		example
implements	MouseListener	
register listener using	void addMouseListener(Object o)	`this.addMouseListener` `(this)`
event handler method(s)	void mouseClicked(MouseEvent event) void mouseReleased(MouseEvent event) void mousePressed(MouseEvent event) void mouseEntered(MouseEvent event) void mouseExited(MouseEvent event)	
useful methods	int getX() int getY() int.getClickCount()	`event.getX()` `event.getY()` `event.getClickCount()`

		example
implements	MouseMotionListener	
register listener using	void addMouseMotionListener(Object o)	`this.addMouseMotion-` `Listener(this)`
event handler method(s)	void mouseDragged(MouseEvent event) void mouseMoved(MouseEvent event)	
useful methods	int getX() int getY()	`event.getX()` `event.getY()`

The different events occur as follows:

`mouseClicked` – the mouse button has been clicked and released without moving the mouse

`mouseReleased` – the mouse button has been released after the mouse has been dragged

`mousePressed` – the mouse button has been pressed

`mouseEntered` – the mouse has entered this window

`mouseExited` – the mouse has left this window

`mouseDragged` – the button has been pressed, held down and the mouse moved. This is preceded by a `mousePressed` event and followed by a `mouseReleased` event.

`mouseMoved` – the mouse has been moved

Programming pitfalls

If you write:

```
if (event.getSource() == "Press me") etc
```

this event will never be detected because this compares an object (`event.getSource()`) with a string. The correct test should probably be:

```
if (event.getSource() == PressMe) etc
```

Note that a number of widgets share the same event handler method (for example, both buttons and text fields cause the same event handler, `actionPerformed`, to be invoked).

Note that `Checkbox` and `Scrollbar` break the standard Java convention for class names.

Appendix E

Rules for names

In Java the name of a variable, a class or a method is known as an identifier. The programmer chooses identifiers. The rules are:

- An identifier can be as long as you like.
- An identifier consists of letters (upper-case and lower-case) and digits (0 to 9).
- An identifier must start with a letter.
- An identifier must not be the same as one of the Java keywords listed in Appendix F.

A letter is defined to be A to Z, a to z, dollar($) or underscore(_). Dollar and underscore are not normally used and are included only for historical reasons. Also included in the category of letters are the letters of many languages of the world.

By convention:

- Class names start with a capital letter and continue in lower-case, for example `Applet`.
- Variable and method names start with a lower-case letter, for example `random`.
- When a name is a combination of words, the new words start with a capital letter, for example `wishYouWereHere`, `drawString`.

Both upper-case and lower-case letters are valid and distinct, so that `mouse` is distinct from `MOUSE` and `Mouse`.

Keywords

These are the Java reserved words. They cannot be used as names by the programmer for variables, methods or classes.

Keyword	See page	Description
abstract	490	Specifies that only part of a class is implemented
boolean	95	Type of variable that can be `true` or `false`
break	103	Used to end a loop or `switch` statement
byte	199	8 bit integer
case	103	Used in `switch` statement to identify one of the cases
cast		Not used (reserved for possible future use)
catch	302	Used to catch an exception
char	276	Type that holds a single character
class	142	Introduces a class description
const		Not used (reserved for possible future use)
continue		Used in a loop to continue
default	105	Used in `switch` to specify the default case
do	124	Used in `do` loop
double	199	Double-precision floating-point data type
else	83	The second alternative in an `if` statement
extends	183	Specifies that one class extends or inherits from another
false[1]	96	Boolean value
final	191	A variable, method or class that cannot be overridden (changed)
finally	311	The last chance part of an exception handler
float	32	Single-precision floating-point data type
for	122	Type of loop
future		Not used (reserved for possible future use)

Keyword	See page	Description
generic		Not used (reserved for possible future use)
goto		Not used (reserved for possible future use)
if	81	Selection statement
implements	493	Specifies that a class implements an interface class
import	485	Specifies use of a package
inner		Not used (reserved for possible future use)
instanceof	513	Tests if an object is an instance of a class
int	32	32 bit integer type
interface	495	A type of class that specifies only how it can be used
long	199	64 bit integer type
native		Type of method that uses machine dependent features
new	146	Creates a new object from a class
null[1]	161	A non-existent object
operator		Not used (reserved for possible future use)
outer		Not used (reserved for possible future use)
package	485	Specifies that a class is part of a named package
private	49	Specifies that a variable or method can only be used by methods in the same class
protected	186	Specifies that a variable or method can only be used by methods in the same class, its subclasses and other classes in the same package
public	49	Specifies that a variable or method can be used by any method
rest		Not used (reserved for possible future use)
return	54	Returns from a method to its invoker
short	199	16 bit integer type
static	159	A variable or method that belongs to a class and not to any of its instantiated objects
super	190	The superclass of the current class
switch	102	Selection statement with several options
synchronized	457	A method that has exclusive usage of an object by a thread
this	153	The current object
throw	306	Create an exception
throws	306	The exceptions that a method can throw
transient		Not used (reserved for possible future use)
true[1]	96	Boolean value
try	302	Specifies statements that may throw an exception
var		Not used (reserved for possible future use)
void	49	A method that returns nothing
volatile		Not used (reserved for possible future use)
while	117	Type of loop

[1] These words are not strictly reserved words. They are literals like the numbers 2010 and 42 (for example). They cannot be used by the programmer to name things.

Appendix G

Visibility (scope rules)

Visibility is the term used to describe what can be accessed (or referred to) by what. Any class can use any `public` class in the world, provided only that it gives its name properly. (This will sometimes involve using an `import` statement.) A class can also inherit from any `public` class in the world, overriding methods or adding methods as required.

A field (method or variable) within a class can be described using one of the following modifiers. This modifier describes what type of access is permitted by other classes. Access to a variable means permission to use the value or change the value of that variable. (Generally, access to variables is undesirable as it violates the principle of information hiding.) Access to a method means the permission to invoke the method.

Suppose that a class is in a particular package. Ranging from most to least accessible, the options for access to a variable or a method are:

1. `public` – accessible from anywhere;
2. `protected` – accessible from any class within this package and also from subclasses in other packages;
3. `default` (no description) – accessible from any class in this package;
4. `private` – accessible only from within this class.

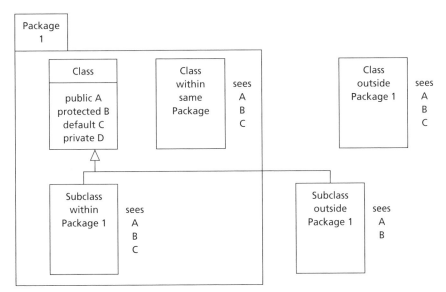

Figure G.1 Java visivility.

This same information is presented in the following table, which illustrates the uniformity of the access scheme:

Variable or method labelled as	Accessible from same class	Accessible from any class in the same package (subclass or not)	Accessible from any subclass (not in same package)	Accessible from any class anywhere
private	yes	no	no	no
default	yes	yes	no	no
protected	yes	yes	yes	no
public	yes	yes	yes	yes

This information is shown graphically in Figure G.1.

Appendix H

Code skeletons

Here we provide skeletons ('bare bones') for the varieties of program that you might want to create with Java. Often, a beginning programmer understands the low-level detail (e.g. using an `if`, a variable, or a method) without being able to create the overall framework. This section is provided to show the high-level structures.

Categories of programs

Essentially, we have applets or free-standing applications.

The majority of applets will be GUI-based, and will use the AWT. We provide two forms:

- the class `AnySmallApplet`, suitable for short applets;
- the class `AnyMVCApplet`, suitable for tackling more complex applets.

Applications are free-standing programs, and we provide three forms:

- The class `SimpleApplication`, which is only suitable for programs of 'Hello World' complexity. It uses console I/O rather than the AWT.
- The class `LargeApplication` for non-AWT applications consisting of classes – all but the most trivial programs will take this form.
- The class `AWTApplication`, for use with AWT applications.

For every AWT form, we have included the event-handling code for a button. For other controls, you need to add the appropriate registration and listener methods.

Applet skeletons

Here is the simple skeleton for small applets which paint shapes on the screen. Classes created by the programmer are not a significant feature at this stage.

```
//simple applet
import java.awt.*;
import java.applet.Applet;
import java.awt.event.*;

public class AnySmallApplet extends Applet
    implements ActionListener {
    // instance variables etc
    private Button aButton;

    public void init() {
        aButton = new Button("press me");
        add(aButton);
        aButton.addActionListener(this);
    }

    public void paint(Graphics g) {
        //code
    }

    public void actionPerformed(ActionEvent event) {
        if (event.getSource() == aButton)
            // respond to button
        repaint(); // if needed
    }
}
```

Now we show the applet structure where the suggested model–view–controller design approach has been used:

```
// MVC Applet
import java.awt.*;
import java.applet.Applet;
import java.awt.event.*;

public class AnyMVCApplet extends Applet
    implements ActionListener {
    // instance variables etc
    private Button aButton;
    private Model aModelInstance;

    public void init() {
        aButton = new Button("press me");
        add(aButton);
        aButton.addActionListener(this);
```

```
                aModelInstance = new Model();
        }


        public void paint(Graphics g) {
            aModelInstance.display(g);
        }


        public void actionPerformed(ActionEvent event) {
            if(event.getSource() == aButton)
                // respond to button, e.g:
            aModelInstance.getSomething();
            repaint(); //if needed
        }
    }


class Model { // start of model class
    // private instance items

    public void setSomething() {
    // code
    }

    public void getSomething() {
        // code
    }

    public void display(Graphics g) {
        // code to display current state
    }
} // end of model class

class Model {    // start of model class
    // private instance items
    public void setSomething() {
    // code
    }
    public void getSomething() {
        // code
    }
    public void display(Graphics g) {
        // code to display current state
    }
}    // end of model class
```

In larger programs, we might choose to move the model class to its own file. If so, it must be specified as:

```
public class Model {
```

We might also need to add any import statements for libraries, which were originally at the top of the single file.

Note that the above is simply a skeleton. It is impossible to provide exact details for such items as parameter and return values for the model. The main point is that in an MVC-based approach, the model is likely to have set and get methods, plus a display method.

● Free-standing applications

First, we will look at non-AWT applications. We show the simplest form consisting of a main method, which you might use to throw together a program which does a trivial task.

```
// Non-AWT trivial application
public class SimpleApplication {
    public static void main(String [] args) {
            // code
    }
}
```

Now we show a non-AWT application which uses a class provided by the programmer. We create an instance, then initiate it by invoking someMethod, which in its turn invokes another method.

```
// non-AWT application with class
public class LargeApplication {
    // private items
    public static void main(String [] args) {
        LargeApplication anInstance = new LargeApplication();
        anInstance.someMethod();
    }
    private void someMethod() {
        // code
        anotherMethod();
    }
    private void anotherMethod() {
        // code
    }
}
```

Finally we look at AWT-based applications. Chapter 18 illustrated the differences between an applet and an application. In the following, we will assume that the model class exists in its own file. We have chosen to build the GUI in a constructor, but could have chosen to do it with an explicit method invocation. The structure takes the form:

```java
// AWT-based application
import java.awt.*;
import java.awt.event.*;

public class AWTApplication extends Frame
    implements ActionListener, WindowListener {
    // instance variables etc
    private Button aButton;
    private Scrollbar aScrollbar;
    private Model aModelInstance;

    public static void main(String [] args) {
        AWTApplication anInstance = new AWTApplication();
        anInstance.setSize(300,200);
        anInstance.setVisible(true);
    }

    public AWTApplication() {      // constructor
        aButton = new Button("press me");
        add(aButton);
        aButton.addActionListener(this);
        aModelInstance = new Model();
        this.addWindowListener(this);      // for windowClosing
    }

    public void paint(Graphics g) {
        aModelInstance.display(g);
    }
    public void actionPerformed(ActionEvent event) {
        if (event.getSource() == aButton)
            // respond to button, e.g:
        aModelInstance.getSomething();
    }

    public void windowClosing(WindowEvent e) {
        System.exit(0);
    }
```

```
//empty WindowListener Methods
public void windowIconified(WindowEvent e) {
}
public void windowOpened(WindowEvent e) {
}
public void windowClosed(WindowEvent e) {
}
public void windowDeiconified(WindowEvent e) {
}
public void windowActivated(WindowEvent e) {
}
public void windowDeactivated(WindowEvent e) {
}

// the Model class is identical to the applet
// example, and is in its own file.
}
```

Appendix I

UML summary

UML, Unified Modeling Language, is a graphical notation for describing object-oriented programs. It is not a method for design, but a notation that can help with designing a program or help to document a program once it is complete. We take the view that these diagrams *can* often help in understanding a program. But if you don't find them useful, then don't use them!

This appendix gives a summary of those aspects of UML used in this book. UML is a large and potentially complex notation and therefore we have only used a part of the notation. Thus the diagrams described and used in this book are:

- collaboration diagrams;
- class diagrams;
- activity diagrams.

● Collaboration diagrams

A collaboration diagram describes the *relationships between objects*. It says which objects use which other objects. An example is shown in Figure I.1. Each object is shown as a rectangular box. Within the box, the name of an object is followed by a colon and then the name of its class. The complete name is underlined. Either the object name or the class name can be omitted. But if the object name is omitted, the colon and class name remain (and this can look rather odd).

Figure I.1 shows two objects – one object is unnamed of the class `PlayBalloon`; the second object is called `myBalloon` of the class `Balloon`. The unnamed object invokes the methods `new`, `changeSize` and `display` on the object `myBalloon`.

Any relationship between two objects is shown as a line connecting their boxes. If desired, method invocations can be shown as small arrows indicating the direction of the invocation; the method name appears alongside the arrow. A special kind of invocation

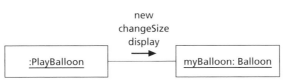

Figure I.1 Example of a collaboration diagram.

is when one object creates another using the Java word `new`. This is shown in the same way as a method invocation. In the illustration (Figure I.1), the unnamed object of the class `PlayBalloon` invokes methods `new`, `changeSize`, and `display` on the object `myBalloon`.

Note that a collaboration diagram presents no information about the order is which things take place – it presents essentially static information about the relationship between objects.

● Class diagrams

A class diagram shows the *inheritance relationships between classes* – the subclasses and superclasses. As illustrated in Figure I.2, each class is shown as a rectangular box that contains its name. To show that a class extends another, a line is drawn from the subclass to the superclass, with the arrowhead pointing to the superclass.

If a class is an abstract class, the name of the class is written in italics. This can be difficult to see, particularly when hand-written. So the name of an abstract class can be followed by the text {abstract} to clarify the meaning (see Figure I.3).

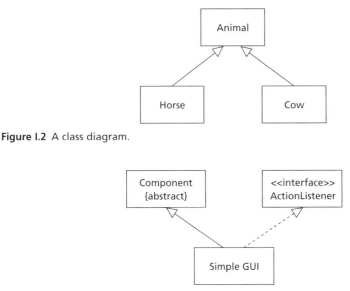

Figure I.2 A class diagram.

Figure I.3 Class diagram showing an abstract class and an interface.

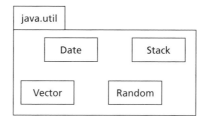

Figure I.4 Example of a class diagram showing details of the class.

Figure I.5 UML diagram showing a package that consists of a number of classes.

An interface is described in the same way as a class – as a box. The difference is that the text `<<interface>>` precedes the name. A class that implements an interface has a dashed line with an arrow leading to the interface box (see Figure I.3).

Classes can be described in more detail, as illustrated in Figure I.4. There are three compartments in this type of diagram. The first compartment holds the class name, the second describes variables and the third describes methods. Any class (static) variables or methods are shown underlined. The visibility of an element can be, optionally, described in a prefix as in Java – public, private, protected or default.

In keeping with information hiding, the diagram can be drawn with the second compartment (the variables) omitted.

Note that a class diagram shows a *static* relationship. It describes how classes inherit from each other, but it says nothing about the sequence of events within a program.

A package can be diagrammed as shown in Figure I.5. It is a rectangle with a tab at the top that holds the package name. Optionally, the classes within a package can be shown within the rectangle.

● Activity diagrams

An activity diagram describes a *sequence of activities*. This matches the usual flow of control within a program as it executes a sequence of statements, including method invocations. An activity diagram can also show:

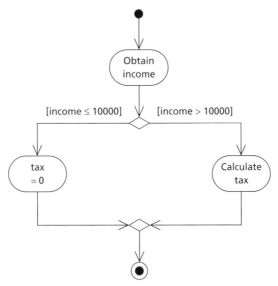

Figure I.6 A UML activity diagram.

● conditions (corresponding to `if` statements)
● loops (corresponding to `for` and `while` statements)
● concurrent activity (corresponding to threads)

Further, as we shall see, an activity diagram can also show which class performs which activity.

A simple activity diagram shows the sequence of actions in a program to calculate tax, Figure I.6. Actions are written in boxes with curved sides. The sequence of actions is shown by the arrows. A sequence starts with a special 'blob' symbol. A sequence ends with a different symbol, as shown.

Figure I.6 also shows the use of a condition. No tax is paid for an income less than or equal to $10,000. You will see the diamond-shaped branch symbol. Associated with each output from the branch is a condition (termed a guard), enclosed in square brackets. If the condition is true the route is taken – just as in a Java `if` statement. If required, the word `else` can appear as the condition, which has the same meaning as in a Java `if` statement.

A condition can also be easily used to describe a loop (repetition) as in a Java `while` or `for` statement. Examples are given in Chapter 8.

Concurrent activities are described as shown in Figure I.7. This describes a program to display two separate animations in a window. The thick horizontal bar (called a fork) means that activities below the bar are carried out concurrently – by different threads in Java. The lower bar (called a join) means that the concurrent activities cease when all the concurrent activities are complete.

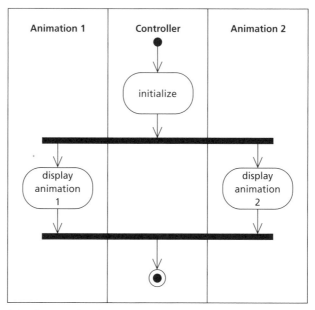

Figure I.7 An activity diagram showing concurrency.

If desired, an activity diagram can show which classes are carrying out the various activities. This is done using a notation called *swimming lanes*. (In a race in a swimming pool, floats are used to define the scope of each participant.) An illustration is shown in the same diagram, Figure I.7. Vertical bars are drawn in the diagram, defining swimming lanes. Activities within a particular swimming lane are carried out by the class whose name appears at the head of the lane.

Appendix J

Swing example code

Here we provide the full code for the Swing applet and application, from Chapter 29. Firstly the applet:

```java
import java.awt.*;
import java.awt.event.*;
import javax.swing.*;
import javax.swing.event.*;

public class SwingAppletDemo extends JApplet
    implements ActionListener, ItemListener,
    ListSelectionListener, ChangeListener {

    private JButton button1, button2, button3, button4;
    private JLabel label1;
    private JCheckBox checkBox1;

    private ButtonGroup radioButtons;
    private JRadioButton hotRadio, warmRadio, coldRadio;

    private JComboBox combo1;

    private JList list1;
    private DefaultListModel listModel;
    private JTextField textField1;

    private JSlider slider1;
```

```java
private JTextArea textArea1;
Paper paper;

public void init() {
    Container c=getContentPane();
    c.setLayout(new FlowLayout() );

    label1= new JLabel("Some basic Swing:");
    c.add(label1);

    checkBox1= new JCheckBox("-A JCheckBox");
    c.add(checkBox1);
    checkBox1.addItemListener(this);

    hotRadio = new JRadioButton("hot",false);
    c.add(hotRadio);
    hotRadio.addItemListener(this);

    warmRadio = new JRadioButton("warm",false);
    c.add(warmRadio);
    warmRadio.addItemListener(this);

    coldRadio = new JRadioButton("cold",false);
    c.add(coldRadio);
    coldRadio.addItemListener(this);

    radioButtons = new ButtonGroup();
    radioButtons.add(hotRadio);
    radioButtons.add(warmRadio);
    radioButtons.add(coldRadio);

    combo1= new JComboBox();
    combo1.addItem("Red");
    combo1.addItem("Yellow");
    combo1.addItem("Blue");
    combo1.addActionListener(this);
    c.add(combo1);

    button1 = new JButton("Message dialog");
    c.add(button1);
    button1.setToolTipText("click to see a message dialog");
    button1.addActionListener(this);
```

```
button2 = new JButton("Confirm dialog");
c.add(button2);
button2.addActionListener(this);

button3 = new JButton("Input dialog");
c.add(button3);
button3.addActionListener(this);

button4 = new JButton("Draw circle");
c.add(button4);
button4.addActionListener(this);

listModel = new DefaultListModel();
listModel.addElement("Mike");
listModel.addElement("Maggie");
listModel.addElement("Matthew");
listModel.addElement("Eleanor");

list1 = new JList(listModel);
list1.setSelectionMode(ListSelectionModel.SINGLE_SELECTION);
c.add(list1);
list1.addListSelectionListener(this);

textField1 = new JTextField(15);
textField1.setText("A JTextField: type here...");
c.add(textField1);
textField1.addActionListener(this);

// a text area in a scroll pane
textArea1 = new JTextArea(" A JTextArea");
textArea1.setLineWrap(true);
JScrollPane areaScrollPane = new JScrollPane(textArea1);
areaScrollPane.setVerticalScrollBarPolicy(
    JScrollPane.VERTICAL_SCROLLBAR_ALWAYS);
areaScrollPane.setHorizontalScrollBarPolicy(
    JScrollPane.HORIZONTAL_SCROLLBAR_ALWAYS);
areaScrollPane.setPreferredSize(new Dimension(100,200));
c.add(areaScrollPane);

// a panel in a scroll pane
paper = new Paper();
JScrollPane paperScrollPane = new JScrollPane(paper);
paperScrollPane.setPreferredSize(new Dimension(100,200));
c.add(paperScrollPane);
```

```java
        slider1 = new JSlider(JSlider.HORIZONTAL, 0, 10, 5);
        slider1.setMajorTickSpacing(10);
        slider1.addChangeListener(this);
        slider1.setMinorTickSpacing(1);
        slider1.setPaintTicks(true);
        slider1.setPaintLabels(true);
        c.add(slider1);
    }

    public void actionPerformed(ActionEvent e) {
    if (e.getSource()== button1) {
        JOptionPane.showMessageDialog(null, "A message:\n"+
                "The Combo state is: " + combo1.getSelectedIndex());
        }

        if (e.getSource()== button2) {
            int userResponse = JOptionPane.showConfirmDialog(null,
                "Delete files?");
            if (userResponse == JOptionPane.NO_OPTION)
                JOptionPane.showMessageDialog(null,
                    "No - Files not deleted!");

            else if (userResponse == JOptionPane.YES_OPTION)
                JOptionPane.showMessageDialog(null,
                    "Yes - Files deleted (just pretending!)");

            else if (userResponse == JOptionPane.CANCEL_OPTION)
                JOptionPane.showMessageDialog(null, "You cancelled");

            else if (userResponse == JOptionPane.CLOSED_OPTION)
                // user closed the dialog - could treat as 'Cancel'
                JOptionPane.showMessageDialog(null, "You closed");

        }

    if (e.getSource()== button3) {

        String bookTitle = JOptionPane.showInputDialog(null,
            "Enter book title");
        if (bookTitle == null)
            JOptionPane.showMessageDialog(null, "You cancelled");
        else
            JOptionPane.showMessageDialog(null, "Title is: "
                + bookTitle);
    }
```

```
    if(e.getSource() == button4) {
        paper.setDiameter(55);
        paper.display();
    }

    if(e.getSource()==combo1){
        int n=combo1.getSelectedIndex();
        JOptionPane.showMessageDialog(null, "combo item number "+
            n + ": the string is: "+combo1.getSelectedItem());
    }

    if (e.getSource()== textField1)
        JOptionPane.showMessageDialog(null,"You hit enter " +
            "on textfield. Text is:\n"+ textField1.getText());
    }

    public void itemStateChanged(ItemEvent e) {
        if (e.getSource() == checkBox1)
                JOptionPane.showMessageDialog(null,
                    "checkBox changed to: "+checkBox1.isSelected());

        if (e.getSource()== hotRadio)
            JOptionPane.showMessageDialog(null, " hot clicked");

        if (e.getSource()== warmRadio)
            JOptionPane.showMessageDialog(null, "warm clicked"+
                coldRadio.isSelected());

        if (e.getSource()== coldRadio)
                JOptionPane.showMessageDialog(null, "cold clicked"+
                    coldRadio.isSelected());
    }

    public void valueChanged(ListSelectionEvent e) {
        if(e.getSource()==list1)
            JOptionPane.showMessageDialog(null,
                "Chose list item number:"+list1.getSelectedIndex());

    }

    public void stateChanged(ChangeEvent e) {
        if (e.getSource()== slider1)
            textArea1.append("\nslider1 is: " + slider1.getValue());
    }
}
```

```
class Paper extends JPanel { // to draw on
    int diameter =400;

    public void setDiameter(int d) {
        diameter = d;
    }

    public void paintComponent(Graphics g) {
        super.paintComponent(g);
        g.drawOval(0,0,diameter,diameter);
        g.drawString("Jpanel drawing", 0, 20);
    }

    public void display() {
        repaint();
    }
}
```

Here is the application code:

```
import javax.swing.*;
import java.awt.event.*;
import java.awt.*;

public class SwingApplicationDemo extends JFrame
    implements ActionListener {
    JMenuBar wholeMenuBar;
    JMenu fileMenu, editMenu;
    JMenuItem openItem, saveItem, copyItem, pasteItem;
    JButton quitButton, rotateButton;
    Container c;

    public SwingApplicationDemo() {
        c=getContentPane();
        c.setLayout(new FlowLayout());
        wholeMenuBar = new JMenuBar();
        setJMenuBar( wholeMenuBar );

        // file menu, with Open, save
        fileMenu = new JMenu("File");

        openItem = new JMenuItem("Open");
        fileMenu.add(openItem);
        openItem.addActionListener(this);
```

```
        saveItem = new JMenuItem("Save");
        fileMenu.add(saveItem);
        saveItem.addActionListener(this);

        wholeMenuBar.add(fileMenu);

        // edit menu, with copy, paste
        editMenu = new JMenu("Edit");

        copyItem = new JMenuItem("Copy");
        editMenu.add(copyItem);
        copyItem.addActionListener(this);

        pasteItem = new JMenuItem( "Paste" );
        editMenu.add( pasteItem );
        pasteItem.addActionListener(this);

        wholeMenuBar.add(editMenu );

        // ovalimage.jpg is 20 by 20 pixels
        Icon ovalIcon = new ImageIcon("ovalimage.jpg");

        rotateButton = new JButton("Rotate", ovalIcon);
        c.add(rotateButton);
        rotateButton.addActionListener(this);

        quitButton = new JButton("Quit");
        c.add(quitButton);
        quitButton.addActionListener(this);

        setSize(200, 200);
        show();
    }

    public void actionPerformed(ActionEvent e) {
        if (e.getSource() == openItem) {
            JFileChooser fileChooser = new JFileChooser();
            int userResponse = fileChooser.showOpenDialog(this);
            if (userResponse == JFileChooser.CANCEL_OPTION )
                JOptionPane.showMessageDialog(null,
                    "User cancelled.");
            else
                JOptionPane.showMessageDialog(null, "User chose" +
                    fileChooser.getSelectedFile());
        }
```

```
        if (e.getSource() == saveItem)
            JOptionPane.showMessageDialog(null, "Save chosen.");
        if (e.getSource() == copyItem)
            JOptionPane.showMessageDialog(null, "Copy chosen.");
        if (e.getSource() == pasteItem)
            JOptionPane.showMessageDialog(null, "Paste chosen.");
        if (e.getSource() == rotateButton)
            JOptionPane.showMessageDialog(null, "Rotate clicked.");
        if(e.getSource() == quitButton)
            System.exit(0);
    }


    public static void main( String args[] ) {
        SwingApplicationDemo app = new SwingApplicationDemo();
        app.setSize( 250, 200 );
        app.show();
    }
}
```

Bibliography

● Java

Please note that all the following books are updated frequently and you should be careful to select the book that describes the version of Java that you are using.

The Java Programming Language, Ken Arnold and James Gosling. Addison-Wesley, Reading, MA, 2nd edition, 1998.
One of the series written by members of the team at Sun who created Java. A definitive source of information on Java. This book describes the language itself (not the libraries). It is very readable, but not for novices.

The Java Language Specification, J. Gosling, B. Joy, G. Steele, G. Brancha. Addison-Wesley, Reading, MA, 2nd edition, 2000.
This is the official specification for the language. It is much more readable than most language specifications, but is not for the faint-hearted!

The Java Class libraries, Patrick Chan, Rosanne Lee, Doug Kramer. Addison-Wesley, Reading, MA. Volume 1 1998, Volume 2 1997.
Useful for reference, the definitive descriptions of the release 1.1 libraries.

The Java Class libraries, supplement for the Java 2 Platform, Patrick Chan, Rosanne Lee, Doug Kramer. Addison-Wesley, 2nd edition, Volume 1, 1999.
The update to the earlier volumes.

http://java.dimensionx.com/tutorial/TOC.html
A Web site that is a tutorial on Java, using the usual hypertext links.

Java in a Nutshell, David Flanagan. O'Reilly & Associates, Sebastopol CA, 3rd edition, 1999.
Written as a reference book. Lists the libraries, with easy referencing. Has a section on the Java language for those who know C++. Useful for reference. Widely used and recommended. But not really suitable for novices.

619

Java: How To Program, H. M. Deitel and P. J. Deitel. Prentice Hall, Englewood Cliffs, NJ, 3rd edition, 1999.
This is very comprehensive and good for reference. Some editions are accompanied by a CD with Borl and JBuilder development system for Java.

Java Gently, Judy Bishop. Addison-Wesley, Reading, MA, 3rd edition, 2000.
A good book for novices. Differs from *Java for Students* in *not* taking a graphical approach to programming.

Just Java, Peter van der Linden. SunSoft Press and Prentice Hall, Englewood Cliffs, NJ, 1998.

Core Java, Volume 1 – Fundamentals, Gary Cornell and Volume 2 – Advanced Features, Gary Cornell and Cay S. Horstmann. SunSoft Press and Prentice Hall, Englewood Cliffs, NJ, 1998. Written by people who work for Sun or who are close to Sun, each book has a unique style and perspective. They are like personal testimonies to the joy of programming in Java. None of these books is for novices to Java programming.

Not Just Java, Peter van der Linden. Sun Microsystems Press and Prentice Hall, Englewood Cliffs, NJ, 1998.
Explains, in a very readable way, the context for Java, the Internet and client/server computing. Written by one of the Java development team.

● Object-oriented programming languages

Java is the latest in a line of object-oriented languages. All share the concepts of encapsulation, classes and inheritance.

Simula Begin, Graham Birtwistle, Ole-Johan Dahl, Bjorn Myrhaug and Kristen Nygaard. Studentliteratur and Auerbach, New York, 1973.
Simula 67 was the first object-oriented language. It was called Simula because it was designed as a language to simulate events. This is the best-known book on Simula.

Smalltalk-80, the Language, Adele Goldberg and David Robson. Addison-Wesley, Reading, MA, 1989.
Smalltalk-80 is the Rolls-Royce of object-oriented languages. It is completely object-oriented – even control structures like repetition and `if` statements are objects. Like Java it supports single inheritance. Like Java it provides a large and comprehensive library that the programmer uses and inherits from to provide facilities including windowing, graphics and data structures. The definitive book on Smalltalk-80.

Problem Solving, Abstraction, and Design using C++, Frank L. Friedman and Elliot B. Koffman, Addison-Wesley, Reading, MA, 1994.
C++ was the most widely-used object-oriented language prior to Java. It has a grammar similar to Java's, but is a much more complex language which supports multiple inheritance. Appendix A describes the main differences between C++ and Java. If you want to know about C++, there are a large number of books. Be warned, some of them are very weighty and formidable! This is the simplest of many books.

● Object-oriented methods

Object-Oriented Systems Design, Edward Yourdon. Prentice Hall International, Englewood Cliffs, NJ, 1994.
A wide-ranging survey of approaches and notations. Very readable. Written very clearly and very readably by one of the gurus of software development. Includes surveys of the various methods for OO design.

Object-Oriented Design with Applications, G. Booch. Benjamin-Cummings, New York, 1990.
An excellent book which introduces the author's view of the process and notation of object-oriented design and also contains five extensive design case studies. Widely regarded as the definitive book on OO design.

Object-Oriented Software Construction, Bertrand Meyer. Prentice Hall, New York, 2nd edition, 1997.
A wonderfully clear exposition of the principles of OOP.

Object Lessons. Lessons Learned in OO Development Projects, Tom Love. SIGS Books, New York, 1993.
Written by a consultant who has seen many successful and unsuccessful projects. He gives the results of his very practical experience. The book begins by identifying the problems of software engineering. As part of this he suggests that successful pieces of software have been written by just two people, young and without using respectable methods. He goes on to look at the expected benefits of OO. The main part of the book is about practical OO methods, including management, 'software component foundries' and how to bring about change.

● Design patterns

Current thinking suggests that many programs need not be designed from scratch but instead they can be designed by looking at a catalogue of patterns. These patterns embody ideas from many previously-written programs. The ideas are ripe for re-use in new programs.

Design Patterns. Elements of Reusable Object-Oriented Software, Erich Gamma, Richard Helm, Ralph Johnson and John Vlissides, Addison-Wesley, Reading, MA, 1995.
This is the original book of patterns, written by the so-called gang-of-four. This is hard going.

Patterns in Java, Volume 1 and Volume 2, Mark Grand, John Wiley and Sons, 1998.
This is more readable – and more directly applicable to Java. But again, it is not easy reading.

Java Design Patterns, A Tutorial, James W. Cooper, Addison Wesley, 2000.
The clearest book on this topic that we have come across.

● UML (Unified Modeling Language)

The books we like best on this topic are:

UML Distilled, Martin Fowler with Kendall Scott, Addison-Wesley, 2000.

Using UML, Perdita Stevens with Rob Pooley, Addison-Wesley, 2000.

● Multithreading

Threads Primer: A Guide to Multithreaded Programming, Bill Lewis and Daniel J. Berg.
SunSoft Press and Prentice Hall, Englewood Cliffs, NJ, 1995.
A book from the SunSoft Press stable, this is comprehensive, but not for the novice.

Principles of Concurrent and Distributed Programming, M. Ben-Ari. Prentice Hall, Englewood
Cliffs, NJ, 1990.
The classic book on concurrency mechanisms.

Parallel Programming: An Introduction, T. Braunl. Prentice Hall, Englewood Cliffs, NJ,
1993.

Concurrent Programming: Fundamental Techniques for Real-Time and Parallel Software Design,
T. Axford. Wiley, New York, 1989.
These are other introductory texts.

● Programmers – their lives and work

There have been several exciting accounts of the personal outlook and work methods of programmers. They give insights into how programming is actually done. They also contribute to
the folklore of programming.

Programmers at Work, Susan Lammers. Microsoft Press, Redmond, WA, 1986.
An example of a book on how programmers actually work. In the book, she reports on inter-
views with notable programmers.

Hackers. Heroes of the Computer Revolution, Steven Levy. Anchor Books, Garden City, NY,
1994.
Another really exciting book which charts the lives of the early 'real programmers'.

Show-Stopper. The Breakneck Race to Create Windows NT and the Next Generation at Microsoft,
G. Pasacal Zachary. The Free Press, New York, 1994.
This is a good read if you are interested in how software projects really get done and what life
is like at Microsoft.

Microsoft Secrets, Michael A. Cusumano and Richard W. Selby. The Free Press, New York
1995.
Describes the methods used at Microsoft.

● Software development

Software Development: Fashioning the Baroque, Darrel Ince. Oxford University Press, Oxford,
1988.
If you would like to know about the problems of (and some of the solutions to) developing
large-scale software, this gives the big picture.

Debugging the Development Process, Steve Maguire. Microsoft Press, Redmond, WA, 1994.
This book has the subtitle 'Practical Strategies for Staying Focused, Hitting Ship Dates and Building Solid Teams'. Life within Microsoft and the lessons that can be learned are well presented in this readable book.

Writing Solid Code, Microsoft's techniques for developing bug-free C Programs, Steve Maguire. Microsoft Press, Redmond, WA, 1993.
A book by a Microsoft programmer which describes techniques for debugging software. The many examples are in the C programming language.

Software Engineering: A Programming Approach, Doug Bell. Prentice Hall, Englewood Cliffs, NJ, 2000.
Software engineering is the term given to the job of developing large programs. This book describes approaches to this task, taking as the reader's starting point a knowledge of programming.

Decline and Fall of the American Programmer, Edward Yourdon. PTR Prentice Hall, Englewood Cliffs, NJ, 1993.
Ed Yourdon is one of the gurus of software development. In this book he gives a very readable account of the problems that he perceives with software development today. The book continues by giving a survey of the possible remedies for the problems. It's altogether a very readable book, free of technicalities and free with opinions. The title reflects the author's opinion that American programmers are under threat from competition from programmers in Asia – who are paid less, but are better!

Rise and Resurrection of the American Programmer, Edward Yourdon. PTR Prentice Hall, Englewood Cliffs, NJ, 1995.
The sequel to *Decline and Fall*, which is much more optimistic about the future of American programmers, provided that they take the initiative and learn about new technologies, like Java.

Glossary

Applet a (usually) small application invoked by a Web browser from a Web page. Sometimes written in Java. The application typically displays graphics, displays animations, plays sounds and video clips, and interacts with the user. The applet is derived from the words 'application' and 'let', meaning small.

Browser *See* Web browser.

Built-in types the types `boolean`, `char`, `byte`, `short`, `int`, `long`, `float` and `double` that are provided ready-made as part of the Java language. They are not true objects.

Byte code the low-level language to which Java programs are compiled. When a Java program is run, byte code is interpreted by the Java Virtual Machine.

Class a unit of programming in an object-oriented language like Java. Represents the abstraction of a number of similar (or identical) objects. Describes the data (variables) and methods that any object contains.

Class method a method that is associated with a class, rather than with any instance (object) of the class.

Extend declare a new class that inherits the behaviour of another class.

Home page the first Web page that you see when you visit a new Web site for an organization or an individual.

HTML (hypertext markup language) describes how information in a file should be displayed on the screen. Also describes the links to other files.

Inheritance the way in which a new class can incorporate the features of an existing class.

Instance an object created from a class.

Interface a Java feature which allows the programmer to specify the interface to a class (the way that the class is to be used), without programming the class itself. This separates the specification of what the class will do from how it will do it.

Internet the world-wide collection of computers connected via telecommunications facilities.

Invoke use a method. (Sometimes the term *call* is used.)

624

Java a general-purpose programming language first designed for constructing Internet applications.

Java Virtual Machine (JVM) a piece of software that allows Java to run on a particular machine. The JVM interprets the byte code produced by the Java compiler.

Method one of the actions associated with an object. A method has a name and may have one or more parameters. (A method is called a *function, procedure* or *subroutine* in other programming languages.) The name 'method' derives from the idea of having a method for doing something.

Navigator a very popular WWW browser produced by Netscape.

Network Computer (NC) a small computer, with very little local storage, that uses the facilities of the Internet. Programs are downloaded from a server computer.

Object a component of a program in an object-oriented language. An object incorporates some data (variables) and the actions (methods) associated with that data.

Overloading providing two or more methods (within the same class) with the same name, but different parameters. There may be a different number of parameters, or the types of the parameters may be different, or both. The Java compiler selects the correct version of the method according to the parameters that are used when the method is invoked.

Overriding providing a method in a subclass that has the same name and parameters as a method in a superclass. The Java run-time system always selects the method of the class that the object belongs to.

Package a way in Java of grouping together a number of related classes. All the names within the class are private, unless a user explicitly refers to the package and the class using an `import` statement. Using packages avoids a potential problem of duplicate names which might otherwise arise, particularly in large pieces of software.

PC (personal computer) an IBM personal computer or, more usually, a clone manufactured by one of many imitators. Uses one of the range of (compatible) Intel processor chips – 386, 486, Pentium etc.

Polymorphism a feature of object-oriented languages in which the appropriate method to act on an object is selected from amongst those methods with the same name.

Subclass a class which inherits variables and methods from the current class.

Superclass a class from which the current class inherits variables and methods.

UML (unified modelling language) a notation for describing the structure of software.

Unicode the 16 bit character code used in Java.

URL (uniform resource locator) the unique address of a file on the Internet. Enables a file to be located, wherever it is in the world.

VRML (virtual reality modelling language) a language for describing three-dimensional scenes in a text format.

Web browser a piece of software that allows a user at a computer to gain access to files at other locations on the Internet. A browser interprets the information embedded in the file which describes how it is to be displayed. The most popular browsers are Netscape Navigator and Internet Explorer.

Web pages a file of information on a computer that can be viewed using a browser on a different computer using the World-Wide Web. The file is divided into convenient pages.

Web site a computer that stores Web pages that are accessible through the Internet.

Widget a button, scrollbar, text field or similar object in a window that supports user interaction by clicking with the mouse. Derived from the words 'Window' and 'gadget'.

World-Wide Web (WWW) or Web the prime means of accessing information on the Internet. The Web defines a standard for the representation of files (including HTML), for the addresses of files anywhere in the world (URLs) and the protocol for communication between computers.

Index